Using Mindfulness to Promote Mental Health in Schools

Using Mindfulness to Promote Mental Health in Schools

EDITED BY

TYLER L. RENSHAW

AND

SHANE R. JIMERSON

OXFORD
UNIVERSITY PRESS

OXFORD
UNIVERSITY PRESS

Oxford University Press is a department of the University of Oxford. It furthers the University's objective of excellence in research, scholarship, and education by publishing worldwide. Oxford is a registered trade mark of Oxford University Press in the UK and in certain other countries.

Published in the United States of America by Oxford University Press
198 Madison Avenue, New York, NY 10016, United States of America.

CIP data is on file at the Library of Congress.

ISBN 9780190880477

DOI: 10.1093/9780190880507.001.0001

The manufacturer's authorized representative in the EU for product safety is Oxford University Press España S.A. of Parque Empresarial San Fernando de Henares, Avenida de Castilla, 2 – 28830 Madrid (www.oup.es/en or product.safety@oup.com). OUP España S.A. also acts as importer into Spain of products made by the manufacturer.

This book is dedicated to school-based mental health professionals and other educators who serve children and families, contributing each day to the well-being of our youth, schools, and communities. We recognize your tireless and important work. And we hope the contents of this book may contribute to your efforts to further support and advocate for children, families, schools, and communities.

We also dedicate this book to those who have informed and inspired us.

For my partner and best friend, Hilary, as well as my children, Carter and Oliver. Your love, support, and presence make life good.

Tyler L. Renshaw

For my wife, Kathryn M. O'Brien, and children Gavin Jimerson and Taite Jimerson, who continue to inspire and inform my efforts and life pursuits.

Shane R. Jimerson

CONTENTS

ACKNOWLEDGMENTS

As with any project of this scope, we feel it is important to acknowledge the efforts of the individuals who contributed to our efforts. First, we would like to recognize the incredible contributions of each of the colleagues who contributed as authors to this important collection of chapters. Second, we recognize the children, families, schools, educators, mental health professionals, and other researchers working in schools who have contributed to the knowledge featured in this book. Third, we recognize and appreciate our colleagues at Oxford University Press, including Sarah Harrington, who helped bring this edited volume to fruition. Finally, we would like to independently recognize the following individuals:

Dr. Renshaw acknowledges the inspiring graduate students he has worked with over the past 13 years, who have helped him think about, research, and practice mindfulness in new and creative directions. Special thanks go to Mary Phan, Caleb Farley, Kris Franzmann, and John Barr for their engagement with mindfulness and related topics during their graduate studies. He would also like to thank Dr. Jimerson for his support not only with this book but also as a professional mentor and friend. And lastly, he acknowledges his other colleagues who have collaborated with him on mindfulness-related presentations and publications. This work has benefited from their investment of time, talent, and wisdom.

Dr. Jimerson would also like to acknowledge the contributions of the graduate students whom he has had the honor of working with at the University of California, Santa Barbara, including Mihya Weber, Chloe Zhang, Alessandra Mittelstet, Lakhvir Kaur, Shemiyah Holland, and Amber Reinke for their ongoing efforts to advance knowledge, science, and services to promote the healthy development and well-being of children at school. He would also like to thank the many talented colleagues with whom he has had the good fortune of collaborating over the years. Finally, he expresses his gratitude to Dr. Renshaw for the opportunity to collaborate on this book and the many opportunities to learn together over the past two decades.

We are grateful for the opportunity to learn from our colleagues and contribute to the future of school professionals supporting the mental health and well-being of students at school.

EDITOR BIOGRAPHIES

Tyler L. Renshaw, PhD, NCSP, LP

Dr. Renshaw is a Professor in the Department of Psychology at Utah State University (USU). He holds a PhD in combined Counseling, Clinical, and School Psychology from the University of California at Santa Barbara and is a Nationally Certified School Psychologist. He is also a credentialed school psychologist and a licensed psychologist in the state of Utah. At USU, Dr. Renshaw serves as the Director of Training for the School Psychology PhD Program, teaches graduate seminars on school-based mental health services, supervises clinical training in schools, and runs a research team known as the School Mental Health Lab. The lab's research aims to improve the accessibility and quality of school-based mental health services, with particular focus on mindfulness-based interventions and brief assessment practices. Dr. Renshaw has authored 130+ scholarly publications and given 150+ professional presentations. He is the current Editor Elect and an Associate Editor for *School Psychology Review*, and he is a prior Editor and Associate Editor for *Assessment for Effective Intervention*. He is a recipient of the Lightner Witmer Award for early-career scholarship in school psychology (APA Division 16) and received the Graduate Faculty Mentor of the Year Award from his college at USU. Dr. Renshaw is also a coauthor of *School Psychology for the 21st Century* (3rd ed.), which is a foundational introductory text in the field of school psychology.

Shane R. Jimerson, PhD, NCSP, CPsychol

Dr. Jimerson is a Professor in the Department of Counseling, Clinical, and School Psychology at the University of California, Santa Barbara. Dr. Jimerson's professional and scholarly activities aim to advance and promote science, practice, and policy relevant to education and school psychology, in an effort to benefit children, families, and communities throughout the world. His scholarship has received extensive funding focused on advancing justice, equity, diversity, and inclusion in mental health supports for children at school. His experience as an editor and author involves work with 400+ publications, including more than 30 books. Dr. Jimerson has chaired and served on numerous boards and advisory committees at the state, national, and international levels, including serving as President of the following: the Society for the Study of School Psychology, the International School Psychology Association, and Division 16 (School Psychology) of the American Psychological Association. He currently serves as Editor for *School Psychology Review* and was previously the Editor of *School Psychology Quarterly*, Editor of *Contemporary School Psychology*, and Senior Editor for International Science for *School Psychology Quarterly*. He has also contributed over 350 presentations during the past 25 years to diverse audiences of students, scholars, and professionals in more than 30 countries. Dr. Jimerson has received numerous honors, including most recently the Tom Oakland Outstanding International Scholar Award from the International School Psychology Association, the Lifetime Contributions Award from the California Association of School Psychologists, an Honorary Doctorate from the University of Liege, Belgium, the Senior Scientist Award from Division 16 (School Psychology) of the American Psychological Association, and the Lifetime Achievement Award from the National Association of School Psychologists.

LIST OF CONTRIBUTORS

Stacy L. Bender PhD is Associate Professor, Department of Counseling, School Psychology, and Sport, University of Massachusetts Boston, MA, US.

Joseph Ciarrochi PhD is a Research Professor, Institute of Positive Psychology and Education, Australian Catholic University, Sydney, Australia.

Clayton R. Cook PhD is Chief Development Officer, CharacterStrong, Auburn, WA, US.

Lisa W. Coyne PhD is Founder and Senior Clinical Consultant, McLean OCD Institute for Children and Adolescents, Belmont, MA, US; and Assistant Professor, Harvard Medical School, Boston, MA, US.

Jacinda K. Dariotis PhD, MAS is Professor, Department of Human Development and Family Studies; Endowed Chair of Family Resilience, College of Agricultural, Consumer and Environmental Sciences; Health Innovation Professor, Department of Biomedical and Translation Sciences, Carle Illinois College of Medicine; University of Illionois Urbana–Champaign, Urbana, IL, US.

Elizabeth Dexter-Mazza PsyD is President, DBT in Schools, LLC, Seattle, WA, US.

Caleb Douglas Farley MS is PhD student, Department of Psychology, Utah State University, Logan, UT, US.

Joshua C. Felver PhD is Associate Professor, Department of Social Work, Binghamton University, NY, US.

Aaron J. Fischer PhD is Professor, Department of Educational Psychology, University of Utah, Salt Lake City, UT, US.

Diana H. Fishbein PhD is Senior Scientist, Frank Porter Graham Child Development Institute, University of North Carolina-Chapel Hill, Chapel Hill, NC, US; and Research Faculty, Department of Human Development and Family Studies, The Pennsylvania State University, University Park, PA, US

Thomas K. Franzmann MS is PhD student, Psychology Department, Utah State University, Logan, UT, US.

Matthew S. Goodman PhD is Licensed Clinical Psychologist, Birmingham Maple Clinic, Troy, MI, US.

Louise Hayes PhD is Adjunct Senior Research Fellow, LaTrobe University, Melbourne, Australia.

Patricia A. Jennings MEd, PhD is Professor, School of Education and Human Development, University of Virginia, Charlottesville, VA, US.

Shane R. Jimerson PhD is Professor, Department of Counseling, Clinical, and School Psychology, University of California, Santa Barbara, Santa Barbara, CA, US.

David A. Klingbeil PhD is Associate Professor, Department of Educational Psychology, University of Wisconsin–Madison, WI, US.

Madeline Larson PhD is Executive Director of Product, CharacterStrong, Auburn, WA, US.

James J. Mazza PhD is Professor, College of Education, University of Washington–Seattle, Seattle, WA, US.

Robert C. McGowan leads government relations and policy for FirstGen Forward, Washington, DC, US.

Rebecca Michel MS is PhD student, Department of Psychology, University of Rhode Island, RI, US.

Mary L. Phan MS is PhD student, Department of Psychology, Utah State University, Logan, UT, US.

Tyler L. Renshaw PhD is Professor, Department of Psychology, Utah State University, Logan, UT, US.

Anthony J. Roberson PhD is Assistant Professor, Department of Psychological & Behavioral Health Sciences, University of Houston–Clear Lake, TX, US.

Erica M. S. Sibinga MD, MHS is Professor of Pediatrics, Johns Hopkins School of Medicine, Baltimore, MD, US.

Randye J. Semple PhD is Professor, Psychiatry and the Behavioral Sciences, Keck School of Medicine, University of Southern California, Los Angeles, CA, US.

Magenta Silberman PhD is Psychologist, Huntsman Mental Health Institute, University of Utah, Salt Lake City, UT, US.

Margaret Sullivan MA is graduate student, Department of Educational Psychology, University of Minnesota, MN, US.

Andrew Jordan Thayer PhD is Founder, Thayer Organizational & Psychological Services, Seattle, WA, US.

Shelley R. Upton, PhD is Director of Assessment Services and staff psychologist, Chicago Psychotherapy, Chicago, IL, US.

Stephanie A. Vinal MS is PhD student, Department of Psychology, Utah State University, Logan, UT, US.

Lindsey Webb PhD, MHS, MS is Assistant Research Professor, Department of Mental Health, Johns Hopkins Bloomberg School of Public Health, Baltimore, MD, US.

Sean N. Weeks PhD is Psychologist, Department of Educational Psychology, University of Utah, UT, US.

PART ONE

Foundations

1

Advancing the Science and Practice of Mindfulness to Support Mental Health in Schools

TYLER L. RENSHAW, SHANE R. JIMERSON, MARY L. PHAN, AND THOMAS K. FRANZMANN ■

The prevalence of mental health issues among youth has significantly increased over recent decades, with more students experiencing anxiety, depression, and other emotional difficulties (Bitsko et al., 2022). This rise in mental health concerns has prompted mental health professionals and educators to explore innovative strategies to support the well-being of youth in schools. One promising approach is the use of mindfulness practices, which aim to promote mental health by fostering emotional regulation, resilience, and overall well-being (Felver et al., 2016; Renshaw & Cook, 2017; Roeser et al., 2022, 2023; Schonert-Reichl & Roeser, 2016). This edited volume aims to advance science and practice on this topic by exploring the foundations and approaches that guide the use of mindfulness practices in schools. More specifically, this chapter provides background information and justification regarding why this book focuses on using mindfulness for promoting mental health in schools. First, the more general case for integrating mental health supports into schools is discussed. Following, the nature and context of mindfulness practices is introduced, with a focus on why these practices may be especially useful for promoting mental health in schools. After the logic for using mindfulness in schools is established, readers are provided with an orientation to the other chapters of this book. Finally, this chapter closes by raising a

Tyler L. Renshaw et al., *Advancing the Science and Practice of Mindfulness to Support Mental Health in Schools*. In: *Using Mindfulness to Promote Mental Health in Schools*. Edited by: Tyler L. Renshaw and Shane R. Jimerson, Oxford University Press. © Oxford University Press (2025). DOI: 10.1093/9780190880507.003.0001 few critical issues related to using mindfulness practices in schools, which readers should consider while reading the other chapters.

MENTAL HEALTH SUPPORTS IN SCHOOLS

To understand the case for integrating mental health supports into schools, it is important to consider the contemporary context of mental health among youth. Across the past two decades, there has been a growing recognition of the critical role mental health plays in the overall well-being and academic success of youth (O'Reilly et al., 2018; US Agency for Healthcare Research and Quality, 2022). Many mental health problems among school-aged children and adolescents are increasingly prevalent, with significant implications for their academic performance, social interactions, and future development (e.g., Lebrun-Harris, 2022; Racine et al., 2021; Twenge et al., 2019). The best available evidence estimates that 17% of youth in the United States have a significant mental health disorder, and that 49% of these youth do not receive treatment from a mental health professional (Whitney & Peterson, 2019). The proportion of youth who could benefit from mental health treatment but do not access it varies drastically across the nation, ranging from a low of 29% in Washington, DC, to a high of 72% in North Carolina (Whitney & Peterson, 2019). The level and scope of this issue have become so concerning that the Biden-Harris Administration declared that "The United States is experiencing an unprecedented youth mental health crisis" and that "tackling [this] mental health crisis [is] a top priority" (The White House, 2023).

Mental health concerns are further compounded for youth identifying with or living in marginalized communities. The American Psychological Association (2021) defines *marginalization* as "relegation to or placement in an unimportant or a depowered position in society" (p. 4). Youth who are marginalized represent a diverse cross-section of the population, including those who identify with minoritized racial, ethnic, sexual, gender, socioeconomic, and other cultural groups. Compared with their majoritized peers, marginalized youth experience more frequent and severe mental health problems—and they have less access to and receive poorer quality mental health care (Alegría et al., 2015; Auerswald et al., 2017; Maura et al., 2017; Rodgers et al., 2022). Common factors contributing to these disparities include the costs of mental health services, stigma associated with seeking help, concerns related to discrimination from providers, insufficient funding for local mental health resources, and the lack of mental health service providers for youth in many communities (Anderson et al., 2017; Robards et al., 2018; Stafford & Draucker, 2020). Research also estimates that, compared with their majoritized peers, marginalized youth are 20–50% less likely to seek help for mental health concerns and 40–80% more likely to drop out of treatment early, likely because of barriers related to their marginalized statuses (Aggarwal et al., 2016). These disparities emphasize the need for not only promoting youth mental health generally, but also for advancing youth mental health equity specifically.

The current landscape of youth mental health—characterized by high problem prevalence rates, low treatment access rates, and unjust disparities—has led many researchers, clinicians, policy makers, and educators to recommend integrating mental health supports into schools (Bradshaw et al., 2023). The intention here is to help more youth access more and better supports by bringing these services to where they already are for many hours during most days, *at school*. Compared with services provided in other settings, mental health services in schools can be more timely, more convenient, less costly, and more efficient (Fazel et al., 2014). Modern school-based mental health services are typically organized around a multitiered system of supports (MTSS) framework, which emphasizes prevention, data-based decision making, and scaling supports to match identified and evolving needs within the school population (Eber et al., 2019). MTSS for school-based mental health commonly consists of three tiers or levels of supports, which have been defined by Merrell et al. (2022, p. 221) as follows:

- *Tier 1* or *universal supports* refers to low-intensity services that are provided to *all* students within a school population, regardless of risk status.
- *Tier 2* or *targeted supports* refers to moderate-intensity services that are provided to *some* students, based on identified risk factors or early indicators of problems.
- *Tier 3* or *intensive supports* refers to high-resource services that are provided to *few* students, based on indicators showing significant risk factors or severe problems.

Research shows that school-based mental health services can benefit students. Meta-analyses have consistently demonstrated that mental health supports across the tiers (i.e., universal, targeted, and intensive) in schools are effective for reducing youths' psychosocial distress and improving their subjective well-being, prosocial behavior, and academic performance (e.g., Cohen et al., 2024; Sanchez et al., 2018; Zhang et al., 2023). There is also emerging evidence that school-based mental health supports may indeed enhance access to services for marginalized youth (e.g., Bains et al., 2016; Bear et al., 2014; Whitaker et al., 2018). Moreover, a recent meta-analysis indicates that youth in both clinical and general populations are now accessing more mental health services in schools than in any other service setting (Duong et al., 2021). Thus, school-based supports via MTSS hold promise as an accessible, effective, and equity-oriented avenue for promoting youth mental health.

MINDFULNESS PRACTICES IN SCHOOLS

As mental health professionals, educators, and researchers seek effective strategies to promote youth mental health in schools, mindfulness practices have emerged as a promising approach (Felver et al., 2013; Renshaw & Cook, 2017; Roeser et al., 2023; Schonert-Reichl & Roeser, 2016). *Mindfulness* is commonly defined as the awareness that arises through paying attention on purpose, in the present moment, and non-judgmentally (Kabat-Zinn, 1994). When considered within the context of education and intervention, this definition of mindfulness can be translated into an applied skill consisting of two core components: present moment awareness of one's subjective experiences, paired with responding with acceptance to the contents of such awareness (Renshaw, 2020). These core mindfulness skills can be learned like any other skill, through effective teaching and training. Mindfulness-based interventions (MBIs), then, are simply any exercise or program or protocol that seeks to train mindfulness skills for the purposes of promoting desirable outcomes (Renshaw et al., 2022).

Mindfulness has its origins in ancient Eastern religious traditions, but it has been incorporated as a secular practice into educational and clinical settings over the past 50 years (Baer, 2003). The history of how mindfulness moved from East to West, and from religious to secular, is long, interesting, and beyond the scope of this chapter (see Kabat-Zinn, 2003 for a brief history). The following describes a few key events that laid the foundation for mindfulness making its way into schools. Beginning in the late 1970s and early 1980s, studies at the University of Massachusetts Medical School evaluated the effects of training adult patients with chronic pain to use mindfulness practices for the sake of decreasing subjective distress and enhancing quality of life (Kabat-Zinn, 1982). The novelty and success of this early work led to the development of a formal group-based treatment known as mindfulness-based stress reduction (MBSR), which became widely used in hospitals for helping patients cope with chronic pain and terminal illness (Shigaki et al., 2006).

Concurrent with the development of MBSR, two other mindfulness-based treatment approaches were being developed by different research teams, who were primarily interested in using mindfulness practices to improve mental health outcomes for clients in outpatient settings. These treatment approaches would later become known as dialectical behavior therapy (DBT; Linehan & Wilks, 2015) and acceptance and commitment therapy (ACT; Wilson et al., 2011), respectively, and were notably different in how they used mindfulness compared with MBSR. Instead of group-based interventions emphasizing formal mindfulness meditations and practices (e.g., mindful breathing, mindful body scan, mindful movement), DBT and ACT started as individualized treatments emphasizing more informal and metaphorical aspects of mindfulness within the context of other evidence-based behavioral interventions.

Throughout the 1990s, MBSR expanded from hospital settings into community settings—and started proving useful for also treating psychological disorders. This evolution eventually led to integrating elements of MBSR with other gold-standard psychosocial treatments with adults, resulting in the development of mindfulness-based cognitive therapy (MBCT) and other similar MBI protocols focused on relapse prevention (e.g., Segal et al., 2002). As the evidence base for using MBIs to improve the mental health of adults accumulated in the early 2000s (Baer, 2003), researchers began to pilot MBIs to promote the mental health of adolescents in clinical settings (e.g., Biegel et al., 2009). Around the same time, some researchers became curious about the potential of MBIs to be used for targeted prevention with children in school settings. The first published study formally evaluating an MBI with youth in schools was conducted by Napoli et al. (2005), who tested the effects of 12 bimonthly mindfulness training sessions on the attention, social skills, and test anxiety of students in grades K–3. Their promising results were the seeds for most of the work on mindfulness in schools that follows throughout this book.

At the same time that MBIs started stepping into schools (circa early 2000s), mindfulness also began making its way into mainstream culture in the United States. Following are some salient examples. About a decade ago, *Time* magazine ran a cover story on "The Mindful Revolution" (Pickert, 2014). There are now over 20 *TED Talks* given by public figures on the nature and benefits of mindfulness (TED, n.d.). A new monthly lifestyle publication, *Mindful Magazine*, was launched and is distributed online and in bookstores and grocery stores around the globe (Mindful, n.d.). Smartphone apps claiming to train or support mindfulness have proliferated—totaling more than 120 at the time this chapter is written (One Mind, n.d.). Mindfulness and MBIs have been embraced by popular-press mental health and medical outlets that provide evidence-based advice to consumers, such as *WebMD* (WebMD, 2022) and *PsychCentral* (Pattermore, 2022). Lastly, several well-regarded health care organizations now provide non-technical guidance on mindfulness practices and its role in physical and mental health promotion, including Nemours Children's Health (2023), Kaiser Permanente (n.d.), and the Mayo Clinic (2022).

The increasing public interest in mindfulness and MBIs is, fortunately, grounded in expanding empirical evidence. Science and scholarship on the benefits of mindfulness practices in schools has developed within the context of the broader spread of mindfulness through mainstream culture. As such practices received more attention from popular press outlets and healthcare organizations, more researchers and funders became curious about investigating its effects on youth mental health and related outcomes in schools. Then, as more research in schools on the topic was funded, conducted, and published, more MBI protocols proliferated, which made mindfulness practices more accessible to mental health professionals and educators interested in implementing these practices in their schools. This cyclical cultural and scientific evolution brings us to the contemporary context, in which mindfulness practices are a mainstay in modern society and well-suited for school-based mental health supports.

MBIs have been shown to offer a range of psychosocial benefits for adults and youth, including reduced psychological distress, improved emotional regulation and subjective well-being, and enhanced cognitive and academic functioning (Klingbeil et al., 2017b; Klingbeil & Renshaw, 2018; Weare, 2015; Zenner et al., 2014; Zoogman et al., 2015). With the increasing recognition of the importance of promoting mental health in schools to facilitate student success, there has been expanding research on the benefits of incorporating mindfulness and MBIs into schools as universal (Tier 1) prevention, and intensive (Tier 3) intervention (e.g., Maynard et al., 2017; Renshaw et al., 2017; Roeser et al., 2022, 2023; Semple et al., 2019). Research reveals that MBIs in schools can be effective not only for students but also for educators and parents (Burgdorf et al., 2019; Carsley et al., 2018; Emerson et al., 2017). MBIs in schools have been shown to promote a variety of small-to-moderate, favorable outcomes that are bigger in scope—benefiting more and different aspects of psychosocial, physical, behavioral, and academic functioning—than other common approaches to school-based mental health promotion (Klingbeil et al., 2017; Phan et al., 2022).

The case for using mindfulness for promoting mental health in schools is largely based on the premises that MBIs are both broadly effective and culturally salient (as discussed above). These points give good reasons for believing that mindfulness practices may be both acceptable and useful across MTSS levels in schools for promoting youth mental health—as well as for promoting the mental health of educators and parents who care for youth (Renshaw, 2020; Renshaw et al., 2022). But this case also relies on one additional important premise: that mindfulness and MBIs may be especially useful for promoting mental health among marginalized youth and in under-resourced schools (Phan et al., 2024; Phan & Renshaw, 2024). In other words, MBIs in schools also hold promise for addressing disparities and advancing mental health equity among youth, which is a critical ethical concern within the broader landscape of youth mental health.

There is, admittedly, sparser evidence for the effectiveness of MBIs with youth who are marginalized compared with their majoritized peers (DeLuca et al., 2018). Yet the evidence that does exist is encouraging and growing, indicating that MBIs can be engaging, acceptable, and effective with diverse populations of youth (Eva & Thayer, 2017; Fung et al., 2016, 2019; Iacono et al., 2022; Jones & Lee, 2022; Mendelson et al., 2010). There are also solid theoretical and practical reasons to expect that MBIs may be particularly effective and feasible for supporting the mental health of diverse youth in under-resourced schools. Some of these reasons include:

- Many mindfulness practices are free and publicly available for use by school-based mental health professionals and educators.
- Mindfulness practices can be adapted to be culturally sensitive while still maintaining their core components.
- Mindfulness practices are scalable and adjustable across MTSS levels, making them appropriate for universal, targeted, and intensive supports.
- Many mindfulness practices require little training and ongoing support, making them feasible to implement for both professionals and paraprofessionals alike.
- Mindfulness practices have been shown to have good social validity with diverse youth and in diverse schools.

Unpacking each of these points is beyond the scope of this chapter. Readers who are interested in diving deeper into these points can review a handful of recent articles that provide background and practice guidelines on how to use mindfulness practices for supporting youth mental health in schools (i.e., Phan et al., 2024; Phan & Renshaw, 2023, 2024; Proulx et al., 2018; Renshaw & Phan, 2024).

USING MINDFULNESS TO PROMOTE MENTAL HEALTH IN SCHOOLS

Now that some background has been provided regarding why this book focuses on using mindfulness for promoting mental health in schools, the following section orients readers to the topics and contents of the chapters. This edited volume aims to provide school-based mental health providers and educational professionals with a well-rounded understanding of how mindfulness practices can be used to promote mental health in schools. The contents of this book draw upon a robust body of literature to explore the mechanisms through which mindfulness supports mental health, examines the evidence base for MBIs in schools, and provides practical guidance for implementing these practices. By synthesizing findings from diverse multidisciplinary studies, this book aims to offer a nuanced perspective on the potential and limitations of mindfulness and MBIs in educational settings. Ultimately, the chapters in this book are intended to be used by professionals, trainers, researchers, and graduate students alike to advance science and inform practice around how to better use mindfulness practices for promoting mental health and well-being in schools.

The contents of this book are organized into two parts. Part I, Foundations covers the foundations of mindfulness, MBIs, and mindfulness assessment and measurement. These chapters describe the context, outline key concepts, and summarize the best available evidence on these topics related to schools. When readers finish Part I, they should be informed about the landscape of the topic and have an intellectual understanding for how mindfulness practices might be used to promote mental health in schools. Part II, Approaches immerses readers more deeply into several approaches to using MBIs in schools. These chapters narrow in on common frameworks, techniques, and strategies that can be employed for using mindfulness practices for prevention and intervention purposes. Each of these chapters includes background information on the approach, a brief review of evidence supporting it, and thorough description of how to go about implementing it with different populations in schools. When readers finish Part II, they should have a better understanding of the many ways mindfulness practices can be used in schools as well as a clearer view of which approaches may (or may not) be well-suited for use in their schools to meet their particular needs. Following is a summary of each chapter, organized by section (see Table 1.1 for a sequential listing of chapters).

Part I: Foundations

In Chapter 2, *Mindfulness-Based Intervention Research With Youth and Students*, David Klingbeil, Aaron Fischer, and Magenta Silberman (2025) offer a detailed review of the significant growth in MBI research for youth over the past two decades. This chapter provides a comprehensive overview of recent evidence for MBIs implemented in school and community settings, with a particular focus on meta-analytic studies. The chapter is organized into three sections. The first section outlines the historical development of MBIs and their evolving application within school environments. The second section presents a synthesis of findings from eight meta-analytic reviews of MBIs targeting youth. These reviews collectively highlight several potential benefits of MBIs, including enhanced emotional regulation, reduced levels of stress and anxiety, improved academic performance,

and caregivers to enhance the effectiveness of MBIs and improve mental health outcomes. McGowan and colleagues conclude by discussing the future of mindfulness assessment, calling for more research on state mindfulness, the development of alternative measurement techniques, and the integration of psychometrically robust self-report measures into the evaluation of therapeutic processes for educators and parents. They caution that the progress of mindfulness research and practice may be hindered without a consensual definition of mindfulness to guide future work. These efforts, they argue, are essential to substantiate claims that adults and caregivers can benefit from MBIs, ultimately enhancing the well-being of both the caregivers and those they support.

Part II: Approaches

In Chapter 6, *Mindfulness-Based Stress Reduction for Youth and Students*, Lindsey Webb and Erica Sibinga (2025) provide a review and synthesis of the well-researched and established MBSR program and its application for youth. The chapter aims to provide comprehensive information on current MBSR programs for young people and offers best practices for implementing MBSR in school settings. The chapter begins with an overview of how MBSR impacts mental health and details the adaptations made to fit the specific needs of students and youth. Webb and Sibinga highlight the significant benefits of MBSR, noting its effectiveness in improving mental and behavioral health in numerous studies. MBSR, when tailored to be age- and culturally appropriate, is presented as an evidence-based, trauma-informed approach that enhances youth mental health, coping skills, and overall well-being. Webb and Sibinga discuss the potential long-term benefits of teaching mindfulness practices to children and adolescents, suggesting that these practices can mitigate the negative impacts of stress and trauma experienced during youth, thus improving physical and mental health in adulthood. Despite the promise of MBSR, the chapter concludes by emphasizing the need for continued rigorous examination and adaptation of MBSR-based programs with youth. This includes examining the components of MBSR, making necessary cultural adaptations, and addressing implementation issues, such as the differences between in-person and technology-based program delivery.

In Chapter 7, *Mindfulness-Based Cognitive Therapy for Children: Cultivating Mental Health in Elementary Schools*, Matthew Goodman and Randye Semple (2025) discuss Mindfulness-Based Cognitive Therapy for Children (MBCT-C), which is a clinical intervention designed to address anxiety and other emotional or behavioral difficulties in youth. This chapter aims to familiarize school-based mental health providers with MBCT-C, offering an overview of its foundations, core aims, and research supporting its effectiveness. The chapter begins by outlining the fundamental principles and goals of MBCT-C, emphasizing its potential to enhance mental health among elementary school students specifically. It reviews research demonstrating the effectiveness of MBCT-C and discusses its practical implementation in school settings, providing a detailed overview of the 12-week program. Goodman and Semple describe a full session in detail and include a clinical vignette showcasing the application of MBCT-C with an anxious student. The chapter also briefly introduces the Mindfulness Matters Program, a variation of MBCT-C designed for use in K–12 classrooms. This program adapts MBCT-C principles to a broader educational context, aiming to integrate mindfulness practices across different grade levels. Goodman and Semple conclude by discussing ways to support mindfulness practices among parents, teachers, and the broader school culture. They highlight the importance of empowering students to develop acceptance and compassion, effectively relate to their thoughts, feelings, and sensations, and make more conscious and wise choices.

In Chapter 8, *Mindful Yoga for Grade School Students*, Jacinda Dariotis and Diana Fishbein (2025) explore the concept and implementation of mindful yoga (MY) in school settings. They address several critical questions, beginning with "What is mindful yoga?" and "Why should we expose students to mindful yoga?" The chapter outlines the benefits of MY, highlighting its positive effects on emotional regulation, stress coping, and cognitive control, including its neurophysiological impacts. Next, the authors discuss "How can mindful yoga be incorporated into schools?" This section shares case studies that demonstrate successful integration of MY into various school environments, showcasing practical applications and benefits observed in real-world settings. To help educators and administrators get started, the chapter answers the questions, "How does one get started with mindful yoga?" and "Where does one locate resources?" The chapter concludes by exploring future directions for MY in schools. The authors propose an agenda for further research and evaluation, emphasizing the need to identify effective components of MY programs and assess the outcomes. They advocate for integrating mindfulness training into teacher preparation programs and other higher education curricula. Overall, Dariotis and Fishbein argue that MY has significant potential as an evidence-based intervention for youth, with ongoing evaluation and research needed to optimize its effectiveness and integration into educational systems.

In Chapter 9, *Dialectical Behavior Therapy Skills in Schools*, James Mazza and Elizabeth Dexter-Mazza (2025) explore the integration of mindfulness strategies into school settings through the framework of DBT skills. Although mindfulness in schools has gained attention in the past two decades, DBT's mindfulness strategies have been implemented in clinical settings with adolescents for even longer. The chapter highlights *DBT Skills in Schools: Skills Training for Emotional Problem Solving for Adolescents* (DBT STEPS-A), which is a universal prevention curriculum designed for middle and high school students. DBT STEPS-A teaches essential DBT skills, with mindfulness serving as the foundational element for acquiring other DBT skills. Mazza and Dexter-Mazza provide an overview of current research on school-based DBT, demonstrating how mindfulness skills contribute to academic and social-emotional learning. The chapter also addresses the current gaps in school-based mindfulness research, noting limitations and barriers to using mindfulness with youth from a DBT perspective. Ultimately, the authors advocate for expanding educational practices to include DBT skills as a proactive approach to helping students achieve their educational goals while improving their social-emotional well-being. Overall, Mazza and Dexter-Mazza argue that incorporating DBT skills into school curricula can significantly enhance students' ability to manage emotions and solve problems, thereby supporting youths' mental health, well-being, and academic success.

In Chapter 10, *DNA-V: The Youth Model of Acceptance and Commitment Therapy for Social-Emotional Learning in Schools*, Louise Hayes and Joseph Ciarrochi (2025) critique the narrow focus on mindfulness solely as formal meditation, advocating instead for a broader approach that integrates mindfulness into daily activities like conversations, sports, or nature walks. They introduce DNA-V, which is an MBI for young people based on ACT principles and evidence-based social-emotional learning (SEL) programs. The chapter presents DNA-V as a systemic model that integrates behaviors, thoughts, and feelings into four psychological processes that emphasize intervening in self and social contexts. These processes serve as a framework for understanding youth well-being and prosocial behavior, guiding interventionists in assessing and enhancing social-emotional skills and mental health. Hayes and Ciarrochi emphasize DNA-V's use of mindfulness and positive psychology techniques to expand youths' skills and strengths through three key processes: the discoverer, the noticer, and the advisor. Ultimately, the DNA-V model seeks to empower young people by equipping them with the skills to engage mindfully in various life situations, fostering resilience, vitality, valued living, emotional regulation, and personal growth. The chapter underscores the importance of integrating mindfulness and SEL into educational practices to promote holistic development and well-being among youth.

In Chapter 11, *Brief Mindfulness Interventions: Soles of the Feet for Students and Guided Mindfulness Practices*, Joshua Felver (2025) discusses two types of brief MBIs designed for school settings: the Soles of the Feet (SoF) curriculum and basic guided mindfulness practices. The chapter emphasizes the advantages of brief MBIs over more intensive programs, highlighting their simplicity and ease of replication in research studies. The simplicity of brief curricular formats also facilitates intervention component analyses, making it easier to understand which parts of MBIs work to bring about behavior change. Felver details the SoF curriculum, which addresses student disruptive behavior across five sessions and has been empirically replicated in several studies. The chapter then reviews basic guided mindfulness practices, which are intended to be used daily, as a straightforward yet potentially effective intervention requiring minimal resource allocation. Empirical evidence supports the positive impact of both the SoF curriculum and daily guided mindfulness practices on student functioning. Given the lack of conclusive data favoring more time- and resource-intensive MBIs over less intensive alternatives, Felver suggests prioritizing briefer and simpler programming in schools to optimize resource efficiency. He concludes by advocating for further research to explore the full extent of benefits offered by brief MBIs compared to their more intensive counterparts in educational settings, anticipating exciting developments in the future.

In Chapter 12, *Mindfulness for Teachers: Evidence-Based Models to Promote Well-Being*, Patricia Jennings (2025) underscores the pivotal role of teachers in fostering supportive classroom environments that enhance students' social, emotional, and academic learning. The chapter reviews current research highlighting the benefits of MBIs tailored for teachers, emphasizing how regular engagement with mindfulness practices improves teachers' emotional regulation and stress management. Jennings discusses contemporary studies demonstrating that teachers trained in mindful awareness and compassion exhibit enhanced abilities to respond consciously to students' needs and challenging behaviors, thereby reducing the likelihood of negative impacts on student relationships and learning outcomes. Evidence supports the positive impact of MBIs on teacher well-being, classroom interactions, and student engagement. Jennings also calls for further research to explore whether MBIs focused on teacher well-being actually influence students' social-emotional competence, academic performance, and behavioral outcomes. Additionally, there is a need for deeper investigation into the causal mechanisms and moderating factors that underpin these findings, helping users of MBIs to better understand how mindfulness practices benefit both teachers and students in educational settings. Overall, the chapter advocates for continued investment in research to expand the evidence base for using mindfulness in education, highlighting its potential to enhance teacher well-being and classroom dynamics while promoting positive student outcomes.

In Chapter 13, *Mindfulness-Based Parent Training*, Stacy Bender (2025) focuses on the framework of mindful parenting and, specifically, mindfulness-based parent training (MBPT). The chapter provides an overview of empirical support for MBPT, highlighting relevant programs and their outcomes. Empirical evidence suggests that MBPT yields positive outcomes for parents, children, and adolescents, making it a promising intervention for addressing family needs within school environments. Bender discusses how mindful parenting promotes mental health and emotional balance by enhancing five dimensions of parent-child relationships: attentive listening, non-judgmental acceptance of self and child, emotional awareness, self-regulation, and compassion. Mindful parenting not only supports children's emotional development but also nurtures a compassionate self-acceptance among parents themselves, which is crucial for fostering a supportive and nurturing family environment. To illustrate how this approach might be used in educational settings, Bender discusses two case examples of MBPT implemented in school settings. The first example details a six-week, one-hour parent group for preschool families. The second example describes a three-week, one-and-a-half-hour parent mindfulness workshop within a school district. Overall, Bender advocates for further exploration and implementation of MBPT in educational settings, emphasizing its role in fostering supportive family-school partnerships and promoting holistic student success.

In Chapter 14, which is the final chapter of the book, *Mindfulness-Based Programs for Classrooms and Schools*, Tyler Renshaw, Shane Jimerson, Caleb Farley, and Thomas Franzmann narrow in on the nature of school-based mindfulness programs (SBMPs). They differentiate SBMPs from other MBIs with youth in schools by their curriculum-based method that has a prevention-oriented purpose, provided to students at the small-group or classroom level. The chapter includes an overview of key features of SMBPs, discussing findings about how programs compare in relation to their general implementation characteristics,

representative sample of U.S. youth aged 4–17 years, indicated that the prevalence of self-reported mindfulness practice increased from .3% in 2012 to 1.6% in 2017 (Wang et al., 2019). Mindfulness usage rates in 2017 were similar for both children (4–11 years) and adolescents (12–17). However, most youth endorsing using mindfulness were female (62%), identified as non-Hispanic White (74%), had parents who were college graduates (58%), and lived with families with incomes above $75,000 (52%; Wang et al., 2019)—suggesting mindfulness practices may be less prevalent among youth identifying with marginalized communities. Presently, the best estimate is that 1–2% of U.S. youth may be exposed to mindfulness, and that youth with more privileged identities and families are more likely to use mindfulness compared with their marginalized peers.

The reasons marginalized youth may have less exposure and engagement with mindfulness and MBIs warrant further exploration. Research with adults shows that those from underrepresented populations tend to engage less with MBIs (Olano et al., 2015). However, studies with adults also suggest that MBIs are more acceptable and have higher completion rates among marginalized populations compared to other treatments (Dutton et al., 2013; Roth & Robbins, 2004). DeLuca et al. (2018) also suggested that the lacking evidence base itself could be a barrier that deters providers from offering MBIs with marginalized youth. School-based mental health providers, educational professionals, and researchers are therefore encouraged to undertake serious efforts to culturally adapt MBIs in order to make them more relevant and available to diverse youth (Phan & Renshaw, 2024; Proulx et al., 2018).

Several chapters in this book offer insight into how to make MBIs culturally sensitive and responsive, yet much more work is needed on this front. For example, researchers and interventionists should carefully consider how intersecting identities (e.g., race, ethnicity, gender, sexuality, socioeconomic status) and experiences with discrimination and marginalization may influence youths' experiences with MBIs. Adapting mindfulness practices to better align with the cultural values and beliefs of youths' families and communities may be especially useful for enhancing their engagement (Phan & Renshaw, 2024). Additionally, individuals with specific disabling conditions may benefit from tailored mindfulness techniques adjusted to their cognitive abilities (Felver & Singh, 2020; Neece et al., 2019). Ultimately, improving the reach of MBIs with marginalized youth in schools will require active consideration of diversity and developmental factors to ensure relevance, accessibility, and engagement across populations.

Third, another future direction for advancing the science and practice of MBIs in schools is intentionally integrating MBIs into targeted prevention efforts. Earlier in this chapter, an overview of modern school-based mental health services was provided, outlining how prevention and intervention are organized via MTSS with three common levels: universal (Tier 1), targeted (Tier 2), and intensive (Tier 3) supports (see the Mental Health Supports in Schools section). Reviews of the research on MBIs with youth in schools illustrate that they are mostly implemented and researched at the universal level (Klingbeil et al., 2017b; Phan & Renshaw, 2024; Renshaw et al., 2023). Notably, these universal (Tier 1) MBIs are largely adaptations of intensive (Tier 3) MBIs that were originally developed and validated outside of schools with clinical populations. Examples of this generalization—adapting Tier 3 interventions for Tier 1 prevention—are illustrated in the chapters in this book on MBSR (see Chapter 6), MBCT-C (see Chapter 7), DBT skills (see Chapter 9), and DNA-V, which is an adaption of the ACT treatment model (see Chapter 10). MBIs in schools at the universal and intensive levels are thus well-grounded in evidence-based intervention frameworks. What remains to address is how to effectively integrate MBIs within targeted prevention.

Targeted (Tier 2) prevention plays a key role within schools as the bridge between universal (Tier 1) and intensive (Tier 3) supports. It is a middle-ground level of support that offers moderate-intensity services to some students based on identified risk factors or early indicators of problems. The goal of targeted prevention is to support students who are exhibiting risk early and efficiently as well as to strengthen their protective factors (Yong & Cheney, 2013), mitigating the potential for worsening risk factors or the development of more chronic and severe problems over time (Merrell et al., 2022). It is estimated that 10–20% of the student population in any given school will not respond to universal prevention and, thus, will need additional support (Brown-Chidsey & Steege, 2010). Tier 2 interventions are designed to provide additional supports in efficient, accessible, and standardized formats that are readily available and can be provided to multiple students within the scope of a school day. Examples of evidence-based targeted prevention for promoting youth mental health in schools include weekly pull-out, small-group, cognitive-behavioral skill instruction (for students at-risk for internalizing concerns) or a daily behavior report card that provides home–school communication about student classroom behavior and is linked to reinforcement contingencies (for students at-risk for externalizing concerns).

Although there has been some discussion of the value of using MBIs as targeted prevention in schools (Renshaw, 2020; Renshaw et al., 2017; Renshaw et al., 2022), there have been no published studies on this topic, to date. This area therefore warrants further exploration in both research and practice. It is possible that MBIs might be integrated into Tier 2 in several ways, modeling after preexisting evidence-based targeted interventions. For instance, mindfulness curricula, like MBSR or DNA-V, could be adapted into a small-group intervention format with preventive aims, similar to how cognitive-behavioral and social-emotional learning curricula have been adapted for use at Tier 2 (Mendez, 2016). As another example, students could be trained in and prompted to use brief mindfulness practices (see Chapter 11) when engaging in off-task behavior in the classroom, similar to how performance feedback and self-management skills are used by teachers for Tier 2 purposes (Yong & Cheney, 2013). Yet another example is that mindfulness practices could be combined with a well-established targeted intervention for the purposes of enhancing the effects of that protocol, similar to how behavioral and social-emotional supports can be combined to improve their benefits for students at Tier 2 (Domitrovich et al., 2010). Those invested in MBIs are encouraged to test these possibilities and substantiate the role of MBIs within targeted prevention in schools.

CONCLUSION

Mindfulness practices are now well-established in many clinical service settings, in several aspects of mainstream culture, and increasingly in schools. Collectively, the contents of this book contribute to advances in science and practice that affirm the value of mindfulness practices to promote the mental health of youth and their caregivers at school. The chapters in this edited volume may be broadly useful for mental health providers and educational professionals who are engaged with school-based programming. This book might also be useful to graduate students, faculty, and applied researchers who are striving for an evidence-based understanding of when, why, and how to best use mindfulness practices in schools. Although mindfulness is clearly a promising approach for supporting mental health in schools, much work is needed to clarify the differential effects of MBIs on particular youth outcomes, to better optimize MBIs as culturally sensitive and responsive practices in schools, and to test the potential of MBIs as targeted (Tier 2) prevention for supporting students with emerging risk.

REFERENCES

Aggarwal, N. K., Pieh, M. C., Dixon, L., Guarnaccia, P., Alegría, M., & Lewis-Fernández, R. (2016). Clinician descriptions of communication strategies to improve treatment engagement by racial/ethnic minorities in mental health services: A systematic review. *Patient Education and Counseling*, *99*(2), 198–209. https://doi.org/10.1016/j.pec.2015.09.002

Alegría, M., Green, J. G., McLaughlin, K. A., Loder, S. (2015). *Disparities in child and adolescent mental health and mental health services in the US.* William T. Grant Foundation. http://cfs.cbcs.usf.edu/projects-research/_docs/Disparities_in_child_and_adolescent_health.pdf

American Psychological Association. (2021). *Equity, diversity, and inclusion: Inclusive language guidelines.* https://www.apa.org/about/apa/equity-diversity-inclusion/language-guidelines.pdf

Anderson, J. K., Howarth, E., Vainre, M., Jones, P., & Humphrey, A. (2017). A scoping literature review of service-level barriers for access and engagement with mental health services for children and young people. *Children and Youth Services Review*, *77*, 164–176. https://doi.org/10.1016/j.childyouth.2017.04.017

Auerswald, C. L., Piatt, A. A., Mirzazadeh, A., & Unicef. (2017). *Research with disadvantaged, vulnerable and/or marginalized adolescents* (Issue Brief No. 6). United Nations Children's Fund. https://www.unicef-irc.org/publications/878-research-with-disadvantaged-vulnerable-and-or-marginalized-adolescents.html

Baer, R. A. (2003). Mindfulness training as clinical intervention: A conceptual and empirical review. *Clinical Psychology: Science and Practice*, *10*, 125–143.

Bains, R. M., & Diallo, A. F. (2016). Mental health services in school-based health centers: Systematic review. *The Journal of School Nursing*, *32*(1), 8–19. https://doi.org/10.1177/1059840515590607

Bear, L., Finer, R., Guo, S., & Lau, A. S. (2014). Building the gateway to success: An appraisal of progress in reaching underserved families and reducing racial disparities in school-based mental health. *Psychological Services, 11*(4), 388–397. http://dx.doi.org/10.1037/a0037969

Bender, S. L. (2025). Mindfulness-based parent training. In T. L. Renshaw & S. R. Jimerson (Eds.), *Using mindfulness to promote mental health in schools*, 255–269. Oxford University Press.

Biegel, G. M., Brown, K. W., Shapiro, S. L., & Schubert, C. M. (2009). Mindfulness-based stress reduction for the treatment of adolescent psychiatric outpatients: A randomized clinical trial. Journal of Consulting and Clinical Psychology, 77(5), 855–856. https://psycnet.apa.org/doi/10.1037/a0016241

Bitsko, R. H., Claussen, A. H., Lichstein, J., Black, L. I., Jones, S. E., Danielson, M. L., . . . Ghandour, R. M. (2022). Mental health surveillance among children—United States, 2013–2019. *Morbidity and Mortality Weekly Report, 71*(2), 1–42. http://dx.doi.org/10.15585/mmwr.su7102a1

Bradshaw, C. P., Evans, S. W., Owens, J. S., & Weist, M. D. (Eds.). (2023). *Handbook of school mental health: Innovations in science and practice* (3rd ed.). Springer.

Brown-Chidsey, R., & Steege, M. (2010). *Response to intervention: Principles and effective strategies*. Guilford.

Burgdorf, V., Szabó, M., & Abbott, M. J. (2019). The effect of mindfulness interventions for parents on parenting stress and youth psychological outcomes: A systematic review and meta-analysis. *Frontiers in Psychology, 10*, 1336. https://doi.org/10.3389/fpsyg.2019.01336

Carsley, D., Khoury, B., & Heath, N. L. (2018). Effectiveness of mindfulness interventions for mental health in schools: A comprehensive meta-analysis. *Mindfulness, 9*, 693–707. https://doi.org/10.1007/s12671-017-0839-2

Cohen, K. A., Ito, S., Ahuvia, I. L., Yang, Y., Zhang, Y., Renshaw, T. L., Larson, M., Cook, C. R., Hill, S., Rapoport, A., Smock, A., Yang, M., & Schleider, J. L. (2024). Brief school-based interventions targeting student mental health or wellbeing: A systematic review and meta-analysis. *Clinical Child and Family Psychology Review*. Advance online. https://doi.org/10.1007/s10567-024-00487-2

Dariotis, J. K., & Fishbein, D. H. (2025). Mindful yoga for grade school students. In T. L. Renshaw & S. R. Jimerson (Eds.), *Using mindfulness to promote mental health in schools*, 163–186. Oxford University Press.

DeLuca, S. M., Kelman, A. R., & Waelde, L. C. (2018). A systematic review of ethnoracial representation and cultural adaptation of mindfulness- and meditation-based interventions. *Psychological Studies, 63*(2), 117–129. https://doi.org/10.1007%2Fs12646-018-0452-z

Domitrovich, C. E., Bradshaw, C. P., Greenberg, M. T., Embry, D., Poduska, J. M., & Ialongo, N. S. (2010). Integrated models of school-based prevention: Logic and theory. *Psychology in the Schools, 47*(1), 71–88. https://doi.org/10.1002/pits.20452

Duong, M. T., Bruns, E. J., Lee, K., Cox, S., Coifman, J., Mayworm, A., & Lyon, A. R. (2021). Rates of mental health service utilization by children and adolescents in schools and other common service settings: A systematic review and meta-analysis. *Administration and Policy in Mental Health and Mental Health Services Research, 48*, 420–439. https://doi.org/10.1007/s10488-020-01080-9

Dutton, M. A., Bermudez, D., Matás, A., Majid, H., & Myers, N. L. (2013). Mindfulness-based stress reduction for low-income, predominantly African American women with PTSD and a history of intimate partner violence. *Cognitive and Behavioral Practice, 20* (1), 23–32. https://doi.org/10.1016/j.cbpra.2011.08.003

Eber, L., Barrett, S., Perales, K., Jeffrey-Pearsall, J., Pohlman, K., Putnam, R., Splett, J., & Weist, M. D. (2019). Advancing education effectiveness: Interconnecting school mental health and school-wide PBIS, Volume 2: An implementation guide. Center for Positive Behavior Interventions and Supports (funded by the Office of Special Education Programs, U.S. Department of Education). University of Oregon Press.

Emerson, L. M., Leyland, A., Hudson, K., Rowse, G., Hanley, P., & Hugh-Jones, S. (2017). Teaching mindfulness to teachers: A systematic review and narrative synthesis. *Mindfulness*, *8*, 1136–1149. https://doi.org/10.1007/s12671-017-0691-4

Eva, A. L., & Thayer, N. M. (2017). Learning to BREATHE: A pilot study of a mindfulness-based intervention to support marginalized youth. *Journal of Evidence-Based Complementary & Alternative Medicine*, *22*(4), 580–591. https://doi.org/10.1177/2156587217696928

Fazel, M., Hoagwood, K., Stephan, S., & Ford, T. (2014). Mental health interventions in schools 1: Mental health interventions in high-income countries. *The Lancet Psychiatry*, *1*(5), 377–387. https://doi.org/10.1016/S2215-0366(14)70312-8

Felver, J. C. (2025). Brief mindfulness interventions: Soles of the Feet for Students and guided mindfulness practices. In T. L. Renshaw & S. R. Jimerson (Eds.), *Using mindfulness to promote mental health in schools*, 223–239. Oxford University Press.

Felver, J. C., Celis-de Hoyos, C. E., Tezanos, K., & Singh, N. N. (2016). A systematic review of mindfulness-based interventions for youth in school settings. *Mindfulness*, *7*, 34–45. https://doi.org/10.1007/s12671-015-0389-4

Felver, J. C., Doerner, E., Jones, J., Kaye, N. C., & Merrell, K. W. (2013). Mindfulness in school psychology: Applications for intervention and professional practice. *Psychology in the Schools*, *50*(6), 531–547. https://doi.org/10.1002/pits.21695

Felver, J. C., and Singh, N. N. (2020). *Mindfulness in the classroom: An evidence-based program to reduce disruptive behavior and increase academic engagement*. New Harbinger.

Fung, J., Guo, S., Jin, J., Bear, L., & Lau, A. (2016). A pilot randomized trial evaluating a school-based mindfulness intervention for ethnic minority youth. *Mindfulness*, *7*(4), 819–828. https://doi.org/10.1007/s12671-016-0519-7

Fung, J., Kim, J. J., Jin, J., Chen, G., Bear, L., & Lau, A. S. (2019). A randomized trial evaluating school-based mindfulness intervention for ethnic minority youth: Exploring mediators and moderators of intervention effects. *Journal of Abnormal Child Psychology*, *47*, 1–19. https://doi.org/10.1007/s10802-018-0425-7

Goodman, M. S., & Semple, R. J. (2025). Mindfulness-based cognitive therapy for children: Cultivating mental health in elementary schools. In T. L. Renshaw & S. R. Jimerson (Eds.), *Using mindfulness to promote mental health in schools*, 139–162. Oxford University Press.

Hayes, L., & Ciarrochi, J. (2025). DNA-V: The youth model of acceptance and commitment therapy for social–emotional learning in schools. In T. L. Renshaw & S. R. Jimerson (Eds.), *Using mindfulness to promote mental health in schools*, 205–222. Oxford University Press.

Iacono, G., Craig, S. L., Crowder, R., Brennan, D. J., & Loveland, E. K. (2022). A qualitative study of the LGBTQ+ youth affirmative mindfulness program for sexual and gender minority youth. *Mindfulness*, *13*, 222–237. https://doi.org/10.1007/s12671-021-01787-2

Jennings, P. A. (2023). Minding the gap: Attending to implementation science and practice in school-based mindfulness program research. *Mindfulness*, *14*, 314–321 https://doi.org/10.1007/s12671-022-02062-8

Jennings, P. A. (2025). Mindfulness for teachers: Evidence-based models to promote well-being. In T. L. Renshaw & S. R. Jimerson (Eds.), *Using mindfulness to promote mental health in schools*, 240–254. Oxford University Press.

Jones, J. M., and Lee, L. H. (2022). Art-based mindfulness at school: A culturally responsive approach to school mental health. *Psychology in the Schools, 59*(10), 2085–2105. https://doi.org/10.1002/pits.22660

Kabat-Zinn, J. (1982). An out-patient program in behavioral medicine for chronic pain patients based on the practice of mindfulness meditation: Theoretical considerations and preliminary results. *General Hospital Psychiatry, 4*, 33–47.

Kabat-Zinn, J. (1994). *Wherever you go, there you are: Mindfulness meditation in everyday life*. Hyperion.

Kabat-Zinn, J. (2003). Mindfulness-based interventions in context: Past, present, and future. *Clinical Psychology: Science and Practice, 10*(2), 144–156. https://doi.org/10.1093/clipsy.bpg016

Kaiser Permanente. (n.d.). *Practicing mindfulness*. https://healthy.kaiserpermanente.org/health-wellness/mindfulness

Klingbeil, D. A., Fischer, A. J., Renshaw, T. L., Bloomfield, B. S., Polakoff, B., Willenbrink, J. B., Copek, R. A., & Chan, K. T. (2017a). Mindfulness-based interventions with youth: A comprehensive meta-analysis of single-subject design studies. *Psychology in the Schools, 54*(1), 70–87. https://doi.org/10.1002/pits.21982

Klingbeil, D. A., Fischer, A. J., & Silberman, M. (2025). Overview of mindfulness-based intervention research with youth and students. In T. L. Renshaw & S. R. Jimerson (Eds.), *Using mindfulness to promote mental health in schools*, 28–49. Oxford University Press.

Klingbeil, D. A., & Renshaw, T. L. (2018). Mindfulness-based interventions for teachers: A meta-analysis of the emerging evidence base. *School Psychology Quarterly, 33*(4), 501–511.

Klingbeil, D. A., Renshaw, T. L., Willenbrink, J. B., Copek, R. A., Chan, K. T., Haddock, A., & Clifton, J. D. (2017b). Mindfulness-based interventions with youth: A comprehensive meta-analysis of group-design studies. *Journal of School Psychology, 63*, 77–103. https://doi.org/10.1016/j.jsp.2017.03.006

Linehan, M. M., & Wilks, C. R. (2015). The course and evolution of dialectical behavior therapy. *American Journal of Psychotherapy, 69*(2), 97–110.

Lebrun-Harris, L. A., Ghandour, R. M., Kogan, M. D., & Warren, M. D. (2022). Five-year trends in US children's health and well-being, 2016–2020. *JAMA Pediatrics, 176* (7), e220056. https://doi.org/10.1001/jamapediatrics.2022.0056

Maura, J., & Weisman de Mamani, A. (2017). Mental health disparities, treatment engagement, and attrition among racial/ethnic minorities with severe mental illness: A review. *Journal of Clinical Psychology in Medical Settings, 24*(3–4), 187–210. https://doi.org/10.1007/s10880-017-9510-2

Maynard, B. R., Solis, M. R., Miller, V. L., & Brendel, K. E. (2017). Mindfulness-based interventions for improving cognition, academic achievement, behavior, and socioemotional functioning of primary and secondary school students. *Campbell Systematic Reviews, 13*(1), 1–144. https://doi.org/10.4073/csr.2017.5

Mayo Clinic. (2022, October 11). *Mindfulness exercises*. https://www.mayoclinic.org/healthy-lifestyle/consumer-health/in-depth/mindfulness-exercises/art-20046356

Mazza, J. J., & Dexter-Mazza, E. (2025). Dialectical behavior therapy skills in schools. In T. L. Renshaw & S. R. Jimerson (Eds.), *Using mindfulness to promote mental health in schools*, 187–204. Oxford University Press.

McGowan, R. C., Michel, R., & Coyne, L. W. (2025). Measures of mindfulness for adults and caregivers. In T. L. Renshaw & S. R. Jimerson (Eds.), *Using mindfulness to promote mental health in schools*, 99–121. Oxford University Press.

Mendelson, T., Greenberg, M. T., Dariotis, J. K., Gould, L. F., Rhoades, B. L., & Leaf, P. J. (2010). Feasibility and preliminary outcomes of a school-based mindfulness intervention for urban youth. *Journal of Abnormal Child Psychology, 38*(7), 985–994. https://doi.org/10.1007/s10802-010-9418-x

Mendez, L. R. (2016). *Cognitive behavioral therapy in schools: A tiered approach to youth mental health services*. Routledge.

Merrell, K. W., Ervin, R. A., Gimpel Peacock, G., & Renshaw, T. L. (2022). *School psychology for the 21st century: Foundations and practices* (3rd ed.). Guilford.

Mindful. (n.d.). *Mindful Magazine*. https://www.mindful.org/magazine/

Napoli, M., Krech, P. R., & Holley, L. C. (2005). Mindfulness training for elementary school students: The attention academy. *Journal of Applied School Psychology, 21*(1), 99–125. https://doi.org/10.1300/J370v21n01_05

Neece, C. L., Chan, N., Klein, K., Roberts, L., & Fenning, R. M. (2019). Mindfulness-based stress reduction for parents of children with developmental delays: Understanding the experiences of Latino families. *Mindfulness, 10*, 1017–1030. https://doi.org/10.1007/s12671-018-1011-3

Nemours Children's Health. (2023). *Mindfulness*. https://kidshealth.org/en/teens/mindfulness.html

Olano, H. A., Kachan, D., Tannenbaum, S. L., Mehta, A., Annane, D. W., & Lee, D. J. (2015). Engagement in mindfulness practices by U.S. adults: Sociodemographic barriers. *Journal of Alternative and Complementary Medicine, 21*(2), 100–102. https://doi.org/10.1089/acm.2014.0269

One Mind. (n.d.). *One Mind PsyberGuide*. https://onemindpsyberguide.org/

O'Reilly, M., Svirydzenka, N., Adams, S., & Dogra, N. (2018). Review of mental health promotion interventions in schools. *Social Psychiatry and Psychiatric Epidemiology, 53* (7), 647–662. https://doi.org/10.1007/s00127-018-1530-1

Pattermore, C. (2022, May 27). *How to get started with practicing mindfulness*. PsychCentral. https://psychcentral.com/health/new-to-mindfulness-how-to-get-started

Phan, M. L., & Renshaw, T. L. (2023). Guidelines for implementing and adapting evidence-based interventions with marginalized youth in schools. *American Journal of Orthopsychiatry, 93*(3), 256–268. https://doi.org/10.1037/ort0000676

Phan, M. L., & Renshaw, T. L. (2024). Guidelines for adapting mindfulness-based school interventions with youth who are racially and ethnically marginalized. *Journal of Educational and Psychological Consultation*. Advance online. https://doi.org/10.1080/10474412.2024.2373462

Phan, M. L., Renshaw, T. L., Caramanico, J., Greeson, J. M., MacKenzie, E., Atkinson-Diaz, Z., Nuske, H. J. (2022). Mindfulness-based school interventions: A systematic review of outcome evidence quality by study design. *Mindfulness, 13*(7), 1591–1613. https://doi.org/10.1007/s12671-022-01885-9

Phan, M. L., Renshaw, T. L., & Farley, C. D. (2024). Guidelines for increasing access to mindfulness-based interventions in under-resourced schools. *Contemporary School Psychology*. Advance online. https://doi.org/10.1007/s40688-024-00508-5

Pickert, K. (2014, January 23). The mindful revolution. *TIME*. https://time.com/1556/the-mindful-revolution/

Proulx, J., Croff, R., Oken, B., Aldwin, C. M., Fleming, C., Bergen-Cico, D., Le T., & Noorani, M. (2018). Considerations for research and development of culturally relevant mindfulness interventions in American minority communities. *Mindfulness, 9*, 361–370. https://doi.org/10.1007/s12671-017-0785-z

Racine, N., McArthur, B. A., Cooke, J. E., Eirich, R., Zhu, J., & Madigan, S. (2021). Global prevalence of depressive and anxiety symptoms in children and adolescents during COVID-19: A meta-analysis. *JAMA Pediatrics, 175*(11), 1142–1150. https://doi.org/10.1001/jamapediatrics.2021.2482

Renshaw, T. L. (2020). Mindfulness-based intervention in schools. In C. Maykel & M. A. Bray (Eds.), *Promoting mind–body health in schools: Interventions for mental health professionals* (pp. 145–160). American Psychological Association. https://doi.org/10.1037/0000157-010

Renshaw, T. L., Barr, J. D., Farley, C. D., Franzmann, T. K., Phan, M. L., Vinal, S. A., Weeks, S. N., & Jimerson, S. R. (2025). Mindfulness-based programs for classrooms and schools. In T. L. Renshaw & S. R. Jimerson (Eds.), *Using mindfulness to promote mental health in schools*. Oxford University Press.

Renshaw, T. L., & Cook, C. R. (2017). Mindfulness in the schools—Historical roots, current trends, and future directions. *Psychology in the Schools, 54*(1), 5–12. https://doi.org/10.1002/pits.21978

Renshaw, T. L., Fischer, A. J., & Klingbeil, D. A. (2017). Mindfulness-based intervention in school psychology. *Contemporary School Psychology, 21*, 299–303. https://doi.org/10.1007/s40688-017-0166-6

Renshaw, T. L., & Jimerson, S. R. (Eds.). *Using mindfulness to promote mental health in schools*. Oxford University Press.

Renshaw, T. L., Jimerson, S. R., Phan, M. L., & Franzmann, T. K. (2025). Advancing the science and practice of mindfulness to support mental health in schools. In T. L. Renshaw & S. R. Jimerson (Eds.), *Using mindfulness to promote mental health in schools*, 3–27. Oxford University Press.

Renshaw, T. L., & Phan, M. L. (2023). Using implementation reporting to advance culturally sensitive and equity focused mindfulness programs in schools. *Mindfulness, 14*, 307–313. https://doi.org/10.1007/s12671-023-02068-w

Renshaw, T. L., Weeks, S. N., Roberson, A. J., Upton, S. R., Barr, J. D., Phan, M. L., & Farley, C. D. (2022). Cultivating mindfulness in schools to promote well-being. In K. Allen, M. J. Furlong, D. Vella-Brodrick ,& S. Suldo (Eds.), *Handbook of positive psychology in schools: Supporting process and practice* (3rd ed.; pp. 135–148). Routledge. https://doi.org/10.4324/9781003013777

Renshaw, T. L., Weeks, S. N., Roberson, A. J., & Vinal, S. (2023). ACT in schools: A public health approach. In M. P. Twohig, M. E. Levin,& J. M. Peterson (Eds.), *Oxford handbook of acceptance and commitment therapy* (pp. 564–583). Oxford. https://doi.org/10.1093/oxfordhb/9780197550076.013.26

Robards, F., Kang, M., Usherwood, T., & Sanci, L. (2018). How marginalized young people access, engage with, and navigate health-care systems in the digital age: Systematic review. *Journal of Adolescent Health, 62*(4), 365–381. https://doi.org/10.1016/j.jadohealth.2017.10.018

Roberson, A. J., & Upton, S. R. (2025). Mindfulness measures for youth and students. In T. L. Renshaw & S. R. Jimerson (Eds.), *Using mindfulness to promote mental health in schools*, 81–98. Oxford University Press.

Roeser, R. W. (2014). The emergence of mindfulness-based interventions in educational settings. In K. W. Brown, J. D. Creswell,& R. M Ryan (Eds.), *Handbook of mindfulness: Theory, research, and practice* (pp. 297–311). Guilford Press.

Roeser, R. W., Galla, B., & Baelen, R. N. (2022). *Mindfulness in schools: Evidence on the impacts of school-based mindfulness programs on student outcomes in P–12 educational settings*. The Pennsylvania State University. https://doi.org/10.31234/osf.io/ascpv

Roeser, R. W., Greenberg, M. T., Frazier, T., Galla, B. M., Semenov, A. D., & Warren, M. T. (2023). Beyond all splits: Envisioning the next generation of science on mindfulness and compassion in schools for students. *Mindfulness, 14*, 239–254. https://doi.org/10.1007/s12671-022-02017-z

Roeser, R. W., Schussler, D., Baelen, R. N., & Galla, B. M. (2023). Mindfulness for students in pre-K to secondary school settings: Current findings, future directions. *Mindfulness, 14*, 233–238. https://doi.org/10.1007/s12671-022-02036-w

Rodgers, C. R. R., Flores, M. W., Bassey, O., Augenblick, J. M., & Cook, B. L. (2022). Racial/ethnic disparity trends in children's mental health care access and expenditures from 2010–2017: Disparities remain despite sweeping policy reform. *Journal of the American Academy of Child & Adolescent Psychiatry, 61*(7), 915–925. https://doi.org/10.1016/j.jaac.2021.09.420

Roth, B., & Robbins, D. (2004). Mindfulness-based stress reduction and health-related quality of life: Findings from a bilingual inner-city patient population. *Psychosomatic Medicine, 66* (1), 113–123. https://doi.org/10.1097/01.PSY.0000097337.00754.09

Schonert-Reichl, K. A. (2023). Encouraging advances in the science on mindfulness and compassion in schools: Current research, lingering questions, and future directions. *Mindfulness, 14*, 300–306. https://doi.org/10.1007/s12671-023-02070-2

Schonert-Reichl, K. A.,& Roeser, R. W. (Eds.). (2016). *Handbook of mindfulness in education: Integrating theory and research into practice*. Springer.

Sanchez, A. L., Cornacchio, D., Poznanski, B., Golik, A. M., Chou, T., & Comer, J. S. (2018). The effectiveness of school-based mental health services for elementary-aged children: A meta-analysis. *Journal of the American Academy of Child & Adolescent Psychiatry, 57*(3), 153–165. https://doi.org/10.1016/j.jaac.2017.11.022

Segal, Z. V., Williams, J. M. G., & Teasdale, J. D. (2002). *Mindfulness-based cognitive therapy for depression: A new approach to relapse prevention*. Guilford.

Semple, R. J., Droutman, V., & Reid, B. A. (2019). Mindfulness goes to school: Things learned (so far) from research and real-world experiences. *Psychology in the Schools, 54*(1), 29–52. https://doi.org/10.1002/pits.22166

Shigaki, C. L., Glass, B., & Schopp, L. H. (2006). Mindfulness-based stress reduction in medical settings. *Journal of Clinical Psychology in Medical Settings, 13*, 209–216.

Stafford, A. M., & Draucker, C. B. (2020). Barriers to and facilitators of mental health treatment engagement among Latina adolescents. *Community Mental Health Journal, 56*, 662–669. https://doi.org/10.1007/s10597-019-00527-0

TED. (n.d.). *TED talks: Discover ideas worth spreading*. https://www.ted.com/talks

Thayer, A. J., Sullivan, M., Larson, M., & Cook, C. R. (2025). Overview of mindfulness-based intervention research with parents and educators. In T. L. Renshaw & S. R. Jimerson (Eds.), *Using mindfulness to promote mental health in schools*, 50–80. Oxford University Press.

The White House. (2023). Biden–Harris Administration announces actions to protect youth mental health, safety & privacy online. Author. https://www.whitehouse.gov/briefing-room/statements-releases/2023/05/23/fact-sheet-biden-harris-administration-announces-actions-to-protect-youth-mental-health-safety-privacy-online/

Twenge, J. M., Cooper, A. B., Joiner, T. E., Duffy, M. E., & Binau, S. G. (2019). Age, period, and cohort trends in mood disorder indicators and suicide-related outcomes in a nationally representative dataset, 2005–2017. *Journal of Abnormal Psychology, 128*(3), 185–199. https://doi.org/10.1037/abn0000410

U.S. Agency for Healthcare Research and Quality (2022). National healthcare quality and disparities report: Child and adolescent mental health. Available from: https://www.ncbi.nlm.nih.gov/books/NBK587174/

Wang, C., Li, K., & Gaylord, S. (2019). Prevalence, patterns, and predictors of meditation use among US children: Results from the National Health Interview Survey. *Complementary Therapies in Medicine, 43*, 271–276. https://doi.org/10.1016/j.ctim.2019.02.004

Webb, L., & Sibinga, E. M. S. (2025). Mindfulness-based stress reduction for youth and students. In T. L. Renshaw & S. R. Jimerson (Eds.), *Using mindfulness to promote mental health in schools*, 125–138. Oxford University Press.

WebMD. (2022, November 7). *What mindfulness can do for you*. https://www.webmd.com/balance/what-is-mindfulness

Weare, K. (2015). Evidence for mindfulness: Impacts on the wellbeing and performance of school staff. *Mindfulness*, 6(2), 197–206. https://doi.org/10.1007/s12671-013-0199-5

Weare, K. (2023). Where have we been and where are we going with mindfulness in schools? *Mindfulness, 14*, 293–299. https://doi.org/10.1007/s12671-023-02086-8

Whitaker, K., Nicodimos, S., Pullmann, M. D., Duong, M. T., Bruns, E. J., Wasse, J. K., & Lyon, A. R. (2018). Predictors of disparities in access and retention in school-based mental health services. *School Mental Health, 10*, 111–121. https://doi.org/10.1007/s12310-017-9233-4

Whitney, D. G., & Peterson, M. D. (2019). US national and state-level prevalence of mental health disorders and disparities of mental health care use in children. *JAMA Pediatrics, 173*(4), 389–391. https://doi.org/10.1001/jamapediatrics.2018.5399

Wilson, K. G., Bordieri, M. J., Flynn, M. K., Lucas, N. N., & Slater, R. M. (2011). Understanding acceptance and commitment therapy in context: A history of similarities and differences with other cognitive behavior therapies. In J. D. Herbert & E. M. Forman (Eds.), *Acceptance and mindfulness in cognitive behavior therapy: Understanding and applying the new therapies* (pp. 233–263). Wiley.

Yong, M., & Cheney, D. A. (2013). Essential features of tier 2 social–behavioral interventions. *Psychology in the Schools, 50*(8), 844–861. https://doi.org/10.1002/pits.21710

Zenner, C., Herrnleben-Kurz, S., & Walach, H. (2014). Mindfulness-based interventions in schools—A systematic review and meta-analysis. *Frontiers in Psychology, 5*, 603. https://doi.org/10.3389/fpsyg.2014.00603.

Zhang, Q., Wang, J., & Neitzel, A. (2023). School-based mental health interventions targeting depression or anxiety: A meta-analysis of rigorous randomized controlled trials for school-aged children and adolescents. *Journal of Youth and Adolescence, 52*(1), 195–217. https://doi.org/10.1007/s10964-022-01684-4

Zoogman, S., Goldberg, S. B., Hoyt, W. T., & Miller, L. (2015). Mindfulness interventio ns with youth: A meta-analysis. *Mindfulness*, 6(2), 290–302. https://doi.org/10.1 007/s12671-013-0260-4

2

Mindfulness-Based Interventions With Youth and Students

DAVID A. KLINGBEIL, AARON J. FISCHER, AND MAGENTA SILBERMAN ■

Research on mindfulness for youth has grown tremendously over the past 20 years (Black, 2015). The number of new intervention studies, systematic reviews, and meta-analyses that appear in the literature makes staying current on the knowledge surrounding mindfulness-based interventions (MBIs) daunting. This chapter provides a contemporary review of evidence for MBIs delivered to youth in schools and community settings. The purpose of the chapter is to provide a brief overview of recent research on MBIs, with a focus on recent meta-analytic work that summarized findings across a number of research studies. The chapter includes three sections. The first describes the history of MBIs and their potential for applications in school settings. The second section summarizes findings from eight published meta-analytic reviews of MBIs with youth. It describes several of the potential benefits of using MBIs for youth. The third section provides a discussion of the implications of these reviews for school-based applications of MBIs.

HISTORY OF MINDFULNESS-BASED INTERVENTIONS AND THEIR APPLICATION IN SCHOOLS

Mindfulness practices have been prevalent in Buddhism throughout history. There are two main branches of Buddhism: Theravad and Mahayana. Tibetan

David A. Klingbeil, Aaron J. Fischer, and Magenta Silberman, *Mindfulness-Based Interventions With Youth and Students*. In: *Using Mindfulness to Promote Mental Health in Schools*. Edited by: Tyler L. Renshaw and Shane R. Jimerson, Oxford University Press. © Oxford University Press (2025). DOI: 10.1093/9780190880507.003.0002

Buddhism, or Vajrayana, is considered part of Mahayana, but it contains distinctly different practices from Zen Buddhism (Cullen, 2011; Smith & Novak, 2003). These varying disciplines have different perspectives that have influenced meditation and other mindfulness practices (Cullen, 2011). In 1979, Jon Kabat-Zinn, who was a student of Buddhism, introduced formal and informal practices of mindfulness into secular settings (Kabat-Zinn, 1982). This work led to the development of mindfulness-based stress reduction (MBSR) and, later, an MBSR training center at the University of Massachusetts Medical Center. MBSR focuses on mindful movement, encouraging body awareness, and utilizing sitting meditation to reduce stress (Cullen, 2011). Based on the seminal research by Kabat-Zinn and others (e.g., Benson, 1975), decades of research on MBIs (e.g., MBSR and mindfulness-based cognitive therapy) has suggested that mindfulness training is beneficial for improving emotional regulation, improving attention, and reducing stress and anxiety in adults (e.g., Baer, 2003; Davis & Hayes, 2011; Khoury et al., 2015). Over the past 20 years, researchers have studied the extension of MBIs to youth in clinical and non-clinical settings (Burke, 2010).

The varying definitions of mindfulness, and what constitutes an MBI, may pose a challenge in the study of MBIs as well as in consuming the literature in this area (Davidson & Kaszniak, 2015; Renshaw et al., 2017). Kabat-Zinn (2003, p. 145) defined mindfulness as "the awareness that emerges through paying attention on purpose, in the present moment, and non-judgmentally to the unfolding of experience moment by moment." The focus on being present and acknowledging one's consciousness are considered the two typical components of contemporary MBIs (Bishop et al., 2004). As the popularity of MBIs grows, there appears to be an increasing number of programs marketed as mindful or mindfulness-based. Young (2016) recommended using the term *mindful awareness* to describe the state of being mindful, using *mindful awareness practices* to describe the strategies that help individuals cultivate mindfulness, and using *mindfulness application* to refer to the way individuals apply their awareness to their daily lives. This chapter uses the term *MBIs* to refer to programs that provide mindful awareness practices to facilitate mindful awareness and improve youth outcomes.

MBIs may include programs that stand as independent intervention or programs that incorporate mindful awareness practices into other interventions. One example of a clinical integration is Segal and colleagues (2002) work on mindfulness-based cognitive therapy (MBCT), which integrates mindfulness practices into traditional cognitive-behavioral therapy for individuals with depression. Within the school system, there is evidence of integration of mindfulness into tiered support models. Schools are increasingly adopting multi-tiered systems of support for addressing students' academic and social-emotional development (Stoiber & Gettinger, 2016). Traditionally, these models emphasize prevention and early intervention, and conceptualize student supports into three tiers: universal, secondary, and tertiary.

Mindfulness awareness practices appear to be well-suited for integration into schools' tiered intervention systems (e.g., Felver et al., 2013; Renshaw et al., 2017).

At the universal level, or Tier 1, all students receive access to school-wide and class-wide academic and behavioral supports (Stoiber & Gettinger, 2016). Several mindfulness-based programs can be conceptualized as providing Tier 1 level of support (Semple et al., 2017). MBIs can be utilized as a school-wide prevention strategy to promote a positive climate, reduce the escalation of problem behavior, and improve the well-being of school staff (Felver et al., 2013; Renshaw et al., 2017). At the Tier 2 level of support, targeted approaches often include small-group programs for students with similar target behaviors. There are a number of MBIs that could be implemented at the Tier 2 level (e.g., Learning to BREATHE; Broderick & Metz, 2009). Finally, at the tertiary level, or Tier 3, students receive individualized interventions to address problem behavior. There are some individualized MBIs available (e.g., Soles of the Feet; Singh et al., 2007); however, research to date reveals less empirical support for the use of MBIs at the individualized level (Renshaw et al., 2017).

PREVIOUS META-ANALYTIC REVIEWS OF MBIS FOR YOUTH

Reviewing the literature of MBIs for youth reveals numerous empirical studies, conceptual articles, systematic reviews, and meta-analyses. Systematic reviews and meta-analyses are especially useful for practitioners seeking a broad overview of what is known about a topic and areas requiring further study (Cooper & Hedges, 2009). Systematic reviews differ from general literature reviews by including a systematic (hence the name) search of the literature using a comprehensive search plan and review protocol for synthesizing information across the articles. When applied to school-based interventions, systematic reviews are useful for identifying trends and variations in the interventions studied, the participants in those studies, the settings in which the interventions were delivered, and the dependent variables measured, and for making general statements about the overall pattern of findings. As mentioned above, there are numerous seminal (e.g., Burke, 2010; Meiklejohn et al., 2012) and more recent systematic reviews (e.g., Black, 2015; Felver et al., 2016) that have made important contributions in the study of MBIs for youth.

Meta-analytic reviews use the same systematic search and coding procedures but add the use of statistical techniques to combine and summarize the results of several studies into an overall effect size. Meta-analytic reviews also provide the option for studying the effects of moderators of the effect size (Cooper & Hedges, 2009). The focus herein is on meta-analytic reviews that provide a quantitative effect size that is useful for evaluating the treatment effects of MBIs. Research on MBIs for youth has rarely compared the effects of MBIs to other active treatments. Until that research exists, effect sizes from meta-analytic reviews can provide an initial guide for comparing the effects of MBIs to the effects of other social-emotional prevention and intervention programs. What follows is a review of eight published meta-analytic reviews that evaluated MBIs for youth (Borquist-Conlon et al., 2019; Carsley et al., 2018; Dunning et al., 2019; Kallapiran et al.,

2015; Klingbeil, Fischer, et al., 2017; Klingbeil, Renshaw, et al., 2017; Zenner et al., 2014; Zoogman et al., 2015). Our chapter covers reviews published before 2019; however, additional reviews have been published since our chapter was written. Readers interested in more recent reviews are encouraged to read Dunning et al. (2023), Mettler et al. (2023), Phillips and Mychailyszyn (2022), among others. A summary of the information contained in the eight meta-analytic reviews is included in Tables 2.1 through 2.3.

SUMMARY OF META-ANALYTIC STUDIES ON MBIS FOR YOUTH

All eight of the published meta-analytic reviews evaluated the use of MBIs for youth. For readers who are less familiar with meta-analyses, there are methodological differences that may not be immediately clear, which makes interpretation of the results difficult (see Table 2.1). Before discussing the results of the meta-analytic reviews further, this section highlights some of the variations in methods to provide context for interpreting the findings. Throughout the remainder of the chapter, the term *primary study* is used to refer to studies that were incorporated into the meta-analytic reviews. The number of primary studies in the eight meta-analytic reviews ranged from 5 (Borquist-Conlon et al., 2019) to 76 (Klingbeil, Renshaw, et al., 2017). Some reasons for this variability are discussed below.

Due to the recent proliferation of MBI research for youth (Black, 2015), the time in which the authors conducted the systematic search would impact the number of primary studies available to the meta-analysts. It is also important to be cognizant of the types of primary studies that were included. For example, two meta-analyses included only randomized controlled trials (Dunning et al., 2019; Kallapiran et al., 2015), five reviews included any group designs (including randomized controlled trials), and one meta-analysis included single-case designs (Klingbeil, Fischer, et al., 2017) that were excluded from the other reviews. Four reviews included unpublished studies such as dissertations (Carsley et al., 2018; Dunning et al., 2019; Kallapiran et al., 2015; Zenner et al., 2014), which may reduce the likelihood that the results are impacted by publication bias (Pigott et al., 2013). It is also important to note that Zoogman et al. (2015) estimated treatment effects using Becker's (1988) *del*, which compares between-group changes from pre-test to post-test. This differed from the standardized mean difference statistics (i.e., d or g) used in the other seven reviews.

Some of the reviews targeted specific populations or outcomes. For example, there were three meta-analytic reviews that focused on the impact of MBIs on mental health outcomes. Borquist-Conlon et al. (2019) reviewed studies conducted only with youth with some type of anxiety diagnosis. Both Carsley and colleagues (2018) and Kallapiran and colleagues (2015) studied the impact of MBIs on broader mental health outcomes, but Carsley and colleagues focused solely on universal interventions that were delivered to general samples of youth in schools. Interpreting the findings from these three studies is not as straightforward as looking at the consistency in reported effect sizes.

Table 2.1. Summary of Meta-Analysis Characteristics

Study	Search Cutoff	Focus	What Research Designs Were Included?	Included Unpublished Studies?	Population	Setting	Other Contemplative Practices Included?	Total Studies (*N*)	Study Quality Indicators
Borquist-Conlon et al. (2019)	February 2016	Effects of MBIs on anxiety outcomes	Between-group designs	Yes	Youth, ages 5–18, with diagnosed anxiety disorders	Any	Yes	5 (188)	Cochrane Collaboration's Risk of Bias Tool (Higgins et al., 2011)
Carsley et al. (2018)	March 2017	Effects of school-based MBIs on mental health and well-being	Between and within-group designs	No	Non-specialized populations of youth, ages 6 to 18	Schools only	No	24 (3,977)	Jadad et al. (1996) criteria
Dunning et al. (2019)	October 2017	Effects of MBIs on cognition and mental health	Randomized controlled trials	Yes	Participants aged 18 years or younger	Any	No	33 (3,666)	Cochrane Collaboration's Risk of Bias Tool (Higgins & Green, 2011)

Kallapiran et al. (2015)	Not Reported	Effects of MBIs on mental health problems	Randomized controlled trials	Yes	Children and adolescents (no age range given), clinical and non-clinical samples	Any	Yes but analyzed separately from MBIs	11 (1,454)	Chambless & Hollon (1996) and Cochrane Collaboration criterion (Higgins & Green, 2006)
Klingbeil, Fischer, et al. (2017)	December 2014	Effects of MBIs from single-case design studies	Single-case designs	No	Youth (no age range given), clinical and non-clinical samples	Any	No	10 (48)	What Works Clearinghouse Criteria (2011)

continued

Table 2.1. Continued

Study	Search Cutoff	Focus	What Research Designs Were Included?	Included Unpublished Studies?	Population	Setting	Other Contemplative Practices Included?	Total Studies (N)	Study Quality Indicators
Klingbeil, Renshaw, et al. (2017)	December 2015	Effects of MBIs delivered to youth in any setting	Between and within-group designs	No	Youth (no age range given), clinical and non-clinical samples	Any	No	76 (6,121)	What Works Clearinghouse Criteria for Single-Case Design (Kratochwill et al., 2010)
Zenner et al. (2014)	August 2012 (database) October 2012 (hand search)	Effects of school-based MBIs targeting psychological aspects.	Included unpublished articles	Yes	Students in grades 1–12	Schools only	No	24 (2,224)	Narratively reviewed design, power, and attrition.
Zoogman et al. (2015)	July 2011	Effects of MBIs for youth	Between and within-group designs	No	Youth (under age 18)	Any	No	20 (1,772)	Jadad et al. (1996) criteria

The impact of methodological variations on the results from the meta-analytic reviews may be best underscored using two examples. First, the largest effect of MBIs was found in a review of single-case designs (Klingbeil, Fischer, et al., 2017; see Table 2.2). That meta-analysis used a design-comparable standardized mean difference for single-case designs (Hedges et al., 2013). Although this effect size is the same metric as Hedges' *g* used in five of the other reviews, the effect sizes found in single-case designs are often much larger than the effect sizes found in between-group designs (Hedges et al., 2013). Therefore, it may be more appropriate to compare the results of that study to other meta-analytic reviews of interventions tested using single-case designs, as opposed to the other, group-design meta-analyses of MBIs reviewed in this chapter.

Second, three of the seven meta-analyses evaluated the impact of MBIs after a follow-up period. Carsley and colleagues (2018) found that the impact of MBIs decreased slightly after a follow-up period, whereas both studies by Klingbeil and colleagues found that the impact of MBIs increased after a follow-up period. This difference may be due to Carsley and colleagues' (2018) focus on school-based MBIs targeting students' mental health outcomes. Taken together, practitioners should consider these types of methodological variations in published meta-analytic reviews when interpreting the results. That said, we believe there are several important questions that can be answered (at least initially) based on the results of these eight meta-analytic reviews.

First, we discuss the types of programs researchers have typically considered as MBIs. Second, we take up the general question of the appropriateness of using MBIs in school settings. Third, we discuss the outcomes that researchers have used MBIs to address. Finally, we evaluate participant and program characteristics that may impact MBI effectiveness.

What Programs Are Considered MBIs?

Perhaps due to the lack of universally accepted definition of an MBI, researchers focused generally on synthesizing the effects of interventions that used mindfulness as the primary therapeutic component. Notably, two reviews (Borquist-Conlon et al., 2019; Kallapiran et al., 2015) also included interventions that use mindfulness as secondary components (e.g., acceptance and commitment therapy and dialectical behavior therapy). These interventions were explicitly excluded from the other reviews.

A variety of MBIs were included in the meta-analytic reviews. MBIs often included formalized training programs such as MBSR and MBCT (which were commonly adapted for youth), formalized programs that were based on MBSR/MBCT (e.g., Learning to BREATHE, Mindfulness in Schools Programme), and programs that included only single aspects of MBSR (e.g., breathing awareness mediation). Mindfulness-based yoga programs were also commonly included in the meta-analytic reviews. There were other MBIs that included a variety of mindfulness activities or exercises. Some of these were formalized programs (e.g., Soles of the Feet), while others appeared to be interventions created by the authors of the primary studies. Given the variability in MBIs included in the meta-analytic reviews, consumers of the literature should evaluate the core therapeutic components included in any program marketed as an MBI to determine whether it fits with the theories of mindfulness practice.

Can Schools Implement MBIs Appropriately?

Given the focus of this book, an important question is whether MBIs are appropriate for use within schools. There have been two meta-analytic reviews focused solely on school settings, showing small effects on a variety of outcomes (Zenner et al., 2014) or on mental health outcomes in particular (Carsley et al., 2017). Klingbeil, Renshaw, and colleagues (2017) found no significant difference in effect sizes derived from studies conducted in schools compared to studies conducted in community or clinical settings. The available evidence suggests that MBIs can be effectively used in schools. We discuss the potential impact of who might deliver the intervention below.

To successfully incorporate MBIs into school settings it is important to consider what factors may hinder school staff and students from participating in the interventions. Dariotis and colleagues (2017) conducted a qualitative research study across three schools to determine common themes that influence students' and teachers' participation in a voluntary school-based mindful yoga program. Some factors that influenced participation were related to the program delivery, including program timing conflicting with students' schedules, features of the physical environment, and logistics of implementing the program (e.g., having to be escorted back to class, integration of boys and girls). Additional factors included: communication with teachers on student attendance and schedule of events, fostering acceptance of the program outside of yoga instruction time (e.g., holding class-wide sessions), optimizing exposure to the intervention, and incentivizing participation for teachers and students.

What Youth Outcomes Can Be Addressed Using MBIs?

Six of the seven meta-analytic reviews of between-group designs presented an overall, aggregate effect size (see Table 2.2). Broadly speaking, it seems the overall effect of MBIs across all outcomes is generally in the small range. This pattern is similar to meta-analytic findings of social-emotional learning programs on a broad array of youth outcomes (Durlak et al., 2011). MBIs appear to have a smaller effect for youth than with clinical or non-clinical adult populations, including teachers (Khoury et al., 2013; Khoury et al., 2015; Klingbeil & Renshaw, 2018). Given the popularity of MBIs, it is important to critically explore the types of outcomes researchers have used MBIs to address. Effect sizes are shown by outcome domain in Table 2.3. In addition to the type of designs, or the focus of the meta-analysis, another source of variation in the outcome domain effects across the meta-analytic reviews relates to how the meta-analytic researchers classified the dependent variables used in the primary studies. For example, two of

Table 2.2. Summary of Overall Effects From Meta-Analyses of Group-Design Studies

Study	Independent Variable(s)	Dependent variables	Post-Treatment			Follow-Up		
			k	Effect Size [95% CI]	*p*	*k*	Effect Size [95% CI]	*p*
Borquist-Conlon et al. (2019)	All eligible	Anxiety	5	$g = 0.62$ [0.20, 1.04]	.004	NR	NR	NR
Carsley et al. (2018)	All eligible	Overall	21	$g = 0.24$ [0.14, 0.34]	< .001	6	$g = 0.17$ (NR)	.079
Dunning et al. (2019)	All eligible	Overall	33	$d = 0.19$ [0.14, 0.23]	< .01			
Kallapiran et al. (2015)	MBSR/MBCT Other MBIs		No Overall No Overall	ES Reported ES Reported				
Klingbeil, Renshaw, et al. (2017)	All eligible	Overall	48	$g = 0.32$ [0.24, 0.40]	< .001	12	$g = 0.40$ [.22, .58]	< .001
Zenner et al. (2014)	All eligible	Overall	19	$g = 0.40$ [0.21, 0.58]	< .001	NR	NR	NR
Zoogman et al. (2015)	All eligible	Overall	20	$del = 0.23$ [0.15, 0.31]	< .001	NR	NR	NR

Table 2.3. Summary of Effect Sizes by Subdomain From Meta-Analyses of Group-Design Studies

Study	Interventions	Subdomain	k	Post-Treatment ES [95% CI]	p
Borquist-Conlon et al. (2019)	All eligible	Anxiety	5	$g = 0.62$ [0.20, 1.04]	< .001
Carsley et al. (2018)	All eligible	Did Not Report		Subdomain Analyses	
Dunning et al. (2019)	All eligible	Mindfulness	11	$d = 0.24$ [0.01, 0.46]	.04
		Social behavior	10	$d = 0.16$ [−0.05, 0.37]	.13
		Negative behavior	11	$d = 0.27$ [0.07, 0.47]	< .01
		Depression	13	$d = 0.27$ [0.06, 0.49]	< .01
		Anxiety/stress	20	$d = 0.16$ [0.04, 0.27]	.01
		Executive functions	15	$d = 0.30$ [0.12, 0.49]	< .01
		Attention	8	$d = 0.19$ [0.04, 0.34]	.02
Kallapiran et al. (2015)	MBSR & MBCT	Anxiety	3	$g = 0.77$ [0.20, 1.34]	< .001
		Depression	1	$g = 0.43$ [0.22, 0.64]	< .001
		Stress	3	$g = 0.33$ [0.04, 0.62]	.020
	Other MBIs	Anxiety	2	$g = 0.89$ [0.37, 1.42]	< .001
		Depression	3	$g = 0.38$ [−0.29, 1.05]	.070
		Stress	2	$g = -0.29$ [−1.53, 0.95]	.010
Klingbeil, Renshaw, et al. (2017)	All eligible	Mindfulness	18	$g = 0.51$ [0.08, 0.94]	.021
		Attention	18	$g = 0.29$ [0.12, 0.46]	.004
		Meta-Cognition	19	$g = 0.40$ [0.01, 0.80]	.045
		Emotion/behavior regulation	49	$g = 0.32$ [0.18, 0.46]	< .001

		Academic achievement	5	$g = 0.39$ [−0.15, 0.94]	.115
		Externalizing problems	9	$g = 0.30$ [0.09, 0.51]	.012
		Internalizing problems	29	$g = 0.39$ [0.27, 0.39]	$< .001$
		Negative emotion and distress	21	$g = 0.25$ [0.12, 0.39]	$< .001$
		Positive emotion and well-being	22	$g = 0.28$ [0.09, .047]	.006
		Physical health	14	$g = 0.28$ [0.17, 0.39]	$< .001$
		Social competence and behavior	12	$g = 0.37$ [0.17, 0.57]	.002
Zenner et al. (2014)	All eligible	Cognitive performance	7	$g = 0.80$ [0.35, 1.26]	$< .05$
		Emotional problems	9	$g = 0.19$ [−0.03, 0.41]	$> .05$
		Stress	7	$g = 0.39$ [0.07, 0.71]	$< .05$
		Resilience	13	$g = 0.36$ [0.09, 0.62]	$< .05$
Zoogman et al. (2015)	All eligible	Psychological symptoms	15	*del* = 0.37 [0.25, 0.49]	$< .001$
		Not psychological symptoms	15	*del* = 0.21 [0.12, 0.29]	$< .001$
		Attention and mindfulness	16	*del* = 0.28 [0.07, 0.49]	.009

the earliest meta-analytic reviews combined measures of mindfulness and other theorized mechanisms of MBIs into one broad category (Zenner et al., 2014; Zoogman et al., 2015). More recent reviews, which had substantially more studies to evaluate, separated the therapeutic mechanism results into narrower categories, such as mindfulness, attention, and executive functioning (Dunning et al., 2019; Klingbeil, Renshaw, et al., 2017).

Mechanisms of Mindfulness

Theories of mindfulness (e.g., Shapiro et al., 2006) posit that the sustained mindfulness awareness practice leads to changes in mindful awareness, attention, emotional regulation, and behavioral flexibility. Klingbeil and colleagues (2017) found that MBIs were associated with medium changes in participants' mindfulness. However, in their review of only randomized-controlled trials, Dunning and colleagues (2019) found a smaller, yet positive effect of MBIs on mindfulness. Changes in mindfulness moderated within-group changes in mental health outcomes in a subset of four studies (Carsley et al., 2018). In addition, MBIs had positive, smaller effects on indices of attention, emotion, and behavioral regulation (Dunning et al., 2019; Klingbeil, Renshaw, et al., 2017; Zenner et al., 2014; Zoogman et al., 2015). These findings are promising in that MBIs result in changes in the mechanisms that are posited to drive mood and behavior changes in youth.

Stress and Mental Health Outcomes

MBIs are commonly described as effective ways to address stress and mental health outcomes. As described earlier in this chapter, there is evidence to suggest that MBIs have a small to moderate, positive effect on reducing negative emotions, stress, and internalizing problems (Borquist-Conlon et al., 2019; Dunning et al., 2019; Kallapiran et al., 2015; Klingbeil, Renshaw, et al., 2017; Zenner et al., 2014).

Subjective Well-Being and Positive Emotions

In addition to reducing mental health symptoms and indices of stress and distress, MBIs have been shown to have small to moderate effects in improving subjective well-being (Carsley et al., 2018). There is also evidence of small effects on indices of positive emotions, coping strategies in response to stress, self-concept, and self-esteem (Klingbeil, Renshaw, et al., 2017; Zenner et al., 2014).

Behavioral Outcomes

Although the focus of this book is on mental health outcomes, we suggest that practitioners are likely interested in the impact of MBIs on other behavioral outcomes. Although studied less commonly than internalizing problems, there is evidence of similar small to moderate effects on reducing externalizing (Klingbeil, Renshaw, et al., 2017) or disruptive behaviors (Klingbeil, Fischer, et al., 2017). Across all of the 33 randomized controlled trials included in their meta-analytic review, Dunning et al. (2019) found that MBIs had a small effect on what they termed "negative behaviors," which included aggression and hostility. MBIs had a small effect on "negative behaviors" in the five studies that used an active control group, but that effect was no longer significant (Dunning et al., 2019). More research is needed on the effects of MBIs on externalizing and other disruptive behaviors.

There is divergent evidence regarding the impact of MBIs on youth's social skills and prosocial behavior. For example, Klingbeil, Renshaw, and colleagues (2017) found that MBIs had a small positive effect on these two outcomes across 12 studies. However, the effect of MBIs on similar social outcomes in 10 randomized controlled trials was not significant (Dunning et al., 2019). At this time, the evidence that MBIs will have an impact on prosocial behaviors or social skills is not convincing.

Finally, there were a small number of primary studies suggesting that MBIs may lead to small positive effects on school functioning or academic achievement outcomes as well as physical health (Klingbeil, Renshaw, et al., 2017; Zenner et al., 2014). These findings fit with contemporary theories of mindfulness (e.g., Shapiro et al., 2006), such that changes in mindfulness will lead to changes in more distal outcomes such as social or academic functioning. Given that MBIs do not train these skills directly, if these more distal outcomes are the desired intervention target, it may be prudent to combine MBIs with other skills or prefer other interventions with more robust evidence.

Which Students Do MBIs Work Best For?

A challenge to interpreting the growing body of literature on MBIs is the divergent evidence on the potential differential effectiveness of MBIs across a variety of student characteristics. Here we highlight the differences reported in the five meta-analytic reviews that examined the differential effects of MBIs related to age, gender, and clinical status.

Age

Zoogman and colleagues (2015) found that age was not a significant predictor of the overall effect size of MBIs. Participant age was also not significantly related to the effect of MBIs on disruptive behavior based on evidence from single-case design studies (Klingbeil, Fischer, et al., 2017). However, age was a significant predictor in two meta-analyses. First, Dunning and colleagues (2019) found that the impact of MBIs on executive functioning was significantly larger for older students across all randomized-controlled trials included in their analysis. Also, when looking specifically at studies with active control groups, MBIs had larger effects on externalizing type behaviors (e.g., aggression, hostility) for younger students (Dunning et al., 2019). Second, Carsley and colleagues (2018) found that the impact of universal MBIs on mental health outcomes was largest for youth in late adolescence (ages 15–18). MBIs had a smaller yet significant effect on mental health outcomes for youth in middle childhood (ages 6–10), but MBIs did not have a significant effect on mental health outcomes for youth in early adolescence (ages 11–14). The divergent findings regarding age make it difficult to draw firm conclusions. Perhaps the most conservative conclusion is that practitioners should look for MBIs shown to have positive benefits for youth who are of similar age to the students with whom they wish to implement an MBI.

Sex

Within primary studies, there is some evidence that MBIs may be more effective for females than males (e.g., Parker et al., 2014). Two meta-analyses evaluated the moderating effect of the percentage of female participants on MBI outcomes. Zoogman et al. (2015) found that the percentage of female students was not a significant predictor of MBI outcomes. Carsley et al. (2018) found that MBIs had similar effects on mental health outcomes between (a) studies that included females only and (b) studies that included both male and female students. In addition, the percentage of females in the studies had a small but significant effect on the within-group effects of MBIs. That said, Carsley et al. (2018, p. 10) were careful to indicate that their finding regarding sex "does not consider the possibility that males in these studies may have shown high effect sizes despite the fact there were fewer of them in the sample." We would add that none of the meta-analytic reviews indicated there was evidence that MBIs were ineffective for males. Additional research is needed to evaluate the relationship between sex and MBIs directly.

Clinical Status

As in MBI research for adults, researchers have evaluated the use of MBIs for clinical and non-clinical populations of youth. There was support for the use of MBIs with clinical populations. For example, Borquist-Conlon and colleagues (2019) found that MBIs were effective for reducing anxiety outcomes for youth with anxiety-related disorders. Klingbeil and colleagues (2017) found that MBIs had a significant effect on reducing problem behaviors for students with developmental disabilities and students with behavioral disorders. MBIs have also been shown to be effective for children and adolescents without a diagnosis (Carsley et al., 2018; Kallapiran et al., 2015; Klingbeil et al., 2017). These results suggest that MBIs can be applied to a wide variety of clinical populations and to those individuals who may have psychological symptoms but do not have a diagnosed psychopathology or disability.

Which MBIs Should Schools Select?

Across the meta-analyses reviewed in this chapter, there is a relatively consistent evidence of small to moderate effects on youth outcomes. Yet, the variability in programs identified as MBIs begs the question, which MBIs should schools implement? Unfortunately, there is little evidence contained within primary studies or the meta-analytic reviews to provide an answer to this question. More primary research studies are needed to evaluate the various components of the interventions, compare the effectiveness of different MBIs, and compare the effects of MBIs to other active treatments rather than no-treatment controls (Carsley et al., 2018; Klingbeil, Renshaw, et al., 2017). When selecting MBIs, practitioners should look for programs with evidence of effectiveness on the outcomes they wish to address and in the age group that the intervention will be delivered. Given the lack of evidence comparing MBIs to other active treatments, practitioners should also consider comparing the effects of MBIs to other known empirically supported treatments for improving the specific outcomes they seek to address.

What Are Primary Considerations for Adopting MBIs in Schools?

Several other contextual factors should be considered when adopting MBIs in schools. These factors relate to the actual implementation of MBIs to improve youth outcomes. Here we focus on considerations that appear particularly relevant: dosage, outside-of-session practice requirements, and who will implement the interventions.

Dosage

One consideration is the amount of time needed to deliver the MBI. Primary studies have evaluated MBIs requiring 15 minutes to 2,400 minutes of formal practice (Klingbeil, Renshaw, et al., 2017). There is divergent evidence whether the dosage (i.e., the number of minutes of formal practice) impacts MBI effects. Dunning et al. (2019) found that more training time led to a larger reduction in problem behaviors. Similarly, Zenner et al. (2014) found that dosage had a small positive impact on MBI effects in school-based programs. However, two meta-analytic reviews of MBIs for youth conducted across settings found that dosage did not have a significant impact on MBI effects (Klingbeil, Renshaw, et al., 2017; Zoogman et al., 2015). Given the differences in the analytic methods used in the four meta-analytic reviews evaluating dosage, it is difficult to determine whether another methodological artifact (e.g., randomized controlled trials or mixing results from school and other settings), the methods of evaluating dosage (e.g., on total duration of formal practice), or some unknown variable confounded the relationship between dosage and MBI effects. As an example, the use of total time as a dosage indicator would equate a program that requires one 90-minute practice session per week with a program that requires three 30-minute sessions per week.

Still, theories of mindfulness suggest that the sustained practice of mindfulness is required to improve outcomes (Kabat-Zinn, 1994). It seems unlikely that a 15-minute MBI would lead to lasting treatment effects due to changes in mindful awareness. Until further research emerges to better inform the necessary dosage of MBIs, practitioners considering the adoption of MBIs may wish to first identify programs that have demonstrated effects on the outcomes and age groups of interest, and then select the program that fits the contextual realities of their school.

Outside-of-session Practice

MBIs often use a variety of mindfulness awareness practices to develop mindfulness in youth (e.g., breath awareness, mindful eating, yoga). For adults, mindfulness theory suggests that developing mindfulness awareness necessary to drive changes in therapeutic outcomes may require sustained informal practice outside of the formal intervention sessions (Davidson, 2010). The impact of individual practice outside of sessions is not yet clear for youth. Zoogman et al. (2015) found slightly larger effects for programs that did not recommend outside-of-session practice ($del = .26$) compared to programs that recommended outside-of-session practice ($del = .21$), although the difference was not statistically significant. That said, leaders in the study of MBIs have suggested that future research focus on quantifying the amount of inside-of-session *and* outside-of-session practice required to improve participant outcomes (Davidson & Kaszniak, 2015). Until that research extends to youth, practitioners should consider the amount of outside-of-session practice recommended within the various MBIs for youth. Some interventions recommend that teachers include additional practice time within the classroom, outside of the formal intervention sessions. Practitioners could evaluate the extent to which classrooms could provide this additional practice and the likelihood that students who receive the intervention are likely to use mindful awareness practices outside of sessions.

Interventionist

Another critical consideration for practitioners is who will deliver the MBI. In the broader mindfulness literature, personal mindfulness practice and training in delivering MBIs appear to be commonly held as requisites for interventionists (Crane et al., 2012; Kabat-Zinn et al., 2011). These two components are connected to what scholars in this area term as the embodiment of mindful awareness (Crane et al., 2012; Cullen, 2011). A recent study of MBSR on a non-clinical sample of adults found that being taught MBSR by a teacher with more training and experience was positively correlated with improvements in well-being and reductions in stress (Ruijgrok-Lupton et al., 2017).

The importance of personal mindfulness practice and training in MBIs can be seen in the program requirements for some school-based MBIs. For example, the Mindfulness in Schools Project, which is a popular school-based MBI in the United Kingdom, requires that teachers of the curriculum complete an eight-week in-person mindfulness course and have maintained a personal practice for at least six months (https://mindfulnessinschools.org). Other programs, such as MBSR (https://www.umassmed.edu/cfm/) and Learning to BREATHE (https://learning2breathe.org), provide workshops for individuals seeking to implement those interventions. Along the same lines, MindUP provides an initial full-day training along with several implementation supports (e.g., booster trainings, on-demand lessons) to schools (https://mindup.org).

Outside of the need for trained interventionists with established personal mindfulness practice, there is evidence that school staff can implement MBIs with similar effectiveness as outside facilitators. Carsley et al. (2018) found slightly larger effects for MBIs delivered by teachers trained to deliver the MBI ($g = .28$) compared to MBIs implemented by outside facilitators ($g = .20$). Whereas, Zoogman and colleagues (2015) found similar effects for MBIs delivered by experienced instructors ($del = .23$) compared to programs delivered by interventionists trained for the study ($del = .22$). Notably, neither meta-analysis appeared to evaluate the personal mindfulness experience of the teachers or outside facilitators who delivered the MBIs.

Overall, findings that school staff can deliver MBIs with similar (or perhaps enhanced) effectiveness as outside facilitators are certainly promising. Using school-staff as interventionists may increase the feasibility and sustainability of MBIs (Broderick et al., 2019). Before adopting an MBI, practitioners should evaluate the criteria for effective delivery of the selected intervention. This will likely include identifying staff with established personal mindfulness practices and, depending on the program, staff who are able to attend the required trainings. In schools where these criteria are difficult to fulfill, another potential option may be to partner with local community organizations that provide training in mindfulness. In order to support high-quality implementation of MBIs in schools, there are two measures that provide a method of quantifying teaching quality, the Mindfulness-Based Interventions: Teaching Assessment Criteria (Crane et al., 2013) and the Teaching Mindfulness in Education Observation Scale (Broderick et al., 2019).

That said, there is no empirical evidence that supports the notion of untrained school staff, without a personal mindfulness practice, delivering MBIs to effectively improve youth outcomes. Simply purchasing an MBI program "off-the-shelf" and implementing it in a school setting is not aligned with current best practices in implementing MBIs (Crane et al., 2017; Kabat-Zinn et al., 2011) and may not result in the desired outcomes.

CONCLUSIONS

MBIs are an increasingly popular method for addressing social-emotional and behavioral outcomes for youth in schools. Several meta-analyses suggest that MBIs are associated with small (Carsley et al., 2018; Klingbeil, Renshaw, et al., 2017) to moderate effects (Borquist-Conlon et al., 2019) across a variety of youth outcomes. Further research is needed to evaluate the components contained within MBIs, determine the necessary dosage of these programs, compare effects among MBIs, and determine situations where MBIs may result in larger effects than other empirically supported treatments. There is a growing body of evidence suggesting MBIs can be effectively used in schools. Yet, more research is needed to guide the implementation of these approaches in school settings. This chapter highlighted general trends regarding the effects of MBIs and potential moderators of effectiveness, summarized from eight recent meta-analytic reviews of MBIs for youth. The results are certainly promising, but practitioners and schools seeking to adopt MBIs must carefully evaluate which MBI may best address the desired youth outcomes and fit the contextual realities of their schools. Finally, as with any school-based intervention, school professionals who implement MBIs should carefully monitor the fidelity of the program implementation and the impact of the MBI on the desired youth outcomes.

REFERENCES

Baer, R. A. (2003). Mindfulness training as a clinical intervention: A conceptual and empirical review. *Clinical Psychology: Science and Practice, 10*, 125–143. https://doi.org/10.1093/clipsy.bpg015

Becker, B. (1988). Synthesizing standardized mean-change measures. *British Journal of Mathematics and Statistical Psychology, 41*, 257–278. https://doi.org/10.1111/j.2044-8317.1988.tb00901.x

Benson, H. (1975). *The relaxation response*. Morrow.

Bishop, S. R., Laur, M., Shapiro, S., Carlson, L., Anderson, N. D., Carmondy, J., & Devins, G. (2004). Mindfulness: A proposed operational definition. *Clinical Psychology: Science and Practice, 11*, 230–241. https://doi.org/10.1093/clipsy.bph077

Black, D. S. (2015). Mindfulness training for children and adolescents: A state-of-the-science review. In K. W. Brown, J. D. Creswell, & R. M. Ryan (Eds.), *Handbook of mindfulness: Theory, research, and practice* (pp. 283–310). Guilford.

Borquist-Conlon, D. S., Maynard, B. R., Brendel, K. E., & Jarina, A. S. (2019). Mindfulness-based interventions for youth with anxiety: A systematic review and meta-analysis. *Research on Social Work Practice, 29*, 195–205. https://doi.org/10.1177/1049731516684961

Broderick, P. C., Frank, J. L., Berrena, E., Schussler, D. L., Kohler, K., Mitra, J., . . . Greenberg, M. T. (2019). Evaluating the quality of mindfulness instruction delivered in school settings: Development and validation of a teacher quality observational rating scale. *Mindfulness, 10*, 36–45. https://doi.org/10.1007/s12671-018-0944-x

Broderick, P. C., & Metz, S. (2009). Learning to BREATHE: A pilot trial of a mindfulness curriculum for adolescents. *Advances in School Mental Health Promotion, 2*, 35–46.

Burke, C. A. (2010). Mindfulness-based approaches with children and adolescents: A preliminary review of current research in an emergent field. *Journal of Child and Family Studies, 19*, 133–144. https://doi.org/10.1007/s10826-009-9282-x

Carsley, D., Khoury, B., & Heath, N. L. (2018). Effectiveness of mindfulness interventions for mental health in schools: A comprehensive meta-analysis. *Mindfulness, 9*, 693–707. https://doi.org/10.1007/s12671-017-0839-2

Chambless, D. L., & Hollon, S. D. (1998). Defining empirically supported therapies. *Journal of consulting and clinical psychology, 66*(1), 7–18. https://doi.org/10.1037//0022-006x.66.1.7

Cooper, H., & Hedges, L. V. (2009). Research synthesis as a scientific process. In H. Cooper, L. V. Hedges, & J. C. Valentine (Eds.), *The handbook of research synthesis and meta-analysis* (pp. 19–36). Russell Sage Foundation.

Crane, R. S., Brewer, J., Feldman, C., Kabat-Zinn, J., Santorelli, S., Williams, J. M. G., & Kuyken, W. (2017). What defines mindfulness-based programs? The warp and the weft. *Psychological Medicine, 47*, 990–999. https://doi.org/10.1017/S0033291716003317

Crane, R. S., Eames, C., Kuyken, W., Hastings, R. P., Williams, J. M. G., Bartley, T., . . . Surawy, C. (2013). Development and validation of the mindfulness-based interventions–teaching assessment criteria (MBI: TAC). *Assessment*, *20*, 681–688. https://doi.org/10.1177/1073191113490790

Crane, R. S., Kuyken, W., Williams, J. M. G., Hastings, R. P., Cooper, L., & Fennell, M. J. V. (2012). Competence in teaching mindfulness-based courses: Concepts, development, and assessment. *Mindfulness*, *3*, 76–84. https://doi.org/10.1007/s12671-011-0073-2

Cullen, M. (2011). Mindfulness-based interventions: An emerging phenomenon. *Mindfulness*, *2*, 186–193. https://doi.org/10.1007/s12671-011-0058-1

Dariotis, J. K., Mirabal-Beltran, R., Cluxton-Keller, F., Gould, L. F., Greenberg, M. T., & Mendelson, T. (2017). A qualitative exploration of implementation factors in a school-based mindfulness and yoga program: Lessons learned from students and teachers. *Psychology in the Schools*, *54*, 53–69. https://doi.org/10.1002/pits.21979

Davidson, R. J. (2010). Empirical explorations of mindfulness: Conceptual and methodological issues. *Emotion*, *10*, 8–11. https://doi.org/10.1037/a0018480

Davidson, R. J., & Kaszniak, A. W. (2015). Conceptual and methodological issues in research on mindfulness and meditation. *American Psychologist*, *70*, 581–592. doi: 10.1037/a0039512

Davis, D. M., & Hayes, J. A. (2011). What are the benefits of mindfulness? A practice review of psychotherapy-related research. *Psychotherapy*, *48*, 198–208. https://doi.org/10.1037/a0022062

Dryden, W., & Still, A. (2006). Historical aspects of mindfulness and self-acceptance in psychotherapy. *Journal of Rational-Emotive and Cognitive-Behavior Therapy*, *24*, 3–28. https://doi.org/10.1007/s10942-006-0026-1

Dunning, D. L., Griffiths, K., Kuyken, W., Crane, C., Foulkes, L., Parker, J., & Dalgleish, T. (2019). The effects of mindfulness-based interventions on cognition and mental health in children and adolescents—A meta-analysis of randomized controlled trials. *The Journal of Child Psychology and Psychiatry*, *60*(3), 244–258. https://doi.org/10.1111/jcpp.12980

Dunning, D., Tudor, K., Radley, L., Dalrymple, N., Funk, J., Vainre, M., . . . Dalgleish, T. (2023). Do mindfulness-based programmes improve the cognitive skills, behaviour and mental health of children and adolescents? An updated meta-analysis of randomised controlled trials. *BMJ Mental Health*, *25*(3), 135–142. https://doi.org/10.1136/ebmental-2022-300464

Durlak, J. A., Weissberg, R. P., Dymnicki, A. B., Taylor, R. D., & Schellinger, K. B. (2011). The impact of enhancing students' social and emotional learning: A meta-analysis of school-based universal interventions. *Child Development*, *82*, 405–432. https://doi.org/10.1111/j.1467-8624.2010.01564.x

Felver, J. C., Celis-de Hoyos, C. E., Tezanos, K., & Singh, N. N. (2016). A systematic review of mindfulness-based interventions for youth in school settings. *Mindfulness*, *7*, 34–45. https://doi.org/10.1007/s12671-015-0389-4

Felver, J. C., Doerner, E., Jones, J., Kaye, N. C., & Merrell, K. W. (2013). Mindfulness in school psychology: Applications for intervention and professional practice. *Psychology in the Schools*, *50*, 531–547. https://doi.org/10.1002/pits.21695

Hedges, L. V., Pustejovsky, J. E., & Shadish, W. R. (2013). A standardized mean difference effect size for multiple baseline designs across individuals. *Research Synthesis Methods*, *4*, 324–341. https://doi.org/10.1002/jrsm.1086

Higgins, J. P., Altman, D. G., Gøtzsche, P. C., Jüni, P., Moher, D., Oxman, A. D., . . . Sterne, J. A. (2011). The Cochrane Collaboration's tool for assessing risk of bias in randomised trials. *BMJ*, No. *343*. https://doi.org/10.1136/bmj.d5928

Jadad, A. R., Moore, R. A., Carroll, D., Jenkinson, C., Reynolds, D. J. M., Gavaghan, D. J., & McQuay, H. J. (1996). Assessing the quality of reports of randomized clinical trials: Is blinding necessary? *Controlled Clinical Trials*, *17*(1), 1–12. https://pubmed.ncbi.nlm.nih.gov/8721797

Kabat-Zinn, J. (1982). An outpatient program in behavioral medicine for chronic pain patients based on the practice of mindfulness meditation: Theoretical considerations and preliminary results. *General Hospital Psychiatry*, *4*, 33–47. https://doi.org/10.1016/0163-8343(82)90026-3

Kabat-Zinn, J. (1994). *Where you go, there you are.* Balance.

Kabat-Zinn, J. (2003). Mindfulness-based interventions in context: Past, present, and future. *Clinical Psychology: Science and Practice*, *10*, 144–156. https://doi.org/10.1093/clipsy.bpg016

Kabat-Zinn, J., Santorelli, S., Blacker, M., Brantley, J., Meleo-Meyer, F., Grossman, P., . . . Stahl, R. (2011). *Training teachers to deliver mindfulness-based stress reduction principles and standards.* http://www.umassmed.edu/cfm/trainingteachers/index.aspx.

Kallapiran, K., Koo, S., Kirubakaran, R., & Hancock, K. (2015). Effectiveness of mindfulness in improving mental health symptoms of children and adolescents: A meta-analysis. *Child and Adolescent Mental Health*, *20*, 182–194. https://doi.org/10.1111/camh.12113

Khoury, B., Lecomte, T., Fortin, G., Masse, M., Therien, P., Bouchard, V., Chapleau, M. A., Paquin, K., & Hoffman, S. G. (2013). Mindfulness-based therapy: A comprehensive meta-analysis. *Clinical Psychology Review*, *33*, 763–771. https://doi.org/10.1016/j.cpr.2013.05.005

Khoury, B., Sharma, M., Rush, S. E., & Fournier, C. (2015). Mindfulness-based stress reduction for healthy individuals: A meta-analysis. *Journal of Psychosomatic Research*, *78*, 519–528. https://doi.org/10.1016/j.jpsychores.2015.03.009

Klingbeil, D. A., Fischer, A. J., Renshaw, T. L., Bloomfield, B. S., Polakoff, B., Willenbrink, J. B., . . . Chan, K. (2017). Effects of mindfulness-based interventions on disruptive behaviors: A meta-analysis of single-case research. *Psychology in the Schools*, *54*, 70–87. https://doi.org/10.10.1002/pits

Klingbeil, D. A., & Renshaw, T. L. (2018). Mindfulness-based interventions for teachers: A meta-analysis of the emerging evidence base. School Psychology Quarterly, 33(4), 501–511. https://psycnet.apa.org/doi/10.1037/spq0000291

Klingbeil, D. A., Renshaw, T. L., Willenbrink, J. B., Copek, R. A., Chan, K. T., Haddock, A., & Clifton, J. (2017). Mindfulness-based interventions with youth: A comprehensive meta-analysis of group design studies. *Journal of School Psychology*, *63*, 77–103. https://doi.org/10.1016/j.jsp.2017.03.006

Kratochwill, T. R., Hitchcock, J., Horner, R. H., Levin, J. R., Odom, S. L., Rindskopf, D. M., & Shadish, W. R. (2010). *Single-case designs technical documentation*. What Works Clearinghouse. https://files.eric.ed.gov/fulltext/ED510743.pdf

Meiklejohn, J., Phillips, C., Freedman, M. L., Griffin, M. L., Biegel, G., Roach, A., . . . Isberg, R. (2012). Integrating mindfulness training into K-12 education: Fostering the resilience of teachers and students. *Mindfulness*, *3*, 291–307. https://doi.org/10.1007/s12671-012-0094-5

Mettler, J., Khoury, B., Zito, S., Sadowski, I., & Health, N. L. (2023). Mindfulness-based programs and school adjustment: A systematic review and meta-analysis. *Journal of School Psychology*, *97*, 43–62. https://doi.org/10.1016/j.jsp.2022.10.007

Parker, A. E., Kupersmidt, J. B., Mathis, E. T., Scull, T. M., & Sims, C. (2014). The impact of mindfulness education on elementary school students: Evaluation of the master mind program. *Advances in School Mental Health Promotion*, *7*, 184–204. https://doi.org/10.1080/1754740X.2014.916497

Phillips, S., & Mychailyszyn, M. (2022). The effect of school-based mindfulness interventions on anxious and depressive symptoms: A meta-analysis. *School Mental Health*, *14*(3), 455–469. https://doi.org/10.1007/s12310-021-09492-0

Pigott, T. D., Valentine, J. C., Polanin, J. R., Williams, R. T., & Canada, D. D. (2013). Outcome-reporting bias in education research. *Educational Researcher*, *42*, 424–432. https://doi.org/10.3102/0013189X13507104

Renshaw, T. L., Fischer, A. J., & Klingbeil, D. A. (2017). Mindfulness-based interventions in school psychology. *Contemporary School Psychology*, *21*, 299–303. https://doi.org/10.1007/s40688-017-0166-6

Ruijgrok-Lupton, P. E., Crane, R. S., & Dorjee, D. (2017). Impact of mindfulness-based teacher training on MBSR participant well-being outcomes and course satisfaction. *Mindfulness*, *9*, 117–128. https://doi.org/10.1007/s12671-017-0750-x

Semple, R. J., Droutman, V., & Reid, B. A. (2017). Mindfulness goes to school: Things learned (so far) from research and real-world experiences. *Psychology in the Schools*, *54*, 29–52. https://doi.org/10.1002/pits

Segal, Z. V., Williams, M. G., & Teasdale, J. D. (2002). *Mindfulness-based cognitive behavior therapy for depression: A new approach to preventing relapse*. Guilford.

Shapiro, S. L., Carlson, L. E., Astin, J. A., & Freedman, B. (2006). Mechanisms of mindfulness. *Journal of Clinical Psychology*, *62*, 373–386. https://doi.org/10.1002/jclp.20237

Singh, N. N., Lancioni, G. E., Singh, S. D., Winton, A. S. W., Sabaawi, M., Wahler, R. G., & Singh, J. (2007). Adolescents with conduct disorder can be mindful of their aggressive behavior. *Journal of Emotional and Behavioral Disorders*, *15*, 56–63. https://doi.org/10.1177/10634266070150010601

Smith, H., & Novak, P. (2003). *Buddhism: A concise introduction*. Harper Collins.

Stoiber, K. C., & Gettinger, M. (2016). Multi-tiered systems of support and evidence-based practices. In S. R. Jimerson, M. K. Burns, & A. M. VanDerHeyden (Eds.), *Handbook of response to intervention* (pp. 121–141). Springer.

Young, S. (2016). What is mindfulness? A contemplative perspective. In K. A. Schonert-Reichl& R. W. Roeser (Eds.), *Handbook of mindfulness in education* (pp. 29–45). Springer.

Zenner, C., Hermleben-Kurz, S., & Walach, H. (2014). Mindfulness-based interventions in schools—A systematic review and meta-analysis. *Frontiers in Psychology*, *5*, 1–20. https://doi.org/10.3389/fpsyg.2014.00603

Zoogman, S., Goldberg, S. B., Hoyt, W. T., & Miller, L. (2015). Mindfulness interventions with youth: A meta-analysis. *Mindfulness*, *6*, 290–302. https://doi.org/10.1007/s12671-013-0260-4

3

Mindfulness-Based Interventions With Parents and Educators

ANDREW JORDAN THAYER, MARGARET SULLIVAN, MADELINE LARSON, AND CLAYTON R. COOK ■

Children experience healthy development and well-being in the context of nurturing, reinforcing, and responsive host environments (Komro et al., 2011). Host environments represent key microsystems in which children spend most of their time, such as home and school. These environments are also home to many children's most proximal adult figures—parents and educators. Research suggests that when the host environment is ill-maintained, and the emotional and mental well-being of parents and educators are compromised, children suffer as a result (Klusmann et al., 2008). Thus, in the interest of protecting and promoting the well-being of children, promoting adult well-being is a potentially effective avenue for research and practice. Several psychologically beneficial theories and practices can be adapted and implemented for parents and educators. Mindfulness-based interventions (MBIs) represent a group of potentially appropriate, feasible, and effective interventions for this population.

The purpose of this chapter is to provide an overview of the research on MBIs with parents and educators as the adults who are most proximal to and influential on the outcomes of children. This chapter is organized by, first, describing the environmental context in which children thrive, with specific emphasis given to the critical role of parents' and educators' well-being. Following this introduction is a review of MBIs with parents—including implications for practice and future work, preceded by a mirror review of MBIs with educators. Throughout

Andrew Jordan Thayer et al., *Mindfulness-Based Interventions With Parents and Educators*. In: *Using Mindfulness to Promote Mental Health in Schools*. Edited by: Tyler L. Renshaw and Shane R. Jimerson, Oxford University Press.
 DOI: 10.1093/9780190880507.003.0003

the chapter, an emphasis is placed on reviewing intervention studies that have examined MBIs delivered specifically to increase adult mindfulness as a way of improving child outcomes. This chapter concludes with a summary that synthesizes the findings and provides recommendations for future research and practice to advance the efficacy and reach of MBIs to increase capacity among caregivers and educators to create more nurturing, reinforcing, and responsive home and school environments for children.

NURTURING ENVIRONMENTS IN WHICH CHILDREN THRIVE

Healthy host environments exhibit three qualities: they are nurturing, reinforcing, and responsive to children's needs. A host environment is nurturing when there are secure relationships between adults and children, and the adults who possess power and authority over the child (e.g., a classroom teacher or a parent) can set and enforce limits compassionately when the child exhibits problem behavior. Nurturing environments prevent abusive and other punitive interactions that undermine healthy relationships and potentially stunt children's social, emotional, physical, and academic development (Biglan et al., 2012). Reinforcing environments are characterized by adults who (a) noncontingently acknowledge a child's intrinsic worth as a person and (b) contingently recognize the energy and effort a child demonstrates as a member of a given setting or place (e.g., classroom or home; Brooks, 2005). Environments with a paucity of reinforcement result in children feeling less connected and belonging, limiting opportunities to motivate and cultivate children's development in key domains of performance (Biglan, 2015). Finally, environments are responsive when adults attend and respond to children's needs as they emerge (Irwin et al. 2007). For example, a responsive teacher is one who notices when a child is upset and responds to this cue by helping the child label the emotion and use a specific coping skill. Responsive environments serve as an antidote to neglect that occurs when children's needs go unnoticed and unmet.

When the primary adults in children's lives—parents and educators—create nurturing, reinforcing, and responsive environments, children develop and grow in healthy ways (Biglan et al., 2012). Both parents and educators, however, experience significant stressors and unwanted experiences that can manifest in negative, punitive interactions that impair relationships with children and unintentionally lead to missed opportunities to reinforce and respond to children's social, emotional, physical, and academic needs (Hinds et al., 2015). This is especially true for children with social, emotional, and behavioral difficulties who may need exceptionally nurturing environments. Many adults may struggle to regulate their thoughts, emotions, and behaviors in response to children's behavioral difficulties (Kokkinos, 2007). As a result, these adults are unable to enact the qualities of nurturing environments that these children with difficulties need. Considering parents and educators are key influences in children's lives, there has been a surge of interest in developing and testing interventions that promote adult well-being as a necessary first step in supporting children's healthy development and functioning.

In particular, researchers of varied disciplines have explored the benefits of mindfulness as a means of improving adult well-being and performance (e.g., Raab, 2014). Within this body of work, there is a subset of researchers investigating mindfulness to improve adult mental health and performance, specifically related to caring for children (e.g., Benn et al., 2012). Mindfulness is traditionally defined as purposeful, non-judgmental, and receptive awareness of two kinds of experiences: present-moment internal (e.g., thoughts, feelings, bodily sensations) and external (e.g., environmental stimuli, setting characteristics, behavior of others) (Kabat-Zinn & Hanh, 2009). Stemming from this definition, mindfulness has two defining features: (a) intentional and purposeful regulation of attention and (b) a relationship with present-moment experiences characterized by openness and willing acceptance (Bishop et al., 2004). It is through these two features or mechanisms that mindfulness is hypothesized to produce a range of potential benefits, including attention and emotion regulation, coping in response to situational stressors (Goldin & Gross, 2010), and improved physical and mental health (e.g., Khoury et al., 2013). Given these potential benefits, mindfulness offers promise to increase the capacity of parents and educators alike to create nurturing, reinforcing, and responsive host environments for children.

CONTEMPORARY MINDFULNESS RESEARCH

Mindfulness research falls into one of two categories. The first category involves studies examining correlates of mindfulness. Typically, these studies are descriptive and correlational in nature and seek to examine associations between mindfulness as an ability, or skill, and other variables of interest, such as mental health, physical health, prosocial functioning, subjective well-being, and vocational performance (Howell et al., 2010). The other category of research involves examining mindfulness as an intervention. In these studies, specific mindfulness-based practices are developed and tested as a form of training, which seeks to alter a person's relationship to present-moment experiences (Hinds et al., 2015). The hypothesis underlying these studies is that a person's ability to be mindful can be improved through specific mindfulness-based practices (e.g., mindful breathing and body scan). In turn, improvements in mindfulness are claimed to enhance one's ability to regulate unwanted experiences, both internal (e.g., thoughts, emotions, or physiological states) and external (e.g., negative interactions with others, stressful situations, failure), without the need to engage in maladaptive behaviors to escape from or confront those experiences (Chu, 2010).

This second category of research moves beyond descriptive, correlational studies to evaluating mindfulness as an intervention for improving adult well-being and performance—often for the purposes of promoting better child outcomes (e.g., Ferraioli & Harris, 2013). Mindfulness-based interventions (MBIs) have demonstrated applicability across multiple contexts in which children reside (e.g., homes, schools, juvenile justice), and there is emerging evidence linking their use to relevant outcomes of interest. Moreover, there has been an emergence of research syntheses (e.g., Shapiro et al., 2007) that provide the opportunity to learn about the potential general and contextual benefits of MBIs when delivered to parents and educators.

This chapter synthesizes the burgeoning research of MBIs for parents and educators to draw conclusions about their effectiveness and usefulness given the current state-of-the-science. This chapter is intended to provide readers with a broad overview of MBIs, illustrations of how MBIs with caregivers should (theoretically) influence the home and school environments of children, and explicit limitations and future directions for continued work regarding MBIs with parents and educators. We begin with a review of research syntheses addressing MBIs for parents, starting first with a discussion of the contextual relevancy of MBIs with this population. We then review each available research synthesis of MBIs with parents, summarizing conclusions from the literature as warranted. After reviewing the research on MBIs with parents, we follow the same structure for reviewing the available research syntheses of MBIs for educators.

OVERVIEW OF MINDFULNESS-BASED INTERVENTIONS WITH PARENTS

The home environment is arguably one of the most important settings for children's development and well-being. Within the home, the relationship between parent and child is "the earliest and most consequential" aspect of this setting (Lee, 2018, p. 1). The care that parents provide is essential to providing a nurturing, reinforcing, and responsive environment. Conversely, inadequate parental care (e.g., emotional neglect, verbal abuse, substance abuse in the home) leads to unhealthy (i.e., unresponsive, punitive) environments that are predictive of a range of negative outcomes, including externalizing behavior problems, substance abuse, lower grades, trauma-related disorders, and physical health problems (Felitti et al., 1998). Numerous parent training programs have been developed to teach parents how to address children's problem behavior and promote healthy development (e.g., Kazdin, 2008). However, research has consistently shown that parent training programs are less effective for parents who experience significant stress and mental health problems, as these parents are less likely to attend and complete the training program, and effectively deliver trained parenting practices (Van den Hoofdakker et al., 2010).

Several studies have shown that parents who demonstrate greater mindfulness are likely to report more positive parenting skills (e.g., Williams & Wahler, 2010). Additionally, these parents report fewer problematic parenting practices (de Bruin et al., 2014). The incorporation of mindfulness practices into parenting provides opportunities for parents to shift their attention from past- and future-thinking to present-moment experiences with their child, as well as to better respond to their child's needs by exercising greater attention and emotion regulation (Duncan et al., 2009). Dumas (2005) referred to the combination of mindfulness with behavior parent training as *mindfulness-based parent training* (MBPT). He describes MBPT as an approach to reduce maladaptive, automatic patterns of interactions between parents and children in order to increase parents' support and use of effective practices. In this way, mindfulness facilitates parents' effective use of positive parenting practices that seek to cultivate a nurturing, reinforcing, and responsive home environment.

Mindful parenting is hypothesized to produce a reduction in emotional reactivity and an increase in responsiveness and consistency to better align parents' actions with their values (Duncan et al., 2009). Mindful parenting is intended to offset the untoward cycle of parental detachment and potential negative interactions with their child or partner using more effective parenting strategies that cultivate a nurturing, reinforcing, and responsive home environment (Dumas, 2005). Recent intervention research has begun to explore mindfulness within the context of the family system, providing some preliminary support for positive effects of parental mindfulness on the parent–child relationship (Coatsworth et al., 2010), parental stress (Haydicky et al., 2015), use of effective parenting practices (Bögels et al., 2014), and child well-being (Neece, 2014).

Popular press has indicated that mindfulness is a revolutionary approach to address many of the problems that parents encounter in the context of raising a child (e.g., Kring, 2013). Some critics have argued, however, that the enthusiasm for mindfulness has outpaced scientific research (e.g., Greenberg & Harris, 2012), suggesting it is not yet clear whether MBIs are effective for promoting parental well-being and effectiveness. Thus, it is important to examine the empirical evidence supporting the use of MBIs to improve parental well-being directly and their ability to manage behaviors, teach expectation, and provide an overall nurturing environment for their children. The evaluation of MBIs with parents has become increasingly common over the last decade, paving the way for research syntheses that examine the nature and effectiveness of MBIs with this population.

Review of Research on MBIs With Parents

This chapter covers a selection of six research syntheses examining the impact of MBIs with parents completed between 2016 and 2018. Each of these syntheses is discussed, in turn, below. Some represent meta-analytic investigations, while others are more consistent with a comprehensive literature review. Important findings emerge across these syntheses that inform the effectiveness of MBIs for parents, the types of practices incorporated into MBIs, and limitations that practitioners should consider when recommending or implementing MBIs with parents. Table 3.1 presents a summary of basic information for each research synthesis, including study sample characteristics, outcomes of interest, highlighted findings from each review, and limitations. Although additional systematic reviews on MBIs with parents have emerged in recent years, the selection of six reviews provided in this chapter offers representative coverage of the topic at hand. Readers interested in additional contemporary reviews beyond the scope of this chapter are referred to Xie et al. (2021), Lee et al. (2022), and Anand et al. (2023).

Townshend, Jordan, Stephenson, and Tsey (2016)

This systematic review evaluated the effectiveness of MBIs in promoting children's, adolescents', and parents' well-being, emotional regulation, attention, quality of the parent-child relationship, resilience, and mindfulness. In total, seven studies

Table 3.1. Research Syntheses of MBIs for Parents

Research Synthesis	Number of studies	Sample Characteristics of Included Studies	Design Features	Outcome Measures	Highlighted Findings	Notable Limitations
Townshend, Jordan, Stephenson, & Tsey (2016)	7 published studies	Study published in English in peer-reviewed journal Children 0–18 years old Three groups: 1. Mothers and 10–14-year olds from a community sample, 2. Parents of children with autism 3. Parents of preschool children Countries: 1. United States 2. Australia	7 out of 7 RCTs Control group: • Waitlist • Home-study	Parent outcomes 1. Emotion awareness and coaching 2. Emotion regulation 3. Parental stress Child outcomes 1. Attention regulation 2. Hyperactivity 3. Behavior problems	Increased family involvement of fathers Increase mindful parenting and rules communication of mothers Reduced symptoms associated with externalizing disorders exhibited by preschool children, particularly attention regulation and attention deficit/hyperactivity Reduced parents' emotional dismissal of their adolescents and preschoolers	Studies with small sample sizes and failure to blind implementer and participants to study condition

continued

Table 3.1. Continued

Cachia, Anderson, & Moore (2016)	10 studies published before February 2015	Study published in English in peer-reviewed journal Parents of children diagnosed with ASD Countries: 1. United States 2. Netherlands 3. Spain	Single-subject (multiple baseline) design; within-subject, repeated measures design; between-group design; mixed design Control group: Not reported	Parent: 1. Subjective stress 2. Physiological stress 3. Depression 4. Psychological flexibility 5. Experiential avoidance 6. Psychological well-being Child: 1. Externalizing behavior 2. Child compliance 3. Aggression 4. Maladaptive behavior 5. Self-injury 6. Disruptive behavior	Consistent reports of reduced stress following mindfulness interventions across all studies, particularly at post intervention Two studies reported indirect, child outcomes, specifically: decreased child aggression, maladaptive behavior; decreased adolescent aggressive and disruptive behavior; and increased adolescent compliance	Only two studies included mindfulness-based interventions that were specific to parenting Studies that included child Outcomes were not peer-reviewed publications, rather two studies within one dissertation; only one Study quality was not distinctly assessed

Rayan & Ahmad (2018)	8 studies published before September 2016	Study published in English Parents of children with disabilities Different groups: 1. Parents 2. Primary care givers 3. Mothers 4. Fathers	Independent with pre-post, Dependent with pre-post, RCT Control group: Skills-based training, None, positive adult development,	Parent Outcomes 1. Parenting stress 2. Psychological distress (i.e., stress, depression, anxiety)	75% reported statistically significant reductions in parenting stress and/or psychological distress, with effect sizes ranging from medium to largeb Of the 6 studies measuring mindfulness levels pre-post, 100% reported improvement in mindfulness scores, 5/6 being statistically significant	Only 1 RCT, which prevents definitive conclusions Studies had small sample sizes (4 out of 8 had an N of 10 or fewer) Heterogeneity of the type, dosage, and implementation of MBIs across studies limits ability to compare outcomes Subjects were primarily mothers

continued

Table 3.1. Continued

Taylor, Cavanagh, & Strauss (2016)	17 studies	Study published in peer reviewed journal in English Explored MBI effectiveness during perinatal period Interventions: 1. Group based 2. Computerized	RCT, dependent with pre-post	Parent Outcomes 1. Depression 2. Anxiety 3. Stress 4. Mindfulness skills	Pre-post analyses reported significant reductions in depression, anxiety, and stress, and significant increases in mindfulness skills (small-medium effects) Effects for depression, stress, and mindfulness remained significant at follow-up	Possible publication bias—smaller studies were associated with larger effect sizes Deviations from mindfulness program and variations in adherence led to homogeneity in treatments

Frantz, Hansen, & Machalicek (2018)	41 studies	Publication in English peer-reviewed journals At least 1 parent of a child with autism spectrum disorder (birth-12) Intervention groups: 1. Psychoeducational 2. Cognitive behavioral therapy 3. MBI 4. Behavioral-based 5. Other	Single case, quasi-experimental, RCT	Parent Outcomes: 1. Stress 2. Depression 3. Self-efficacy	4 of the 41 studies (9.8%) included mindfulness-based interventions All 4 studies included parental stress as an outcome variable, 100% reported significant decrease in stress 3 of the 4 included parental depression as an outcome variable, 100% reported significant decrease in depression	Intervention types are immensely varied, and this narrow breadth of research limits definitive findings Only 77.44% of participants met inclusion criteria of having a child with ASD diagnosis, and authors could not extract individual participant data

continued

Table 3.1. Continued

Alexander (2018)	7 studies	Groups: 1. Mothers only 2. Mothers and fathers Countries: 1. United States 2. U.K. 3. Chile	3 out of 7 RCTs 4 out of 7 descriptive studies	Parent outcomes: 1. Symptoms of parental depression	100% of RCTs reported a statistically significant reduction in depression symptoms post mindfulness-based parenting interventions, with range of medium—high effect sizes.	Study samples lack cultural, racial, and economic diversity, primarily consisting of White, affluent, highly educated women Heterogeneity in intervention type and implementation, and measurement tools affect generalizability

met inclusion criteria and were subjected to data extraction to glean and codify information for analyses. Regarding study target populations, three subgroups emerged: (1) mothers and 10–14-year old youth from a community sample, (2) parents of children with autism, and (3) parents of preschool children. The review focused on randomized-controlled trials and included comparisons with waitlist or active control groups. Outcome variables included both parent and child measures. Authors noted that, although programs had different names, all programs integrated mindfulness with parenting either by drawing on Kabat-Zinn's mindfulness-based stress reduction (MBSR; Kabat-Zinn, 2003) or Gottman and colleagues' work on emotional awareness (Gottman et al., 1996). MBIs included in the review drew on MBSR, mindfulness-based cognitive therapy, mindfulness-based cognitive behavior therapy, dialectical behavior therapy, and acceptance commitment therapy (ACT). MBIs had a minimum duration of one to two hours per week for six to eight weeks. Findings from the included studies indicated that MBIs may reduce parental stress, increase parents' emotional awareness of their children, and reduce children's symptoms associated with externalizing disorders, particularly regarding symptoms of attention deficit/hyperactivity disorder. Further, findings showed that MBIs reduced parents' emotional dismissal of their adolescents and preschoolers. Regarding study quality, authors indicated that studies were of "low to moderate" quality, indicating that it is difficult to draw definitive conclusions about MBI effectiveness. The interpretation of findings should be considered in light of key limitations, including small sample sizes, multiple significance testing without adjustments to the criterion level for statistical significance, and lack of blinding the participants to their experimental condition by researchers.

Cachia, Anderson, and Moore (2016)

This systematic review investigated the efficacy of MBIs in reducing stress and increasing psychological well-being in parents of children with autism spectrum disorder (ASD). In total, 10 studies met inclusion criteria and were subjected to specific data extraction to glean and codify information from each of the studies. Outcome variables included parent subjective stress, physiological stress response, depression, psychological flexibility, experiential avoidance, and psychological well-being. Two studies included in the review also assessed indirect effects of parent-focused MBIs on child and adolescent behavior. Regarding study design, half of the studies employed a within-subject, repeated-measures design, while the second half of the studies utilized between-group, mixed, or single-subject designs. Regarding the nature of MBIs, authors noted that there was significant overlap in the elements of mindfulness used across intervention. Three studies were based on an ACT program, one included both a mindfulness-based phase and an ACT phase, and the remaining six studies reported on mindfulness-only intervention programs.

Contact hours of program delivery varied across studies, ranging from less than 12 contact hours to over 36 contact hours. Most interventions consisted of eight to nine sessions and included daily practice. A strength of this review was that it recorded whether treatment fidelity was assessed within each study, including different measures of fidelity and consistency of treatment outcomes when certain fidelity elements were present. Results consistently indicated reduced stress following parent-focused MBIs, particularly at post-intervention; the largest effects were found when teachers received explicit training in mindfulness as part of treatment fidelity. Regarding additional parent-level outcomes, studies showed decreased self-reported depression, subjective and physiological stress, and increased psychological well-being. Furthermore, two studies reported increased parent psychological flexibility and decreased experiential avoidance, specifically in relation to the use of ACT. An additional two studies investigated the indirect effect of parent-focused MBIs on the behavior of children diagnosed with ASD, with studies demonstrating a decrease in child aggression and maladaptive behavior. Findings also showed an increase in adolescent compliance during and following parent mindfulness intervention. These findings should be considered in light of a couple limitations, namely that only two studies included MBIs that were specific to parenting (i.e., the explicitly connected mindfulness skills to parenting practices, whereas other studies only taught general mindfulness skills), and only one dissertation (comprising two studies) assessed the indirect effects of parent mindfulness intervention on child behavior in a specific population (i.e., parents of children diagnosed with ASD). It is also noteworthy that study quality was not directly evaluated and, thus, could diminish the defensibility of study results.

Rayan and Ahmad (2018)

Rayan and Ahmad (2018) conducted what appears to be the first review synthesizing existing literature on the use of MBIs to address parental stress and psychological distress in parents of children with disabilities. Eight studies met inclusion criteria for this review. Most of the studies reported improvements in parent psychological health and parenting stress post-MBI, with medium to large effect sizes. In cases where there was a comparison group, those receiving MBI had better outcomes than those who received a different intervention (e.g., parenting skills intervention with no mindfulness component). These findings seem to endorse the use of MBIs to ameliorate parent symptoms. Interestingly, the two studies that did not improve parent stress used interventions focusing solely on stress reduction, with no parenting content. This further suggests that the integration of mindfulness practices into parenting skills and everyday life may be a key element in successful MBIs with parents. These findings must be viewed in context of the several notable limitations across the eight studies, including small sample sizes, a paucity of experimental designs, and heterogeneity of MBIs. The authors suggested that future studies should address improvements to study quality and focus more on the relative effectiveness of different MBIs.

Taylor, Cavanagh, and Strauss (2016)

Taylor and colleagues (2016) conducted a systematic review on the effects of MBI on depression, anxiety, stress, and mindfulness of expecting mothers during the perinatal period. Seventeen studies met inclusion criteria for this review.

Pre-post analyses reported significant increases in mindfulness skills and significant reductions in depression, anxiety, and stress, with effect sizes varying from small to medium. Effect sizes for anxiety and depression were higher when this meta-analysis was restricted to studies with participants exhibiting high levels of depression and anxiety at baseline, which aligns with the research in other clinical populations (e.g., Hofmann et al., 2010). In contrast, an examination of only studies within this meta-analysis that involved "healthy" participants yielded small-to-moderate effects of MBIs on anxiety and depression (mean *g* range: .36–.51). No significant between-group effects of MBIs were identified when compared to controlled conditions, which included treatment as usual and partial control (i.e., received attention and some aspects of treatment but not hypothesized core components). The authors suspected that variation in frequency, duration, and overall fidelity of implementation of the MBIs may be responsible for these negligible differences. Consequently, Taylor and colleagues emphasized the exploration of "active ingredients" of MBIs as a key focus for future research. They also contributed to the growing collective conclusion that a general improvement in study quality is needed when testing MBIs, to enhance the internal validity of findings.

Frantz, Hansen, and Machalicek (2018)

Frantz and colleagues (2018) took a broader, more encompassing approach, with a systematic review of various interventions to improve the well-being of parents with children who have autism spectrum disorder (ASD). Interventions are broken down into five separate categories in this review: CBT, psychoeducational, MBIs, behavioral-based, and other. Effects on the outcome variables of parental stress, depression, and self-efficacy are examined. Of the 41 studies included in this review, only 4 included MBIs as a treatment. In all four studies, MBIs were associated with a significant decrease in parental stress. Of the three studies that included parental depression as an outcome variable, MBIs were associated with a significant decrease in depression. No MBI studies measured parent self-efficacy. Although there were few studies including MBIs, mindfulness intervention studies were among the highest quality and most effective, with 75% using a randomized group design and 50% reporting medium to large effect sizes. Although only a few studies in this review evaluated MBIs, the results support their use as effective treatments to reduce stress and depression in parents of children with ASD.

Alexander (2018)

Alexander (2018) took an integrative approach to reviewing the relationship between MBIs and depression symptoms in parents by reviewing both randomized controlled trials and cross-sectional descriptive studies. Three RCTs and four descriptive studies met inclusion criteria for this review, and findings were consistent across methodologies. RCT results showed that MBIs decreased depression in all three studies (effect sizes ranging from moderate to large). Descriptive studies substantiated this finding, as all four studies reported that general mindfulness was inversely correlated with depression symptoms (in one study, $r = -.51, p < .001$). Alexander cautioned that generalizability may be greatly affected by the sample characteristics, as most participants in all seven studies were white, affluent, highly educated women. An additional factor limiting generalizability was the inconsistency in measurement tools across studies. Nonetheless, Alexander highlighted the strength of evidence linking MBIs to increased parent well-being, and she advocates for the mobilization of MBIs as a method to not only improve parent mental health but to improve the well-being of entire families.

Summary of Findings for MBIs With Parents

Overall, MBIs appear to offer some promise to improve parental outcomes, such as emotional awareness, sensitivity, and communication. Also, there appears to be evidence supporting the use of MBIs to reduce parents' self-reported stress and mental health problems, such as anxiety and depression. Considering the importance of parental mental health for healthy child development, the potential to generalize these improvements to other parent samples and populations warrants further investigation into parent-focused MBIs. As we mentioned at the outset of this chapter, parents' mental health impacts their ability to effectively and appropriately regulate their emotions and attention to provide the most nurturing environment possible. Without a nurturing environment, children's development can negatively cascade, potentially resulting in increased parental conflicts and worsening mental health problems. MBIs demonstrate preliminary evidence for breaking this undesirable cycle.

The evidence is only preliminary, however, as it is not clear from these reviews the extent to which MBIs resulted in improving parents' capacity to create nurturing, reinforcing, and responsive environments for children. In theory, the relationship between MBIs improving parental health that cascades into improved environments is reasonable. Unfortunately, many of the studies included within these research syntheses did not concurrently examine parent and child outcomes. In fact, out of the 90 included studies, only 9 appeared to have gathered child outcome data regarding a small set of outcome variables (e.g., externalizing behaviors, maladaptive behaviors, attention). The remaining 81 studies focused exclusively on parent outcomes. Of those that investigated child outcomes, the results are at least promising. Significant improvements in two child outcomes—reduction in externalizing behaviors (e.g., aggression) and increased attention—were reported across the nine studies. Thus, positive and general conclusions about the effectiveness of MBIs for parents-only can be made, but less is known regarding whether parent-focused MBIs indirectly influence child outcomes. Greater attention is needed in future research to assess these links to support the appropriateness of parent-focused MBIs as a tool to increase parents' capacity to be responsive, develop healthy relationships with their children, and provide a nurturing environment.

Results are further tempered by the fact that publication bias is likely present in this literature. Most of the research syntheses did not include "gray" or unpublished literature, which is more likely to include studies with non-significant findings. Although sometimes studies are not published because their design and overall quality are poor, some high-quality studies demonstrate null findings. A future synthesis could replicate the searches used in the reviewed syntheses and include unpublished findings to see if the inclusion of these studies alters outcomes.

A critical improvement that can be made in parent-focused MBI research, and one that practitioners can also address in their work, is the lack of treatment integrity assessment in the reviewed studies. Treatment integrity is a multifaceted concept that can be broadly understood as the degree to which a particular intervention was implemented as designed for a particular problem and for a particular population (Perepletchikova, 2011). Research cannot provide definitive conclusions about treatment effectiveness without some measure of how well the treatment components (e.g., frequency, duration, intensity) aligned with the intended benefactor of the intervention; otherwise, an intervention delivered according to protocol that appears ineffective may have, for example, been simply mismatched or matched theoretically but lacking dosage or any other possible combination of treatment elements needed to bring about a desired outcome. Indeed, this inability to determine the true effectiveness of an intervention is why some researchers advocate for the inclusion of treatment integrity data and conclusions as part of a requirement for ethical research conduct and dissemination (e.g., Bond et al., 2011). Thus, we encourage researchers and practitioners to consider that the effectiveness of a parent-focused MBI likely hinges on it being delivered with integrity. The reviewed syntheses were unable to determine the relationship between integrity and outcomes, because most studies did not report integrity outcomes.

OVERVIEW OF MINDFULNESS-BASED INTERVENTIONS WITH EDUCATORS

Teachers are widely recognized as a vital asset to a well-functioning society (Vesely et al., 2013). Notwithstanding the societal importance of the teaching profession, it is regarded as one of the most demanding and stressful occupations (Kyriacou, 2001). Many teachers feel unprepared, unsupported, and unable to meet the demands of their positions (Renard, 2003). Yet, contemporary teachers confront growing societal expectations to accomplish more with less, as exemplified by higher accountability standards for student outcomes with an ever-changing and increasingly diverse body of students (Emery & Vandenberg, 2010). This increased pressure, combined with ineffective emotion regulation for dealing with the stress inherent in the job, can lead to burnout, which has wide-reaching impact on teachers themselves and, consequentially, the students they serve (Pillay et al., 2005).

Teacher stress and burnout are real concerns; recent survey data indicated that teacher-reported job satisfaction was at an all-time low in 2012 (Markow & Pieters, 2012). Teachers reporting lower satisfaction also reported higher levels of occupational stress and were more likely to indicate that they would leave the teaching profession within five years (Markow & Cooper, 2008). Estimates of retention indicate that up to 50% of new teachers leave the profession within five years, with similar percentages observed internationally (Roffey, 2012). In addition to attrition, chronic stress can lead to a host of negative outcomes for both teachers and the students they serve. Teachers who are stressed and burned out experience more difficulties with classroom management and deliver lower quality instruction (Oberle & Schonert-Reichl, 2016). Chronic difficulties managing daily stress may lead to a series of experiences referred to as the *burnout cascade*, characterized by increases in emotional exhaustion (e.g., feeling tired, overextended, and emotionally and physically drained), depersonalization (e.g., callous, unfeeling response to students), and job dissatisfaction (Oberle & Schonert-Reichl, 2016).

Chronic stress can also have negative impacts on overall health, with higher rates of depression and illness, decreased hippocampal functioning, and lower perceived personal and professional efficacy (Roffey, 2012). Finally, teacher stress and reduced teacher efficacy contribute to lower student achievement, poorer teacher-student interactions and relationships, reduced support of students in the classroom, and less positive classrooms (Hoglund et al., 2015). Recent research demonstrated a contagion effect of teachers' stress on students, in which burned-out teachers were more likely to have students who had higher levels of morning cortisol, indicating that the students in their classes were experiencing higher levels of stress in anticipation of going to school (Oberle & Schonert-Reichl, 2016).

The success of initiatives addressing classroom and school climate, student achievement, and student social-emotional competence has been argued to be dependent on the well-being of teachers who are frontline implementers (Gu & Day, 2007). Teachers must navigate challenging or emotionally provocative situations daily and are limited in their options for self-regulation when they must remain in the classroom while calming down. To function well in schools with accountability requirements and high expectations for student well-being and academic outcomes, teachers must be able to manage stress, cope effectively with ongoing change, and seek and provide social support (Cook et al., 2017).

Because of mounting evidence demonstrating the negative impact of teacher stress and burnout, more recent research has shifted away from documenting causes, correlates, and outcomes of teacher stress and burnout toward an intentional focus on developing and examining the impact of interventions targeting the promotion of teacher well-being. Many of these interventions focus on mindfulness training (e.g., Jennings et al., 2013). The empirical findings obtained from these studies point to the importance and promise of targeting teachers with intervention as a way of promoting their well-being and effectiveness. Research examining interventions to promote teacher well-being is emerging, with considerable room for further research to develop innovative supports, replicate findings on existing programs, and examine mediators and moderators impacting outcomes.

Table 3.2. Research Syntheses of MBIs for Teachers

Research Synthesis	Number of Studies	Sample Characteristics of Included Studies	Design Features	Outcome Measures	Findings	Notable Limitations
Emerson et al. (2017)	13 studies across 12 publications since 2004	Countries of Origin: USA, Canada, UK Education Service Levels: Preservice, Primary, Secondary % Female (range): 69.7–97.4	Group Design: Independent with pre-post, qualitative interviews, qualitative focus groups, mixed-designs Control Group: None, non-active, waitlist	1. Stress 2. Emotion Regulation 3. Self-efficacy 4. Mindfulness and self-compassion	Approximately 50% of studies reported significant improvements in stress and burnout More than 50% reported significant improvements in emotion regulation, although mixed results were apparent based on study quality MBIs were largely effective in teaching mindfulness and boosting self-compassion in almost 40% of studies	Publication bias not directly assessed No moderator or mediator analyses to test their self-efficacy theory or other variables of interest

continued

Table 3.2. CONTINUED

Research Synthesis	Number of Studies	Sample Characteristics of Included Studies	Design Features	Outcome Measures	Findings	Notable Limitations
Hwang et al. (2017)	16 studies across 16 publications since 2015	Countries of Origin: Not reported Education Service Levels: preschool, primary, secondary, specialist, administration; % Female (average): 59.4	Group Design: RCT, Independent with pre-post, Dependent with pre-post, Single-subject Control Group: None, waitlist	Stress, well-being, mindfulness, self-compassion, psychological symptoms and burnout, classroom organization, affective attention, depression, anxiety, psychological distress	Reduced psychological problems and symptoms in nearly every study Improvements in teachers' affect and positive word choice in the classroom; Improvements in classroom management skills	Inconsistent reporting of calculated effect sizes Due to small literature, study quality was not assessed; results may be moderated based on study design

Lomas et al. (2017)	17 studies across 17 publications since 2008	Countries cf Origin: Not reported Education Service Levels: preschool, primary, secondary, university % Female (average): Not reported	Group Design: RCT, independent with pre-post, dependent with pre-post Control Group: None, Business-as-usual, Waitlist, Active-control	1.Anxiety 2. Burnout & resilience 3. Compassion & empathy 4. Depression 5. Distress & anger 6. Emotional regulation 7. Health 8. Job performance 9. Mindfulness & Awareness 10. Stress & Strain 11. Well-being & Satisfaction	86% of studies demonstrated positive MBI related improvements. General health was the second most common outcome observed, with over 60% of studies demonstrating improvements; Improvements in resiliency, which helps protect against burnout and increased demands in the teaching profession, were observed in 57% of studies	Majority of included studies were considered "weak" in study quality Clinical interventions may not be suitable for educational contexts Focused mostly on negative indicators of well-being

continued

Table 3.2. Continued

Research Synthesis	Number of Studies	Sample Characteristics of Included Studies	Design Features	Outcome Measures	Findings	Notable Limitations
Klingbeil & Renshaw (2018)	29 studies published since April 2018	Countries of Origin: Not reported Education Service Levels: primary, secondary % Female (range): 57–100	Group Design: RCT, Independent with pre-post Control Group: Not reported	1. Mindfulness 2. Mechanisms of mindfulness 3. Psychological well-being 4. Psychological Distress 5. Psychological indicators 6. Classroom climate & Instructional practices	Exploration of potential moderators included if the study incorporated randomization, who facilitated the intervention, and overall intervention dosage: none were related to the observed effect sizes. Some publication bias was observed despite the authors searching dissertations and theses, suggesting that some of the effects may be a bit smaller than observed	Studies had to focus exclusively on educators; studies that included teachers within a larger occupational treatment group were excluded Several outcomes were combined into broad categories which limits specificity of treatment outcomes

Review of Research on MBIs With Educators

This chapter covers a selection of four comprehensive research syntheses examining the impact of MBIs with educators completed between 2017 and 2018. Each review adopted a slightly different approach to synthesizing the literature, and the findings from each review differed depending on the focus or purpose of the included studies. By identifying common elements across these research syntheses, however, it is possible to generate tentative general findings about the appropriateness and effectiveness of MBIs for teachers. Table 3.2 presents basic information, including study sample characteristics, outcomes of interest, and general findings from each review. Although additional systematic reviews on MBIs with educators have emerged in recent years, the selection of four reviews provided in this chapter offers representative coverage of the topic at hand. Readers interested in additional contemporary reviews beyond the scope of this chapter are referred to Zarate et al. (2019) and Gómez-Olmedo et al. (2020).

Emerson et al. (2017)

Emerson and colleagues (2017) explored the utility of MBIs in boosting teachers' skills of emotion regulation and perceived self-efficacy, which were hypothesized to result in reduced stress and improved classroom and workload management. Thirteen studies across multiple levels of education (i.e., primary, secondary, and post-secondary) and several countries were included. Studies used mixed designs, including pre-post treatment and control groups with follow-up interviews, and tracked improvements in participants' stress, emotion regulation, self-efficacy, and self-compassion and mindfulness skills. Results were inconsistent. MBIs appeared effective, on average, for a small majority of participants, with the largest effects found in teachers' perceived stress. It is noteworthy that these large effects were not accompanied by increases in self-efficacy, despite Emerson and colleagues hypothesizing self-efficacy as a mediating effect that reduces stress. That is, they suggested that mindfulness leads to increased self-efficacy, which in turn leads to decreased stress. The data did not support this mediation hypothesis and, instead, suggested that teachers can benefit from the stress-reducing effects of mindfulness (e.g., reduction in burnout, improved non-reactivity) without experiencing an increase in their self-efficacy. Five studies did report changes in teacher self-efficacy, however, with a range of effect sizes (d) from .07 to .87, suggesting that when MBIs do affect self-efficacy, they are associated with positive and desirable changes. Overall, this review suggested that MBIs could be potentially useful as stress-reduction techniques for teachers. Furthermore, the variability across studies in the proportion of teachers reporting positive changes and where positive changes occurred (e.g., self-efficacy vs. perceived stress) indicated that more research is needed to clarify the mechanisms of improvement.

Hwang, Bartlett, Greben, and Hand (2017)

Hwang and colleagues (2017) also examined the impact of mindfulness on self-efficacy and self-compassion, while exploring educators' related improvements in psychological distress (e.g., intensity and frequency of depression and/or anxiety symptoms), well-being, and classroom practices. Potential moderators of MBI effectiveness included who received the MBI, for how long, and who delivered it. Sixteen studies were included in their review, most of which were RCTs. Across studies, Hwang and colleagues (2017) observed improvements across several domains of teacher functioning and well-being. Decreases in symptoms of depression and anxiety were observed in nearly every study (*d* range = 0.61–1.06 for depression, 0.71–0.89 for anxiety). These were accompanied by improvements in self-efficacy (*d* range = 0.52–0.66) and reported coping skills (*d* range = 0.57–0.70). A common theme across several qualitative studies that were included was that teachers felt more able to pause and cope with aversive classroom situations (e.g., aggressive student behavior) in healthy ways that were not reactive and automatic; these same teachers reported noticing improved relationships with students. Although not directly tested, the results from the quantitative and qualitative studies included in this review suggest that MBIs affect internal mechanisms (i.e., subjective perceptions and experiences, such as sense of openness between student and teacher) and external mechanisms (i.e., observable experiences and behaviors, such as the frequency of student problem and compliance behaviors) of student-teacher relationships that promote nurturing, responsive, and reinforcing environments.

The generalizability of these findings is limited by the fact that the duration of MBIs varied substantially. Some interventions lasted six weeks with minimal prior training, others included an MBI training period followed by an eight-to-ten-week practice period, and still another study implemented the MBI for three years plus a follow-up year during which the sustainability of mindfulness practices and effects were assessed. Since MBIs for educators is still an emerging area of research, Hwang and colleagues were unable to investigate if the duration of intervention moderated outcomes. In addition, studies targeted a broad range of educators, including specialists such as paraprofessionals and school psychologists, as well as administrative staff. Hwang and colleagues purposefully defined "educators" broadly to increase their reach across the literature, yet by capturing studies investigating school staff with very different responsibilities, they were also unable to investigate if MBIs were more effective for some roles than for others, such as for teachers versus principals. Finally, studies were implemented by a variety of individuals. In some cases, studies did not explicitly identify who facilitated the MBI implementation, making it difficult to draw inferences about how effective MBIs are when implemented by a researcher compared to, for example, a school-based clinician.

Lomas, Medina, Ivtzan, Rupprecht, and Eiroa-Orosa (2017)

Lomas and colleagues (2017) produced a very similar synthesis as Hwang and colleagues (2017). Across 17 studies, they examined MBIs in relation to impacts on in-service teachers' stress, burnout, and well-being factors, such as life satisfaction. Their results were consistent with Hwang and colleagues (2017). MBIs were associated with improvements across 11 outcome domains, including mindfulness, general health, general well-being, and job performance. Nearly all studies reported improvements in mindfulness skills, which were believed to translate into improvements in other areas of functioning for teachers, and most of these studies demonstrated simultaneous improvements in at least one other outcome domain (e.g., job performance or emotional regulation). Perhaps the most interesting findings from this synthesis are the notable improvements in several dimensions of in-service teachers' resiliency, including improvements in empathy toward others, sleep, and stress regulation. These are foundational skills and habits that help protect individuals from succumbing to increased internal and external pressures. Thus, MBIs may be fruitful not just for short-term stress management but also for enhancing educators' long-term performance and coping.

Despite the promising findings from Lomas et al.'s (2017) review, we caution that conclusions like these need to be bolstered by future studies because, based on the ratings of study quality in this review, most studies were using MBIs that were initially developed for clinical settings. This creates potential issues when generalizing these findings to schools because (a) treatments founded and evaluated within clinical contexts may rely on factors not apparent in educational contexts (e.g., dedicated, uninterrupted session time) and (b) measures of effectiveness may have been more aligned with valued clinical outcomes as opposed to educational outcomes. In addition, the overall quality of study designs was questionable—or not enough information was reported in studies to accurately assess study quality, warranting a need for higher quality investigation. A final limitation from this synthesis is that effect sizes were not calculated, nor were data provided to allow us to calculate effect sizes ourselves. This limits our understanding of the magnitude of effects observed in these studies and how they might compare to other studies.

Klingbeil and Renshaw (2018)

Klingbeil and Renshaw (2018) conducted the most recent and perhaps most comprehensive review of MBIs with teachers to date. It included the largest number of studies ($k = 29$) and used an outcome categorization scheme similar to that of Lomas and colleagues (2017) to help draw conclusions about broad health and work performance outcomes. They also used more broad inclusion criteria—specifically, incorporation of unpublished studies such as dissertations—to achieve minimum statistical power to explore potential moderating factors accounting for results seen in previous syntheses. Overall, Klingbeil and Renshaw (2018) observed moderate improvements in teachers' mindfulness ($g = .69$), psychological well-being and distress ($g = .43$ and $.55$, respectively), classroom practices ($g = .31$), and theoretical mechanisms (e.g., emotional processing and regulation, sustained attention) linking the practice of mindfulness to other teacher behaviors and qualities ($g = .44$). There was still notable variability in the effects between studies, though. Klingbeil and Renshaw (2018) conducted exploratory analyses to determine potential variables that might moderate this variability. Studies that incorporated randomization to determine intervention and control groups did not produce different effects than non-randomized studies. Similarly, there were no differences between interventions that were implemented by the intervention developer themselves and studies that used another facilitator, such as school-based staff. These findings are promising, as they suggest that MBIs can be effective for a wide variety of teacher outcomes and that these effects do not appear to be moderated by who leads the intervention, yet they do not clarify any potential sources of differential effectiveness among MBIs.

Summary of Findings for MBIS With Educators

Overall, these four comprehensive research syntheses demonstrate the promise of MBIs for teaching mindfulness to and improving the well-being of educators. All reviews demonstrated that improvements in stress and negative psychological symptoms are generally observed upon completion of an MBI. Additionally, when improvements in stress were observed, they were accompanied by further improvements in components of resiliency, which can help inoculate teachers against future stress and burnout.

However, findings for some resiliency-related constructs, such as self-efficacy, were not consistent. As Emerson and colleagues (2017) hypothesized, mindfulness may lead to improvements in self-efficacy, which then cascades into improved teacher practices, classroom and workload management, and improved student-teacher relationships. Yet, self-efficacy did not always improve after completing an MBI, and nearly every study within this synthesis reported no change in teachers' classroom or workload management skills. Teachers reported improvements in student-teacher relationships, but this was explored in only one study and relied on subjective reporting without any behavioral observations to corroborate these improvements. As such, we do not yet see evidence to validate the purported mediating relationship from improved teacher well-being to improved management practices to improved student outcomes.

In contrast, Hwang and colleagues (2017) did observe that MBIs improved self-efficacy along with other notable improvements in outcomes. It is unclear why conclusions about the impact of MBIs on target variables such as self-efficacy differed across syntheses. A potential explanation for these differences is that not enough studies in the literature evaluated MBIs in relation to certain outcomes. Low frequency within the literature could make certain variables highly susceptible to differences in how the syntheses conducted their literature searches. For example, self-efficacy was included in 38% of studies reviewed by Emerson and colleagues (2017), and 44% of studies reviewed by Hwang and colleagues (2017), with only some overlap in included studies. If the studies included in these syntheses are considered samples of a larger population of studies (as is assumed for reviews and meta-analyses), then it is possible that such low prevalence means there is not enough literature yet to reliably determine how MBIs affect self-efficacy. This same dearth of research could also underpin conclusions about other outcomes, such as the discrepancies in the effects on classroom management skills observed by Emerson et al. (2017; null effects) and Klingbeil and Renshaw (2018; positive effects).

Another potential explanation for different outcomes is that MBIs may need to directly address the putative mechanisms of mindfulness that boost educator classroom practices. Klingbeil and Renshaw (2018) determined that MBIs positively impact mechanisms of mindfulness (e.g., selective attention), yet MBIs had a weaker (although still positive) impact on classroom management and instructional practices. As such, MBIs may include core components that strengthen mindfulness skills and mechanisms (e.g., selective attention) without explicitly drawing links to how these improved outcomes can be transferred to classrooms (e.g., demonstrating how selective attention can improve classroom management). As such, educators may become more mindful while not necessarily becoming more mindful educators, leading to disparate outcomes across studies and syntheses.

A third explanation for different outcomes links to a consistent limitation across all four syntheses: few studies reported implementation integrity. Only one meta-analysis (Klingbeil & Renshaw, 2018) incorporated enough studies that reported integrity to test if implementation integrity moderated intervention effects—finding the effect was not significant. However, there are notable limitations. First, the studies in this meta-analysis reported intervention dosage, which is just one aspect of treatment integrity (Perepletchikova, 2011). Second, this moderator analysis may have been underpowered to observe small-to-moderate, but no less important, effects. Like primary studies, statistical power is a concern in meta-analyses (Valentine et al., 2010), and arguably more so, given that the unit of analysis for moderators in most meta-analyses is the study itself and not participant sample size. Therefore, it is difficult to rule out implementation integrity as a potential explanation for MBI outcomes.

CONCLUSION

Children need nurturing, responsive, and reinforcing environments in order to develop and thrive. Parents and educators represent vital role models and influencers within a child's ecology. MBIs may be beneficial for parents and educators alike, improving their ability to attend and respond to children's needs. Current syntheses suggest that MBIs improve parents' and educators' ability to be mindful, while also evidencing some other benefits, including stress reduction and improvements in mental health. What is still unclear is how the effects of MBIs are moderated by implementation integrity and how the exclusion of "gray literature" in most of the syntheses influences conclusions regarding effectiveness. Recommendations for future research in primary studies include assessment of treatment integrity, specific identification and measurement of theoretical mechanisms of mindfulness that produce proximal changes in caregivers and distal changes in children, and consistent measurement across studies. Recommendations for future meta-analytic research include incorporating "gray literature" and assessing moderators (e.g., intervention facilitator effects, intervention setting, differences in participant demographics) to account for discrepancies in study outcomes. Combined, these improvements in research would help to solidify MBI's active ingredients, as well as determine the contexts in which parent and educator MBIs have optimal potential to promote positive child outcomes.

REFERENCES

*Denotes meta-analyses and reviews summarized in the chapter

*Alexander, K. (2018). Integrative review of the relationship between mindfulness-based parenting interventions and depression symptoms in parents. *Journal of Obstetric, Gynecologic & Neonatal Nursing, 47*(2), 184–190. doi: https://doi.org/10.1016/j.jogn.2017.11.013

Anand, L., Sadowski, I., Per, M., & Khoury, B. (2023). Mindful parenting: A meta-analytic review of intrapersonal and interpersonal parental outcomes. *Current Psychology, 42*(10), 8367–8383.

Benn, R., Akiva, T., Arel, S., & Roeser, R. W. (2012). Mindfulness training effects for parents and educators of children with special needs. *Developmental Psychology, 48*(5), 1476–1487. Doi: 10.1037/a0027537.

Biglan, A. (2015). *The nurture effect: How the science of human behavior can improve our lives and our world.* New Harbinger Publications.

Biglan, A., Flay, B. R., Embry, D. D., & Sandler, I. N. (2012). The critical role of nurturing environments for promoting human well-being. *American Psychologist, 67*(4), 257–271. doi:10.1037/a0026796

Bishop, S. R., Lau, M., Shapiro, S., Carlson, L., Anderson, N. D., Carmody, J., . . . Devins, G. (2004). Mindfulness: A proposed operational definition. *Clinical Psychology: Science and Practice, 11*(3), 230–241. https://doi.org/10.1093/clipsy.bph077

Bond, G. R., Becker, D. R., & Drake, R. E. (2011). Measurement of fidelity of implementation of evidence-based practices: Case example of the IPS Fidelity Scale. *Clinical Psychology: Science and Practice, 18*(2), 126–141. https://doi.org/10.1111/j.1468-2850.2011.01244.x

Bögels, S.M., Hellemans, J., van Deursen, S., Römer, M., & van der Meulen, R. (2014). Mindful parenting in mental health care: effects on parental and child psychopathology, parental stress, parenting, coparenting, and marital functioning. *Mindfulness, 5*(5), 536–551. https://doi.org/10.1007/s12671-013-0209-7

Brooks, R.B. (2005). The power of parenting. In S. Goldstein & R. B. Brooks (Eds.), *Handbook of resilience in children* (pp. 297–314). Springer.

*Cachia, R. L., Anderson, A., & Moore, D. W. (2016). Mindfulness, stress and well-being in parents of children with autism spectrum disorder: A systematic review. *Journal of Child and Family Studies, 25*(1), 1–14. https://doi.org/10.1007/s10826-015-0193-8

Chu, L. C. (2010). The benefits of meditation vis-à-vis emotional intelligence, perceived stress and negative mental health. *Stress and Health: Journal of the International Society for the Investigation of Stress, 26*(2), 169–180. https://doi.org/10.1002/smi.1289

Coatsworth, J. D., Duncan, L. G., Greenberg, M. T., & Nix, R. L. (2010). Changing parent's mindfulness, child management skills and relationship quality with their youth: Results from a randomized pilot intervention trial. *Journal of Child and Family Studies, 19*(2), 203–217. https://doi.org/10.1007/s10826-009-9304-8

Cook, C. R., Grady, E. A., Long, A. C., Renshaw, T., Codding, R. S., Fiat, A., & Larson, M. (2017). Evaluating the impact of increasing general education teachers' ratio of positive-to-negative interactions on students' classroom behavior. *Journal of Positive Behavior Interventions*, *19*(2), 67–77. https://doi.org/10.1177%2F1098300716679137

de Bruin, E. I., Zijlstra, B. J., Geurtzen, N., van Zundert, R. M., van de Weijer-bergsma, E., Hartman, E. E., . . . Bögels, S. M. (2014). Mindful parenting assessed further: Psychometric properties of the Dutch version of the Interpersonal Mindfulness in Parenting Scale (IM-P). *Mindfulness*, *5*(2), 200–212. doi: 10.1007/s12671-012-0168-4

Dumas, J. E. (2005). Mindfulness-based parent training: Strategies to lessen the grip of automaticity in families with disruptive children. *Journal of Clinical Child and Adolescent Psychology*, *34*(4), 779–791. doi: 10.1207/s15374424jccp3404_20

Duncan, L. G., Coatsworth, J. D., & Greenberg, M. T. (2009). Pilot study to gauge acceptability of a mindfulness-based, family-focused preventive intervention. *The Journal of Primary Prevention*, *30*(5), 605–618. https://doi.org/10.1007/s10935-009-0185-9

*Emerson, L. M., Leyland, A., Hudson, K., Rowse, G., Hanley, P., & Hugh-Jones, S. (2017). Teaching mindfulness to teachers: A systematic review and narrative synthesis. *Mindfulness*, *8*(5), 1136–1149. doi: https://doi.org/10.1007/s12671-017-0691-4

Emery, D. W., & Vandenberg, B. (2010). Special education teacher burnout and ACT. *International Journal of Special Education*, *25*(3), 119–131.

Felitti, V. J., Anda, R. F., Nordenberg, D., Williamson, D. F., Spitz, A. M., Edwards, V., & Marks, J. S. (1998). Relationship of childhood abuse and household dysfunction to many of the leading causes of death in adults: The Adverse Childhood Experiences (ACE) Study. *American Journal of Preventive Medicine*, *14*(4), 245–258. https://doi.org/10.1016/S0749-3797(98)00017-8

Ferraioli, S. J., & Harris, S. L. (2013). Comparative effects of mindfulness and skills-based parent training programs for parents of children with autism: Feasibility and preliminary outcome data. *Mindfulness*, *4*(2), 89–101. doi: 10.1007/s12671-012-0099-0

*Frantz, R., Hansen, S. G., & Machalicek, W. (2018). Interventions to promote well-being in parents of children with autism: A systematic review. *Review Journal of Autism and Developmental Disorders*, *5*(1), 58–77. doi: https://doi.org/10.1007/s4048

Goldin, P. R., & Gross, J. J. (2010). Effects of mindfulness-based stress reduction (MBSR) on emotion regulation in social anxiety disorder. *Emotion*, *10*(1), 83–91. https://psycnet.apa.org/doi/10.1037/a0018441

Gómez-Olmedo, A. M., Valor, C., & Carrero, I. (2020). Mindfulness in education for sustainable development to nurture socioemotional competencies: A systematic review and meta-analysis. *Environmental Education Research*, *26*(11), 1527–1555.

Gottman, J. M., Katz, L. F., & Hooven, C. (1996). Parental meta-emotion philosophy and the emotional life of families: Theoretical models and preliminary data. *Journal of Family Psychology*, *10*(3), 243–268. https://psycnet.apa.org/doi/10.1037/0893-3200.10.3.243

Greenberg, M. T., & Harris, A. R. (2012). Nurturing mindfulness in children and youth: Current state of research. *Child Development Perspectives*, *6*(2), 161–166. doi: 10.1111/j.1750-8606.2011.00215.x

Gu, Q., & Day, C. (2007). Teachers resilience: A necessary condition for effectiveness. *Teaching and Teacher Education*, *23*(8), 1302–1316. https://doi.org/10.1016/j.tate.2006.06.006

Haydicky, J., Shecter, C., Wiener, J., & Ducharme, J. M. (2015). Evaluation of MBCT for adolescents with ADHD and their parents: Impact on individual and family functioning. *Journal of Child and Family Studies*, *24*(1), 76–94. https://doi.org/10.1007/s10826-013-9815-1

Hinds, E., Jones, L. B., Gau, J. M., Forrester, K. K., & Biglan, A. (2015). Teacher distress and the role of experiential avoidance. *Psychology in the Schools, 52*(3), 284–297. https://doi.org/10.1002/pits.21821

Hofmann, S. G., Sawyer, A. T., Witt, A. A., & Oh, D. (2010). The effect of mindfulness-based therapy on anxiety and depression: A meta-analytic review. *Journal of Consulting and Clinical Psychology, 78*(2), 169–183. doi: 10.1037/a0018555

Hoglund, W. L., Klingle, K. E., & Hosan, N. E. (2015). Classroom risks and resources: Teacher burnout, classroom quality and children's adjustment in high needs elementary schools. *Journal of School Psychology, 53*(5), 337–357. https://doi.org/10.1016/j.jsp.2015.06.002

Howell, A. J., Digdon, N. L., & Buro, K. (2010). Mindfulness predicts sleep-related self-regulation and well-being. *Personality and Individual Differences, 48*(4), 419–424. https://doi.org/10.1016/j.paid.2009.11.009

*Hwang, Y. S., Bartlett, B., Greben, M., & Hand, K. (2017). A systematic review of mindfulness interventions for in-service teachers: A tool to enhance teacher wellbeing and performance. *Teaching and Teacher Education, 64*, 26–42. https://doi.org/10.1016/j.tate.2017.01.015

Irwin, L. G., Siddiqi, A., & Hertzman, C. (2007). *Early child development: A powerful equalizer. Final Report to the World Health Organization's Commission on the Social Determinants of Health.* Early Child Development Knowledge Network. Retrieved from https://www.who.int/social_determinants/resources/ecd_kn_report_07_2007.pdf

Jennings, P. A., Frank, J. L., Snowberg, K. E., Coccia, M. A., & Greenberg, M. T. (2013). Improving classroom learning environments by Cultivating Awareness and Resilience in Education (CARE): Results of a randomized controlled trial. *School Psychology Quarterly, 28*(4), 374–390. https://psycnet.apa.org/doi/10.1037/spq0000035

Kabat-Zinn, J. (2003). Mindfulness-based stress reduction (MBSR). *Constructivism in the Human Sciences, 8*(2), 73–83.

Kabat-Zinn, J., & Hanh, T. N. (2009). *Full catastrophe living: Using the wisdom of your body and mind to face stress, pain, and illness.* Delta.

Kazdin, A. E. (2008). *Parent management training: Treatment for oppositional, aggressive, and antisocial behavior in children and adolescents.* Oxford University Press.

Khoury, B., Lecomte, T., Fortin, G., Masse, M., Therien, P., Bouchard, V., . . . Hofmann, S. G. (2013). Mindfulness-based therapy: A comprehensive meta-analysis. *Clinical Psychology Review, 33*(6), 763–771. https://doi.org/10.1016/j.cpr.2013.05.005

*Klingbeil, D. A., & Renshaw, T. L. (2018). Mindfulness-based interventions for teachers: A meta-analysis of the emerging evidence base. *School Psychology Quarterly, 33*(4), 501–511. doi: http://dx.doi.org/10.1037/spq0000291

Klusmann, U., Kunter, M., Trautwein, U., Lüdtke, O., & Baumert, J. (2008). Teachers' occupational well-being and quality of instruction: The important role of self-regulatory patterns. *Journal of Educational Psychology, 100*(3), 702–715. doi:10.1037/0022-0663.100.3.702

Kokkinos, C. M. (2007). Job stressors, personality and burnout in primary school teachers. *British Journal of Educational Psychology, 77*(1), 229–243. https://doi.org/10.1348/000709905X90344

Komro, K. A., Flay, B. R., & Biglan, A. (2011). Creating nurturing environments: A science-based framework for promoting child health and development within high-poverty neighborhoods. *Clinical Child and Family Psychology Review*, *14*(2), 111–134. doi:10.1007/s10567-011-0095-2

Kring, L. (2013, December 14). The 5 main tenets of mindful parenting. Retrieved from https://www.huffpost.com/entry/the-5-main-tenets-of-mindful-parenting_b_4086080

Kyriacou, C. (2001). Teacher stress: Directions for future research. *Educational Review*, *53*(1), 27–35. https://doi.org/10.1080/00131910120033628

Lee, C. S., Ng, K. H., Chan, P. C., & Peng, X. (2022). Effectiveness of mindfulness parent training on parenting stress and children's ADHD-related behaviors: A systematic review and meta-analysis. *Hong Kong Journal of Occupational Therapy*, *35*(1), 3–24.

Lee, S. S. (2018). Perspectives on parenting behavior: Origins, mechanisms, and future opportunities: Editorial for the supplement on parenting. *Journal of Clinical Child & Adolescent Psychology*, *47:sup1*, S1–S4, doi:10.1080/15374416.2018.1511433

∗Lomas, T., Medina, J. C., Ivtzan, I., Rupprecht, S., & Eiroa-Orosa, F. J. (2017). The impact of mindfulness on the wellbeing and performance of educators: A systematic review of the empirical literature. *Teaching and Teacher Education*, *61*, 132–141. doi: https://doi.org/10.1016/j.tate.2016.10.008

Markow, D., & Cooper, M. (2008). The MetLife survey of the American teacher: Past, present, and future. *Education Resources Information Center (ERIC) ED504457*.

Markow, D., & Pieters, A. (2012). The MetLife survey of the American teacher: Teachers, parents and the economy. Metlife. Retrieved from https://files.eric.ed.gov/fulltext/ED530021.pdf

Neece, C. L. (2014). Mindfulness-based stress reduction for parents of young children with developmental delays: Implications for parental mental health and child behavior problems. *Journal of Applied Research in Intellectual Disabilities*, *27*(2), 174–186. https://doi.org/10.1111/jar.12064

Oberle, E., & Schonert-Reichl, K. A. (2016). Stress contagion in the classroom? The link between classroom teacher burnout and morning cortisol in elementary school students. *Social Science & Medicine*, *159*, 30–37. https://doi.org/10.1016/j.socscimed.2016.04.031

Perepletchikova, F. (2011). On the topic of treatment integrity. *Clinical Psychology: Science and Practice*, *18*(2), 148–153. https://doi.org/10.1111/j.1468-2850.2011.01246.x

Pillay, H., Goddard, R., & Wilss, L. (2005). Well-being, burnout and competence: Implications for teachers. *Australian Journal of Teacher Education*, *30*(2), 22–33.

Raab, K. (2014). Mindfulness, self-compassion, and empathy among health care professionals: A review of the literature. *Journal of Health Care Chaplaincy*, *20*(3), 95–108. https://doi.org/10.1080/08854726.2014.913876

∗Rayan, A., & Ahmad, M. (2018). Mindfulness and parenting distress among parents of children with disabilities: A literature review. *Perspectives in Psychiatric Care*, *54*(2), 324–330. doi: 10.1111/ppc.12217

Renard, L. (2003). Setting new teachers up for failure . . . or success. *Educational Leadership*, *60*(8), 62–64.

Roffey, S. (2012). Pupil wellbeing—teacher wellbeing: Two sides of the same coin? *Educational and Child Psychology, 29*(4), 8–17.

Shapiro, S. L., Brown, K. W., & Biegel, G. M. (2007). Teaching self-care to caregivers: Effects of mindfulness-based stress reduction on the mental health of therapists in training. *Training and Education in Professional Psychology, 1*(2), 105–115. doi: 10.1037/1931-3918.1.2.105

*Taylor, B. L., Cavanagh, K., & Strauss, C. (2016). The effectiveness of mindfulness-based interventions in the perinatal period: A systematic review and meta-analysis. *PloS one, 11*(5), e0155720.

*Townshend, K., Jordan, Z., Stephenson, M., & Tsey, K. (2016). The effectiveness of mindful parenting programs in promoting parents' and children's wellbeing: A systematic review. *JBI Database of Systematic Reviews and Implementation Reports, 14*(3), 139–180. doi: 10.11124/JBISRIR-2016-2314

Valentine, J. C., Pigott, T. D., & Rothstein, H. R. (2010). How many studies do you need? A primer on statistical power for meta-analysis. *Journal of Educational and Behavioral Statistics, 35*(2), 215–247. https://doi.org/10.3102%2F1076998609346961

van den Hoofdakker, B. J., Nauta, M. H., van der Veen-mulders, L., Sytema, S., Emmelkamp, P. M. G., Minderaa, R. B., & Hoekstra, P. J. (2010). Behavioral parent training as an adjunct to routine care in children with ADHD: Moderators of treatment response. *Journal of Pediatric Psychology, 35*(3), 317–326. https://doi.org/10.1093/jpepsy/jsp060

Vesely, A. K., Saklofske, D. H., & Leschied, A. D. (2013). Teachers—the vital resource: The contribution of emotional intelligence to teacher efficacy and well-being. *Canadian Journal of School Psychology, 28*(1), 71–89. https://doi.org/10.1177%2F0829573512468855

Williams, K. L., & Wahler, R. G. (2010). Are mindful parents more authoritative and less authoritarian? An analysis of clinic-referred mothers. *Journal of Child and Family Studies, 19*(2), 230–235. https://doi.org/10.1007/s10826-009-9309-3

Xie, Q. W., Dai, X., Lyu, R., & Lu, S. (2021). Effects of mindfulness-based parallel-group interventions on family functioning and child and parent mental health: A systematic review and meta-analysis. *Mindfulness, 12*(12), 2843–2864.

Zarate, K., Maggin, D. M., & Passmore, A. (2019). Meta-analysis of mindfulness training on teacher well-being. *Psychology in the Schools, 56*(10), 1700–1715.

4

Mindfulness Measures for Youth and Students

ANTHONY J. ROBERSON AND SHELLEY R. UPTON ■

Although mindfulness practices have deep roots in ancient Buddhist traditions, pragmatic interest in reappropriating mindfulness as "therapy" has exploded in the past few decades, both in scientific study and society at large (Harrington & Dunne, 2015). Many acceptance- and mindfulness-based interventions (MBIs) have been developed in recent years, including mindfulness-based stress reduction, mindfulness-based cognitive therapy, and others that integrate components of mindfulness within a broader therapeutic framework (e.g., acceptance and commitment therapy). Treatment studies have found encouraging empirical evidence in support of their effectiveness with youth in clinical and school settings (Klingbeil et al., 2017b), suggesting improved process outcomes (i.e., desirable changes in acceptance and mindfulness) as well as improvements in well-being behavior and symptoms of disorder, including anxiety and depression (Biegel et al., 2009), conduct problems (Klingbeil et al., 2017a), and chronic pain (Wicksell et al., 2007).

While the benefits of MBIs with youth are promising, controversy around the assessment methodology used in treatment studies has also grown (Davidson & Kaszniak, 2015; Grossman, 2011). This chapter provides a brief review of the key issues in this debate as well as a summative appraisal of the strengths and weaknesses of 11 available mindfulness measures for youth. We aim to synthesize the available information in a way that is especially useful for practitioners in becoming more critical consumers of the literature and to help inform their own instrument selection process for summative assessment or progress monitoring MBIs with youth.

Anthony J. Roberson and Shelley R. Upton, *Mindfulness Measures for Youth and Students*. In: *Using Mindfulness to Promote Mental Health in Schools*. Edited by: Tyler L. Renshaw and Shane R. Jimerson, Oxford University Press.
 DOI: 10.1093/9780190880507.003.0004

Note that some excellent recent review articles aimed to accomplish similar goals as this chapter but were relatively limited in their scope of discussed measures (see Eklund et al., 2017; Goodman et al., 2017). This chapter supplements these articles by extending the range of reviewed measures to include both mindfulness and psychological (in)flexibility scales. Psychological flexibility can be understood as a broad construct that includes mindfulness but extends beyond it and relates to both cognitions and overt behavior. The phenomena of cognitive fusion and experiential avoidance have been identified as two key mechanisms underlying disorder from psychological inflexibility (Fletcher & Hayes, 2005). Cognitive fusion is present when someone views their thoughts and feelings as literal directions for action, whereas experiential avoidance is characterized by engaging in action with the goal of altering the frequency or severity of private events (Hayes et al., 2006). These processes are negatively reinforcing in the short term but may result in damaging long-term behavioral outcomes (Hayes et al., 2006; Hayes et al., 2011). Taken together, measures of cognitive fusion and experiential avoidance can be understood as representing mindless (as opposed to mindful) behavior. We believe that incorporating discussion of psychological inflexibility assessment is an important enhancement to a comprehensive review of mindfulness-related measures for youth.

CHALLENGES OF MEASURING MINDFULNESS WITH YOUTH

One of the central issues with mindfulness research is the often loosely applied label of "mindfulness" itself. A widely agreed upon definition of mindfulness conceptualizes it as a conscious act of present moment awareness, where one observes each moment with acceptance, non-judgment, and kindness (Bishop et al., 2004; Kabat-Zinn, 1994). However, measure developers frequently emphasize certain aspects of this definition over others, as is evident in the measures reviewed in this chapter. Researchers may also focus instead on measuring proxy mindfulness constructs, such as compassion or executive control, that are closely related but theoretically distinct from mindfulness itself (Zenner et al., 2014; Zoogman et al., 2015). Much of the youth mindfulness literature has also suffered from "jingle-jangle" fallacies, where multiple scales may purport to measure "mindfulness" but in fact use conceptually different item content that actually relates to alternate constructs (i.e., jingle fallacy; Thorndike, 1904). Likewise, different scales may carry distinct labels but actually measure the same construct (i.e., jangle fallacy; Kelley, 1927). This ambiguity around what information is actually being captured with various instruments makes drawing sound conclusions from treatment studies challenging and calls into question the true strength of construct validation evidence that is available for most measures. While it is important that practitioners select mindfulness measures with strong support for their technical adequacy (i.e., reliability and validity characteristics) and conceptual alignment with the MBI being implemented, this may be difficult if the scale labeling is inaccurate or inconsistent.

Another issue with mindfulness measurement for youth is the developmental appropriateness of item content. Many of the commonly used instruments are simply modified versions of preexisting adult measures that largely employ the same item content verbatim. While some obvious changes are made (e.g., removing an item about driving from the adult Mindful Attention Awareness Scale [MAAS] for the adolescent [MAAS-A] and child [MAAS-C] versions), using mostly the same item content makes a major assumption that youth experience mindfulness in the same ways that adults do. Psychobiological mindfulness research with adults suggests that prefrontal and fronto-limbic brain areas are implicated in the use of important skills associated with mindfulness practice, including awareness of one's own thoughts and feelings as well as manual emotion regulation (Chiesa et al., 2013; Davidson, 2002). However, because these neural structures do not typically mature until adulthood (Gogtay et al., 2004), it may be unreasonable to expect children and adolescents to demonstrate the same behaviors in the same way. While MBI research with youth is certainly growing, far more work has been done with adult populations to this point and researchers must be careful not to overgeneralize the findings. Because of this, it is important that future research utilizes multidimensional mindfulness scales with youth to monitor the particular domains of change from MBI to clarify if systematic differences exist in individuals' experience of mindfulness across development.

While not strictly the only method available to measure mindfulness, at present, self-report behavior rating scales are by far the most commonly used assessment approach (Goodman et al., 2017). Although self-report mindfulness measures are quick and easy to administer, score, and interpret, they suffer from several drawbacks. For instance, it is well established that responding on any self-report instrument is colored by many factors, including social desirability bias, idiosyncratic item interpretations, or tendencies to give all high or all low ratings. Further, respondents may hear the terminology used during an MBI and be influenced on how to respond to rating scales that use the same language (e.g., "non-judgment," "awareness"). In addition, there is much debate regarding item valence; particularly, whether or not the lack of "mindless" behaviors (e.g., walking into a room and forgetting why you came in) constitutes an affirmative presence of mindfulness (cf. Brown, Ryan, et al., 2011; Grossman, 2011). In the majority of available measures, some or all of the items are negatively worded, typically requiring reverse-scoring before scale scores can be obtained. This procedure assumes that not acting mindlessly in everyday life is indicative of being mindful, which is inconsistent with the understanding of mindfulness as deliberate action. Moreover, empirical study of the correspondence between positive and negative variants of the same mindfulness scale items show large associations, but more than half of the variance in scores is left unaccounted for (Brown & Ryan, 2003). This finding suggests that, for practical purposes, positive and negative items are not in fact strictly measuring "two sides of the same coin." Other studies have provided further evidence of this disconnect, noting that not only do respondents give differential ratings to positive versus negative items, but that further systematic differences in responding are found between those who have more versus less previous training with mindfulness meditation (Van Dam et al., 2009).

Most current measures also focus exclusively on measuring trait mindfulness, where the items are indicative of general behavior trends in everyday life, similar to personality characteristics. On the other hand, state mindfulness pertains to the ability to actively cultivate non-judgmental attention awareness during meditative practice. While this is an important aspect of mindfulness training and a primary goal of most MBIs, some evidence suggests it holds little relation to the trait mindfulness more commonly measured by available self-report measures (Thompson & Waltz, 2007). This raises concerns that the core evidence for MBIs with youth perhaps does not align as directly with the intervention targets as we might hope. Unfortunately, we were able to find only one published state mindfulness instrument with validation data from a youth sample (i.e., State Mindfulness Scale for Physical Activity; Ullrich-French, Cox, et al., 2017), indicating significant opportunity for future research to improve and develop such measures.

Finally, because mindfulness is a complex and multifaceted construct, blunt measurement of general "mindfulness" obscures the particular components that are changing during MBI or driving changes in other outcomes. Three popular measures of youth mindfulness—the Child and Adolescent Mindfulness Measure (CAMM), MAAS-A, and MAAS-C—only produce a single overall score indicative of general mindfulness. Although, more recently developed measures have incorporated multiple subscales, opening the door to assessing specific change components that might aid in creating more precisely targeted intervention decisions.

In the next section, we consider 11 available measures for assessing mindfulness (and lack of) and psychological inflexibility with youth. This is not intended as an exhaustive systematic review of all published studies for these instruments, but rather a summary discussion of the key features and supporting evidence for their interpretation and use. A summary of the key characteristics for each of the 11 measures reviewed below is provided in Table 4.1. We hope this chapter is useful as a quick reference for practitioners and stimulates critical consideration of the merits and drawbacks of each when using mindfulness intervention in schools.

CURRENTLY AVAILABLE MINDFULNESS MEASURES FOR YOUTH

Child and Adolescent Mindfulness Measure

The CAMM is a 10-item unidimensional, self-report mindfulness measure for youth ages 10–17 years (Greco et al., 2011). Individuals respond to the items on a 5-point relative-frequency-based scale, ranging from 0 = Never True to 4 = Always True. The item content was grounded in a multidimensional understanding of mindfulness and is based on the Kentucky Inventory of Mindfulness Scale (KIMS; Baer et al., 2004). The three facets of mindfulness on which the items are based are (1) acting with awareness (e.g., "At school, I walk from class to class without noticing what I'm doing"), (2) accepting without judgment (e.g., "I get upset with myself for having feelings that don't make sense"), and (3) observing

Table 4.1. Summary of Mindfulness Measures for Youth and Students

Measure	Citation	Ages	# of Items	Construct Measured	Subscales
CAMM	Greco et al., 2011	10–17 years	10 items	Trait mindfulness	*None*
MAAS-A	Brown et al., 2011	14–18 years	14 items	Trait mindfulness	*None*
MAAS-C	Benn, *unpublished*	9–13 years	15 items	Trait mindfulness	*None*
MTASA	West et al., 2005	11–19 years	32 items	Trait mindfulness	1) Accepting Experience, 2) Active Attention, 3) Awareness and Observation, 4) Healthy Self-Regulation
CHIME-A	Johnson et al., 2017	11–17 years	25 items	Trait mindfulness	1) Accepting and Nonjudgmental Orientation, 2) Acting with Awareness, 3) Awareness of External Experiences, 4) Awareness of Internal Experiences, 5) Decentering and Nonreactivity, 6) Insightful Understanding, 7) Openness to Experience, 8) Relativity of Thoughts
AAMS	Droutman, 2015	11–25 years	19 items	Trait mindfulness	1) Attention and Awareness, 2) Non-Reactivity, 3) Non-judgmental Orientation, 4) Self-Acceptance

continued

Table 4.1. CONTINUED

Measure	Citation	Ages	# of Items	Construct Measured	Subscales
MICA	Briere, 2011	8–18 years	25 items	Trait mindfulness	1) Acceptance of Internal Experience, 2) Equanimity, 3) Meta-cognitive Awareness, 4) Present-Centered Awareness, 5) Self-Acceptance
MSQ	Renshaw, 2016	6th–8th grade	15 items	School-specific trait mindfulness	1) Mindful Acceptance, 2) Mindful Attention, 3) Approach and Persistence
SMS-PA	Ullrich-French et al., 2017	10–13 years	12 items	State mindfulness	1) State Mindfulness of the Mind and 2) State Mindfulness of the Body
AFQ-Y	Greco et al., 2008	9–17 years	17 items	Psychological inflexibility	*None*
AFQ-Y8	Greco et al., 2008	9–17 years	8 items	Psychological inflexibility	*None*

(e.g., "I think about things that happened in the past instead of thinking about things that are happening right now"). These items use uniformly negative wording and are reverse-coded to produce a single score that reflects an overall level of mindful behavior, or lack of mind-less behavior.

In a study examining the validity of the CAMM, good internal consistency ($\alpha = .81$; Greco et al., 2011) was reported. Additionally, it was found that scores on the CAMM are positively correlated to a small degree with measures of social skills ($r = .14$), academic competence ($r = .25$), and quality of life ($r = .25$). Furthermore, scores on the CAMM have medium to large negative association with somatic complaints ($r = -.40$), internalizing symptoms ($r = -.50$), externalizing symptoms ($r = -.37$), thought suppression ($r = -.58$), psychological inflexibility ($r = -.60$), and a small correlation with problematic behaviors ($r = -.22$; Greco et al., 2011). Although the CAMM has not been validated with a clinical youth population, it has been validated with diverse international samples. For example, Saggino and colleagues (2017) validated the measure with Italian youth. They found that the CAMM demonstrated good internal consistency ($\alpha = .75$), which was improved with the removal of two items: "At school, I walk from class to class without noticing what I'm doing" and "I push away thoughts that I don't like" ($\alpha = .79$; Saggino et al., 2017). The CAMM has also been validated with French (Dion et al., 2017), Catalan (Viñas et al., 2015), and Dutch (de Bruin et al., 2014) adolescents, providing some support for its use with these populations as well.

Mindful Attention Awareness Scale for Adolescents

The MAAS-A is a 14-item unidimensional, self-report trait mindfulness measure for youth ages 14–18 years (Brown, West, et al., 2011). Individuals respond to the items on a 6-point relative-frequency based scale, ranging from 1 = Almost Always to 6 = Almost Never. This measure was adapted from the widely used adult MAAS (Brown & Ryan, 2003), which reflects one major facet of mindfulness: being "present" (e.g., "I find myself doing things without paying attention"). The MAAS-A has one fewer item than the MAAS, excluding "I drive places on 'automatic pilot' and then wonder why I went there." The items in the MAAS-A are worded negatively and reverse-coded, so that higher scores indicate greater levels of trait mindfulness.

The initial development study demonstrated that the MAAS-A items have a unidimensional factor structure and adequate internal consistency ($\alpha = .82$; Brown et al., 2011). The MAAS-A also showed high test-retest reliability over a 3–4 week period (intraclass correlation = .79; Brown et al., 2011). Scores on the MAAS-A had small to moderate positive correlations with agreeableness ($r = .23$), conscientiousness ($r = .23$), positive affect ($r = .22$), life satisfaction ($r = .34$), wellness ($r = .30$), happiness ($r = .23$), and self-regulation ($r = .39$), as well as small to moderate negative correlations with neuroticism ($r = -.42$), negative affect ($r = -.41$), and substance use ($r = -.23$). In a second study utilizing a clinical sample, scores on the MAAS-A improved significantly following participation in mindfulness-based stress reduction (MBSR), characterized by a medium effect size ($d = 0.61$). These scores were also moderately associated with improved self-esteem and reduced stress, anxiety, and other psychological functioning, suggesting that the MAAS-A is sensitive to changes in mindfulness and that increased scores are related to improvements in other psychological outcomes.

Mindful Attention Awareness Scale for Children

The MAAS-C is a 15-item unidimensional, self-report trait mindfulness measure for youth ages 9–13 years (Benn, *unpublished*). Individuals respond to the items on a 6-point relative-frequency based scale, ranging from 1 = Almost Always to 6 = Almost Never. As with the MAAS-A, items are negatively worded and reverse-scored, so that higher scores indicate a greater level of trait mindfulness; however, the MAAS-C's item wording is more developmentally appropriate for younger children. The item content is reflective of being present (e.g., "I find myself doing things without paying attention," "I could be feeling a certain way and not realize it until later"). It is important to note that while the MAAS-A removed the item related to driving ("I drive places on 'automatic pilot' and then wonder why I went there"), the MAAS-C changes the language to "I walk into a room, and then wonder why I went there"—thus retaining the same number of items (15) as the adult MAAS.

Although modified by Benn in 2004, the MAAS-C underwent its first validation study in 2014 (Lawlor et al., 2014). Exploratory factor analysis demonstrated that the MAAS-C items represent a single latent factor with adequate internal consistency ($\alpha = .84$). There were no significant gender differences found; however, there were significant grade differences, where fifth-grade students scored reliably higher on the MAAS-C than those in seventh grade. This suggests that levels of mindfulness may not be stable across childhood development or that the measure may be biased across developmental levels of respondents. Scores on the MAAS-C had small to medium correlation with measures of school self-concept ($r = .22$), optimism ($r = .34$), positive affect ($r = .19$), autonomy ($r = .18$), academic efficacy ($r = .16$), and personal achievement ($r = .16$), as well as medium to large negative correlation with measures of anxiety ($r = -.39$), depression ($r = -.47$), negative affect ($r = -.52$), and rumination ($r = -.56$).

Mindful Thinking and Action Scale for Adolescents

The MTASA is a 32-item multidimensional, self-report trait mindfulness measure appropriate for youth ages 11–19 years (West et al., 2005). The items use a 5-point relative-frequency based response scale, ranging from 1 = Never to 5 = Almost Always. Early factor analytic evidence suggests that the items can be meaningfully decomposed into four specific domains of mindfulness: (1) accepting experience (e.g., "It is interesting to sit quietly"), (2) active attention (e.g., "I plan before I act on my ideas"), (3) awareness and observation (e.g., "I feel my moods in my body"), and (4) healthy self-regulation (HSR; e.g., "Others could describe me as patient with myself"; West et al., 2005). The MTASA uses a mix of positively and negatively worded items, in which negative items are reverse-coded to calculate total scores for each domain. The authors note that the item content is written at a fourth-grade reading level and is developmentally appropriate for younger respondents as well as contextually appropriate for individuals with more limited autonomy, such as incarcerated youth or those in residential treatment facilities (Coyne et al., 2008; West et al., 2005).

Although scale development research is relatively scarce for the MTASA, it has been studied alongside three other mindfulness measures with a sample of 600 high school students (West, 2008). In terms of reliability, estimates suggest that the MTASA's total mindfulness score has acceptable internal consistency ($\alpha = .85$), yet internal consistency for the four domain-specific subscales range widely, from weak ($\alpha = .47$) to acceptable ($\alpha = .84$). Test-retest reliability was strong for the total mindfulness score ($r = .81$). The MTASA also showed small to moderate correlations with several adult mindfulness measures in this study, including scales from the Five Facet Mindfulness Questionnaire ($r = .15$–$.56$; Baer et al., 2006), KIMS ($r = .10$–$.40$), and the MAAS ($r = .42$). Other researchers have found that the 12-item HSR subscale shows moderate to large positive correlation with the CAMM and MAAS-A measures, though the other subscales have not been as well validated (Brown et al., 2011; de Bruin et al., 2011; de Bruin et al., 2014). The HSR subscale has also been used as an outcome measure of MBI with incarcerated adolescents, where it demonstrated significant positive change from pre-intervention ($M = 43.6$) to post-intervention ($M = 48.7$), while scores on the adult MAAS did not change (Himelstein et al., 2012).

Comprehensive Inventory of Mindfulness Experiences—Adolescents

The CHIME-A is a 25-item multidimensional, self-report trait mindfulness measure for adolescents that uses both positively and negatively worded items (Johnson et al., 2017). The authors derived the CHIME-A from the 37-item adult CHIME measure (Bergomi et al., 2014) to create an instrument more developmentally appropriate for youth. Respondents are asked to endorse how often each statement is true of them on a 5-point relative-frequency based scale, ranging from 1 = Never True to 5 = Always True. Johnson et al. (2017) conducted a series of studies with four distinct samples of youth between ages 11 and 17 years to explore the factor structure, refine item content, and investigate reliability and validity characteristics of the measure.

Exploratory and confirmatory factor analyses supported the presence of 8 subdomains of mindfulness among the items, including (1) accepting and nonjudgmental orientation (e.g., "I notice my mistakes without giving myself a hard time"), (2) acting with awareness (e.g., "I get distracted by memories or daydreams"), (3) awareness of external experiences (e.g., "I notice sounds in my environment, such as birds chirping or cars passing"), (4) awareness of internal experiences (e.g., "When my mood changes, I notice it straight away"), (5) decentering and non-reactivity (e.g., "I am able to notice my thoughts and feelings without getting tangled up in them"), (6) insightful understanding (e.g., "When I have given myself a hard time without needing to, I can laugh about it"), (7) openness to experience (e.g., "I try to avoid emotional pain as much as possible"), and (8) relativity of thoughts (e.g., "I realize my thoughts aren't always facts"). Estimates of internal consistency for the subscales were in the acceptable or near acceptable range ($\alpha = .65–.77$), but the total mindfulness score consistently showed weak item-total correlations across competing models. For this reason, the authors do not recommend use of the overall total score (Johnson et al., 2017). Despite the questionable reliability of the overall scale, some evidence of construct validity was suggested from a moderate positive correlation between the CHIME-A and CAMM total scores ($r = .35$). Further, the 8 CHIME-A subscales collectively accounted for a large portion of the variance in the CAMM total score (39%) as well as with convergent measures of emotional dysregulation (54%), rumination (41%), and self-criticism (29%).

Adolescent and Adult Mindfulness Scale

The AAMS (formerly named the Mindfulness Scale for Pre-Teens, Teens, and Adults) is a 19-item multidimensional, self-report trait mindfulness measure that has been investigated with individuals from ages 9 to 25 years and recommended for use with individuals 11 years and older (Droutman, 2015). The measure contains a mix of both positively and negatively worded items that use a five-point relative-frequency based response scale, ranging from 1 = Never True to 5 = Always True. A suite of five studies has been conducted as part of the initial development and validation efforts for the AAMS (Droutman et al., 2018). Exploratory and confirmatory factor analyses suggested the items can be separated into four subdomains: (1) attention and awareness (e.g., "I notice when my moods begin to change"), (2) non-reactivity (e.g., "When you realize that you missed something important in a class or during a lecture or a work meeting, how often do you get angry with self?"), (3) non-judgmental orientation (e.g., "I make judgments about whether my thoughts are good or bad"), and (4) self-acceptance (e.g., "The emotions I feel sometimes seem wrong"). The authors recommend averaging items within each domain to obtain subscale scores, followed by summing the averages to obtain a higher-order mindfulness score. Estimates of reliability suggest that all scores have at least adequate internal consistency ($\alpha > .70$). The overall factor structure and scale reliabilities were consistently adequate across multiple samples.

In terms of construct validity evidence across samples, moderate to large correlations with the CAMM were found for the AAMS mindfulness ($r = .59–.62$), self-acceptance ($r = .62–.66$), non-reactive ($r = .31$), and non-judgmental ($r = .40–.51$) scores, but only trivial correlations with the attention and awareness score ($r = –.03$ to $–.06$). Correlations with a measure of emotional regulation were moderate to large for the AAMS mindfulness ($r = .37–.55$) and self-accepting

($r = .35–.54$) scores, small to moderate for non-reactive ($r = .21–.43$) and non-judgmental ($r = .12–.37$) scores, but borderline trivial for attention and awareness ($r \leq .10$). Associations with a measure of self-compassion were in the trivial to small range for all AAMS scores ($r \leq .28$).

Mindfulness Inventory for Children and Adolescents

The MICA is a 25-item multidimensional, self-report measure of trait mindfulness appropriate for youth ages 8 to 18 years (Briere, 2011). Items are both positively and negatively worded. Respondents indicate how true each item statement is of them on a 5-point Likert-type scale, ranging from 1 = Disagree a lot to 5 = Agree a lot. In contrast with the other measures described here, the MICA's structural characteristics and construct validity have not been formally evaluated in an empirical study. The author drew from theoretical guidance and expertise in Buddhist mindfulness concepts to produce item content relating to five subdomains of mindfulness: (1) acceptance of internal experience, (2) equanimity, (3) metacognitive awareness, (4) present-centered awareness, and (5) self-acceptance. Although still in the experimental stages, a recent pilot study of an elementary school mindfulness program suggested that greater pre- to post-intervention changes were captured by the MICA ($\eta^2 = .24$) compared to the CAMM ($\eta^2 = .14$).

Mindful Student Questionnaire

The 15-item MSQ is a multidimensional, self-report measure of youths' school-specific mindfulness (Renshaw, 2017a). Presently, only the initial development and validation study has been conducted with a convenience sample of 278 adolescents in grades 6–8. Respondents indicate the relative frequency in which they engage in each behavior described on a four-point scale, ranging from 1 = Almost Never to 4 = Almost Always. All items are positively worded and require no reverse scoring. Results from exploratory factor analysis suggest that the items can be broken into three meaningful subscales: (1) Mindful Acceptance (e.g., "When I am feeling bad at school, I still stay calm"), (2) Mindful Attention (e.g., "When I am at school, I notice when my thoughts come and go"), and (3) Approach and Persistence (e.g., "When I am doing something hard at school, I try to do the best I can"). All scales demonstrated adequate internal consistency ($\alpha = .77–.90$). A higher-order composite mindfulness scale can be computed from summing item scores from the Mindful Acceptance and Mindful Attention subscales, but scores from the Approach and Persistence subscale should not be included. Evidence of convergent validity for all three scales was found with four measures of subjective well-being, including joy of learning ($r = .28–.53$), school connectedness ($r = .19–.42$), educational purpose ($r = .28–.50$), and academic efficacy ($r = .27–.55$), as well as student perception of their academic achievement ($r = .02–.30$). The MSQ has yet to be co-validated along with other existing mindfulness measures, limiting the available evidence for its construct validity to theory. Importantly, the MSQ is the only measure currently available to our knowledge that incorporates items that are all directly worded and do not require reverse-coding, thus representing a truly positive conception of trait mindfulness behavior at school.

State Mindfulness Scale–Physical Activity

The State Mindfulness Scale for Physical Activity (SMS-PA) is a 12-item, self-report measure intended for youth shortly after they engage in a physical activity with only one validation study available to date (Ullrich-French et al., 2017). The SMS-PA was based on Tanay and Berstein's original State Mindfulness Scale (2013) and has item content relating to two domains: State Mindfulness of the Mind (e.g., "I noticed thoughts come and go") and State Mindfulness of the Body (e.g., "I felt present in my body"). Respondents indicate how much they experienced the phenomenon described in each item on a 5-point scale ranging from 0 = Not at all to 4 = Very much. After partitioning proportions of uniquely reliable variance in the two possible subscales from an overall general state mindfulness factor, the developers found that only the general factor had adequate reliability ($\omega_H = .91$) while the subscales offered very little unique information over and above the general factor (Mind $\omega_{HS} = .17$; Body $\omega_{HS} = .10$). This implies that an overall total score might be favored rather than subscale scores with this population. They also found strong positive intercorrelations between the three scores from the measure ($r = .75$–$.94$), as well as positive associations with external scores such as moderately strong correlation with state engagement ($r = .29$–$.48$) and small to moderate correlations with intrinsic motivation for, regulation for, and enjoyment of physical activity ($r = .22$–$.48$). The SMS-PA has also been translated to Spanish (Ullrich-French, González Hernández et al., 2017).

Avoidance and Fusion Questionnaire for Youth

The Avoidance and Fusion Questionnaire for Youth (AFQ-Y) is a 17-item unidimensional, self-report measure of psychological inflexibility for youth (Greco et al., 2008). Individuals respond on a 5-point relative-frequency based scale, ranging from 0 = Not at all True to 4 = Very True. This measure was developed as a robust clinical measure of cognitive fusion and experiential avoidance—processes that maintain psychological inflexibility as described in the beginning of this chapter. Most of the items are negatively worded, and those that are positively worded are reverse-coded to generate a score reflecting overall psychological inflexibility (Greco et al., 2008). Greco and colleagues (2008) initially developed 50 items and reduced these through expert feedback and exploratory factor analysis to 25 items. The content of these items were based on the items present in the adult Acceptance and Action Questionnaire (AAQ; Hayes et al., 2004). An additional exploratory factor analysis with the 25 items was conducted with 346 youth, and results revealed a unidimensional factor structure

(Greco et al., 2008). Items selected for the final 17-item version were based on subsequent principal factors analysis. Internal consistency was determined to be adequate ($\alpha = .90$). Scores on the AFQ-Y correlated with anxiety ($r = .58$), behavior problems ($r = .11$), somatic symptoms ($r = .37–.45$), thought suppression ($r = .53$), and combined internalizing and externalizing behavioral functioning ($r = .64$), as well as negatively correlated with quality of life ($r = -.30$ to $-.39$), scores on the CAMM ($r = -.53$), social skills ($r = -.13$), and academic competence ($r = -.15$ to $-.19$). Importantly, correlations between the AFQ-Y and measures of symptoms and functioning reduced somewhat but remained significant (medium effect for somatic symptoms, combined internalizing/externalizing behavior, and thought suppression; small effect for quality of life and social skills) after controlling for scores on the CAMM—suggesting that the AFQ-Y is measuring a construct that includes but is broader than mindfulness alone (Greco et al., 2008). The AFQ-Y has been validated with Spanish-speaking youth, and the results of this study yielded a two-factor structure of cognitive fusion and experiential avoidance (Valdivia-Salas et al., 2017).

Avoidance and Fusion Questionnaire for Youth–Short Form

The Avoidance and Fusion Questionnaire for Youth–Short Form (AFQ-Y8) is an eight-item unidimensional, self-report measure of psychological inflexibility for youth (Greco et al., 2011). Individuals respond on a 5-point relative-frequency based scale, ranging from 0 = Not at all True to 4 = Very True. The AFQ-Y8 was developed as a brief screener version of the AFQ-Y and similarly measures cognitive fusion and experiential avoidance. As with the AFQ-Y, most of the items are negatively worded, and those that are positively worded are reverse-coded to generate a score indicative of psychological inflexibility (Greco et al., 2008). The eight items of the AFQ-Y8 were selected for having the strongest factor loadings out of all items on the AFQ-Y. Exploratory factor analysis was used to determine that the AFQ-Y8 items relate to a single factor with adequate internal consistency ($\alpha = .83$).

Commensurate with the AFQ-Y, scores on the AFQ-Y8 were positively correlated with anxiety ($r = .56$), behavior problems ($r = .14$), somatic symptoms ($r = .39–.42$), suppression ($r = .46$), and other psychological functioning ($r = .63$), as well as negatively correlated with measures of quality of life ($r = -.29$ to $-.43$), social skills ($r = -.18$), academic competence ($r = -.11$ to $-.17$), and the CAMM ($r = -.44$; Greco et al., 2008). Renshaw (2017b) aimed to determine the utility of the AFQ-Y8 as an appropriate mental health screener within a secondary school setting with a sample of 219 adolescent students (M age = 16.3). The full AFQ-Y was used to establish a comparison between the short and the long versions. The AFQ-Y8 displayed good data-model fit, consisted of robust factor loadings (i.e., > .50), and had strong latent construct reliability ($H = .90$). Additionally, bivariate correlation analyses suggested that both versions produced strong positive associations with measures of anxiety ($r = .63$) and depression ($r = .64$), and moderately positive associations with measures of academic problems ($r = .45$). The second phase of data analysis consisted of receiver operating characteristic (ROC) curve analyses. This analysis determined that the AFQ-Y8 had excellent discriminatory ability for classifying students with and without clinical levels of depression and anxiety. A cutoff score of 15 was determined to be optimal in identifying individuals with these disorders. Using this cutoff score, Renshaw (2017b) was able to identify 86% and 92% of students with clinical levels of depression and anxiety, respectively. Furthermore, follow-up t-tests confirmed that, compared to students with scores below the cutoff value, students with AFQ-Y8 scores greater than the cutoff value had much higher levels of self-reported depression, anxiety, and academic problems (Renshaw, 2017b).

CONCLUSION

This chapter provided an overview of some of the key challenges in measuring mindfulness and psychological flexibility and reviewed 11 available self-report instruments intended for use with youth. While none of these measures are perfect, they each possess variable strengths and weaknesses that should be carefully considered before they are selected for use in schools. In addition to considering basic validation evidence, it is most critical that practitioners select assessment measures that closely match the skills targeted in their chosen MBI. Given the limitations in the self-report rating scale methodology discussed here, we encourage exploration of alternative modes of data collection to supplement and enhance the information gathered from these measures. Methods such as an objective breath-counting task have garnered initial support in the adult literature as a potentially useful way of assessing state mindfulness (Levinson et al., 2014) and may be well-suited for study with youth. Further, use of experiential reports at one or more points throughout the day has gained popularity in adult studies (Moore et al., 2016) and could potentially be used with youth in schools as well. Extension of the widely used check-in/check-out procedure could incorporate student report of their current state on a few targeted mindfulness items or in a diary format to more sensitively capture the variability in mindfulness experience in school settings at regular intervals during the day. We hope that school-based practitioners and researchers alike have found this chapter a useful reference and motivator to explore the utility of evidence-based mindfulness assessment in the important work they do for youth.

REFERENCES

Baer, R. A., Smith, G. T., & Allen, K. B. (2004). Assessment of mindfulness by self-report: The Kentucky Inventory of Mindfulness Skills. *Assessment, 11*, 191–206. doi:10.1177/1073191104268029

Baer, R. A., Smith, G. T., Hopkins, J., Krietemeyer, J., & Toney, L. (2006). Using self-report assessment methods to explore facets of mindfulness. *Assessment, 13*, 27–45. doi:10.1177/1073191105283504

Benn, R. (2004). *Modified mindful attention awareness scale*. Unpublished raw data.

Bergomi, C., Tschacher, W, & Kupper, Z. (2014). Konstruktion und erste Validierung eines Fragebogens zur umfassenden Erfassung von Achtsamkeit [construction and initial validation of a questionnaire for the comprehensive investigation of mindfulness]. *Diagnostica, 60*, 111–125. doi:10.1026/0012-1924/a000109

Biegel, G. M., Brown, K. W., Shapiro, S. L., & Schubert, C. M. (2009). Mindfulness-based stress reduction for the treatment of adolescent psychiatric outpatients: A randomized clinical trial. *Journal of Consulting and Clinical Psychology, 77*, 855–866. doi:10.1037/a0016241

Bishop, S. R., Lau, M., Shapiro, S., Carlson, L., Anderson, N. D., Carmody, J., & . . Devins, G. (2004). Mindfulness: A proposed operational definition. *Clinical Psychology: Science and Practice, 11*, 230–241. doi:10.1093/clipsy/bph077

Briere, J. (2011). *Mindfulness inventory for children and adolescents*. Unpublished assessment inventory. University of Southern California.

Brown, K. W., & Ryan, R. M. (2003). The benefits of being present: Mindfulness and its role in psychological well-being. *Journal of Personality and Social Psychology, 84*, 822–848. doi:10.1037/0022-3514.84.4.822

Brown, K. W., Ryan, R. M., Loverich, T. M., Biegel, G. M., & West, A. M. (2011). Out of the armchair and into the streets: Measuring mindfulness advances knowledge and improves interventions: Reply to Grossman (2011). *Psychological Assessment, 23*, 1041–1046 doi:10.1037/a0025781

Brown, K. W., West, A. M., Loverich, T. M., & Biegel, G. M. (2011). Assessing adolescent mindfulness: Validation of an adapted Mindful Attention Awareness Scale in adolescent normative and psychiatric populations. *Psychological Assessment, 23*, 1023–1033. doi:10.1037/a0021338

Chiesa, A., Serretti, A., & Jakobsen, J. C. (2013). Mindfulness: Top-down or bottom-up emotion regulation strategy? *Clinical Psychology Review, 33*, 82–96. doi:10.1016/j.cpr.2012.10.006

Coyne, L. W., Cheron, D., & Ehrenreich, J. T. (2008). Assessment of acceptance and mindfulness processes in youth. In L. A. Greco & S. C. Hayes (Eds.), Acceptance & mindfulness treatments for children & adolescents: A practitioner's guide (pp. 37–59). New Harbinger.

Davidson, R. J. (2002). Anxiety and affective style: Role of prefrontal cortex and amygdala. *Biological Psychiatry, 51*, 68–80.

Davidson, R. J., & Kaszniak, A. (2015). Conceptual and methodological issues in research on mindfulness and meditation. *American Psychologist, 70*, 581–592. doi:10.1037/a0039512

de Bruin, E. I., Zijlstra, B. H., & Bögels, S. M. (2014). The meaning of mindfulness in children and adolescents: Further validation of the Child and Adolescent Mindfulness Measure (CAMM) in two independent samples from The Netherlands. *Mindfulness*, 5, 422–430. doi:10.1007/s12671-013-0196-8

de Bruin, E. I., Zijlstra, B. J., van de Weijer-bergsma, E., & Bögels, S. M. (2011). The mindful attention awareness scale for adolescents (MAAS-A): Psychometric properties in a Dutch sample. *Mindfulness, 2*, 201–211. doi:10.1007/s12671-011-0061-6

Dion, J., Paquette, L., Daigneault, I., Godbout, N., & Hébert, M. (2017). Validation of the French version of the Child and Adolescent Mindfulness Measure (CAMM) among samples of French and indigenous youth. *Mindfulness, 9*, 645–653. doi:10.1007/s12671-017-0807-x

Droutman, V. (2015). *Mindfulness scale for pre-teens, teens and adults.* In R. J. Semple (Chair), *Clinical Applications of Mindfulness.* Research symposium conducted at the Bridging the Hearts and Minds of Youth: Mindfulness and Compassion in Clinical Practice, Education, and Research conference in San Diego, California.

Droutman, V., Golub, I., Oganesyan, A., & Read, S. (2018). Development and initial validation of the Adolescent and Adult Mindfulness Scale (AAMS). *Personality and Individual Differences, 123,* 34–43. doi:10.1016/j.paid.2017.10.037

Eklund, K., O'Malley, M., & Meyer, L. (2017). Gauging mindfulness in children and youth: School-based applications. *Psychology in the Schools, 54,* 101–114. doi:10.1002/pits.21983

Fletcher, L., & Hayes, S. C. (2005). Relational frame theory, acceptance and commitment therapy, and a functional analytic definition of mindfulness. *Journal of Rational-Emotive and Cognitive-Behavioral Therapy, 23,* 315–336. doi:10.1007/s10942-005-0017-7

Gogtay, N., Giedd, J. N., Lusk, L., Hayashi, K. M., Greenstein, D., Vaituzis, A. C., . . . Thompson, P. M. (2004). Dynamic mapping of human cortical development during childhood through early adulthood. Proceedings of the National Academy of Sciences of the United States of America, *101,* 8174–8179. doi:10.1073/pnas.0402680101

Goodman, M. S., Madni, L. A., & Semple, R. J. (2017). Measuring mindfulness in youth: Review of current assessments, challenges, and future directions. *Mindfulness, 8,* 1409–1420. doi:10.1007/s12671-017-0719-9

Greco, L. A., Baer, R. A., & Smith, G. T. (2011). Assessing mindfulness in children and adolescents: Development and validation of the Child and Adolescent Mindfulness Measure (CAMM). *Psychological Assessment, 23,* 606–614. doi:10.1037/a0022819

Greco, L. A., Lambert, W., & Baer, R. A. (2008). Psychological inflexibility in childhood and adolescence: Development and evaluation of the Avoidance and Fusion Questionnaire for Youth. *Psychological Assessment, 20,* 93–102. doi:10.1037/1040-3590.20.2.93

Grossman, P. (2011). Defining mindfulness by how poorly I think I pay attention during everyday awareness and other intractable problems for psychology's (re)invention of mindfulness: Comment on Brown et al. (2011). *Psychological Assessment, 23,* 1034–1040. doi:10.1037/a0022713

Harrington, A., & Dunne, J. D. (2015). When mindfulness is therapy: Ethical qualms, historical perspectives. *American Psychologist, 70,* 621–631. doi:10.1037/a0039460

Hayes, S. C., Luoma, J. B., Bond, F. W., Masuda, A., & Lillis, J. (2006). Acceptance and commitment therapy: Model, processes and outcomes. *Behaviour Research and Therapy, 44,* 1–25. doi:10.1016/j.brat.2005.06.006

Hayes, S. C., Strosahl, K. D., & Wilson, K. G. (2011). *Acceptance and commitment therapy: The process and practice of mindful change* (2nd ed.). Guilford.

Hayes, S. C., Strosahl, K. D., Wilson, K. G., Bissett, R. T., Pistorello, J., Toarmino, D., & McCurry, S. M. (2004). Measuring experiential avoidance: A preliminary test of a working model. *The Psychological Record, 54,* 553–578.

Himelstein, S., Hastings, A., Shaprio, S., & Heery, M. (2012). Mindfulness training for self-regulation and stress with incarcerated youth: A pilot study. *Probation Journal, 59,* 151–165.

Johnson, C., Burke, C., Brinkman, S., & Wade, T. (2017). Development and validation of a multifactor mindfulness scale in youth: The Comprehensive Inventory of Mindfulness

Experiences–Adolescents (CHIME-A). *Psychological Assessment, 29*, 264–281. doi:10.1037/pas0000342

Kabat-Zinn, J. (1994). Wherever you go, there you are: Mindfulness meditation in everyday life. Hyperion.

Kelley, T. L. (1927). *Interpretation of educational measurements*. World Book.

Klingbeil, D. A., Fischer, A. J., Renshaw, T. L., Bloomfield, B. S., Polakoff, B., Willenbrink, J. B., Copek, R. A., & Chan, K. T. (2017a). Effects of mindfulness-based intervention on disruptive behavior: A meta-analysis of single-case research. *Psychology in the Schools, 54*, 70–87. doi:10.1002/pits.21982

Klingbeil, D. A., Renshaw, T. L., Willenbrink, J. B., Copek, R. A., Chan, K. T., Haddock, A., Yassine, J., & Clifton, J. (2017b). Mindfulness-based interventions with youth: A comprehensive meta-analysis of group-design studies. *Journal of School Psychology, 63*, 77–103. doi:10.1016/j.jsp.2017.03.006

Lawlor, M. S., Schonert-Reichl, K. A., Gadermann, A. M., & Zumbo, B. D. (2014). A validation study of the Mindful Attention Awareness Scale adapted for children. *Mindfulness, 5*, 730–741. doi:10.1007/s12671-013-0228-4

Levinson, D. B., Stoll, E. L., Kindy, S. D., Merry, H. L., & Davidson, R. J. (2014). A mind you can count on: Validating breath counting as a behavioral measure of mindfulness. *Frontiers in Psychology, 5*, Article 1202, 1–10. doi:10.3389/fpsyg.2014.01202

Moore, R. C., Depp, C. A., Wetherell, J. L., & Lenze, E. J. (2016). Ecological momentary assessment versus standard assessment instruments for measuring mindfulness, depressed mood, and anxiety among older adults. *Journal of Psychiatric Research, 75*, 116–123. doi:10.1016/j.jpsychires.2016.01.011

Renshaw, T. L. (2017a). Preliminary development and validation of the Mindful Student Questionnaire. *Assessment for Effective Intervention, 42*, 168–175. doi:10.1177/1534508416678971

Renshaw, T. L. (2017b). Screening for psychological inflexibility: Initial validation of the Avoidance and Fusion Questionnaire for Youth as a school mental health screener. *Journal of Psychoeducational Assessment, 35*, 482–493. doi:10.1177/0734282916644096

Saggino, A., Bartoccini, A., Sergi, M. R., Romanelli, R., Macchia, A., & Tommasi, M. (2017). Assessing mindfulness on samples of Italian children and adolescents: The validation of the Italian version of the Child and Adolescent Mindfulness Measure. *Mindfulness, 8*, 1364–1372. doi:10.1007/s12671-017-0712-3

Tanay, G., & Bernstein, A. (2013). State Mindfulness Scale (SMS): Development and initial validation. *Psychological Assessment, 25*, 1286–1299. doi:10.1037/a0034044

Thompson, B. L., & Waltz, J. (2007). Everyday mindfulness and mindfulness meditation: Overlapping constructs or not? *Personality and Individual Differences, 43*, 1875–1885. doi:10.1016/j.paid.2007.06.017

Thorndike, E. L. (1904). *An introduction to the theory of mental and social measurements*. Teachers College, Columbia University.

Ullrich-French, S., Cox, A. E., Cole, A. N., Cooper, B. R., & Gotch, C. (2017). Initial validity evidence for the State Mindfulness Scale for Physical Activity with youth. *Measurement in Physical Education and Exercise Science, 21*, 177–189. doi:10.1080/1091367X.2017.1321543

Ullrich-French, S., González Hernández, J., & Hildago Montesinos, M. D. (2017). Validity evidence for the adaptation of the State Mindfulness Scale for Physical Activity

(SMS-PA) in Spanish youth. *Psicothema, 29*, 119–125. doi:10.7334/psicothema2016.204

Valdivia-Salas, S., Martín-Albo, J., Zaldivar, P., Lombas, A. S., & Jiménez, T. I. (2017). Spanish validation of the Avoidance and Fusion Questionnaire for Youth (AFQ-Y). *Assessment, 24*, 919–931. doi:10.1177/1073191116632338

Van Dam, N. T., Earleywine, M., & Danoff-Burg, S. (2009). Differential item function across meditators and non-meditators on the Five Facet Mindfulness Questionnaire. *Personality and Individual Differences, 47*, 516–521. doi:10.1016/j.paid.2009.05.005

Viñas, F., Malo, S., González, M., Navarro, D., & Casas, F. (2015). Assessing mindfulness on a sample of Catalan-speaking Spanish adolescents: Validation of the Catalan version of the Child and Adolescent Mindfulness Measure. *The Spanish Journal of Psychology, 18*, e46, 1–8. doi:10.1017/sjp.2015.48

West, A. M. (2008). Mindfulness and well-being in adolescence: An exploration of four mindfulness measures with an adolescent sample [Unpublished doctoral dissertation]. Central Michigan University, Mount Pleasant.

West, A. M., Sbraga, T. P., & Poole, D. A. (2005). *Measuring mindfulness in youth: Development of the Mindful Thinking and Action Scale for Adolescents.* Unpublished manuscript. Central Michigan University, Mount Pleasant.

Wicksell, R. K., Melin, L., & Olsson, G. L. (2007). Exposure and acceptance in the rehabilitation of adolescents with idiopathic chronic pain—A pilot study. *European Journal of Pain, 11*, 267–274. doi:10.1016/j.ejpain.2006.02.012

Zenner, C., Hermleben-Kurz, S., & Walach, H. (2014). Mindfulness-based interventions in schools—A systematic review and meta-analysis. *Frontiers in Psychology, 5*, 1–20. doi:10.3389/fpsyg.2014.00603

Zoogman, S., Goldberg, S. B., Hoyt, W. T., & Miller, L. (2015). Mindfulness interventions with youth: A meta-analysis. *Mindfulness, 6*, 290–302. doi:10.1007/s12671-013-0260-4

5

Measures of Mindfulness for Adults and Caregivers

ROBERT C. MCGOWAN, REBECCA MICHEL, AND LISA W. COYNE

This chapter provides an introduction to commonly used mindfulness measures for adults and caregivers, including parents and educators. It begins with an overview of the competing mindfulness conceptions that have shaped instrument development and briefly outlines other constructs related to mindfulness. After discussing the importance of psychometrically valid mindfulness measures, this chapter presents an overview of contemporary assessments and reviews the eight most commonly used instruments, focusing on the psychometric properties of each. It also reviews a less frequently used state mindfulness instrument, hoping to stimulate research in this largely neglected area of the field. The chapter concludes with a discussion of the future of mindfulness assessment, emphasizing future directions for researchers and schools.

COMPETING CONCEPTIONS OF MINDFULNESS

A Buddhist concept, mindfulness is over twenty-five hundred years old. Jon Kabat-Zinn (1990) developed a more secularized mindfulness concept from Buddhism that mental health professionals utilize independently of its spiritual origins (Baer, 2003). The exponential growth in mindfulness research since the 1980s in education, law, business, and leadership (Williams & Kabat-Zinn, 2011) has produced multiple mindfulness conceptualizations, but methodological problems plagued early mindfulness research (Baer, 2003; Kabat-Zinn, 2003). Many early investigators used vague definitions of mindfulness in their studies, yet the accumulation

Robert C. McGowan, Rebecca Michel, and Lisa W. Coyne, *Measures of Mindfulness for Adults and Caregivers*. In: *Using Mindfulness to Promote Mental Health in Schools*. Edited by: Tyler L. Renshaw and Shane R. Jimerson, Oxford University Press. © Oxford University Press (2025). DOI: 10.1093/9780190880507.003.0005 of evidence from several studies made it possible to create a more concrete definition of mindfulness (Kabat-Zinn, 2003). This concrete definition greatly reduced methodological and measurement problems.

Buddhist texts describe mindfulness as the ability to attend to an object, whether it is present or absent, and associate this ability with the recollection or retention of past and present information (Williams & Kabat-Zinn, 2011). Some researchers fear that introducing a Westernized conceptualization of mindfulness may de-nature or de-contextualize the original construct of mindfulness. For example, Williams and Kabat-Zinn (2011) argue that in equating mindfulness with present-centered, non-judgmental awareness, researchers neglect the recollective nature of mindfulness emphasized in Buddhist texts. Kabat-Zinn (2003) argues that mindfulness is not unique to Buddhism, but that it inheres in human behavior, making it a universal practice. Kabat-Zinn's (1990) early mindfulness conceptualization emphasizes attention to moment-to-moment experiences.

Due to the relaxed state that mindfulness often induces, some scholars, practitioners, and laypeople conflate mindfulness and relaxation (Dimidjian & Linehan, 2003). Although the practices are similar, relaxation is not mindfulness' purpose. At times, experts may discourage persons engaging in a mindfulness exercise from shifting physical positions, which may cause muscle or joint pain, and encourage them to attend to the discomfort and associated thoughts, such as, "This is unbearable" or "I need to move" (Baer, 2003). Attending to discomfort and distressing emotions during mindfulness exercises may increase physiological arousal and evoke racing thoughts, muscle tension, and other sensations inconsistent with relaxation (Epel et al., 2009). For this reason, non-judgmental observation of experience, rather than relaxation, is a key facet of mindfulness.

Langer and Moldoveanu (2002) describe mindfulness as the process of drawing novel distinctions. They prioritize the novelty of whatever the viewer is noticing. Through mindfulness, individuals gain a greater sensitivity to their environment, a greater openness to new information, a greater ability to create new categories for structuring perception, and a greater awareness of multiple perspectives in problem-solving. For Langer and Moldoveanu (2002), mindfulness interventions involve working with external material and considering information from multiple perspectives to increase creativity. Langer and Moldoveanu's (2002) definition of mindfulness generated controversy among researchers due to its emphasis on novel information and goals. In contrast, Baer (2003) describes mindfulness as being an internal experience involving non-judgmental observation, with less emphasis on goal-directed behavior.

Bishop and colleagues (2004) present a consensual definition of mindfulness that was composed during multiple meetings of scholars who assembled to identify key components of mindfulness. Their definition proposes two components of mindfulness: self-regulation of attention and curious, open, and accepting present-moment orientation. Many investigators suggest that researchers have largely adopted Bishop and colleagues' (2004) definition. It is noteworthy that self-regulation of attention and openness to present-moment experience feature prominently in the commonly used adult mindfulness measures reviewed in this chapter. Despite this, Bishop and colleagues (2004) would argue that many of these measures conflate mindfulness with elements of related constructs (e.g., patience, calmness) and are based on a false notion of mindfulness as a trait. For these reasons, Bishop and colleagues would suggest that the most commonly used adult mindfulness measures are thereby limited in their ability to aid in both the refinement and understanding of the construct.

IMPORTANCE OF ADULT MINDFULNESS ASSESSMENT

Developing psychometrically sound mindfulness measures for adults is important for many reasons. In a managed care context, insurance companies require mental health professionals to use evidence-based treatments to receive reimbursement for services. Numerous studies have demonstrated both the efficacy and effectiveness of mindfulness-based treatments for several populations (e.g., Brown & Ryan, 2003). Without psychometrically sound assessments, neither researchers nor practitioners can demonstrate the contribution of mindfulness-based variables to outcomes. Practitioners who are unable to convince insurance companies that mindfulness-based treatments are both evidence-based and related to clinical progress might not receive reimbursement for services and therefore may discontinue their use. Insofar as psychometrically sound mindfulness assessments help demonstrate that mindfulness-based treatments and variables are related to outcomes, these assessments are indispensable to mental health practitioners.

Beyond demonstrating the impact of mindfulness-based interventions, psychometrically valid mindfulness assessments allow practitioners to predict and improve outcomes relevant to adults and caregivers who work with youths. For example, studies suggest that caregiver mindfulness training increases the quality of parent-child interactions and reduces client and familial stress (e.g., Gershy et al., 2017). A study by Parent and colleagues (2016) suggests that parent dispositional mindfulness is associated with lower levels of negative parenting practices and internalizing and externalizing psychological problems. These findings suggest that cultivating mindfulness in caregivers may improve client outcomes and reduce psychopathology-induced familial strain.

Further, a substantial number of studies have found a relationship between mindfulness and other constructs related to well-being. Research has found significant, small to moderate positive correlations between mindfulness and conscientiousness, emotional intelligence, openness to experience, positive affect, life satisfaction, self-esteem, and psychological well-being (e.g., Mesmer-Magnus et al., 2017). In addition, significant, small to moderate negative correlations are reported between mindfulness and neuroticism, social anxiety, depression, rumination, worry, negative affect, and perceptions of cognitive failures (e.g., Mesmer-Magnus et al., 2017). Given the associations between mindfulness and outcome-related constructs, practitioners should continue refining mindfulness-based interventions, which requires the development and validation of mindfulness assessments.

SHARED CHARACTERISTICS OF ADULT MINDFULNESS MEASURES

The eight most commonly used mindfulness measures share several characteristics. Each of the instruments is a self-report measure exhibiting robust psychometric properties. Every measure referenced in this chapter uses a Likert-type scale to record participant responses, and apart from the Toronto Mindfulness Scale (TMS) and the State Mindfulness Scale (SMS), each inventory assesses dispositional mindfulness instead of state mindfulness. Finally, each scale incorporates key elements of the secularized Buddhist understanding of mindfulness as the ability to attend to an object, advanced by Kabat-Zinn (1990). Key elements of Kabat-Zinn's mindfulness conception (e.g., non-judgment, sustained attention, present-focus) sometimes coexist with elements of other mindfulness conceptualizations (e.g., curiosity, creativity, openness to various perspectives) in commonly used mindfulness measures.

Despite their similarities, the most commonly used mindfulness measures differ in their construct representation. Certain instruments, such as the Five Facet Mindfulness Questionnaire (FFMQ) and Kentucky Inventory of Mindfulness Skills (KIMS), treat mindfulness as a multifaceted construct and report scores for each facet. Other measures, including the Philadelphia Mindfulness Scale (PHLMS) and the Mindful Attention Awareness Scale (MAAS), assess mindfulness along a single dimension.

Having outlined the shared characteristics of the eight most commonly used mindfulness measures, the following section offers a brief review of each instrument. To facilitate practitioner selection of appropriate instruments, this review focuses on measure structure and psychometrics. Measure inclusion and ordering reflects the number of citations generated by each instrument's associated article on Google Scholar and frequency of appearance in systematic reviews (e.g., Bergomi et al., 2013; Qu et al., 2015). The basic characteristics of the eight most commonly used adult mindfulness measures are summarized in Table 5.1.

REVIEW OF COMMONLY USED ADULT MINDFULNESS MEASURES

Mindful Attention Awareness Scale (MAAS)

The MAAS (Brown & Ryan, 2003) is a 15-item trait measure assessing a single mindfulness factor: Attention. A validated, five-item state version of the MAAS is also available (Brown & Ryan, 2003). Several studies support the one-dimensional structure of the MAAS (e.g., Carlson & Brown, 2005; Mackillop & Anderson, 2007). Unlike other measures, the MAAS uses negatively formulated items exclusively. MAAS items include: "I find myself doing things without paying attention" and "I forget a person's name almost as soon as I've been told it for the first time." Respondents report the frequency with which they have the experience captured by the statement on a 6-point response scale, with "1" indicating that they have the

Table 5.1. Basic Characteristics of Most Commonly Used Adult Mindfulness Measures

Measure Name	Author(s)	Number of Items	State or Trait Measure	Scales/Constructs	Number of Scores	Notable Features
Mindful Attention Awareness Scale (MAAS)	Brown & Ryan (2003)	15 (5 for Short Form)	Trait	Attention	1 (total score)	Exclusively uses negatively formulated items; Validated state version available
Five Facet Mindfulness Questionnaire (FFMQ)	Baer et al. (2006)	39	Trait	Observing; Describing; Acting with Awareness; Non-judging of Inner Experience	6 (one per subscale, one total score)	Composite of MAAS, FMI, KIMS, CAMS-R, and SMQ items
Kentucky Inventory of Mindfulness Skills (KIMS)	Baer et al. (2004)	39	Trait	Observing; Describing; Acting with Awareness; Accepting without Judgment	4 (one per subscale)	Assesses four "mindfulness skills" (Rooted in DBT)
Toronto Mindfulness Scale (TMS)	Lau et al. (2006)	13	State	Curiosity; De-centering	3 (one per subscale, one total score)	Validated trait version available

continued

Table 5.1. CONTINUED

Measure Name	Author(s)	Number of Items	State or Trait Measure	Scales/Constructs	Number of Scores	Notable Features
Cognitive and Affective Mindfulness Scale-Revised (CAMS-R)	Feldman et al. (2007)	12	Trait	Attention; Present-focus; Awareness; Acceptance	1 (total score)	Assesses willingness/capacity for mindfulness
Philadelphia Mindfulness Scale (PHLMS)	Cardaciotto et al. (2008)	20	Trait	Present-moment Awareness; Non-judgmental Acceptance	3 (one per subscale, one total score)	N/A
Freiburg Mindfulness Inventory (FMI)	Buchheld et al. (2001)	30 (14 for Short Form)	Trait	Attention; Non-judgment; Openness; Insightful Understanding	1 (total score)	Only appropriate for use with experienced meditators
Southampton Mindfulness Questionnaire (SMQ)	Chadwick et al. (2008)	16	Trait	De-centered Awareness vs. Reacting to Difficult Cognitions; Attention vs. Experiential Avoidance; Acceptance vs. Judgment; Release of Difficult Cognitions vs. Rumination	1 (total score)	All items use the same stem: "Usually when I experience distressing thoughts and images . . . "

experience "almost always" and "6" indicating that they "almost never" have the experience. Consistent with the scale's single-factor structure, the measure yields one total score. Higher scores reflect higher levels of trait mindfulness.

Brown and Ryan (2003) utilized seven samples (five college samples, one community sample, and one national sample) for MAAS item selection and scale construction. Each sample was between 62% and 66% female and 63% to 93% Caucasian (M_{age} = 19.0–43.3 years; Brown & Ryan, 2003). Later studies utilized 18 independent samples to establish norms for the MAAS (Brown & Ryan, 2003). Four samples comprise 436 community adults (MAAS $M = 4.20$, $SD = .69$), while the fourteen remaining samples comprise 2,277 college students (MAAS $M = 3.83$, $SD = .70$). Additionally, Carlson and Brown (2005) have validated the scale with a sample of cancer patients ($N = 122$, $M_{age} = 49.55$, $SD_{age} = 12.81$, % female = 67.21).

The MAAS exhibits excellent reliability. Brown and Ryan (2003) report internal consistency values ranging from .80 to .87 across seven independent samples and good test-retest reliability. Several other studies attest to the MAAS's good internal consistency, with alpha values ranging from .80 to .89 (Christopher & Gilbert, 2010; Frewen et al., 2008; MacKillop & Anderson, 2007; Schmertz et al., 2009). Christopher and Gilbert (2010) also report excellent test-retest reliability for the MAAS over a one-month interval ($r = .81$), while Frewen and colleagues (2008) report an intraclass correlation coefficient of .25 for the MAAS.

Several studies indicate that the MAAS has excellent discriminant, convergent, concurrent, and predictive validity. Brown and Ryan (2003) found significant, moderate to large positive correlations between MAAS and emotional intelligence, openness to experience, positive affect, vitality, autonomy, competence, relatedness, self-esteem, and the Mindfulness/Mindlessness Scale (MMS). They also found significant, moderate to large negative correlations between MAAS and social anxiety, negative affect, absorption, neuroticism, depression, anxiety, reported physical symptoms, somatization, and medical visit frequency (Brown & Ryan, 2003). Carlson and Brown (2005) report significant, moderate negative correlations between MAAS scores and mood disturbance and symptoms of stress in cancer outpatients. The MAAS also exhibits high content validity, insofar as theory, inductive and deductive methods of item generation, and the use of both exploratory and confirmatory factor analyses support the consistency of its dimensionality (Qu et al., 2015).

Five Facet Mindfulness Questionnaire (FFMQ)

The FFMQ (Baer et al., 2006) is a comprehensive trait mindfulness questionnaire developed following a factor-analytic study of 112 items from five other mindfulness measures: MAAS, Freiburg Mindfulness Inventory (FMI), Kentucky Inventory of Mindfulness Skills (KIMS), Cognitive and Affective Mindfulness Scale-Revised (CAMS-R), and Southampton Mindfulness Questionnaire (SMQ). The FFMQ's 39 items are organized into 5 subscales: Observing, Describing, Acting with Awareness, Non-judging of Inner Experience, and Non-reactivity to Inner Experience. FFMQ items include: "I watch my feelings without getting lost in them" (Non-reactivity to Inner Experience), "I do jobs or tasks automatically without being aware of what I'm doing" (Acting with Awareness), "I can easily put my beliefs, opinions, and expectations into words" (Describing), "I tell myself I shouldn't be feeling the way I'm feeling" (Non-judging of Inner Experience), and "I pay attention to sounds, such as clocks ticking, birds chirping, or cars passing" (Observing). Respondents report the extent to which each statement is true of them on a 5-point Likert-type scale, with "1" indicating that the statement is "never or very rarely true" and "5" indicating that the statement is "very often or always true." The questionnaire produces scores for each of the five subscales, as well as a total score.

Baer and colleagues (2006) used two samples of undergraduate psychology students for FFMQ item selection and scale development. Sample one ($N = 613$) had a mean age of 20.5 years, and participants in this sample were 70% female and 90% Caucasian. Sample two ($N = 268$) had a mean age of 18.9 years, and participants in this sample were 77% female and 90% Caucasian. Baer and colleagues (2006) used exploratory factor analysis (EFA) and data from sample one to identify the facets of mindfulness, while the researchers used confirmatory factor analysis (CFA) and the data from sample two to assess the replicability of the five-factor structure derived from the EFA performed on sample one's data.

The FFMQ has robust psychometric characteristics. In a sample of non-meditators, the measure exhibited adequate to good internal consistency reliability, with alpha coefficients ranging from .75 to .91 (Baer et al., 2006). Subsequent studies corroborate Baer and colleagues' (2006) findings, suggesting that the FFMQ and its subscales exhibit adequate to good internal consistency reliability, with alpha coefficients for the full measure ranging from .85 (Andrei et al., 2016) to .946 (Richards, 2013, p. 66) and alpha coefficients for the subscales ranging from .67 (Baer et al., 2008) to .963 (Richards, 2013, p. 66).

The FFMQ also demonstrates high discriminant, convergent, and concurrent validity. Qu and colleagues (2015) suggest that mindfulness as measured by the FFMQ differs from other, similar constructs, such as self-compassion, and is convergent with mindfulness as measured by the MAAS, FMI, KIMS, CAMS-R, and SMQ. Qu and colleagues (2015) also argue that the use of regression analyses and comparisons with psychological symptoms and well-being outcomes support the measure's concurrent validity. Moreover, several studies have found significant, moderate to large positive correlations with self-regulation, emotional intelligence, and openness to experience, as well as moderate to large negative correlations with thought suppression, alexithymia (i.e., inability to recognize or describe one's own emotions), and experiential avoidance (Baer et al., 2006; Baer et al., 2008; Brown & Ryan, 2003). In experienced meditators, the five facets positively correlated with psychological well-being and negatively correlated with psychological distress (Baer et al., 2008; Carmody & Baer, 2008). Furthermore, Curtiss and Klemanski (2014) report significant, moderate to large positive correlations between FFMQ subscales and a measure of psychological flexibility, as well as significant, low to moderate negative correlations between FFMQ subscales and measures of affect intensity, worry, general distress, and lack of emotional awareness.

Kentucky Inventory of Mindfulness Skills (KIMS)

The KIMS (Baer et al., 2004) is a 39-item trait measure targeting 4 "mindfulness skills" from a dialectical behavior therapy (DBT) perspective: Observing, Describing, Acting with Awareness, and Accepting without Judgment. Items from the KIMS include: "I notice the smells and aromas of things" (Observe), "It's hard for me to find the words to describe what I'm thinking" (Describe), "I tend to do several things at once rather than focusing on one thing at a time" (Act with Awareness), and "I criticize myself for having irrational or inappropriate emotions" (Accept without Judgment). Respondents report the extent to which each statement is generally true of them on a 5-point Likert-type scale, with "1" indicating that the statement is "never or very rarely true" and "5" indicating that the statement is "very often or always true." The measure yields a score for each subscale, but the measure does not provide a total score.

Baer et al. (2004) developed the KIMS using two nonclinical samples ($N = 205$, 215) and a clinical sample of patients with borderline personality disorder ($N = 26$). The first nonclinical sample ($N = 205$) was 60% female, 85% Caucasian, and consisted of undergraduates aged 18 to 22 years. The second nonclinical sample ($N = 215$) was demographically similar to the first nonclinical sample. The clinical sample ($N = 26$; $M_{age} = 36$ years) consisted of 25 Caucasian males and one Caucasian female. Most individuals in the clinical sample had comorbid psychiatric diagnoses, including major depressive disorder, PTSD, and bipolar II disorder.

The KIMS demonstrates adequate to good reliability. During test development, Baer and colleagues (2004) reported internal consistency values of .91 and .85 (Observe), .84 and .86 (Describe), .83 and .76 (Act with Awareness), and .87 (Accept without Judgment). Correlations between KIMS subscales were modest yet significant, except for a nonsignificant correlation between Observe and Act with Awareness ($r = .09$). Baer and colleagues (2004) speculate that inexperienced meditators may be more likely to judge attended-to experiences. KIMS subscales demonstrated adequate to good test-retest reliabilities during development, with correlations of .65 (Observe), .81 (Describe), .86 (Act with Awareness), and .83 (Accept without Judgment; Baer et al., 2004).

The KIMS also demonstrates adequate content, discriminant, and convergent validity. Five practicing psychologists and six doctoral students trained in DBT assessed each item's content validity. Interrater agreement on the assignment of the final 39 items to each of the mindfulness skills categories by the psychologists and doctoral students ranged from 64% to 100% ($M = 86\%$), indicating to Baer and colleagues (2004) that the measure exhibits adequate content validity. Baer and colleagues (2004) report significant, moderate to large positive correlations between KIMS subscales and openness to experience, conscientiousness, emotional intelligence, absorption, and life satisfaction, as well as significant, moderate to large negative correlations between KIMS subscales and neuroticism, psychopathology, alexithymia, experiential avoidance, and dissociative experiences. Further, regarding convergent construct validity, Baer and colleagues (2004) found significant, moderate to large positive correlations between MAAS scores and KIMS Describe, Act with Awareness, and Accept without Judgment scores. Finally, the clinical sample scored significantly lower than both nonclinical samples on KIMS Describe, Act with Awareness, and Accept without Judgment, suggesting that these three subscales demonstrate adequate discriminant validity, given the negative correlation between mindfulness skills and psychological symptoms (Baer et al., 2004).

Toronto Mindfulness Scale (TMS)

The TMS (Lau et al., 2006) is a 13-item state measure assessing two facets of mindfulness: Curiosity and Decentering. A validated trait version of the scale is also available (Davis et al., 2009). Items from the state TMS include: "I was curious to see what my mind was up to from moment to moment" (Curiosity) and "I experienced myself as separate from my changing thoughts and feelings" (Decentering). Respondents report the extent to which they believe each statement reflects their experiences during a mindfulness activity on a 5-point Likert-type scale, with "0" indicating that the statement captures their experiences "not at all" and "4" indicating that the statement captures their experiences "very much." The measure yields a score for each of the two subscales and a total score.

Lau and colleagues (2006) recruited 390 participants (55% female; $M_{age} = 40.8$ years) for TMS development. Lau et al. (2006) assigned participants to groups based on previous meditation experience. The nonmeditator group ($N = 158$) and the meditator group ($N = 232$) did not differ significantly in terms of age or gender. Following the removal of outliers and participants demonstrating untenable response sets, 374 participants contributed data to scale development. The researchers evaluated the scale's validity using a different, clinical sample of 99 individuals (68% female; $M_{age} = 46.68$ years) recruited from MBSR programs. Clients in the clinical sample presented with general stress, anxiety, depression, chronic pain, diabetes, multiple sclerosis, and cancer.

The TMS demonstrates adequate to excellent internal consistency reliability. Lau and colleagues (2006) report alpha coefficients of .95 (total scale), .86 (Curiosity), and .87 (De-centering). The average item-total correlation was .53, while item variances ranged from .32 to .67. The Curiosity subscale demonstrated an item-level variance to measurement error ratio of .57, while the Decentering subscale demonstrated a ratio of .27 (Lau et al., 2006). Andrei and colleagues (2016) report internal consistency values of .86 and .88 (Curiosity) and .73 and .76 (De-centering).

The TMS also demonstrates adequate convergent and predictive validity, high discriminant validity, and low content validity. Lau and colleagues (2006) report significant, small to moderate positive correlations between TMS and absorption, internal state awareness, awareness of surroundings, reflective self-awareness, openness to experience, psychological mindedness (i.e., one's ability to see how one's thoughts, feelings, and behaviors relate to one another), and self-consciousness, as well as significant, small negative correlations with cognitive failures (i.e., lapses in perception, memory, and motor function resulting from inattention). In a clinical sample, Lau and colleagues (2006) found significant decreases in symptoms and perceived stress and a significant increase in TMS scores following MBSR. Moreover, Andrei and colleagues (2016) found positive, moderate correlations between TMS Curiosity, FFMQ Observe, and PHLMS Awareness, as well as between TMS De-centering and FFMQ Non-reactivity and FFMQ Observe, suggesting that the TMS has adequate concurrent validity. Furthermore, the TMS predicted performance on simultaneously administered measures of acceptance, absorption, positive and negative affect, worry, rumination, reflection, private and public self-consciousness, and reappraisal (Andrei et al., 2016). Despite these findings, Qu and colleagues (2015) report that theory, the deductive method of item generation, and factor-analytic procedures result in inconsistent dimensions, suggesting that the measure demonstrates poor content validity.

Cognitive and Affective Mindfulness Scale–Revised (CAMS-R)

The CAMS-R (Feldman et al., 2007) is a 12-item trait measure assessing 4 facets of mindfulness: Attention, Present-focus, Awareness, and Acceptance. The CAMS-R's items differ from those of other measures in that they assess willingness or capacity for mindfulness (Bergomi et al., 2013). Willingness or capacity for mindfulness differs from the construct of trait mindfulness assessed by other measures in that the former reflects the extent to which an individual might successfully practice mindfulness with proper instruction, while the latter reflects the extent to which one incorporates mindfulness techniques and attitudes into daily living. Items from the CAMS-R include: "It is easy for me to concentrate on what I am doing" (Attention), "I am preoccupied by the future" (Present-focus), "I try to notice my thoughts without judging them" (Awareness), and "I can tolerate emotional pain" (Acceptance). Respondents report the extent to which they believe each statement is true of them on a 4-point Likert-type scale, with "1" indicating that the statement is "rarely or not at all true" and "4" indicating that the statement is "almost always true." The measure yields one total score, with no subscale scores. Higher scores indicate greater capacities for mindfulness.

Feldman and colleagues (2007) used two samples of university students to develop their scale. Sample 1 ($N = 250$) was 64% female and 36% male ($M_{age} =$ 19.31 years). Sample 1's ethnic composition was as follows: 56% White/Caucasian, 18% Hispanic/Latino, 9% Black/African American, 6% Asian American, and 11% other/mixed heritage. Sample 2 ($N = 298$) was 61% female and 39% male ($M_{age} =$ 18.74 years). Sample 2's ethnic composition was as follows: 56% White/Caucasian, 21% Hispanic/Latino, 7% Black/African American, 7% Asian American, and 9% other/mixed heritage.

The CAMS-R demonstrates adequate internal consistency reliability. Feldman and colleagues (2007) report alpha values of .74 and .77 (entire scale), .79 and .81 (Attention), .53 and .47 (Present-focus), .42 and .46 (Awareness), and .56 and .66 (Acceptance). Because internal consistency is related to number of items (John & Benet-Martinez, 2000), lower values for three of the four three-item subscales (i.e.,

Present-focus, Awareness, and Acceptance) are not surprising. Schmertz and colleagues (2009) report entire-scale alpha values of .76 and .85 for two independent samples.

Studies consistently demonstrate the CAMS-R's concurrent, convergent, and discriminant validity. Feldman and colleagues (2007) report significant, moderate to large positive correlations between the CAMS-R and MAAS, FMI, and measures of well-being, attention to feelings, clarity of feelings, mood repair, distraction, plan rehearsal, problem analysis, and cognitive flexibility. In addition, significant, moderate to large negative correlations are reported between CAMS-R and measures of general distress (anxiety and depression), anxious arousal, anhedonic depression, worry, rumination, reflection, brooding, experiential avoidance, thought suppression, outcome fantasy, and stagnant deliberation (Feldman et al., 2007). Two other studies suggest that the CAMS-R is a better predictor of psychological distress than the MAAS, KIMS, FMI, and SMQ (Baer et al., 2006; Thompson & Waltz, 2007).

Philadelphia Mindfulness Scale (PHLMS)

The PHLMS (Cardaciotto et al., 2008) is a 20-item trait measure assessing two orthogonal facets of mindfulness: Present-moment Awareness (of perceptions and feelings) and Non-judgmental Acceptance (experiential avoidance). Items from the PHLMS include: "When someone asks how I am feeling, I can identify my emotions easily" (Awareness), and "I tell myself that I shouldn't have certain thoughts" (Acceptance). Respondents report the frequency with which they have had the experience reflected by each statement in the past week on a 5-point Likert-type scale, with "1" indicating that the statement is "rarely or very rarely true" and "5" indicating that the statement is "very often or always true." The measure yields an overall score and scores for each of the 2 10-item subscales.

Cardaciotto et al. (2008) developed the PHLMS using 2 nonclinical samples (N = 204, 559), and 3 clinical samples (N = 52 mixed psychiatric outpatients, 30 inpatients with eating disorders, 78 student counseling center outpatients). The general student sample (N = 559) included 270 males and 283 females (M_{age} = 20.12 years). The sample's racial composition was as follows: 64% White/Caucasian/European Descent, 19% Asian/Pacific Islander, 8% Black/African American/Caribbean American, 5% multiracial, 2% Hispanic/Latino/Latina, 1% Native American, and 1% "other" or race not listed.

Numerous studies attest to the PHLMS' internal consistency reliability. Across their samples, Cardaciotto and colleagues (2008) calculated alpha values of .81, .75, .75, and .85 for the Awareness subscale and .85, .82, .75, and .90 for the Acceptance subscale. Inter-item correlations ranged from .01 to .50 for the Awareness subscale and from −.04 to .67 for the Acceptance subscale. Corrected item-to-total correlations ranged from .10 to .62 for the Awareness subscale and from .23 to .67 for the Acceptance subscale (Cardaciotto et al., 2008). Andrei and colleagues (2016) found alpha values of .73 and .76 for Present-moment Awareness and alpha values of .86 and .88 for Non-judgmental Acceptance.

The PHLMS exhibits high content validity (Qu et al., 2015). Cardaciotto and colleagues (2008) found significant, moderate to large positive correlations between the PHLMS Awareness subscale and measures of mindfulness awareness/attention and reflection, while the PHLMS Acceptance subscale was positively correlated (with moderate correlations) with measures of acceptance/willingness, happiness, and quality of life, as well as negatively correlated (with low to moderate correlations) with measures of thought suppression and rumination. The PHLMS Acceptance subscale was also negatively correlated with social desirability, depression, anxiety, and hopelessness (Cardaciotto et al., 2008). Research indicating that PHLMS subscales are moderately to strongly positively correlated with similar subscales on the KIMS and FFMQ provides further evidence that the PHLMS exhibits high content validity (Andrei et al., 2016; Cardaciotto et al., 2008).

Freiburg Mindfulness Inventory (FMI)

The FMI (Buchheld et al., 2001) is a 30-item trait measure assessing 4 facets of mindfulness: Attention, Non-Judgment, Openness, and Insightful Understanding. A psychometrically robust, 14-item short form of the FMI is also available (Walach et al., 2006). Items from the FMI include: "I easily get lost in my thoughts and feelings" (Attention), "I accept myself as I am" (Non-judgment), "I avoid unpleasant feelings" (Openness), and "I consider things from different perspectives" (Insightful Understanding). Respondents report the extent to which they believe that the statements characterized them over a fixed period on a 4-point Likert-type scale, with "1" indicating that the statement has "rarely" characterized them and "4" indicating that the statement has "almost always" characterized them. The measure provides one total score, with no subscale scores.

Buchheld et al. (2001) provide detailed demographic information for their general sample ($N = 115$). The sample was 69% female and 31% male ($M_{age} = 43$ years). Participants reported an average of five years of insight meditation experience, but 21% of the participants had been practicing for less than one year. Roughly 28% of the respondents reported meditating once daily. Additionally, Walach et al. (2006) validated the FMI with a clinical sample ($N = 117$) of inpatients and outpatients. Diagnoses in the clinical sample varied extensively but excluded psychosis.

The FMI demonstrates excellent internal consistency. Buchheld and colleagues (2001) report alpha values of .93 and .94 (entire scale), .90 (Attention), .82 (Non-judgment), .81 (Openness), and .76 (Insightful Understanding). They also report interitem correlations of .32 and .33 for the FMI at two different times (Buchheld et al., 2001). Walach and colleagues (2006) found an alpha value of .86 with the FMI short form and demonstrated an extremely large correlation between the FMI short and long forms ($r = .95$).

Several studies attest to the FMI's good validity. Buchheld and colleagues (2001) note that participant FMI scores increased significantly following insight meditation retreats. Though the FMI demonstrated good validity during development,

Buchheld and colleagues (2001) note that the scale may be appropriate for use only with experienced meditators. Inexperienced meditators are likely to misinterpret ambiguous items dealing with bodily awareness and attention to unpleasant mental states, such as, "I sense my body, whether eating, cooking, cleaning or talking" and "I see how I create my own suffering" (Buchheld et al., 2001). Walach and colleagues (2006) report significant, moderate to large positive correlations between the FMI and measures of private self-awareness, self-knowledge, and meditation experience, as well as significant, moderate negative correlations between the FMI and measures of absorption, the Dissociative Experiences Scale, and the Symptom Checklist-90.

Southampton Mindfulness Questionnaire (SMQ)

The SMQ (Chadwick et al., 2008) is a 16-item trait measure assessing 4 bipolar mindfulness constructs: (1) De-centered Awareness vs. Reacting to Difficult Cognitions, (2) Attention vs. Experiential Avoidance, (3) Acceptance vs. Judgment, and (4) Release of Difficult Cognitions vs. Rumination. Each item from the SMQ begins with the phrase, "Usually when I experience distressing thoughts and images . . . " and continues with clauses including, "I am able just to notice them without reacting" and "I find it so unpleasant I have to distract myself and not notice them." Respondents report the extent to which they agree with each statement on a 7-point Likert scale, with "0" indicating that they "strongly disagree" with the statement and "6" indicating that they "strongly agree" with the statement. Consistent with its single-factor structure, the measure yields one total mindfulness score.

Chadwick and colleagues (2008) used both a clinical sample ($N = 122$) and a non-clinical sample ($N = 134$) in the SMQ's validation. Both samples were recruited using convenience and snowball methodologies. The clinical sample consisted of 78 men and 44 women ($M_{age} = 31$ years), who were experiencing psychosis and distressing delusions. The clinical sample also included 11 inpatients. The non-clinical sample consisted of a group of meditators ($N = 83$; $M_{age} = 47$ years) and a group of non-meditators ($N = 51$; $M_{age} = 47$ years). Fifty of the meditators were women, and fifty-one of the non-meditators were women.

Chadwick and colleagues (2008) report alpha values of .89 (non-clinical sample) and .82 (clinical sample). Item-total correlations ranged from .34 to .67 ($M = .54$; Chadwick et al., 2008). Similarly, Baer and colleagues (2006) found an alpha value of .85 for the SMQ in a sample of 613 undergraduates. These results suggest that the SMQ has adequate internal consistency reliability.

The SMQ exhibits adequate concurrent validity, high convergent validity, and low content validity. Chadwick and colleagues (2008) suggest that the SMQ differentiates meditators from non-meditators and members of clinical samples from members of non-clinical samples. Moreover, the SMQ differentiated between regular and non-regular meditators. Chadwick and colleagues (2008) also report significant, large positive correlations between SMQ and MAAS scores in both clinical and non-clinical samples, as well as significant, large positive correlations between SMQ scores and measures of positive mood and positive affect. They also report significant, large negative correlations with negative affect (Chadwick et al., 2008). Baer and colleagues (2006) found significant, moderate to large positive correlations between SMQ and MAAS, FMI, KIMS, CAMS-R, and measures of emotional intelligence and self-compassion. In addition, significant, moderate to large negative correlations have been reported between SMQ and measures of psychological symptoms, neuroticism, thought suppression, emotional regulation difficulties, alexithymia, dissociation, experiential avoidance, and absent-mindedness (Baer et al., 2006).

STATE MINDFULNESS MEASURES FOR ADULTS

The above review suggests that researchers have developed several promising mindfulness measures for adults and caregivers, but it is noteworthy that apart from the TMS and the state version of the MAAS, the most commonly used instruments reviewed above assess trait mindfulness. Findings that measures of state and trait mindfulness have little to no relationship highlight the need for state mindfulness assessments (Thompson & Waltz, 2007). Without adequate state mindfulness measures, the field cannot examine the relationship of state mindfulness to other, clinically relevant constructs or develop evidence-based interventions founded on this construct. At the time of publication, we identified only one well-known state measure other than the TMS and the state version of the MAAS, and we briefly review this inventory below, with the interest of stimulating further research in this largely neglected area of the field.

State Mindfulness Scale (SMS)

The SMS (Tanay & Bernstein, 2013) is a 21-item state measure assessing two levels of mindfulness: State Mindfulness of Mind and State Mindfulness of Body. Despite the measure's reliance on a two-level model of state mindfulness, Tanay and Bernstein (2013) maintain that the SMS assesses mindfulness as a unidimensional construct, which incorporates both the objects of mindful attention as well as the quality of *how* one is mindful of these objects. The two-level model underlying the SMS seeks to capture elements of both the traditional Buddhist concept of mindfulness and Bishop and colleagues' (2004) consensual definition of mindfulness. Sample items from the SMS include: "I noticed pleasant and unpleasant emotions" (State Mindfulness of Mind) and "I noticed various sensations caused by my surroundings (e.g., heat, coolness, the wind on my face)" (State Mindfulness of Body). Respondents report the extent to which each statement is consistent with their recent experiences using a 5-point Likert-type scale, with "1" indicating that the statement is "not at all" consistent and "4" indicating that the statement matches one's recent experiences "very well." The scale produces subscale scores for each of the two levels of mindfulness, as well as a total score.

Tanay and Bernstein (2013) used three samples in the development of the SMS. Sample A ($N = 193$) was 74% female ($M_{age} = 24$ years) and had the following religious/ethnic composition: 77% Jewish, 9% Muslim Arabs, 9% Christian Arabs, 1% Druze, and 4% no religious/ethnic affiliation. Sample B ($N = 57$) was 65% female ($M_{age} = 25$ years) and had the following religious/ethnic composition: 95% Jewish and 5% Christian or Muslim Arabs. Sample C consisted of two cohorts from a single study. Cohort 1 ($N = 130$) was 65% female ($M_{age} = 30$ years) and had the following religious/ethnic composition: 91% Jewish, 6% Muslim Arabs, and 3% Christian Arabs. Cohort 2 ($N = 86$) was 64% female ($M_{age} = 33$ years) and had the following religious/ethnic composition: 79% Jewish, 9% Muslim Arabs, 4% Christian Arabs, and 8% Druze.

The SMS demonstrates excellent internal consistency reliability and strong test-retest reliability. Tanay and Bernstein (2013) report alpha values of .95 for the full scale, .95 for the Mindfulness of Body scale, and .90 for the Mindfulness of Mind scale. Tanay and colleagues (2012) likewise report an alpha value of .92 for the SMS full scale, adding that the scale demonstrated strong one-week test-retest reliability ($r = .72$).

The SMS also demonstrates adequate convergent, discriminant, and construct validity. Tanay and Bernstein (2013) found significant, moderate correlations between both SMS subscales and TMS Total Score, TMS Decentering, TMS Curiosity, and FFMQ Observe. Interestingly, Tanay and Bernstein (2013) found non-significant correlations between both SMS subscales and the trait MAAS, which the authors cite as evidence that the SMS assesses state mindfulness rather than the unrelated construct of trait mindfulness. With respect to SMS construct validity, Tanay and Bernstein (2013) report that individuals who engaged in mindfulness meditation practice received significantly higher SMS scores immediately after the intervention than their counterparts who did not participate in the intervention. Moreover, the elevated SMS scores observed in the experimental group were not observed among control condition participants over time, indicating that the changes in SMS scores were unique to the intervention (Tanay & Bernstein, 2013).

FUTURE DIRECTIONS FOR ADULT MINDFULNESS ASSESSMENT

Directions for Researchers

Though researchers have developed several promising mindfulness instruments for adults and caregivers, the field must still overcome many challenges. First, researchers should continue developing psychometrically sound state mindfulness measures. Though the TMS and SMS represent a promising first step in the development of state inventories, both researchers and practitioners seem to neglect these scales, as only the TMS appeared on our list of commonly used measures. It is unclear whether this is due to the TMS having both a state and a trait version. The SMS generated significantly fewer references on Google Scholar and did not appear in any of the systematic reviews referenced during this chapter's development. Ultimately, a more diverse set of measures will help researchers to refine state mindfulness as a construct, and an increased understanding of state mindfulness might help both researchers and practitioners to identify and implement evidence-based mindfulness interventions.

Second, further research should focus on the development and validation of non-self-report mindfulness measures. Several researchers have articulated concerns that social desirability bias and significant differences in semantic understandings of mindfulness items across populations may decrease the construct validity of self-report mindfulness measures (e.g., Bergomi et al., 2013). Despite demonstrations of current measures' validity (Baer et al., 2009), the misinterpretation of items by inexperienced meditators (Baer et al., 2006) and significant, low to moderate positive correlations between mindfulness scores and social desirability (Brown & Ryan, 2003; Cardaciotto et al., 2008) suggest that the field would benefit from the development of alternative measurement techniques, such as structured interviews and behavior rating scales completed by an informant.

Recognizing the problems with self-report mindfulness measures, researchers have begun studying procedures that reduce assessment recall bias. One promising family of procedures is ecological momentary assessment (EMA). EMA methods capture a representative sample of an individual's experience through repeated assessment in naturalistic settings (Shiffman et al., 2008). EMA methods may incorporate mobile technologies (e.g., cell phones) or low-tech methods of responding (e.g., journals) in measure administration. EMA devices prompt participants to complete measures either when thoughts, feelings, or behaviors occur (event-based sampling) or at predetermined intervals (time-based sampling). Practitioners may also use both sampling methods simultaneously to identify behavioral antecedents (Shiffman et al., 2008).

Researchers recently compared the sensitivity of a paper-and-pencil mindfulness measure to an EMA mindfulness measure in a clinical sample (Moore et al., 2016). Both measures assessed mindfulness using CAMS-R items. While the paper survey and the EMA measure did not differ significantly with respect to internal consistency, they did differ with respect to their change sensitivity. Patients who participated in MBSR were significantly more mindful than patients participating in health education when researchers compared EMA measure scores, but the two groups did not differ on mindfulness when researchers compared paper survey scores. Moreover, Depp and colleagues (2012) suggest that EMA measures exhibit better convergent validity (with respect to clinician ratings) than paper surveys, further emphasizing the possible benefits of EMA for mindfulness research. Before practitioners implement EMA in applied contexts, however, future studies should seek to replicate Moore and colleagues' (2016) and Depp and colleagues' (2012) findings in demographically diverse samples using different mindfulness scales, technologies, and sampling procedures.

Furthermore, researchers should implement the same consensual definition of mindfulness across all studies of the construct. Despite reasonably well-received attempts to operationalize mindfulness (e.g., Bishop et al., 2004), researchers frequently conflate the construct of mindfulness with common correlates and benefits of mindfulness (e.g., calmness, patience, self-knowledge) and treat mindfulness as a trait rather than as a state (Bishop et al., 2004). When researchers develop mindfulness measures that reflect these "impure" concepts of mindfulness, they greatly reduce the construct validity of their scales (Bishop et al., 2004). The conflation of operational features with common correlates and potential benefits hinders meaningful comparisons between various scales, thereby impeding refinement of the construct (Bishop et al., 2004). Lack of agreement in this area may impede basic research of the mechanisms of mindfulness, the development of mindfulness-based interventions, and an understanding of how mindfulness buffers against psychopathology.

Lastly, researchers should consistently implement self-report measures in the evaluation of the process effects of mindfulness-based interventions (MBIs) with teachers and parents. Although a few studies have included mindfulness measures in their procedures (e.g., Rayan & Ahmad, 2017), the majority of MBIs do not assess pre-post intervention changes in mindfulness and consequently fail to demonstrate that increased mindfulness was directly related to MBI outcomes (e.g., Taylor et al., 2016). Neither researchers nor practitioners can refine promising interventions without understanding the mechanisms by which these interventions function, and for this reason, the development of efficacious and effective MBIs depends largely on the use of psychometrically sound measures to evaluate mindfulness as a process variable. Subsequent research that consistently fails to establish mindfulness as a key factor in MBI effectiveness may suggest that MBIs are effective not because they induce changes in mindfulness per se but rather because they incorporate other, more procedurally significant factors. Such a scenario would essentially indicate that "mindfulness-based" interventions are not truly grounded in modifications to mindfulness. In this case, researchers and practitioners could then focus their efforts on developing treatments that emphasize more procedurally significant factors and thereby enhance client outcomes.

Directions for Schools

The current, most popular technique for measuring mindfulness in schools is through self-report. Researchers have gained much insight into mindfulness through studies utilizing self-report measures (Baer et al., 2004, 2006; Bergomi et al., 2013). Providing information via self-report may be efficient and convenient for participants in school settings, as data-collection resources are often limited. However, educators involved in school mindfulness training may also benefit from EMA. EMA's naturalistic nature may allow teachers to integrate mindfulness assessment into their lives. Teachers are responsible for maintaining a classroom devoid of conflict and disruptive behavior and promoting smooth activity transitions, appropriate emotional expression, and individual support

(LaParo & Pianta, 2003). Personal mindfulness practice is crucial for teachers, because mindful practices can contribute to a positive classroom atmosphere, and EMA may allow teachers to assess the extent to which they are successfully incorporating mindful practices into classroom activities, without disrupting those activities.

Mental flexibility is one benefit of mindfulness, and challenging classroom environments demand mental flexibility (Roeser et al., 2012). Studies have shown that mindfulness can also promote emotional regulation (Bishop et al., 2004). Emotional regulation is key for teachers, as they are expected to exhibit interest and enthusiasm, while managing negative emotions and stressors associated with burnout (Chang, 2009). When teachers experience frustration or anger at work, they are seldom able to leave class to collect themselves (Roeser et al., 2012). EMA may allow teachers to assess their own mindfulness both within and outside of the classroom. EMA may also allow researchers to study what teachers do, think, and feel over time in response to mindfulness-based intervention in schools. It is noteworthy that teachers report enjoying EMA methodologies because they are "convenient, portable, practical, simple, quick, consistent, [and] fascinating to students" (Carson et al., 2010, p. 170). Researchers may also consider supplementing EMA with journals, although this more time-consuming procedure might discourage teachers from fully participating in studies of mindfulness in schools (cf., Carson et al., 2010).

CONCLUSION

The development of psychometrically sound mindfulness measures for adults and caregivers is crucial if mental health practitioners are to improve outcomes through the development and refinement of MBIs. Fortunately for researchers, practitioners, and clients alike, the eight most commonly used adult mindfulness measures demonstrate robust psychometric properties and are appropriate for use with a variety of populations, including parents and educators. Future mindfulness research should focus on the validation of the distinct construct of state mindfulness, the development and use of alternative mindfulness measurement techniques, and the incorporation of psychometrically robust self-report measures into the evaluation of therapeutic process effects in educators and parents receiving MBIs. Ultimately, efforts to refine the construct of mindfulness, understand its mechanisms, and develop and implement effective interventions may falter if neither researchers nor practitioners allow a consensual definition of mindfulness to guide their work. Heeding these directions for future work may therefore help to substantiate claims that adults and caregivers can benefit from practicing mindfulness. These recommendations for improving assessment may also contribute to a more rigorous understanding of the utility of MBIs in schools, insofar as mindfulness can increase student engagement, decrease teacher burnout, and promote emotional regulation and mental flexibility in teachers, which may allow them to handle difficult classroom situations better.

REFERENCES

Andrei, F., Vesely, A., & Siegling, A. B. (2016). An examination of concurrent and incremental validity of four mindfulness scales, *Journal of Psychopathology and Behavioral Assessment, 38*, 559–571. doi:10.1007/s10862-016-9546-x

Baer, R. A. (2003). Mindfulness training as a clinical intervention: A conceptual and empirical review. *Clinical Psychology: Science and Practice, 10*, 125–143. doi:10.1093/clipsy.bpg015

Baer, R. A., Smith, G. T., & Allen, K. B. (2004). Assessment of mindfulness by self-report: The Kentucky inventory of mindfulness skills. *Assessment, 11*, 191–206. doi:10.1177/1073191104268029

Baer, R. A., Smith, G. T., Hopkins, J., Krietemeyer, J., & Toney, L. (2006). Using self-report assessment methods to explore facets of mindfulness. *Assessment, 13*, 27–45. doi:10.1177/1073191105283504

Baer, R. A., Smith, G. T., Lykins, E., Button, D., Krietemeyer, J., . . . Williams, J. M. G. (2008). Construct validity of the five facet mindfulness questionnaire in meditating and nonmeditating samples. *Assessment, 15*, 329–342. doi:10.1177/1073191107313003

Baer, R. A., Walsh, E., & Lykins, E. L. (2009). Assessment of mindfulness. In F. Didonna (Ed.), *Clinical handbook of mindfulness* (pp. 153–168). Springer.

Bergomi, C., Tschacher, W., & Kupper, Z. (2013). The assessment of mindfulness with self-report measures: existing scales and open issues. *Mindfulness, 4*, 191–202. doi:10.1007/s12671-012-0110-9

Bishop, S. R., Lau, M., Shapiro, S., Carlson, L., Anderson, N. D., Carmody, J., . . . Devins, G. (2004). Mindfulness: A proposed operational definition. *Clinical Psychology: Science and Practice, 11*, 230–241. doi:10.1093/clipsy.bph077

Brown, K. W., & Ryan, R. M. (2003). The benefits of being present: Mindfulness and its role in psychological well-being. *Journal of Personality and Social Psychology, 84*, 822–848. doi:10.1037/0022-3514.84.4.822

Buchheld, N., Grossman, P., & Walach, H. (2001). Measuring mindfulness in insight meditation (Vipassana) and meditation-based psychotherapy: The development of the Freiburg mindfulness inventory (FMI). *Journal for Meditation and Meditation Research, 1*, 11–34. Retrieved from http://www.smmr.de/journal-for-meditation-and-meditation-research-2/

Cardaciotto, L., Herbert, J. D., Forman, E. M., Moitra, E., & Farrow, V. (2008). The assessment of present-moment awareness and acceptance the Philadelphia Mindfulness Scale. *Assessment, 15*, 204–223. doi:10.1177/1073191107311467

Carlson, L. E., & Brown, K. W. (2005). Validation of the mindful attention awareness scale in a cancer population. *Journal of Psychosomatic Research, 58*, 29–33. doi:10.1016/j.jpsychores.2004.04.366

Carmody, J., & Baer, R. A. (2008). Relationships between mindfulness practice and levels of mindfulness, medical and psychological symptoms and well-being in a mindfulness-based stress reduction program. *Journal of Behavioral Medicine, 31*, 23–33. doi:10.1007/s10865-007-9130-7

Carson, R. L., Weiss, H. M., & Templin, T. J. (2010). Ecological momentary assessment: A research method for studying the daily lives of teachers. *International*

Journal of Research & Method in Education, 33, 165–182. doi:10.1080/1743727X.2010.484548

Chadwick, P., Hember, M., Symes, J., Peters, E., Kuipers, E., & Dagnan, D. (2008). Responding mindfully to unpleasant thoughts and images: Reliability and validity of the Southampton mindfulness questionnaire (SMQ). *British Journal of Clinical Psychology, 47*, 451–455. doi:10.1348/014466508X314891

Chang, M. L. (2009). An appraisal perspective of teacher burnout: Examining the emotional work of teachers. *Educational Psychology Review, 21*, 193–218. doi:10.1007/s10648-009-9106-y

Christopher, M. S., & Gilbert, B. D. (2010). Incremental validity of components of mindfulness in the prediction of satisfaction with life and depression. *Current Psychology, 29*, 10–23. doi:10.1007/s12144-009-9067-9

Curtiss, J., & Klemanski, D. H. (2014). Factor analysis of the five facet mindfulness questionnaire in a heterogeneous clinical sample. *Journal of Psychopathology and Behavioral Assessment, 36*, 683–694. doi:10.1007/s10862-014-9429-y

Davis, K. M., Lau, M. A., & Cairns, D. R. (2009). Development and preliminary validation of a trait version of the Toronto Mindfulness Scale. *Journal of Cognitive Psychotherapy, 23*, 185–197. doi:10.1891/0889-8391.23.3.185

Depp, C. A., Kim, D. H., Vergel de Dios, L., Wang, V., & Ceglowski, J. (2012). A pilot study of mood ratings captured by mobile phone versus paper-and-pencil mood charts in bipolar disorder. *Journal of Dual Diagnosis, 8*, 326–332. doi:10.1080/15504263.2012.723318

Dimidjian, S., & Linehan, M. M. (2003). Defining an agenda for future research on the clinical application of mindfulness practice. *Clinical Psychology: Science and Practice, 10*, 166–171. doi:10.1093/clipsy/bpg019

Epel, E., Daubenmier, J., Moskowitz, J. T., Folkman, S., & Blackburn, E. (2009). Can meditation slow rate of cellular aging? Cognitive stress, mindfulness, and telomeres. *Annals of the New York Academy of Sciences, 1172*, 34–53. doi:10.1111/j.1749-6632.2009.04414.x

Feldman, G., Hayes, A., Kumar, S., & Laurenceau, J.-P. (2007). Mindfulness and emotion regulation: The development and initial validation of the cognitive and affective mindfulness scale-revised (CAMS-R). *Journal of Psychopathology and Behavioral Assessment, 29*, 177–190. doi:10.1007/s10862-006-9035-8

Frewen, P. A., Evans, E. M., Maraj, N., Dozois, D. J., & Partridge, K. (2008). Letting go: Mindfulness and negative automatic thinking. *Cognitive Therapy and Research, 32*, 758–774. doi:10.1007/s10608-007-9142-1

Gershy, N., Meehan, K. B., Omer, H., Papouchis, N., & Irit, S. S. (2017). Randomized clinical trial of mindfulness skills augmentation in parent training. *Child & Youth Care Forum, 46*, 783–803. doi:10.1007/s10566-017-9411-4

John, O. P., & Benet-Martinez, V. (2000). Measurement: Reliability, construct validation, and scale construction. In H. T. Reis and C. M. Judd (Eds.), *Handbook of research methods in social and personality psychology* (pp. 339–369). New York: Cambridge.

Kabat-Zinn, J. (1990). *Full catastrophe living: Using the wisdom of your body and mind to face stress, pain, and illness*. Bantam Doubleday Dell.

Kabat-Zinn, J. (2003). Mindfulness-based interventions in context: Past, present, and future. *Clinical Psychology: Science and Practice, 10*, 144–156. doi:10.1093/clipsy/bpg016

Langer, E. J., & Moldoveanu, M. (2002). The construct of mindfulness. *Journal of Social Issues*, *56*, 1–9. doi:10.1111/0022-4537.00148

LaParo, K. M., & Pianta, R. C. (2003). *CLASS: Classroom Assessment Scoring System.* University of Virginia Press.

Lau, M. A., Bishop, S. R., Segal, Z. V., Buis, T., Anderson, N. D., . . . Devins, G. (2006). The Toronto mindfulness scale: Development and validation. *Journal of Clinical Psychology*, *62*, 1445–1467. doi:10.1002/jclp.20326

MacKillop, J., & Anderson, E. J. (2007). Further psychometric validation of the mindful attention awareness scale (MAAS). *Journal of Psychopathology and Behavioral Assessment*, *29*, 289–293. doi:10.1007/s10862-007-9045-1

Mesmer-Magnus, J., Manapragada, A., Viswesvaran, C., & Allen, J. W. (2017). Trait mindfulness at work: A meta-analysis of the personal and professional correlates of trait mindfulness. *Human Performance*, *30*, 79–98. doi:10.1080/08959285.2017.1307842

Moore, R. C., Depp, C. A., Wetherell, J. L., & Lenze, E. J. (2016). Ecological momentary assessment versus standard assessment instruments for measuring mindfulness, depressed mood, and anxiety among older adults. *Journal of Psychiatric Research*, *75*, 116–123. doi:10.1016/j.jpsychires.2016.01.011

Parent, J., Mckee, L. G., Rough, J. N., & Forehand, R. (2016). The association of parent mindfulness with parenting and youth psychopathology across three developmental stages. *Journal of Abnormal Child Psychology*, *44*, 191–202. doi:10.1007/s10802-015-9978-x

Qu, Y. E., Dasborough, M. T., & Todorova, G. (2015). Which mindfulness measures to choose to use? *Industrial and Organizational Psychology*, *8*, 710–723. doi:10.1017/iop.2015.105

Rayan, A., & Ahmad, M. (2017). Effectiveness of mindfulness-based intervention on perceived stress, anxiety, and depression among parents of children with autism spectrum disorder. *Mindfulness*, *8*, 677–690. doi:10.1007/s12671-016-0595-8

Richards, D. (2013). *A randomized control study of brief mindfulness with undergraduates on self-compassion, mindfulness, and thought suppression* (Doctoral dissertation). Retrieved from ProQuest Information and Learning. (UMI 3562161)

Roeser, R. W., Skinner, E., Beers, J., & Jennings, P. A. (2012). Mindfulness training and teachers' professional development: An emerging area of research and practice. *Child Development Perspectives*, *6*, 167–173. doi:10.1111/j.1750-8606.2012.00238.x

Schmertz, S. K., Anderson, P. L., & Robins, D. L. (2009). The relation between self-report mindfulness and performance on tasks of sustained attention. *Journal of Psychopathology and Behavioral Assessment*, *31*, 60–66. doi:10.1007/s10862-008-9086-0

Shiffman, S., Stone, A. A., & Hufford, M. R. (2008). Ecological momentary assessment. *Annual Review of Clinical Psychology*, *4*, 1–32. doi:10.1146/annurev.clinpsy.3.022806.091415

Tanay, G., & Bernstein, A. (2013). State Mindfulness Scale (SMS): development and initial validation. *Psychological Assessment*, *25*, 1286–1299. doi:10.1037/a0034044

Tanay, G., Lotan, G., & Bernstein, A. (2012). Salutary proximal processes and distal mood and anxiety vulnerability outcomes of mindfulness training: A pilot preventive intervention. *Behavior Therapy*, *43*, 492–505. doi:10.1016/j.beth.2011.06.003

Taylor, C., Harrison, J., Haimovitz, K., Oberle, E., Thomson, K., Schonert-Reichl, K., & Roeser, R. W. (2016). Examining ways that a mindfulness-based intervention reduces stress in public school teachers: A mixed-methods study. *Mindfulness*, *7*, 115–129. doi:10.1007/s12671-015-0425-4

Thompson, B. L. & Waltz, J. (2007). Everyday mindfulness and mindfulness meditation: Overlapping constructs or not? *Personality and Individual Differences*, *43*, 1875–1885. doi:10.1016/j.paid.2007.06.017

Walach, H., Buchheld, N., Buttenmuller, V., Kleinknecht, N., & Schmidt, S. (2006). Measuring mindfulness—The Freiburg Mindfulness Inventory (FMI). *Personality and Individual Differences*, *40*, 1543–1555. doi:10.1016/j.paid.2005.11.025

Williams, J. M., & Kabat-Zinn, J. (2011). Mindfulness: Diverse perspectives on its meaning, origins, and multiple applications at the intersection of science and dharma. *Contemporary Buddhism*, *12*, 1–18. doi:10.1080/14639947.2011.564811

PART TWO

Approaches

6

Mindfulness-Based Stress Reduction for Youth and Students

LINDSEY WEBB AND ERICA M. S. SIBINGA ■

Mindfulness-based stress reduction (MBSR) is one of the most well-researched and well-established mindfulness programs used in the West. Created by Jon Kabat-Zinn in 1979, MBSR was developed as an adjunct to allopathic treatment for adults with chronic pain (Kabat-Zinn, 1982; Kabat-Zinn, 1990). Adult MBSR programs consist of 8 weekly sessions, with a duration of approximately 2.5 hours per session, include a day-long retreat, and recommend the use of mindfulness practices by participants at home for about 45 minutes a day, 6 days per week for the duration of the program and beyond (Kabat-Zinn, 1990). The goal of the MBSR program is to enhance participants' innate capacity for mindfulness, which can be described as non-judgmental awareness of present-moment experience. MBSR program content includes learning about the mind-body connection, experiential instruction in a variety of mindfulness meditation practices, and discussing the potential barriers to using mindfulness practices in the participants' daily lives (Grossman et al., 2004; Kabat-Zinn, 1990). Formal mindfulness practices that are typically taught in MBSR include breath awareness meditation, walking meditation, meditation on sound, the body scan, gentle yoga, and loving-kindness meditation (Kabat-Zinn, 1990).

Since its creation, MBSR has been expanded to and studied in adult populations dealing with other chronic conditions, such as cancer (e.g., Carlson et al., 2023; Speca et al., 2000), heart disease (e.g., Tacon et al., 2003), and fibromyalgia (e.g., Grossman et al., 2007). Several meta-analyses have been conducted to synthesize

Lindsey Webb and Erica M. S. Sibinga, *Mindfulness-Based Stress Reduction for Youth and Students*. In: *Using Mindfulness to Promote Mental Health in Schools*. Edited by: Tyler L. Renshaw and Shane R. Jimerson, Oxford University Press.
 DOI: 10.1093/9780190880507.003.0006

the research on the impact of MBSR on the psychological health of adult populations. In meta-analyses of studies in healthy adults, those with chronic medical diseases, and other clinical populations, mindfulness-based interventions, such as MBSR, have been shown to have moderate to strong effects on reducing symptoms of depression, anxiety, stress, and pain (e.g., Bohlmeijer et al., 2010; Goyal et al., 2014; Khoury et al., 2015; Virgili, 2015). The purpose of this chapter is to provide information on current MBSR programs for youth and best practices for those who might be interested in implementing MBSR in a school setting. The following sections will review how MBSR impacts mental health and how it has been modified to fit the needs of students and youth. We will then discuss important issues of consideration when implementing MBSR in schools.

MBSR'S MECHANISMS OF EFFECT

The mechanisms of MBSR's salutatory effects in adults are not entirely clear, with different disciplines describing a variety of changes due to MBSR but no overarching, fully explanatory answer. Here, we will touch briefly on research on the mechanisms of MBSR's effect in adults. While this body of evidence is important, it is unclear how and if it applies to MBSR for children and youth, given the significant differences in development, psychology, neurobiology, and physiology between adults and youth. Currently, very little is known about MBSR's mechanism of effect in children and youth; thus, the best we can do is generalize from what is known about adults.

As mentioned earlier, there is robust evidence for MBSR's benefit related to common psychological symptoms of anxiety and depression (e.g., Goyal et al., 2014). Further, Jain and colleagues' (2007) RCT of mindfulness meditation compared to relaxation in 83 young adults shows that mindfulness meditation moderately reduces rumination, and that the decrease in rumination is at least partially responsible for the reduction in psychological distress. In addition, there is cumulative evidence to suggest that mindfulness-based interventions produce improvements in cognitive outcomes, such as attention regulation and executive function (e.g., see the meta-analysis by Chiesa et al., 2011).

The physiology of stress has been a focus of mindfulness research for many years and includes the body's hormonal and biochemical substances, immune and inflammatory mediators, and autonomic nervous system. A recent meta-analysis of the impact of mindfulness-based interventions on stress physiology shows a small to medium positive impact. In particular, this review identified 45 RCTs comparing mindfulness meditation to active control programs and found that meditation improved the following outcomes: cortisol, C-reactive protein, blood pressure, heart rate, triglycerides, and tumor necrosis factor-alpha (Pascoe et al., 2017).

In an attempt to better understand the impact of MBSR on mental health and well-being, there has been increasing attention on MBSR's impact on neurobiology and brain functioning.

A review of the research in adults shows that mindfulness practice is associated with changes in both specific areas of the brain (e.g., hippocampus and amygdala) as well as in how brain regions are connected to one another. These changes are observed even at rest in the default mode network, with evidence that mindfulness leads to changes in both executive function ("top-down") and emotional reactivity ("bottom-up") pathways (Marchand, 2014).

Britton and Sydnor (2015) posit that current research on the prefrontal cortex supports the theory that meditation can strengthen some functions of the prefrontal cortex. Specifically, they discuss the role of focused-attention meditation (i.e., paying direct, prolonged attention to a specific anchor) and open-monitoring meditation (i.e., prolonged attention to any and all stimuli that reach the senses). The content of MBSR training focuses on focused-attention meditation for the first four sessions, and then shifts to open-monitoring meditation techniques in the second half of the course (Santorelli & Kabat-Zinn, 2003). Research on these two types of meditation have linked them to areas of the prefrontal cortex, such as the dorsal attention system, the dorsal anterior cingulate cortex, and parts of the limbic system including the amygdala (Britton & Sydnor, 2015). Youth in middle childhood are tasked with balancing internal needs and goals with social expectations and rules that can sometimes be at odds with each other (Markus & Nurius, 1984). This development of self-regulation is extended into adolescence with testing of boundaries and development of personal identity (Steinberg et al., 2018). Hypofrontality, or reduced self-regulation, can lead to a host of negative outcomes later in life. The prefrontal cortex develops in youth until approximately age 25, making it susceptible to both positive and negative stimuli affecting its development. Mindfulness meditations commonly used in MBSR aim to decrease hypofrontality and increase self-regulation (Britton & Sydnor, 2015).

FOCUSING MBSR ON YOUTH AND STUDENTS

Given the strong evidence base for MBSR's positive impact on psychological outcomes and functioning in adults (described earlier), mindfulness programming for children and youth has become increasingly popular over the past 10 years. Studies of MBSR for youth have focused on programming for those approximately 10–20 years old. This developmental period of middle childhood through early adulthood will be the focus of this chapter. The following sections will discuss how MBSR has been modified for implementation within schools and provides examples of prior successful MBSR programs. Moreover, we will discuss the evidence for school-based MBSR.

Modifying MBSR for Youth

MBSR is a highly structured, evidence-based mindfulness program, with recommended instructor training and a published facilitator guide for adult programs (Santorelli et al., 2003). To address the specific developmental needs of children and adolescents, some common modifications have been made to the implementation of MBSR. Typically, individual sessions are shortened from the adult program (2.5 hours) to both adapt to youths' attention spans and to fit into schools' class schedules. For school programs with much shorter classes, additional sessions are usually added to ensure that all key concepts are reviewed with students. Depending on the age of the students, sessions are more experiential and less didactic than adult programs, with age-appropriate activities and more concrete language to express mindfulness concepts. Finally, content and examples may be modified to be more relatable to students and the overall culture and climate of the school. For example, discussion of celebrities who use mindfulness, like Kobe Bryant and Russell Simmons, can be given to students as motivating examples, along with the incorporation of culturally relevant writings and poetry/lyrics, like JusTme's song "D.F.Y.L. (Don't Flip Your Lid)." All of these adjustments to the MBSR curriculum are important to make the program acceptable for youth, and to meet them where they are developmentally and culturally.

MBSR Adapted for Youth

One youth MBSR program with strong research support for participant benefit has come from the Johns Hopkins School of Medicine in Baltimore, Maryland. The program was first adapted from MBSR in 2006 for use with clinical populations, specifically HIV-infected and at-risk adolescents (Sibinga et al., 2008; Sibinga et al., 2011), with school-based programming starting in 2009 (Sibinga et al., 2013; Sibinga et al., 2016). Adaptation of the MBSR curriculum for youth was conducted iteratively by racially diverse, well-trained, and experienced MBSR instructors, leading to a culturally sensitive, trauma-informed curriculum. While the structure, content, and sequence of the curriculum remained relatively unchanged from the original (adult) version of MBSR, there was a need to adjust the program language and logistics. Consistent with the youth's developmental stage, the language of the course was made more concrete and straightforward, without changing the underlying concepts or ideas. Some examples of the logistics that were modified are starting with very brief mindfulness practices of a few minutes and building over subsequent classes to 20+ minute practices, shortening class duration (to 8 2-hour sessions plus 1 3-hour retreat in the clinic setting; 12 ~50-minute sessions in the school setting), and providing snacks (Sibinga et al., 2011; Sibinga et al., 2013).

The youth MBSR program has been found to be beneficial for HIV-infected and at-risk youth in clinical settings. Randomized controlled trials (RCTs) comparing the MBSR program (eight weekly two-hour sessions and one three-hour retreat) with a matched age-appropriate health education program have found that MBSR participants showed large improvements in psychological functioning and coping, conflict avoidance and reduced aggression, enhanced self-regulation, improved cognitive accuracy in emotional settings, and improved HIV medication adherence (Kerrigan et al., 2018; Sibinga et al., 2011, 2014, 2022; Webb et al., 2018). Further, participant responses to post-intervention interviews showed that youth used program techniques in ways that are meaningful and behaviorally advantageous from their perspective. For example, in reference to the program, one youth participant said, "I've actually practiced it the other day. I was about to get in an argument. I just sat there and I took three breaths and did my own little counting in my head and took three more breaths. And I was actually calm and left the argument—just let it be" (Sibinga et al., 2014, p. 216). Not only does this illustrate the participant's mindfulness skill of noticing a stressful moment and implementing a brief mindfulness technique, it also shows the preferred choice to leave the argument and illustrates how this choice felt positive to the participant.

This version of the MBSR program has also been adapted to and studied in school settings, consisting of 12 weekly 50-minute sessions to fit the school schedule. An initial pilot RCT of 41 middle-school male students randomly assigned participants to either the MBSR or an age-appropriate, time- and attention-matched general health education program. Findings from the study support the effectiveness of the MBSR program in improving psychological functioning, by moderately decreasing rumination and strongly impacting anxiety symptoms, as well as reducing the stress hormone salivary cortisol's rise at borderline significance among MBSR participants (Sibinga et al., 2013).

A subsequent, larger RCT (n = 300) was conducted in Baltimore City Public Schools. The adapted MBSR course was taught by two racially diverse, trained, and experienced MBSR instructors, who met weekly to discuss challenges and ensure the smooth implementation of the program across schools. The health education control program was taught by racially diverse, trained, and experienced health educators. Like the previous implementation in schools (Sibinga et al., 2013), the MBSR curriculum included 12 weekly sessions in both study arms. However, class session times ranged from 45 to 75 minutes, depending on the time allotted by the individual school. With this implementation, additional concrete activities were added to the curriculum. For example, the "mind jar" activity involved students filling jars with water and glitter to metaphorically demonstrate thoughts swirling in a stressed and active mind (i.e., a shaken jar), compared to the calming of thoughts once the jar is still and allowed to settle down. Analysis of the first year of the program implemented in two public schools shows a small but significant benefit for the MBSR participants, with improved psychological functioning (Sibinga et al., 2016). Specifically, students in the MBSR program (compared to students in the general health class) had lower depression symptoms, hostility, negative emotions, rumination, maladaptive coping strategies, somatization, and post-traumatic stress disorder symptoms (Sibinga et al., 2016). This program illustrates how specific adaptations can be made to MBSR to fit into the school setting and to address developmental needs of students, while maintaining the core conceptual and practice components of the original (adult) MBSR curriculum. By maintaining the core MBSR components, this adapted program has demonstrated the ability to significantly improve mental health and self-regulation in students and youth in urban settings.

An MBSR program for youth called MBSR for Teens (MBSR-T) has also been shown to be acceptable and effective. In a RCT of 102 youth in outpatient psychiatric care, MBSR-T participants showed significant improvement in self-reported outcomes compared to treatment-as-usual, including strong impacts on anxiety, depression, and somatic distress, a moderate impact on self-esteem, and a small impact on sleep quality. Additionally, MBSR-T participants were more likely to have significant improvements in the severity of their diagnoses (Biegel et al., 2009). Like the other MBSR programs for youth (described earlier), MBSR-T was designed to address the challenges that are unique to adolescence, and made similar logistic modifications (e.g., shortened session duration, removal of the day-long retreat; Biegel et al., 2009).

Learning to BREATHE

Another popular MBSR-based program for schools, Learning to BREATHE (L2B), was created to address emotion regulation in adolescence (Broderick, 2013). While the curriculum is based on MBSR, it centers on six lessons built around the BREATHE acronym: body awareness (Body); understanding and working with thoughts (Reflections); understanding and working with feelings (Emotions); integrating awareness of thoughts, feelings, and bodily sensations (Attention); reducing harmful self-judgments (Tenderness); and integrating mindful awareness into daily life (Healthy habits; Bluth et al., 2016; Metz et al., 2013). The L2B program has been offered in private, public, residential, and alternative schools (Broderick & Frank, 2014; Eva & Thayer, 2017). The 6 lessons in the L2B curriculum can be presented in 6, 12, or 18 sessions, and each lesson includes several group activities and opportunities for in-class mindfulness meditation (Broderick & Frank, 2014; Broderick & Metz, 2009). As with other MBSR-based programs, students in the L2B program typically receive a workbook and a CD to promote home practice (Broderick & Metz, 2009).

One study of the L2B program took place in a private high school for girls in suburban Pennsylvania (Broderick & Metz, 2009). Girls in the senior class were given the L2B program and were compared to girls in the junior class who received their usual school courses. For this implementation of the program, 6 sessions were given twice a week, with each session length ranging from 32 to 43 minutes. Results from the study of this program showed that the girls in the L2B condition had moderately lower negative mood at the end of the program than the junior girls in the education-as-usual condition. Additionally, girls in the L2B condition had moderately higher feelings of relaxation, self-acceptance, and calmness than girls in the junior class (Broderick & Metz, 2009). Although this study is suggestive of program benefit, there are substantial study design limitations, such as the lack of participant randomization and potential confounding of both age and differences between tasks and stresses of junior and senior years in high school. Thus, these findings should be interpreted cautiously.

L2B has also been tested in smaller studies of minority and at-risk youth populations. Results from these studies have shown feasibility and acceptability, and some preliminary support for the effectiveness of the program in slightly lowering internalizing and externalizing problems (Fung et al., 2016), and, in a small RCT with an active control, largely impacting depressive symptoms (Bluth et al., 2016). Taken together, these findings show that L2B is a feasible and acceptable MBSR-based program that is likely to have psychological benefit.

Additional School-Based MBSR Programs

A number of other modified MBSR programs have been implemented in schools, including .b (Kuyken et al., 2013; see Chapter 14), Breathing Awareness Meditation (BAM: Barnes et al., 2004), and MindfulKids (Weijer-Bergsma et al., 2014). The amount of research support for these programs vary considerably; however, the body of research on these programs continues to grow. The popularity of school-based MBSR programs has spread internationally, with programs being implemented in schools in India (Anand & Sharma, 2011; Anila & Dhanalakshmi, 2016), the UK (Bennett & Dorjee, 2016), and Australia (Johnson et al., 2016). Despite the popularity of these MBSR-based programs, more research is needed to evaluate program implementation and real-world effectiveness.

Reviews Support School-Based MBSR

Meta-analyses examining school-based mindfulness programs serve to pool results to reveal overarching findings in the body of research literature. A meta-analysis of mindfulness programs for youth found that, while all mindfulness programs had small effect sizes, MBSR-based programs have a greater effect size than other mindfulness intervention types (Zoogman et al., 2015). Additionally, a meta-analysis examining impacts of MBSR on anxiety symptoms among youth samples (primarily implemented in schools) found that MBSR significantly reduced anxiety symptoms compared to control conditions (Zhou et al., 2020). And in another review of school-based mindfulness programs, MBSR was listed as the mindfulness-based intervention with the greatest amount of empirical support for its effectiveness (Felver et al., 2016). However, this review underscored a critical issue in the research on MBSR in schools—specifically, that research has not yet been conducted to understand the specific components of the original MBSR program for adults that are effective in addressing stress and mental well-being. Moreover, with the translation of the original (adult) version of MBSR to multiple versions suitable for youth in school, it is difficult to know whether a component analysis of these adapted programs would be a representative test of the original MBSR components (Felver et al., 2016). Regardless, it seems safe to conclude that school-based MBSR programs have benefited by basing their curricula and programming on the original, evidence-based MBSR program for adults.

CONSIDERATIONS WHEN IMPLEMENTING MBSR IN SCHOOLS

When implementing MBSR within a school setting, many logistical factors need to be considered. Selection of individuals to teach MBSR programs to students should be handled with care and considerable attention to a potential instructor's experience with mindfulness and with working with youth in school settings. For the most part, MBSR-based programs for youth are led by instructors who have gone through formal training in the adult MBSR curriculum, such as from the Center for Mindfulness at the University of Massachusetts Medical School, the University of California at San Diego, or Brown University. Additionally, it is felt to be important that the instructor have an established personal mindfulness practice to enhance his or her own capacity to provide astute moment-to-moment mindfulness instruction. By having this consistent firsthand experience with mindfulness practices being taught to youth, the instructor can better articulate the potential challenges and benefits of a particular practice. Also, understanding child and adolescent development and learning styles can be crucial to an instructor's ability to effectively communicate, teach, and, perhaps most importantly, model mindfulness practices to youth. Being able to translate and inhabit mindfulness-related concepts in a way that resonates with students is likely vital to the success of MBSR-based programming in schools.

As an extension of this ability to embody and translate mindfulness, when implementing an MBSR program in schools, culture should be taken into account, including that of individual students, classrooms, and schools as a whole. Considering what background and experiences students are bringing with them into the classroom is important when instructors are asking youth to self-reflect. For example, trauma history has been a focus of concern in mindfulness and meditation literature and should be handled with care and expertise (Treleaven, 2018). Many of the schools in which the adapted MBSR program has been studied are in low-income, urban areas, where many students face chronic stressors and may have experienced trauma. One small adjustment made to in-class sessions is to offer students an option of gently resting their eyes on the horizon, if they did not feel comfortable closing their eyes during practices. Another modification is having instructors being aware of youths' relative positioning for yoga or body work to prevent students from ending up in uncomfortable or vulnerable positions as a posture unfolds, for example having students face inward in a circle for sun salutation or downward dog practices. These examples are not the only adjustments that can or should be made when implementing MBSR in schools. We also recommend that instructors be trained to recognize the signs of trauma as well as how to appropriately handle students expressing trauma symptoms, so they can better meet students where they are and create a safe environment for reflection and mindfulness meditation practices. Instructors should also apply cultural awareness to the examples or activities being utilized with students. For example, instructors would do well to ask themselves: Can a student relate to the individuals pictured in student workbooks? Are the references to pop culture or examples of stressors included in the curriculum easily recognized by students? One way to ensure cultural relevance and appropriateness is to do a focus group with students or have teachers and parents from the school look through the MBSR curriculum and give feedback prior to implementation.

In addition to the cultural background of individual students, there is the climate of the classroom and the school to consider. Successful MBSR groups are based on creating a safe space in which to practice mindfulness and have discussion about the skills being taught. As one might imagine, many times the environment in a classroom and that of a mindfulness retreat can be at extreme odds. Stressed teachers, rows of desks, and strict consequences for rule infractions can run counter to creating a space that supports reducing stress and supporting open awareness in youth. If the MBSR instructor is not the classroom teacher, then creating a respectful working relationship with the classroom teacher is key to creating a successful MBSR group. Prioritizing communication with teachers will help MBSR instructors to better understand classroom rules and incorporate them, along with the teacher's support, into the group (e.g., getting permission to move desks into a circle). If a MBSR program is bringing in instructors from outside the school to implement the program, respect for the teacher and their space is very important. Teachers put great amounts of time and thought into creating a learning environment for their students that is stable from day to day. It is therefore wise and respectful to ask teachers if things in their classroom can be moved, written on, or used prior to doing so. It can be a good idea to involve the teacher in MBSR sessions as well, as often times teachers will report that they would like to learn more about the stress reduction techniques being taught to students. Cultivating a positive relationship between MBSR instructors and teachers is also key to addressing any behavioral issues that may arise among students during the course of intervention, and in creating a group that can both adequately teach MBSR and comfortably fit within the classroom's routine.

Finally, the optimal mode of delivery for MBSR programs in schools is a growing question. Most often, programs that have proven effective are provided by a trained MBSR instructor, who implements the curriculum face-to-face with students. However, hiring enough instructors with the appropriate training and experience to serve multiple classrooms or an entire school can be difficult and expensive. Moreover, integrating additional in-person programming into the school day typically means that schools need to shift their curriculum for students receiving the extra program. At times, these scheduling concerns could be addressed by offering the MBSR programming before or after school. However, this option may not be feasible for all students or their parents.

Another way to address these scheduling issues is to have an online MBSR-based program for schools. One such program founded on the core concepts of MBSR is Inner Explorer, which includes programs for preschool through kindergarten, elementary school, and middle school (Bakosh et al., 2016; Semple et al., 2017). Unlike typical in-person MBSR programs, Inner Explorer includes eight weeks of daily sessions that are only about five to ten minutes in length. Each session is pre-recorded and played by the classroom teacher, eliminating need for outside mindfulness instructors (Bakosh et al., 2016). This online-based intervention format also allows for a greater amount of flexibility, as classroom teachers can choose when to implement the recordings into their class schedule (Semple et al., 2017). In a pilot study of the Inner Explorer program, some preliminary support was found for the program's effectiveness in improving science and reading grades (Bakosh et al., 2016). Despite the obvious feasibility benefits of this type of delivery format, it is important to remember that it is not yet known how the impact of an MBSR-based program may change with the absence of a trained instructor. Moreover, it is unclear how other logistical differences (i.e., shorter sessions) may impact the effect of MBSR on youth outcomes (Semple et al., 2017). Further research is therefore needed to understand the components of MBSR that are effective for improving youth mental health, and how those components may be adjusted to differing populations and settings while maintaining their effectiveness.

CONCLUSIONS

MBSR adapted for students and youth has shown significant and salient benefit for improving mental and behavioral health in a number of research studies. Implemented in age- and culturally appropriate ways, MBSR can be considered an evidence-based, trauma-informed approach to improving youths' mental health, coping, and well-being. It is plausible that teaching mindfulness practices and concepts during childhood and adolescence may reduce the negative impact of stress and trauma experienced during youth (Whitaker et al., 2014), which could have long-lasting impact on adult physical and mental health (Ortiz & Sibinga, 2017). Further, empowering youth with mindfulness skills they can use to de-escalate confrontation has the potential to reduce conflicts and their negative residua more broadly and over time. Despite the significant potential for benefit, there is need for continued and on-going rigorous assessment of MBSR-based programming with students and youth, especially as it relates to component analyses, cultural adaptations, and other implementation issues (e.g., in-person versus technology-based program delivery).

REFERENCES

Anand, U., & Sharma, M. P. (2011). Impact of a mindfulness-based stress reduction program on stress and well-being in adolescents: A study at a school setting. *Journal of Indian Association for Child and Adolescent Mental Health*, *7*(3), 79–97.

Anila, M. M., & Dhanalakshmi, D. (2016). Mindfulness based stress reduction for reducing anxiety, enhancing self-control and improving academic performance among adolescent students. *Indian Journal of Positive Psychology*, *7*(4), 390–397. doi: 10.15614/ijpp%2F2016%2Fv7i4%2F133842

Bakosh, L. S., Snow, R. M., Tobias, J. M., Houlihan, J. L., & Barbosa-Leiker, C. (2016). Maximizing mindful learning: Mindful awareness intervention improves elementary school students' quarterly grades. *Mindfulness*, *7*, 59–67. doi: 10.1007/s12671-015-0387-6

Barnes, V. A., Davis, H. C., Murzynowski, J. B., & Treiber, F. A. (2004). Impact of meditation on resting and ambulatory blood pressure and heart rate in youth. *Psychosomatic Medicine*, *66*, 909–914. doi: 10.1097/01.psy.0000145902.91749.35

Bennett, K., & Dorjee, D. (2016). The impact of a mindfulness-based stress reduction course (MBSR) on well-being and academic attainment of sixth-form students. *Mindfulness*, *7*, 105–114. doi: 10.1007/s12671-015-0430-7

Biegel, G. M., Brown, K. W., Shapiro, S. L., & Schubert, C. M. (2009). Mindfulness-based stress reduction for the treatment of adolescent psychiatric outpatients: A randomized clinical trial. *Journal of Consulting and Clinical Psychology*, *77*(5), 855–866. doi: 10.1037/a0016241

Bluth, K., Campo, R. A., Pruteanu-Malinici, S., Reams, A., Mullarkey, M., & Broderick, P. A. (2016). A school-based mindfulness pilot study for ethnically diverse at-risk adolescents. *Mindfulness*, *7*(1), 90–104. doi: 10.1007/s12671-014-0376-1

Bohlmeijer, E., Prenger, R., Taal, E., & Cuijpers, P. (2010). The effects of mindfulness-based stress reduction therapy on mental health of adults with chronic medical disease: A meta-analysis. *Journal of Psychosomatic Research*, *68*, 539–544. doi: 10.1016/j.jpsychores.2009.10.005

Britton, W., & Sydnor, A. (2015). Neurobiological models of meditation practices: Implications for applications with youth. In C. Willard & A. Salzman (Eds.), *Teaching mindfulness skills to kids and teens* (pp. 402–426). Guilford Press.

Broderick, P. (2013). *Learning to BREATHE: A mindfulness curriculum for adolescents to cultivate emotion regulation, attention, and performance*. New Harbinger Press.

Broderick, P. C., & Frank, J. L. (2014). Learning to BREATHE: An intervention to foster mindfulness in adolescence. *New Directions for Youth Development*, *2014*(142), 31–44. doi: 10.1002/yd.20095

Broderick, P. C., & Metz, S. (2009). Learning to BREATHE: A pilot trial of a mindfulness curriculum for adolescents. *Advances in School Mental Health Promotion*, *2*(1), 35–46. doi: 10.1080/1754730X.2009.9715696

Carlson, L. E., Ismaila, N., Addington, E. L., Asher, G. N., Atreya, C., Balneaves, L. G., Bradt, J., Fuller-Shavel, N., Goodman, J., Hoffman, C. J., Huston, A. (2021, October 1). Integrative oncology care of symptoms of anxiety and depression in adults with cancer: Society for integrative oncology–ASCO guideline. *Journal of Clinical Oncology*, *41*(28):4562–4591.

Chiesa, A., Calati, R., & Serretti, A. (2011). Does mindfulness training improve cognitive abilities? A systematic review of neuropsychological findings. *Clinical Psychology Review*, *31*(3), 449–464. doi:10.1016/j.cpr.2010.11.003

Eva, A. L., & Thayer, N. M. (2017). Learning to BREATHE: A pilot study of a mindfulness-based intervention to support marginalized youth. *Journal of Evidence-Based Complementary & Alternative Medicine*, *22*(4), 580–591. doi:10.1177/2156587217696928

Felver, J. C., Hoyos, C. E. C., Tezanos, K., & Singh, N. N. (2016). A systematic review of mindfulness-based interventions for youth in school settings. *Mindfulness*, *7*, 34–45. doi: 10.1007/s12671-015-0389-4

Fung, J., Guo, S., Jin, J., Bear, L., & Lau, A. (2016). A pilot randomized trial evaluating a school-based mindfulness intervention for ethnic minority youth. *Mindfulness*, *7*(4), 819–828. doi: 10.1007/s12671-016-0519-7

Goyal, M., Singh, S., Sibinga, E. M. S., Gould, N. F., Rowland-Seymour, A., Sharma, R. . . . Haythornthwaite, J. A. (2014). Meditation programs for psychological stress and well-being: A systematic review and meta-analysis. *JAMA Internal Medicine, 174*(3), 357–368. doi: 10.1001/jamainternmed.2013.13018

Grossman, P., Niemann, L., Schmidt, S., & Walach, H. (2004). Mindfulness-based stress reduction and health benefits: A meta-analysis. *Journal of Psychosomatic Research, 57*(1), 35–43. doi: 10.1016/S0022-3999(03)00573-7

Grossman, P., Tiefenthaler-Gilmer, U., Raysz, A., & Kesper, U. (2007). Mindfulness training as an intervention for fibromyalgia: Evidence of postintervention and 3-year follow-up benefits in well-being. *Psychotherapy and Psychosomatics, 76*(4), 226–233. doi: 10.1159/000101501

Jain, S., Shapiro, S. L., Swanick, S., Roesch, S. C., Mills, P. J., Bell, I., & Schwartz, G. E. (2007). A randomized controlled trial of mindfulness meditation versus relaxation training: Effects on distress, positive states of mind, rumination, and distraction. *Annals of Behavioral Medicine, 33*(1), 11–21. doi:10.1207/s15324796abm3301_2

Johnson, C., Burke, C., Brinkman, S., & Wade, T. (2016). Effectiveness of a school-based mindfulness program for transdiagnostic prevention in young adolescents. *Behaviour Research and Therapy, 81*, 1–11. doi: 10.1016/j.brat.2016.03.002

Kabat-Zinn, J. (1982). An outpatient program in behavioral medicine for chronic pain patients based on the practice of mindfulness meditation: Theoretical considerations and preliminary results. *General Hospital Psychiatry, 4*(1), 33–47.

Kabat-Zinn, J. (1990). *Full catastrophe living: Using the wisdom of your body and mind to face stress, pain, and illness*. Bantam Books.

Kerrigan, D., Grieb, S. M., Ellen, J., Sibinga, E. (2018, November 2). Exploring the dynamics of ART adherence in the context of a mindfulness instruction intervention among youth living with HIV in Baltimore, Maryland. *AIDS Care, 30*(11):1400–1405.

Khoury, B., Sharma, M., Rush, S. E., & Fournier, C. (2015). Mindfulness-based stress reduction for healthy individuals: A meta-analysis. *Journal of Psychosomatic Research, 78*, 519–528. doi: 10.1016/j.jpsychores.2015.03.009

Kuyken, W., Weare, K., Ukoumunne, O. C., Vicary, R., Motton, N., Burnett, R. . . . Huppert, F. (2013). Effectiveness of the mindfulness in schools programme: Non-randomised controlled feasibility study. *The British Journal of Psychiatry, 203*, 126–131. doi: 10.1192/bjp.bp.113.126649

Marchand, W. R. (2014). Neural mechanisms of mindfulness and meditation: Evidence from neuroimaging studies. *World Journal of Radiology, 6*(7), 471–479. doi:10.4329/wjr.v6.i7.471

Markus, H. J., & Nurius, P. S. (1984). Self-understanding and self-regulation in middle childhood. In W. A. Collins (Ed.), *Development during middle childhood: The years from six to twelve* (pp. 147–183). National Academy Press.

Metz, S. M., Frank, J. L., Reibel, D., Cantrell, T., Sanders, R., & Broderick, P. C. (2013). The effectiveness of the Learning to BREATHE program on adolescent emotion regulation. *Research in Human Development, 10*(3), 252–272. doi: 10.1080/15427609.2013.818488

Ortiz, R., & Sibinga, E. (2017). The role of mindfulness in reducing the adverse effects of childhood stress and trauma. *Children, 4*(3), 16. doi:10.3390/children4030016

Pascoe, M. C., Thompson, D. R., Jenkins, Z. M., & Ski, C. F. (2017). Mindfulness mediates the physiological markers of stress: Systematic review and meta-analysis. *Journal of Psychiatric Research, 95*, 156–178. doi:10.1016/j.jpsychires.2017.08.004

Santorelli, S. F., & Kabat-Zinn, J. (2003). *MBSR curriculum guide and supporting materials: Mindfulness-based stress reduction professional training*. Center for Mindfulness.

Semple, R. J., Droutman, V., & Reid, B. A. (2017). Mindfulness goes to school: Things learned (so far) from research and real-world experiences. *Psychology in the Schools*, *54*(1), 29–51. doi: 10.1002/pits.21981

Sibinga, E. M. S., Kerrigan, D., Stewart, M., Johnson, K., Magyari, T., & Ellen, J. M. (2011). Mindfulness-based stress reduction for urban youth. *The Journal of Alternative and Complementary Medicine*, *17*(3), 213–218. doi: 10.1089/acm.2009.0605

Sibinga, E., Perry-Parrish, C., Chung, S., Johnson, S. B., Smith, M., & Ellen, J. M. (2013). School-based mindfulness instruction for urban male youth: A small randomized controlled trial. *Preventive Medicine*, *57*, 799–801. doi: 10.1016/j.ypmed.2013.08.027

Sibinga, E. M., Perry-Parrish, C., Thorpe, K., Mika, M., & Ellen, J. M. (2014). A small mixed-method RCT of mindfulness instruction for urban youth. *Explore*, *10*(3), 180–186. doi: 10.1016/j.explore.2014.02.006

Sibinga, E., Stewart, M., Magyari, T., Welsh, C. K., Hutton, N., & Ellen, J. M. (2008). Mindfulness-based stress reduction for HIV-infected youth: A pilot study. *Explore*, *4*(1), 36–37. doi:10.1016/j.explore.2007.10.002

Sibinga, E. M. S., Webb, L., Ghazarian, S., & Ellen, J. M. (2016). School-based mindfulness instruction: An RCT. *Pediatrics*, *137*(1), 1–8. doi: 10.1542/peds.2015-2532

Sibinga E. M., Webb L., Perin J., Tepper V., Kerrigan D., Grieb S., Denison J., Ellen J. (2022, December 2). Mindfulness instruction for medication adherence among adolescents and young adults living with HIV: A randomized controlled trial. *AIDS Care*. 2022, *34*(12), 1619–1627.

Speca, M., Carlson, L. E., Goodey, E., & Angen, M. (2000). A randomized, wait-list controlled clinical trial: The effect of a mindfulness meditation-based stress reduction program on mood and symptoms of stress in cancer outpatients. *Psychosomatic Medicine*, *62*(5), 613–622. doi:10.1097/00006842-20009000-00004

Steinberg, L., Icenogle, G., Shulman, E. P., Breiner, K., Chein, J., Bacchini, D. . . . Takash, H. M. S. (2018). Around the world, adolescence is a time of heightened sensation seeking and immature self-regulation. *Developmental Science*, *21*(e12532), 1–13. doi: 10.1111/desc.12532

Tacon, A. M., McComb, J., Caldera, Y., & Randolph, P. (2003). Mindfulness meditation, anxiety reduction and heart disease: A pilot study. *Family and Community Health*, *26*(1), 25–33. doi:10.1097/00003727-200302000-00004

Treleaven, D. A. (2018). *Trauma-sensitive mindfulness: Practices for safe and transformative healing*. W.W. Norton & Company.

Virgili, M. (2015). Mindfulness-based interventions reduce psychological distress in working adults: A meta-analysis of intervention studies. *Mindfulness*, *6*, 326–337. doi: 10.1007/s12671-013-0264-0

Webb, L., Perry-Parrish, C., Ellen, J., & Sibinga, E. (2018). Mindfulness instruction for HIV- infected youth: A randomized controlled trial. *AIDS Care*, *30*(6), 688–695. doi:10.1080/09540121.2017.1394434

Weijer-Bergsma, E., Langenberg, G., Brandsma, R., Oort, F. J., & Bogels, S. M. (2014). The effectiveness of a school-based mindfulness training as a program to prevent stress in elementary school children. *Mindfulness*, *5*, 238–248. doi: 10.1007/s12671-012-0171-9

Whitaker, R. C., Dearth-Wesley, T., Gooze, R. A., Becker, B. D., Gallagher, K. C., McEwen, B. S. (2014, October 1). Adverse childhood experiences, dispositional mindfulness, and adult health. *Preventive Medicine*, *67*, 147–153.

Zhou, X., Guo, J., Lu, G., Chen, C., Xie, Z., Liu, J., & Zhang, C. (2020). Effects of mindfulness-based stress reduction on anxiety symptoms in young people: A systematic review and meta-analysis. *Psychiatry Research, 289*, 113002. doi: 10.1016/j.psychres.2020.113002

Zoogman, S., Goldberg, S. B., Hoyt, W. T., & Miller, L. (2015). Mindfulness interventions with youth: A meta-analysis. *Mindfulness*, *6*, 290–302. doi: 10.1007/s12671-013-0260-4

7

Mindfulness-Based Cognitive Therapy for Children

Cultivating Mental Health in Elementary Schools

MATTHEW S. GOODMAN AND RANDYE J. SEMPLE ■

Like the school playground at recess, the mind of a student can be a busy place. Thoughts whiz around like balls flying through the air; attention jumps from topic to topic, as if swinging from the monkey bars; a tug-of-war breaks out between conflicting emotions. Students with anxiety are especially prone to this chaotic mental landscape. They often ruminate excessively about the past and future, have difficulty paying attention, and become self-critical toward their thoughts and feelings. In 2020, more than 6.7 million children (9.2%) had been diagnosed with an anxiety disorder (Lebrun-Harris et al., 2022).

Children with anxiety have benefited from cognitive-behavioral therapies (CBT) by learning to identify, challenge, and restructure their thoughts. In doing so, they alter the content of their thinking. For example, a self-critical student might instead focus on thoughts that more realistically boost self-esteem. While CBT is effective for some, around 40% of youth with anxiety disorders do not respond well to traditional cognitive-behavioral interventions (James et al., 2015). Mindfulness-based therapies offer an alternative approach. Instead of changing the content of their thoughts, children change their relationship to them. Mindful attention aims to bring awareness to racing thoughts, focus the jumping "monkey mind," and step out of the tug-of-war with inner experiences. Instead of being caught up in the cognitive chaos of their "inner playgrounds," students observe it from a distance; then, they are free to make more skillful behavioral choices. Complementing mindfulness-based therapies with some CBT skills diversifies

Matthew S. Goodman and Randye J. Semple, *Mindfulness-Based Cognitive Therapy for Children*. In: *Using Mindfulness to Promote Mental Health in Schools*. Edited by: Tyler L. Renshaw and Shane R. Jimerson, Oxford University Press.
 DOI: 10.1093/9780190880507.003.0007

coping mechanisms and bolsters resiliency (Madni et al., 2019; Semple & Madni, 2015).

This chapter describes a mindfulness-based clinical intervention for children: Mindfulness-Based Cognitive Therapy for Children (MBCT-C; Semple & Lee, 2011). The chapter introduces MBCT-C to school-based mental health providers treating students with anxiety and other emotional or behavioral difficulties. This chapter begins with an overview of the foundations and core aims of MBCT-C, and then briefly reviews research support for its effectiveness. The chapter also includes a discussion of the implementation of MBCT-C in schools and offers a brief review of the 12-week program. One full session is described to illustrate the content of the program, along with a clinical vignette in which MBCT-C is implemented with a single anxious student. The chapter also includes a brief description of the Mindfulness Matters Program, which is a variation of MBCT-C that is intended for use in K-12 classrooms. The chapter concludes with a discussion of ways to support mindfulness practices among parents, teachers, and the broader school culture.

FOUNDATIONS OF MBCT-C AND ADAPTATIONS FROM ADULT MINDFULNESS PROGRAMS

MBCT-C was modeled on mindfulness-based stress reduction (MBSR; Kabat-Zinn, 1990) and Mindfulness-Based Cognitive Therapy (MBCT; Segal et al., 2013). While it shares a similar theoretical basis and aims, MBCT-C is developmentally appropriate for elementary- and middle-school-aged children. MBCT-C makes three fundamental distinctions between children and adults that inform its approach to teaching mindfulness. First, children are at an earlier level of cognitive and affective development. Their capacity to observe internal experiences with meta-cognitive awareness and use language to describe those experiences is still emerging (Gogtay et al., 2004). Second, children have less capacity for sustained attention than adults do. Third, children are more physically and emotionally dependent on parents, teachers, and other adult relationships.

To allow children an experiential understanding of mindfulness despite their less developed cognitive skills, MBCT-C teaches mindfulness through the five senses. Children develop concentration and present-focused awareness by paying attention to their moment-to-moment sensory experiences. They later reflect on these experiences using non-judgmental, descriptive language. To accommodate children's attentional capacity, clinic-based sessions are 90 minutes. In school settings, 45 minutes or less may be more appropriate. Longer periods of mindfulness practice are replaced with shorter activities that are repeated frequently. Children begin by experiencing three mindful breaths and eventually work up to 10 minutes or more of breath, body, or sensory-based mindfulness practices. Activities are lively and diversified, such as drawing and moving, to meet the energetic and creative needs of young children. Similar to CBT, MBCT-C includes weekly home practice assignments. Parental involvement with the child's home-based practices is strongly encouraged. Children take home summary information and home practice assignments after each session, so that parents can track progress and practice alongside their child. MBCT-C facilitators may choose to hold information and practice sessions for parents or adult caregivers.

MBCT-C CORE CONCEPTS AND AIMS

A key distinction between traditional cognitive approaches and contemporary mindfulness-based approaches is that children are not taught to change their thoughts. Attempts to alter the form or frequency of thoughts, emotions, or body sensations may actually amplify their intensity and lead to greater psychological suffering (Hayes et al., 2011; Wenzlaff & Wegner, 2000). Instead, in mindfulness-based approaches, children practice acceptance of thoughts and emotions just as they are. They learn that thoughts and emotions are not always facts. For example, a child with anxiety might have persistent thoughts about failing an upcoming test. Rather than engaging with the thoughts as evidence of reality or attempting to restructure their content, the child learns to "de-center" from them—she sees that thoughts are "just thoughts," that they do not always represent reality, and that they are always changing. Children also learn to pay attention to their tendencies to judge experiences as positive or negative. They practice becoming aware of their own judgmental thoughts and words, learning to observe and use more descriptive language to understand their experiences. Children discover that they have choices in how to respond to the events in their lives. Thus, the core aims of MBCT-C are to: (a) develop greater awareness of thoughts, feelings, and body sensations; (b) cultivate de-centering from thoughts and feelings; (c) distinguish judging from noting; and (d) learn to make more thoughtful choices when responding to people and events. Through these aims, facilitators guide children to experience thoughts as "just thoughts," better manage their emotional responses, and choose their behaviors with more intention and skill.

FIVE IMPORTANT POINTS OF MBCT-C

Five important points form the foundation of this approach. First, MBCT-C is not a spiritual practice. While mindfulness-based therapies have borrowed elements from Buddhist practices, there is nothing inherently religious or spiritual about MBCT-C. Children are taught simply to pay attention to the present moment and treat themselves and others with more kindness. Second, MBCT-C is not a conventional cognitive therapy. Cognitive approaches teach students to change their thoughts and behaviors; MBCT-C teaches children how to relate to their thoughts in a more wholesome way. Third, MBCT-C and traditional cognitive therapy are paradoxical models of acceptance and change. While MBCT-C integrates certain cognitive principles and practices, the notion that students can change through acceptance is not part of traditional cognitive approaches. Fourth, MBCT-C challenges the facilitator to be mindful of and abandon their own desire for change. This can be one of the most difficult, yet important, aspects of delivering MBCT-C, as mental health professionals are trained to help children change. Although acceptance and change are seemingly contradictory goals, acceptance (i.e., recognition of what is happening in each moment—which also changes moment-by-moment) is both a precursor to and a catalyst for change. Carl Rogers (1961) noted, "the curious paradox is that when I accept myself just as I am, then I can change" (p. 17). In MBCT-C, we use the word "acceptance" not as a passive resignation to fate, but rather as a wholehearted acceptance of what *is* in any given moment. We also recognize that what *is* changes from moment to moment. So, in order to accept the present moment, we must let go of the previous moment—and continue doing so, moment by moment. Essentially, in cultivating acceptance, we are practicing seeing clearly and letting go—over and over again. Lastly, MBCT-C offers facilitators opportunities to incorporate mindfulness into their own lives. Like the adult programs from which it is derived, the developers of MBCT-C strongly advocate that mindfulness must be understood experientially in order to be taught effectively. A facilitator's own mindfulness practice allows her to embody the interventions in ways that go beyond simply teaching the activities.

RESEARCH SUPPORT FOR MBCT-C

The initial open trial development study of MBCT-C demonstrated feasibility, acceptability, and reductions in internalizing and externalizing symptoms with children ages 7 and 8, albeit with a small sample ($n = 5$; Semple et al., 2005). A subsequent randomized controlled trial of the 12-session MBCT-C program with low-income, ethnic minority children found small to medium treatment effects for improved attention (Cohen's $d = .46$) and decreased behavior problems (Cohen's $d = .27$). A subgroup of youth ($n = 6$) with clinically elevated anxiety showed medium to large reductions in state anxiety (Cohen's $d = .64$), attentional problems (Cohen's $d = .60$), and behavioral problems (Cohen's $d = .69$; Semple et al., 2010). Findings from other studies suggest that MBCT-C may enhance emotional resiliency (Esmaeilian et al., 2018), reduce symptoms of anxiety and depression (Cotton et al., 2016; Esmaeilian et al., 2013, 2018; Jang & Shin, 2019; Syeda & Andrews, 2021), reduce bullying behaviors (Faraji et al., 2019), reduce internalizing problems (Wright et al., 2019), strengthen neural networks involved in interoception (i.e., awareness of internal body sensations) and social-emotional processing (Strawn et al., 2016), and enhance functional connectivity strength in the frontal and limbic areas of the brain in youth who are at risk for bipolar disorder (Qin et al., 2021). Positive effects of MBCT-C have been observed for youth presenting with a variety of behavioral health concerns, including traumatized children hospitalized for both psychiatric reasons (Kostova et al., 2019) and medical reasons (Abedini et al., 2020).

CONTEXT: HOW AND WHERE TO USE MBCT-C

Since MBCT-C is a clinical intervention, it is typically implemented by psychologists, school counselors, social workers, and other trained mental health professionals. MBCT-C is not a classroom program led by general education teachers (see the Mindfulness Matters Program section in this chapter for a classroom-friendly adaptation of MBCT-C). School-based clinicians can implement MBCT-C individually or as a group, during or after the school day. In a group setting, it is recommended to have about six to eight students. This allows for a diversity of experience to be shared while maintaining group intimacy. One or two adults can lead an MBCT-C group. While it may be desirable to assemble groups with homogenous clinical issues, this is usually not feasible or necessary, as mindfulness-based cognitive and social-emotional skills can be helpful in addressing a variety of clinical symptoms and behaviors.

Whether conducted individually or as a group, the facilitator is an active participant and is encouraged to share his own experiences of mindfulness activities. For example, the facilitator might share, "I noticed that my mind wandered while listening to sounds in the room. I also noticed that my mind judged the sound of the fan as 'annoying.' Then, after congratulating myself for noting this, I returned my attention again to experiencing sounds, moment-by-moment." As usual in any clinical group setting, facilitators cultivate a mindful space. This might mean using a dedicated room each week—setting it up with appropriate materials (e.g., yoga mats), or posting guidelines and other materials in the room. Ideally, MBCT-C groups are conducted with members sitting in a circle on the floor or in chairs. It is important to foster a sense of safety during sessions. Like other therapies, MBCT-C facilitators make clear the expectation that group discussions remain confidential.

The MBCT-C manual (Semple & Lee, 2011) lists suggested materials for each therapy session and includes printable session handouts (e.g., poems), session summaries, and home practice worksheets for each session. There are a few basic materials, however, that may be helpful for every facilitator to have. Examples of these include the following: yoga mats and firm pillows or cushions for sitting on the floor (e.g., a *zafu*), three-ring binders for handouts and homework, mindfulness bells (e.g., *tingsha* bells are a student favorite), and a "Worry Warts Wastebasket," which is a small container placed just inside the door of the therapy room. Students are encouraged to write down any worried thoughts they might be having—and then choose what to do with the pieces of paper over the course of the session: let go of them, pick them up on the way out, or leave them behind in the wastebasket.

OVERVIEW OF THE MBCT-C PROGRAM

MBCT-C is a 12-week program that is implemented once weekly. School-based facilitators will likely need to adapt MBCT-C to the school schedule, available resources, and student needs. For example, the facilitator might conduct 30-minute sessions over 36 weeks instead of 90-minute sessions over 12 weeks. He might substitute materials listed in the treatment manual for those readily available at school; images, scents, sounds, food, and other objects mentioned in the manual can all be creatively interchanged. Individual sessions can be tailored to each student's needs. Children differ in their attention spans, need for structure, ability to transition between activities, and rate of intellectual and experiential understanding of the material. Some children may thrive in a quiet classroom setting, while others may benefit from environments with more sensory stimulation (e.g., using pillows, blankets, hammocks, or conducting the groups outdoors). All students will also learn better in an environment where they feel safe.

The aims of the initial phase of MBCT-C (sessions 1–3) are to introduce mindfulness, establish program expectations, review guidelines for participation, and address barriers to home practice. Students also learn to cultivate mindfulness of the breath and body. The middle phase of MBCT-C (sessions 4–10) focuses on teaching mindful awareness through the senses (sights, sounds, tastes, smells, and touch). Students learn to differentiate thoughts, feelings, and body sensations. They learn to notice habitual reactions and automatic judgments and practice approaching their experiences with curiosity and acceptance. Students use descriptive, non-judgmental language to identify objects of attention. They learn that they can choose how to respond to situations. The termination phase of MBCT-C (sessions 11–12) focuses on maintaining and integrating mindfulness into everyday life. Following each experiential activity, the facilitator—drawing from her own experiences of mindfulness—leads guided inquiries to help encourage reflection and enhance learning. Three-minute mindful breathing practices and basic mindful movements are done at the beginning and end of most sessions.

The following section provides a brief description of the primary aims and interventions for each session. Table 7.1 provides an overview of the theme, key points, mindfulness activities, session handouts, and home practices for each of the 12 sessions.

Session 1: Being on Automatic Pilot

The opening session begins with getting to know the group members, then establishing group guidelines, and providing an overview of the program. Fostering a sense of safety and cohesiveness is a key aim of the first session. Students are introduced to the concepts of mindfulness and being on "autopilot." The facilitator elicits autopilot-like experiences from the children, for example, eating breakfast while watching television and then not remembering what was just eaten. Students are challenged to cultivate present-moment awareness by passing half-filled and full cups of water back and forth. They are introduced to mindfulness of the breath through a brief breathing activity. Facilitators engage students in a writing activity using the prompt "draw whatever mindfulness means to you." Students may place this artwork on the front of their binders. The same activity will be repeated at the end of the program (Session 11).

Table 7.1. Overview of the 12-Session MBCT-C Program

	Session and Theme	Key Points	In-Session Practices	Poems, Stories, and Other Handouts	Home Practices
1	Being on Automatic Pilot	• We live much of our lives on automatic pilot • Mindfulness exists, and it is a different, more helpful way of being in the world	• Getting to Know You • Discovering Awareness in a Cup • What Mindfulness Means to Me • Taking Three Mindful Breaths	• Mindful Breathing Is the Best Practice • Mindfulness Is Cultivating Attention	• Mindful Breathing Lying Down • Mindful Breathing Sitting Up • Living with Awareness
2	Being Mindful Is Simple, But It Is Not Easy!	• Living with awareness isn't easy, so why are we doing this anyway? • We give attention to the barriers to practice • Understanding the importance of practice • Bringing awareness to the breath and body	• Taking Three Mindful Breaths • Raisin Mindfulness • Mindfully Moooving Sloowly • Taking Three Mindful Breaths	• Flight from the Shadow • Practicing Mindful Awareness • Instructions for Mindful Breathing	• Living with Awareness • Mindful Breathing • Mindful Eating

continued

Table 7.1. Continued

3	Who Am I?	• Thoughts arise in the present, but are often about the past or future • Thoughts may not be accurate to the present reality • Thoughts are not facts	• Taking Three Mindful Breaths • Mindfulness of the Body • Hey, I Have Thoughts, Feelings, and Body Sensations! • Listening to the Sounds of Silence • Taking Three Mindful Breaths	• Have You Ever Gotten a Thought? • Breathing • Who Am I?	• Mindful Breathing • Mindfulness of the Body • Pleasant Events
4	A Taste of Mindfulness	• We have thoughts, feelings, and body sensations, but these are not who we are • Thoughts, feelings, and body sensations are not exactly the same as the events they describe	• Introduction to Three-Minute Breathing Space • Opening to One Orange • Mindful Yoga Movements • Three-Minute Breathing Space	• Ode to a Grape • Three-Minute Breathing Space	• Three-Minute Breathing Space • Mindful Yoga Movements • Tasting Fruits

5	Music to Our Ears	• Thoughts, feelings, and body sensations often color how we experience the world • With our thoughts, we create individual and unique relationships and experiences • Awareness holds it all	• Three-Minute Breathing Space • Do You Hear What I Hear? • Mindfulness of the Body • Three-Minute Breathing Space	• The Door	• Three-Minute Breathing Space • Mindfulness of the Body • Mindful Listening
6	Sound Expressions	• Practicing mindful awareness helps us recognize that thoughts, feelings, and body sensations influence how we express ourselves • We can choose to express ourselves with mindful awareness	• Three-Minute Breathing Space • Sounding Out Emotions—Mindfully • Mindful Yoga Movements • Three-Minute Breathing Space	• Hearing	• Three-Minute Breathing Space • Mindful Yoga Movements • Unpleasant Sounds

continued

Table 7.1. CONTINUED

7	Practice Looking	• Judging is not the same as noting • If we simply observe experiences rather than judge them, the experience may change • We can choose to observe or note our experiences instead of judge them	• Three-Minute Breathing Space • Visualizing with Clarity • Mindful Yoga Movements • Seeing What Is in the Mind's Eye • Three-Minute Breathing Space	• Looking	• Three-Minute Breathing Space • Seeing the Little Details • Stressful Events
8	Strengthening the Muscle of Attention	• Judging often changes how we experience the world • Becoming more aware of judgments may change how we relate to thoughts and feelings • Discovering "choice points"	• Three-Minute Breathing Space • Seeing Through Illusions • Moving Mindfully • Seeing What Is Not There • Three-Minute Breathing Space	• Choices	• Three-Minute Breathing Space • Choosing to Be Aware • Seeing Five New Things
9	Touching the World with Mindfulness	• We have little control over most events that occur • We do have choices in how we respond to events • Choice points exist only in the present moment • Bringing greater awareness to this moment, we may see more choice points	• Three-Minute Breathing Space • Being in Touch • Mindfulness of the Body • Three-Minute Breathing Space	• Touch	• Three-Minute Breathing Space • Mindfulness of the Body • Mindful Touching

10	What the Nose Knows	• We often react to events by moving toward things we like or judge as "good" and moving away from things we don't like or judge as "bad" • Judging an experience may interfere with seeing clearly what is present in each moment • We have choices in how we respond to events	• Three-Minute Breathing Space • Judging Stinks! • Mindful Yoga Movements • Three-Minute Breathing Space	• To Be or Not to Be • Things We Can Learn from a Dog	• Three-Minute Breathing Space • Mindful Yoga Movements • Mindful Smelling
11	Life Is Not a Rehearsal	• Mindfulness is available in everyday life • We can practice mindful awareness using all our senses	• Three-Minute Breathing Space • Thoughts Are Not Facts • Feelings Are Not Facts Either • Raisin Mindfulness • Mindfulness Is . . . Three-Minute Breathing Space	• Slow Dance • Letter to My Self	• Three-Minute Breathing Space • Letter to My Self

continued

Table 7.1. Continued

12	Living With Presence, Compassion, and Awareness	• Mindful awareness can be helpful in our daily lives • Bringing greater awareness to our lives is a personal choice • Living with awareness requires commitment, compassion, and continued daily practice	• Three-Minute Breathing Space • Exploring Everyday Mindfulness • Program Evaluation (optional) • Three-Minute Breathing Space • Graduation Ceremony • Graduation Party! • Three-Minute Breathing Space	• Little Gidding • Living with Presence, Compassion, and Awareness • Letter from Therapist to Child • Daily Practice Calendar • Program Evaluation Questionnaire (optional)
	Three-Month Follow-Up	• Support for maintaining a daily practice of mindful awareness	• No session • Therapist mails Letter to My Self and Daily Practice Calendar to each child	• Letter to My Self (written by the child after session 11) • Three-Month Follow-Up Letter from Therapist to Child • Daily Practice Calendar

Note. Reprinted by permission from Semple & Lee (2011). *Mindfulness-Based Cognitive Therapy for Anxious Children.* New Harbinger Publications. Table 2. Overview of the Twelve Sessions and Follow-Up (pp. 79–82).

Session 2: Being Mindful Is Simple, but It Is Not Easy!

Facilitators and students discuss why it might be important to practice mindfulness outside of therapy. Facilitators address current or anticipated obstacles to consistent practice. Students practice observing body sensations and engage in mindful movement activities. They explore mindfulness in the sense of taste by mindfully eating one raisin.

Session 3: Who Am I?

Students observe the nature of thoughts as being focused on either the past or the future. They are oriented to the notion that thoughts are "just thoughts." Students begin to distinguish among thoughts, feelings, and body sensations—exploring how they are interrelated. Concentration is further cultivated by listening to the ringing of bells—and to the silence between the sounds.

Session 4: A Taste of Mindfulness

Students begin to consider how thoughts, feelings, memories, expectations, and beliefs influence how they interpret their experiences and the choices they make. For example, a student's beliefs about a peer might influence her interactions with that person. A student's expectations about the taste of broccoli might affect his decision to try it. Students mindfully eat an orange and observe how their memories influence the present experience.

Session 5: Music to Our Ears

By listening to music, students continue to strengthen present-focused attention while noting thoughts, emotions, and body sensations. The subjectivity of experience is explored by observing that each student has unique reactions to the same stimulus.

Session 6: Sound Expressions

Instead of listening to music, students create their own. They use small "instruments" (e.g., wooden spoons, partially filled water bottle, pet's squeak toy) or use the body (e.g., humming, clapping hands, tapping fingers) to creatively express their emotional states through sound. Students take turns being the "conductor" or being "orchestra musicians."

Session 7: Practice Looking

Students practice "seeing clearly" by mindfully observing different images. They notice automatic judgments, learn to differentiate judging and noting, and consider how their cognitive and emotional responses "color" their perceptions of the image. Drawing activities are used to elicit similar reflections.

Session 8: Strengthening the Muscle of Attention

Students observe optical illusions and learn to see in a different way by drawing the negative spaces within and around a three-dimensional object. They learn that what they pay attention to influences what they see, and explore how this translates into everyday experiences. Students are introduced to "choice points." These are moments in which choices can be made about how to respond—in real time—to thoughts and feelings or to situational events.

Session 9: Touching the World With Mindfulness

Students practice mindfulness of tactile sensations and notice how judgments might influence their experiences. They continue to build awareness of thoughts, emotions, and body sensations—beginning to discover that bringing awareness to experiences in this moment brings opportunities to discover their choice points.

Session 10: What the Nose Knows

Students notice automatic judgments, emotions, and memories as they explore various scents with mindful awareness. They practice using descriptive rather than judgmental language to describe the scents. The ability to observe our judgmental "autopilot" responses is again joined with the concept of choice points.

Session 11: Life Is Not a Rehearsal

Mindfulness is explored in the context of everyday life. Through guided practice, students see how their emotional states affect how they interpret events. Students learn that their thoughts, beliefs, and expectations about a situation may be inconsistent with what is actually happening. Students are reminded that all thoughts are "just thoughts"—even the scared, angry, sad, or worried thoughts. Similarly, emotions have a quality of impermanence about them and do not need to be pushed away or judged harshly. Emotions come and go and, like ocean waves, cannot be captured or pushed away. Students consider various areas of their lives where cultivating mindfulness might be helpful, such as in their relationships with family or friends, playing sports, or focusing in the classroom. Students repeat the drawing activity using the prompt, "draw whatever mindfulness means to you," as was done in Session 1. After comparing the two drawings and reflecting on what changed in 11 weeks, they place this artwork on the back of their mindfulness binders.

Session 12: Living With Presence, Compassion, and Awareness

Students reflect on what they learned in the program. They share ways to continue bringing presence and compassion into their own lives, as well as being more present and compassionate with others. The facilitator may choose to hold a "graduation ceremony" where certificates or small tokens (e.g., a polished stone) are distributed to students to celebrate their hard work and serve as a reminder of the skills they have cultivated.

EXAMPLE MBCT-C SESSION ACTIVITY

This section describes a sample activity from Session 10, *What the Nose Knows* (Semple & Lee, 2011, pp. 203–210). The session begins with a *Three-Minute Breathing Space*. Students engage in the sensory-focused activity, *Judging Stinks!*, which brings mindful awareness to the sense of smell. This is followed by mindful yoga movements and another *Three-Minute Breathing Space*. The session concludes with the facilitator eliciting a summary of the session from the participants, reading a short handout, "*Things We Can Learn From a Dog*," and reviewing home practices for the coming week. An optional activity is to complete the *Feely Faces Scale* at the beginning and the end of the session as a way of checking in with themselves to note their current mood.

We next describe the *Judging Stinks!* activity. While scripts are provided for learning purposes, the facilitator is encouraged to draw from his own mindfulness practice and use his own words while guiding the activities and post-activity inquiries.

Materials and Setup

Prior to Session 10, the facilitator gathers an assortment of scents. These can include bold scents that might evoke both positive and negative judgments. Examples include vinegar, peppermint, chocolate, onions or garlic, moist dirt, pungent cheeses, camphor, lotions, or scented candles. Of course, the facilitator should check with parents beforehand to ascertain if any child might have allergies to any scent. Students sit in a circle. A chart can be created during the post-activity inquiry, so that students may identify their thoughts, emotions, body sensations, and other observations that were noted during the activity.

Mindfulness Activity: Judging Stinks!

This activity is intended to help children notice the quick, often habituated judgments they make about their experiences, develop curiosity toward those experiences, and practice using descriptive versus judgmental language. Students learn that we frequently judge objects, people, and events as either positive or negative. Less commonly, we experience neutral or no judgment. Consequently, we reactively move toward experiences that we judge favorably, and move away from those we judge unfavorably. With mindful awareness, children practice observing their judgments, staying present, and paying attention to their experiences with curiosity, patience, and kindness.

The facilitator begins by passing around the scents one at a time and inviting children to smell each one with mindful attention to the thoughts, feelings, body sensations, and any judgments or memories that arise when smelling each scent. Students are invited to describe the scent with one word using descriptive, versus judgmental, language. For example, instead of describing the scent as "gross," the student might be encouraged to use a more descriptive word, such as "bitter" or "rancid." The facilitator might offer a list of adjectives that describe scents. Providing a list of vocabulary words is useful with many of the other activities as well. Following is a sample script used to guide this activity:

> *The world around us is filled with scents. We often don't notice all of these scents or how our bodies and minds react to them. For example, when we smell pizza in the cafeteria, we may feel excited. Our mouths might start to water as we imagine how delicious it will be. Our actual experience of eating the pizza, however, is not always the same as how we imagine it. Similarly, when we smell something we judge as unpleasant, we may cringe, feel disgusted, or remember an unpleasant memory associated with that scent. Sometimes, the memories, emotions, and judgments we have about a smell are different from the actual smell itself! Our mind likes to add additional flavors—those positive or negative judgments—to the scent itself.*

Post-Activity Inquiry

The facilitator invites children to describe their experiences of smelling each scent. As the students share, the facilitator creates a chart to identify each part of the experience, as illustrated in Table 7.2. Post-activity inquiries elicit three levels of observation. The first is, "What thoughts, feelings, and body sensations did you experience?" The second is, "How was that different than what you do every day?" The third is, "How might doing this be useful to you in your daily life?" Examples of inquiries that might be used by the facilitator include:

- *Describe the thoughts, feelings, and body sensations you experienced when smelling each scent.*
- *Did you notice any judging thoughts arise? What body sensations were associated with this?*
- *Did you notice any memories? Did this affect your ability to be fully present with the scent?*
- *Did you notice yourself moving* toward *or* away *from any of the scents? In other words, did you want more of some and less of others?*

Table 7.2. Example Chart to Use with the Inquiry Following the Judging Stinks! Activity

	Scent	Description of Smell	Thoughts	Feelings	Body Sensations	Memories	Judgments
Student 1	Dirt	Tangy, musty	This smells like the creek down the street.	Disgust, fear	Tightening of throat, nose wrinkles	Getting pushed into the mud by another kid	I don't like this at all.
Student 2	Dirt	Fresh, almost fruity	This smells like the playground after it rains.	Happy, excited	Slowing of breath, lips smile	Playing on the playground	This is my favorite scent—it reminds me of playing in the rain.

- *How do you think moving* toward *or* away *from experiences affects how we respond to events in our everyday life?*
- *How might thoughts and judgments about a smell get in the way of how we respond to it? How does this relate to other situations that you encounter in your everyday life?*

USING MBCT-C WITH INDIVIDUAL STUDENTS: A CLINICAL VIGNETTE

Melody is a ten-year-old female attending fifth grade at an urban public elementary school. She was referred to the school psychologist, Dr. Z, after her classroom teacher noticed that Melody had difficulty paying attention in class, appeared nervous and fidgety, and was having difficulty forming relationships with other students. The school psychologist assessed Melody and found clinically elevated generalized anxiety. Dr. Z also found deficits in executive functioning, poor emotion-regulation skills, and low levels of mindfulness on the Mindful Attention Awareness Scale for Children (MAAS-C; Lawlor et al., 2014). Melody has been meeting with Dr. Z for individual weekly therapy to learn mindfulness skills to better manage her anxiety and attention problems. In Session 10, *What the Nose Knows*, Dr. Z begins the session with the *Three-Minute Breathing Space*. She then guides the *Judging Stinks!* activity. Dr. Z and Melody engage in the following dialogue.

DR. Z: What do you notice about the scent you are holding [dirt]?
MELODY: It's gross! I don't like it [Melody scrunches her nose].
DR. Z: When you went like *this* with your nose [Dr. Z mirrors the disgust displayed in Melody's face], what other body sensations were you aware of?
MELODY: I noticed that I get a lump in my throat.
DR. Z: Would you be willing to "hang out" with that experience for a minute, Melody?
MELODY: [Closes eyes and focuses on the sensations in her throat].
DR. Z: What did you notice?
MELODY: Well, first my throat became tighter, and then it started to relax.
DR. Z: So, the sensation changed over time?
MELODY: [Nods head].
DR. Z: That's an interesting observation. If you continue to pay attention, you might notice that your thoughts, emotions, and sensations are always changing. What emotions or thoughts do you notice as you smell the dirt?
MELODY: It reminds me of a time when another kid pushed me into the mud. It makes me angry. I don't like to think about it.
DR. Z: Certain memories are difficult to think about, especially things that might bring up anger in us. It's perfectly okay to feel angry. It's a normal

human emotion—one that everyone experiences. Let's try giving that anger a hug, like this [Dr. Z models giving herself a hug].

MELODY: [Follows along with Dr. Z].

DR. Z: There is also a difference between *being* angry and *feeling* angry. Remember that emotions are temporary experiences—they don't define who we are. Try saying "I am angry" and "I feel angry" and notice the difference in your body.

MELODY: [Follows the prompt].

DR. Z: What did you notice?

MELODY: When I say that I *am* angry, my chest tightens even more and I feel heavy on the inside. When I say that I *feel* angry, I feel a little lighter.

DR. Z: That's a great observation. Is that feeling of anger related to the thoughts and body sensations that you described earlier?

MELODY: Well, when I feel angry, I start to feel that tightness in my throat and chest. I think about the kid pushing me and it makes it feel even worse. Then I just can't stop thinking about it.

DR. Z: I see—so there is a link between thoughts and feelings, where one kind of fuels the other?

MELODY: [Nods].

DR. Z: Let's try something else. As you notice this happening in your body right now, see if you can also notice what happens with your breath.

MELODY: [Focuses on breath].

DR. Z: What did you notice?

MELODY: When I get angry, my breath speeds up. Then, when I pay attention to my breath, it starts to slow down. The tightness in my chest and throat is still there, but I feel a little calmer—it doesn't scare me as much and I can focus better.

DR. Z: That's right. Instead of "sticking" to the sensation in your throat and chest, or that feeling of anger, you can choose to take a step back from it. When we learn to make friends with our experiences, we may have more energy to focus our attention where we want.

MELODY: [Nods].

DR. Z: Now, let's return to smelling this object again. Practice experiencing the scent, as best you can, staying with it moment-by-moment.

MELODY: [Smells the dirt again].

DR. Z: How would you describe the scent now—pretend I have never smelled it before.

MELODY: It smells moist. It also has a fruity smell to it.

DR. Z: It sounds like you discovered something new.

MELODY: Yes. At first, I didn't want to smell it at all because it reminded me of being pushed in the mud. Now it smells a little different than I thought.

DR. Z: It sounds like your memories and expectations about the scent were not the same as the experience itself. Your thoughts "colored" your experience. How might knowing this relate to other events in your everyday life?

MELODY: Well, I guess my imagination can take over. Sometimes I worry a lot about things, like a conversation with a friend, and it turns out different. My mind always thinks about the worst possible situation.

DR. Z: Our minds are very good at that! We often remember the past or imagine the future—but those thoughts aren't always accurate to what's happening right now. We've already learned that thoughts are not facts. What do you think you might do when your mind continues to "stick" to thoughts about the past or future?

MELODY: I guess I can just recognize that my mind is wandering off, or "sticking" to something. Then come back to my breathing—or whatever I want to focus on.

DR. Z: That's right—and as we have talked about, it takes a lot of practice to teach our minds to do this. We have to build our "muscle" of attention. Shall we practice doing this again with the *Three-Minute Breathing Space?*

Vignette Summary

Melody had a strong negative judgment when smelling the dirt, which was related to a previous negative experience. She stated that she "[didn't] like it" and labeled it as "gross." Dr. Z began by reflecting Melody's facial expression to help encourage greater body awareness. She asked Melody to continue sitting with this emotion to heighten awareness of body sensations, thoughts, and feelings. Dr. Z emphasized the transient nature of these experiences after Melody noted that her body sensations changed over time. Dr. Z and Melody discussed the memory that triggered feelings of anger. Dr. Z introduced the notion of "common humanity" (i.e., that anger is a shared human emotion) and encouraged self-compassion. Melody practiced saying "I *feel* angry" versus "I *am* angry," which helps create space between the emotion and the person experiencing it. Melody and Dr. Z explored the connection among the memory (i.e., thought), the feelings of anger, and the physiological sensations of Melody's throat and chest tightening. Melody was again encouraged to be present with the experience while directing attention to the breath. Melody learned that she could use the breath to redirect her attention from "sticking" to these thoughts and emotions. Dr. Z invited Melody to bring this same present-focused attention to smelling the dirt again, whereupon Melody used descriptive rather than judgmental language. They discussed how memories and expectations can "color" present-moment experiences. Melody recognized that she ruminates about future events—which are often different from what she had imagined. Dr. Z reinforced the notion that thoughts are not facts. Dr. Z and Melody talked about what to do when the mind "sticks" to thoughts. As mindfulness is learned experientially, Dr. Z closed with another *Three-Minute Breathing Space*, during which she continued to guide Melody in observing her moment-by-moment experiences.

ADAPTING MBCT-C TO THE CLASSROOM: THE MINDFULNESS MATTERS PROGRAM

Classroom teachers may be interested in using the MBCT-C approach in a general education setting. The Mindfulness Matters Program (MMP; Semple & Willard, 2019) is a non-clinical adaptation of MBCT-C for K–12 students. MMP offers dozens of mindfulness activities within a flexible framework that can be implemented by classroom teachers. It is not a structured program—it is more like a "choose your own adventure" book. Its aims and approaches are similar to those of MBCT-C, in that students enhance mindful awareness through the five senses, learn to relate to themselves and others with more kindness, and make more skillful choices. Teachers are also guided in selecting and sequencing activities for groups struggling with specific challenges: stress and anxiety, depression, attention problems, behavioral and emotion regulation issues, and trauma. The aim of the program is to provide teachers with resources to address common emotional and behavioral problems and bolster social-emotional resilience. Activity variations make MMP age-appropriate for both adolescents and younger children.

WIDENING THE MINDFULNESS CIRCLE: GETTING TEACHERS AND PARENTS INVOLVED

Students do not function apart from their environment. They are embedded within multiple systems that contribute to psychosocial functioning and well-being. Bronfenbrenner's (1992) Ecological Systems Theory states that the student's home and school environments (the microsystem) are the most proximal system of influence. Progress within therapy is often dependent in part on the child's environment. Therefore, it is helpful for parents, teachers, and other adults to learn the same skillful behaviors that we aim to teach our children.

Facilitators conducting MBCT-C are encouraged to conduct information sessions for parents, individually or in a group, to provide the rationale and an overview of the curriculum. Parent sessions include several introductory mindfulness practices, a review of the aims and approaches of MBCT-C, a description of the school- and home-based activities, the written summaries and handouts that accompany each session, and discussion about incorporating mindfulness into everyday life. The school may also consider hosting a drop-in mindfulness practice group for parents. Over the course of MBCT-C, facilitators update parents on the themes and practices their child is learning. The child is assigned weekly home practices and handouts that parents are encouraged to review. Children are also encouraged to lead a few mindfulness practices at home—teaching their parents and siblings what they learn in the groups. Examples include breathing practices, mindful walking, or mindfully eating dinner.

A growing number of schools are becoming interested in mindfulness training for teachers and other staff members. Facilitators of MBCT-C might consider leading mindfulness orientations, workshops, or drop-in groups for teachers and other staff. There are also numerous organizations that train teachers and school staff in mindfulness, either locally or via online programs. Mindful Schools (www.mindfulschools.org) is one well-known program that offers both in-person and on-line training. We recommend beginning with volunteer teachers or other staff members who have an interest in learning mindfulness. Mindfulness is an ongoing practice and a way of being—not just a lesson plan—so teachers must be invested in these practices for their own personal and professional development. Maintaining a personal mindfulness practice is helpful for both therapists delivering MBCT-C and general education teachers drawing from other mindfulness curricula, such as the MMP.

CONCLUSIONS

MBCT-C is a structured clinical program that teaches mindful awareness to elementary school-aged youth with clinically elevated emotional or behavioral difficulties. Adaptations may be made to use MBCT-C with middle-school students by adjusting language, activities, and length of sessions. This program should be facilitated by trained mental health professionals. Other mindfulness programs such as the MMP (Semple & Willard, 2019), Stressed Teens (Biegel, 2009), and Making Friends with Yourself: A Mindful Self-Compassion program for teens (Bluth, 2017), are better suited for non-clinical populations and can be implemented by teachers with high school students.

MBCT-C is meant to be facilitated by a trained mental health professional in either a group or individual format. Implementing MBCT-C in a school setting requires flexibility with time, pace, environment, materials, and the unique learning needs of each student. The facilitator's own mindfulness practice is the foundation for guiding the activities and inquiries. Teaching mindfulness to parents, teachers, and other staff members can provide additional support to students and help foster a school culture of mindfulness and compassion.

Just like the school playground, children's minds will always be a place filled with a multitude of experiences and constant change. Watching from a distance, they can smile at its frantic exuberance. Knowing this is its nature, maintaining a carefully cultivated mindfulness and compassion, they can remain calm in the midst of the chaos. In teaching mindfulness, we empower students to relate to their minds in a more skillful way. Mindfulness can help children find their own space of acceptance and compassion and make wiser, more conscious choices.

REFERENCES

Abedini, S., Habibi, M., Abedini, N., Achenbach, T. M., & Semple, R. J. (2020). A randomized clinical trial of a modified Mindfulness-Based Cognitive Therapy for children hospitalized with cancer. *Mindfulness*, *12*, 141–151. https://doi.org/10.1007/s12671-020-01506-3

Biegel, G. M. (2009). *The stress reduction workbook for teens: Mindfulness skills to help you deal with stress*. New Harbinger Publications.

Bluth, K. (2017). *The self-compassion workbook for teens: Mindfulness and compassion skills to overcome self-criticism and embrace who you are*. New Harbinger Publications.

Bronfenbrenner, U. (1992). Ecological systems theory. In R. Vasta (Ed.), *Six theories of child development: Revised formulations and current issues* (pp. 187–249). Jessica Kingsley Publishers.

Cotton, S., Luberto, C. M., Sears, R. W., Strawn, J. R., Stahl, L., Wasson, R. S., . . . Delbello, M. P. (2016). Mindfulness-Based Cognitive Therapy for youth with anxiety disorders at risk for bipolar disorder: A pilot trial. *Early Intervention in Psychiatry*, *10*, 426–434. doi.org/10.1111/eip.12216

Esmaeilian, N., Dehghani, M., Dehghani, Z., & Lee, J. (2018). Mindfulness-Based Cognitive Therapy enhances emotional resiliency in children with divorced parents. *Mindfulness*, *9*(4), 1052–1062. doi:10.1007/s12671-017-0840-9

Esmaeilian, N., Tahmassian, K., Dehghani, M., & Mootabi, F. (2013). Effectiveness of Mindfulness-Based Cognitive Therapy on depression symptoms in children with divorced parents. *Journal of Clinical Psychology*, *5*(3), 47–57. doi.org/10.1007/s12671-017-0840-9

Faraji, M., Talepasand, S., & Boogar, I. (2019). Effectiveness of Mindfulness-Based Cognitive Therapy for child on bullying behaviors among children. *International Archives of Health Sciences*, *6*(1), 52. https://doi.org/10.4103/iahs.iahs_54_18

Gogtay, N., Giedd, J. N., Lusk, L., Hayashi, K. M., Greenstein, D., Vaituzis, A. C., . . . Rapoport, J. L. (2004). Dynamic mapping of human cortical development during childhood through early adulthood. *Proceedings of the National Academy of Sciences*, *101*(21), 8174–8179.

Hayes, S. C., Strosahl, K. D., & Wilson, K. G. (2011). *Acceptance and commitment therapy: The process and practice of mindful change*. Guilford Press.

James, A. C., James, G., Cowdrey, F. A., Soler, A., & Choke, A. (2015). Cognitive behavioural therapy for anxiety disorders in children and adolescents. *Cochrane Database of Systematic Reviews*, *2015*(2), Article CD004690. doi.org/10.1002/14651858.CD004690.pub4

Jang, J. Y., & Shin, H. K. (2019). The effects of Mindfulness-Based Cognitive Therapy (MBCT-C) on middle school students anxiety and mindfulness. *Korean Journal of Youth Studies*, *26*(8), 53–78. https://doi.org/10.21509/KJYS.2019.08.26.8.53

Kabat-Zinn, J. (1990). *Full catastrophe living*. Bantam Doubleday Dell.

Kostova, Z., Sarmiento, I., Fulwiler, C., & Semple, R. J. (2019, October 25). *Implementing Mindfulness-Based Cognitive Therapy for Children (MBCT-C) with history of trauma in inpatient settings: A pilot study*. European Society for Trauma and Dissociation Conference: The Legacy of Trauma and Dissociation—Body and Mind in a New Perspective, Rome, Italy.

Lawlor, M. S., Schonert-Reichl, K. A., Gadermann, A. M., & Zumbo, B. D. (2014). A validation study of the mindful attention awareness scale adapted for children. *Mindfulness*, *5*, 730–741. doi.org/10.1007/s12671-013-0228-4

Lebrun-Harris, L. A., Ghandour, R. M., Kogan, M. D., & Warren, M. D. (2022). Five-year trends in US children's health and well-being, 2016–2020. *JAMA Pediatrics*, *176*(7), e220056. https://doi.org/10.1001/jamapediatrics.2022.0056

Madni, L. A., Goodman, M. S., & Semple, R. J. (2019). Anxiety and depression. In V. G. Carrión & J. Rettger (Eds.), *Applied mindfulness: Approaches in mental health for children and adolescents* (pp. 75–97). American Psychiatric Association Publishing.

Qin, K., Lei, D., Yang, J., Li, W., Tallman, M. J., Duran, L. R. P., . . . Delbello, M. P. (2021). Network-level functional topological changes after Mindfulness-Based Cognitive Therapy in mood dysregulated adolescents at familial risk for bipolar disorder: A pilot study. *BMC Psychiatry, 21*(1). https://doi.org/10.1186/s12888-021-03211-4

Rogers, C. (1961). *On becoming a person: A therapist's view of psychotherapy*. Houghton Mifflin Harcourt.

Segal, Z. V., Williams, J. M. G., & Teasdale, J. D. (2013). *Mindfulness-Based Cognitive Therapy for depression* (2nd ed.). Guilford.

Semple, R. J., & Lee, J. (2011). *Mindfulness-Based Cognitive Therapy for anxious children: A manual for treating childhood anxiety*. New Harbinger Publications.

Semple, R. J., Lee, J., Rosa, D., & Miller, L. F. (2010). A randomized trial of Mindfulness-Based Cognitive Therapy for Children: Promoting mindful attention to enhance social-emotional resiliency in children. *Journal of Child and Family Studies, 19*, 218–229. doi.org/10.1007/s10826-009-9301-y

Semple, R. J., & Madni, L. A. (2015). Treating childhood trauma with mindfulness. In V. M. Follette, J. Briere, D. Rozelle, J. W. Hopper, & D. I. Rome (Eds.), *Mindfulness-oriented interventions for trauma: Integrating contemplative practices* (pp. 284–300). Guilford.

Semple, R. J., Reid, E. F. G., & Miller, L. (2005). Treating anxiety with mindfulness: An open trial of mindfulness training for anxious children. *Journal of Cognitive Psychotherapy: An International Quarterly, 19*, 379–392. doi.org/10.1891/jcop.2005.19.4.379

Semple, R. J., & Willard, C. (2019). *The Mindfulness Matters program for children and adolescents: Strategies, activities, and techniques for therapists and teachers*. Guilford Press.

Strawn, J. R., Cotton, S., Luberto, C. M., Patino, L. R., Stahl, L. A., Weber, W. A., . . . DelBello, M. P. (2016). Neural function before and after Mindfulness-Based Cognitive Therapy in anxious adolescents at risk for developing bipolar disorder. *Journal of Child and Adolescent Psychopharmacology, 26*, 372–379. doi.org/10.1089/cap.2015.0054

Syeda, M. M., & Andrews Jac, J. W. (2021). Mindfulness-Based Cognitive Therapy as a targeted group intervention: Examining children's changes in anxiety symptoms and mindfulness. *Journal of Child and Family Studies, 30*(4), 1002–1015. https://doi.org/https://doi.org/10.1007/s10826-021-01924-4

Wenzlaff, R. M., & Wegner, D. M. (2000). Thought suppression. *Annual Review of Psychology, 51*, 59–91. doi.org/10.1146/annurev.psych.51.1.59

Wright, K. M., Roberts, R., & Proeve, M. J. (2019). Mindfulness-Based Cognitive Therapy for Children (MBCT-C) for prevention of internalizing difficulties: A small randomized controlled trial with Australian primary school children. *Mindfulness, 10*, 2277–2293. https://doi.org/10.1007/s12671-019-01193-9

8

Mindful Yoga for Grade School Students

JACINDA K. DARIOTIS AND DIANA H. FISHBEIN ■

How might mindful yoga programs in schools make a difference for youth? The evidence base demonstrating positive impacts of mindful yoga on students is growing. The literature shows that compromised self-regulation skills predict worse student outcomes, including poor academic performance and school dropout, in part due to negative responses to stress (Reynolds et al., 2001). Given that stress is one of the leading social determinants of compromised chronic health conditions in later childhood, adolescence, and adulthood (Felitti et al., 1998), teaching coping strategies in early childhood is essential to preventing the cascade of negative health outcomes that accumulate across development. Movement and meditation, which are key components of mindful yoga, have been shown to decrease distraction and impulsivity as well as improve attention and positive coping (Dariotis et al., 2016a, 2016b; Greenberg & Harris, 2012; Mendelson et al., 2010; Weare, 2013; Zoogman et al., 2014). By teaching coping strategies that are translatable to school and afterschool settings, home environments, and beyond, the impact of mindful yoga programs has the potential to be transformative by holistically improving youths' lives across contexts. Moreover, relative to other programs that require intensive time commitment, complex curricula, and substantial training and materials, mindful yoga programs are relatively cost-effective and sustainable, and can therefore be readily incorporated into the school day.

This chapter is divided into several sections framed as answers to pivotal questions. First, we ask, "What is mindful yoga?" and "Why should we expose students to mindful yoga?" This section briefly overviews the benefits of mindful yoga programs in terms of emotional regulation, stress coping, and cognitive control (including neurophysiology). Second, we ask, "How can mindful yoga be in-

Jacinda K. Dariotis and Diana H. Fishbein, *Mindful Yoga for Grade School Students*. In: *Using Mindfulness to Promote Mental Health in Schools*. Edited by: Tyler L. Renshaw and Shane R. Jimerson, Oxford University Press. © Oxford University Press (2025). DOI: 10.1093/9780190880507.003.0008

corporated into schools?" This section describes several case studies that have successfully incorporated mindful yoga into schools. Third, we ask, "How does one get started with mindful yoga?" and "Where does one locate resources?" This section provides suggestions about partnerships and resources for those interested in incorporating mindful yoga programs into schools. Finally, we ask, "What are future directions for mindful yoga in schools?" This section discusses an agenda for this work, including the need to research and evaluate which mindful yoga program components are effective in "moving the needle" regarding outcomes and the effects of systemic approaches to implementation, such as integrating training into teacher preparation programs.

WHAT IS MINDFUL YOGA? AND WHY SHOULD WE EXPOSE STUDENTS TO MINDFUL YOGA?

Nature of Mindful Yoga

Mindfulness encompasses a set of mental practices that cultivate attention regulation and the related capacity to bring non-judgmental awareness to whatever is occurring in the present moment (Kabat-Zinn et al., 1992; Kabat-Zinn, 2003; Ricard et al., 2014). Similarly, yoga encompasses somatic-based practices (e.g., postures, mindful awareness, breathing) that aim to promote mindfulness and self-regulation (Schmalzl et al., 2015). Thus, mindful yoga integrates the physical practice of poses with mindfulness. Yoga has eight limbs, or domains of practice (Iyengar, 1966), several of which are not appropriate for school-based programs because they require consistent practice and mastery-level skills (e.g., the practice of withdrawing of senses in Pratyahara).

Typically, mindful yoga begins with several minutes of centering, in which participants settle into the present moment by quietly breathing. This is followed by structured breath work (e.g., ocean breathing; three-point breathing) and yoga-based poses (e.g., a sequence known as "sun salutations" that involves moving major muscles of the body). Silent, guided reflection or meditation is used to train participants to attend to something neutral and not cognitively energetic (e.g., breath or sound). Some programs incorporate additional elements, such as discussion (e.g., how to manage stress), "homework" (e.g., breathing techniques and poses to practice), and guided imagery (e.g., Holistic Life Foundation, see Gould et al., 2014, for seven core activities; Khalsa & Butzer, 2016). Many of these core components, which are discussed in more detail below, have been found to exert significant independent and, possibly, synergistic positive effects on stress physiology (Brown & Gerbarg, 2009) and clinical conditions (e.g., anxiety, depression, fibromyalgia, irritable bowel syndrome; Fjorback et al., 2013; Jerath et al., 2015).

Khalsa and Butzer (2016) reviewed 47 yoga programs conducted in schools and reported that the vast majority of programs lasted 12 weeks, with most programs ranging between 4 and 16 weeks. Sessions typically lasted between 30 and 60 minutes, with 30 and 45 minutes as the most frequently reported durations (Khalsa & Butzer, 2016). Similarly, in their review of mindfulness-based interventions with youth in school settings, Felver and colleagues (2016) reported that across 25 studies, the average number of sessions was 17.5, with an average session duration of 36.8 minutes over an average treatment duration of 8.2 weeks. School-based prevention and intervention programs tend to be "one-and-done," meaning implementers go to schools, conduct the program for a certain period of time, and then the program ends with the conclusion of a grant award. Moving toward a systematic approach, where programming is integrated into the culture and curriculum of a classroom or school, is a more sustainable direction for the field. Mindful yoga program components (e.g., breathing practice, mindful moment, stretches) are amenable to being incorporated into traditional academic curricula and daily practices within school settings.

Although it is important for a trained and certified instructor to implement initial programming and train teachers how to implement intervention components in the classroom, mindful yoga is relatively easy for teachers to learn and implement and is conducive to self-practice. Expensive equipment is not needed, so programming can be sustained with low cost. Mindful yoga can be practiced in a chair, standing, or laying down and can be modified for almost all populations of students—making it accessible for nearly everyone. The skills of mindful yoga can be practiced in combination (e.g., breathing and poses; breathing and meditation) or separated, depending on needs and constraints (e.g., time, space). Breath work can be practiced anytime and anywhere; balancing poses can be used to still the mind that may be racing or ruminating on negative thoughts.

Mindful yoga is feasible, cost-effective, and translatable to settings beyond the session in which it is taught. For example, breath work learned in session can be used by a student in the classroom during test-taking to downregulate or de-stress. Some schools and workplaces have implemented "mindfulness moment" initiatives (Duggan & Julliard, 2018), taking a few minutes at the start or end of a day, meeting, or class to focus on breathing and quieting the mind. Mindful moments may involve specific practices like a mindful body scan (i.e., walking through the body from toes to head, relaxing each part along the way) or simply provide a calm and serene space for students and employees to engage in a variety of mindfulness practices. These efforts demonstrate the scalability of mindful yoga to the whole school, as discussed later in this chapter.

Students have reported that the skills they learned during mindful yoga translate well to test-taking situations, where reducing anxiety is important (Dariotis et al., 2016b). Although they did not participate in the mindful yoga themselves, some teachers found creative ways to integrate what students were learning into their classrooms. For example, students reported using neck rolls during standardized school tests to stay awake, and that doing stretches, dog pose, and deep breathing to calm down and stay awake during testing was helpful. In one fifth-grade classroom, only three students chose not to participate in the mindful yoga program. During the state standardized assessments, one student who attended the yoga program would lead the classroom in a practice. In another classroom, students nominated a student to lead the class in a demonstration, and if the students could not decide, the teacher would make the selection. The break was for six minutes, and the class would practice yoga for three of those minutes; the remaining time was spent talking about how they were doing and reacting to being tested. The class repeated this exercise across three days of testing. Remembering back to previous years of testing without this yoga break, students recounted that they would just sit at their desks quietly, eat a snack, and not talk. As one fifth-grade male remarked, "[I am] happier to like do the test. More confident like when some question, when you get like angry 'cuz you didn't know something. You know like you are more calm. It made me be more calm" (Dariotis et al., 2016b). This anecdote exemplifies how classroom teachers have empowered students to use skills learned in mindful yoga outside of the program.

Other examples of using skills learned outside the program include the use of *mudras* (hand gestures) to help reduce frustration during test-taking, turning away from distracting classmates to avoid getting more upset (referred to in the program as "diversion" and "set shifting"), and imagining themselves practicing "Sunrise" (i.e., a sequence of poses that works the entire body and includes forward folds, lunges, downward facing dog, plank, push-up, and a backbend) in class to reduce stress. Students gave many examples of how mindful yoga helped them manage stress when interacting with peers and at home with siblings. They also described how they taught breathing techniques and poses to family members, helping others with their ailments (Dariotis et al., 2016b).

Benefits of Mindful Yoga

Given that emotion dysregulation is a hallmark of externalizing behaviors and affective disorders among youth, there is a vital need for novel interventions, such as mindful yoga, to improve the clinical outcomes that prevent many youths from reaching critical developmental benchmarks. Mindful yoga can improve youth outcomes via its effects on strengthening regulatory controls, reducing stress, and enhancing sleep quality, which, in turn, improves "top-down" cognitive control over intrusive thoughts and emotional or stress responses. Mindful yoga interventions may be especially helpful to youth exposed to trauma and other adverse childhood experiences (ACEs), because it provides them with positive coping techniques that promote emotional and behavioral regulation. Many negative behavioral and psychological outcomes (e.g., poorer academic performance, high rates of dropout, unplanned pregnancies, substance abuse, and mental health issues) are related to poor regulation of emotion and behavior (Eisenberg et al., 2010; Fox & Calkins, 2003; Schore, 2005), and impaired stress reactivity underlies these types of dysregulation (McEwen & Morrison, 2013).

Studies increasingly reveal that improvements in stress reactivity processes lead to a greater ability to adaptively respond to social and developmental demands in youth (Bierman et al., 2008; Blair et al., 2014; Fishbein et al., 2006; Hsu et al., 2014; Stuss, 2011; Tracy & Osipowicz, 2011; Venkatakrishnan & Sandrini, 2012). Mindfulness-based interventions, including mindful yoga, have potential to improve aberrant physiological stress responses underlying emotion dysregulation and, in turn, lead to more positive affective and behavioral outcomes.

There is growing empirical evidence among youth and adults that mindfulness and mindful yoga interventions improve well-being, overall health (e.g., mood, distress, blood pressure), and prosocial behavior by stabilizing responses to stress; improving emotional and cognitive regulation; and enhancing attention, awareness, and compassion (Carlson, 2012; Dariotis et al., 2016a, 2016b, 2023a; Flook et al., 2015; Goldin & Gross, 2010; Holzel et al., 2011a, 2011b; Khalsa et al., 2012; Pilkington et al., 2005; Schonert-Reichl et al., 2015; Teper et al., 2013). Multiple meta-analyses present convincing evidence that mindfulness and yoga enhance adult psychological well-being (Khoury et al., 2013; Tomasino et al., 2014; Vøllestad et al., 2012; Zenner et al., 2014), and an increasing number of studies with pre-, primary, and secondary school-aged youth are establishing similar effects with children and adolescents (Carsley et al., 2018; Dunning et al., 2019; Klingbeil et al., 2017).

Emotion regulation is a key protective process that helps reduce behavioral and psychological problems stemming from adversity and trauma exposure (Fishbein, 2000; Tull et al., 2015). Exposure to adversity—from poverty and discrimination to suffering child maltreatment or witnessing violence—can profoundly impair development of stress, executive cognitive function, and sleep systems that underlie regulation of emotion (Briere et al., 2010). Thus, severely adverse life circumstances can alter physiological stress responses, undermine executive control (e.g., attention, mindful awareness), and disrupt sleeping patterns, which, independently and collectively, can sabotage development of adequate self-regulation (Hofmann et al., 2012). The resulting emotional dysregulation often manifests in a range of risky behaviors (e.g., aggression, impulsivity, poor social relationships, substance misuse, gambling; Ernst et al., 2006) that may compromise educational outcomes—leading to school suspensions and high school drop out that, in turn, predict underemployment, unemployment, incarceration, and other negative outcomes.

Mindful yoga interventions have potential to improve the mechanisms underlying emotion dysregulation and optimize developmental trajectories. For example, studies among adults with various clinical syndromes and in different settings demonstrate that mindfulness and yoga (together and separately) have beneficial effects on psychological well-being, stress responses, sleep patterns, and even cardiovascular and immune systems (Davis et al., 2007; Feldman et al., 2007; Kristeller et al., 2006). Similarly, a review of 28 yoga studies in school contexts found positive changes in multiple outcomes for students, including decreased anxiety, hyperactivity, hostility, aggression, blood pressure, and heart rate, as well as improved social skills, classroom behavior, attention, academic engagement, psychological well-being, and sleep (Felver et al., 2016).

Mindful yoga programs, however, may have differential utility for youth who vary in certain characteristics prior to intervention. Preexisting conditions that influence outcomes are called "moderators." Identifying moderators that interact with an intervention provides important information about individuals or subgroups that are less likely to respond well. This information can then be used to further refine programs to benefit more recipients. For example, when examining student outcomes after a mindful yoga program, Gould and colleagues (2012) found that intervention students reporting high baseline levels of depressive symptoms also reported more impulsive action and problematic responses to stress at post-assessment relative to intervention and control peers reporting fewer depressive symptoms and control peers reporting similarly high depressive symptoms. These findings suggest that mindful yoga interventions may work well in isolation for some students, but that they may need to be paired with more intensive interventions (e.g., cognitive behavioral therapy) for students who are experiencing high degrees of psychological distress. Other baseline conditions, such as level of cognitive function, history of trauma, and socioeconomic status, may also influence outcomes and, thus, warrant further examination in mindfulness studies.

Equally as important as identifying moderators is the elucidation of mediating conditions that may contribute to favorable versus poor intervention outcomes. Mediators are conditions (whether preexisting or not) that change in response to intervention and help to explain an intervention's effect. An understanding of mediators provides vital information on how program components specifically work to improve the functioning of a mechanism that underlies the behavior we seek to prevent or strengthen. Toward that end, empirical studies on the neuroscience of mindfulness are yielding rich information on how mindfulness works to improve psychological, cognitive, and behavioral health (Paulson et al., 2013). For example, both neuroimaging and electrophysiological studies with adults suggest that mindfulness produced through yoga influences the neurobiological mechanisms that target regulatory and affective processes (Davidson et al., 2003; Gard et al., 2014; Pagnoni et al., 2008; Rocha et al., 2012). Mindfulness and yoga are hypothesized to lead to enhanced attentional control, sensory processing (Hölzel et al., 2011b; Tang et al., 2007), and "top-down" cognitive-emotive regulation (Goldin & Gross, 2010). These enhancements then lead to reductions in psychiatric symptoms, trauma, and substance abuse (Farb et al., 2012; Garland et al., 2020). Regulation of emotions and stress reactivity are key protective processes that aid in reducing or managing substance abuse as well as psychiatric and traumatic stress symptoms (Fishbein, 2000; Tull et al., 2015). Maturation of the prefrontal neural circuit subserves this developmental integration, thereby promoting the ability to exert effortful control over behavior in emotional contexts. In this way, yoga and mindfulness exert higher-order changes that can be measured downstream (Froeliger et al., 2012; Garland et al., 2013; Rocha et al., 2012). These processes are particularly relevant during adolescence, when discrepancies in the pace of neurobiological development may lead to a disconnect between emotional regulation and behavioral constraint (Steinberg, 2005). In effect, such interventions are thought to attenuate or normalize the behavioral and psychophysiological conditions that otherwise predispose adolescents to risky behaviors.

HOW TO INTEGRATE MINDFUL YOGA INTO SCHOOLS?

Different methods can be used to incorporate mindful yoga into schools. One way is to conduct the program during the school day and implement it either as part of the curriculum (systemic programming) or as a pull-out program ("one-and-done" programming) that students volunteer to attend in lieu of lunch, resource, gym, or other elective class time. Alternatives are to offer programs after school for students who opt to stay later or universal school-wide programing integrated throughout the regular school day. Described below are case studies of these different types of mindful yoga programs.

School-Based "One-and-Done" Programs

One example of a "one-and-done" program is that provided by Holistic Life Foundation Inc. (HLF). HLF is a non-profit organization in Baltimore City that offers mindfulness and mindful yoga classes aimed at improving emotional and academic outcomes among inner-city youth. Most of the youth served by HLF are African American and live in low-income, high-crime neighborhoods. The HLF founders were born and raised in Baltimore City, are of African American and Latinx descent, and have strong ties to the community. Designed for an urban youth population, HLF's curriculum—called *Stress Reduction and Mindfulness*—aims to empower youth with tools and skills for self-regulation of behaviors, thoughts, and emotions. In particular, the program is geared toward countering the psychological and cognitive effects of chronic stress exposure by cultivating a state of calm attention and mindful awareness. HLF's program is based on well-established principles of contemplative practices, with a focus on meditation, breath work, and physical poses and other mindfulness techniques (e.g., set-shifting, present moment focus). A typical session starts with a brief meditation exercise of focusing on the breath to "center" (becoming present-moment focused), followed by physical yoga poses and then breathing exercises. Afterward, a selected topic is discussed (e.g., stress, love, consequences) and the instructors conclude with a guided meditation (e.g., mindful body scan) while lying down (corpse pose). These practices begin at a basic level and increase in complexity over time. Participants are given assignments between sessions to reinforce lessons.

HLF has a lengthy track record of providing mindfulness and yoga programming for this largely low-income, largely minority children and adolescent population. The curriculum was manualized in 2007 and has since been refined and updated based on previous findings. Studies of this program were the first randomized control trials (RCTs) assessing school-based mindfulness and mindful yoga for urban youth. School-based studies on HLF's programming included a CDC-funded pilot RCT of 97 fourth- and fifth-graders (Mendelson et al., 2010), a NIDA-funded R34 RCT of 252 fifth- and sixth-graders (Dariotis et al., 2016a, 2016b, 2017; Mendelson et al., 2013), a pilot RCT of 92 alternative high school students at risk for dropping out (Prenoveau et al., 2018), and an NCCIH-funded study of 210 ninth-graders (Dariotis et al., 2023a, 2023b; Rose et al., in press). In the first study, the HLF curriculum was taught to fourth- and fifth-graders over 48 sessions (four times a week for 12 weeks) in two schools, with another two schools serving as waitlist controls (Mendelson et al., 2010). Among fourth- and fifth-grade students, this program has enhanced emotional regulation and cognitive outcomes (Gould et al., 2012; Mendelson et al., 2010). In the second RCT, fifth- and sixth-graders received the program across 32 sessions (two times a week for 16 weeks) in three schools, with an additional three schools serving as controls (Dariotis et al., 2016a, 2016b, 2017; Mendelson et al., 2013). In the third RCT, ninth- through twelfth-grade students at two high schools received HLF programming for 12 weeks and students at two other high schools did not receive programming (Prenoveau et al., 2018). In the fourth RCT, ninth-graders reported enhanced emotional intelligence, a mindset shift toward cognitive control, use of program skills in other contexts, and use of sharing skills with others.

Altogether, study findings describe core program components, a rigorous observational fidelity coding system (Gould et al., 2014), and implementation barriers and facilitators from the perspective of HLF (Mendelson et al., 2013). Qualitative data from fifth- and sixth-graders showed that students remembered and used program skills involving breath work in their daily lives and described improved emotional regulation (Dariotis et al., 2016b) and stress reactions (Dariotis et al., 2016a). Students reported learning coping strategies, retaining and using program skills involving breath work and poses, and having knowledge about health benefits of these techniques that promoted self-utilization and sharing of skills. They also reported having keener emotional appraisals that, coupled with new and improved emotional regulation skills, helped de-escalate negative emotions, promote calm, and reduce stress. Additionally, students noted realistic and optimistic expectations for future impact of acquired program skills (Dariotis et al., 2016b). It is noteworthy that findings from HLF's evaluation studies highlight the pervasive nature of stress and trauma in the target population (e.g., by middle school, 52–93% of students had seen drug deals, 68–93% had heard gunshots, and 73–81% had witnessed beatings). Overall, quantitative and qualitative data suggest significant change in students' emotion regulation in response to HLF's school-based programming (Dariotis et al., 2016b; Gould et al., 2012; Mendelson et al., 2010), which parallels changes produced by other mindfulness-based intervention programs.

Whole-School Programs

Mindful Moment Initiatives

In 2014, HLF initiated a Mindful Moment Program (MMP), a whole-school program that has now been integrated into several schools (Semple et al., 2017). MMP involves 15 minutes of guided practice (e.g., yoga poses, meditation, and other mindfulness activities) twice a day (https://hlfinc.org/programs-services/mindful-moment-program/). The program begins with a few weeks of instructor-led classes, followed by guidance using audio recordings via the school's loudspeaker system. Additionally, schools have provided a devoted space for "mindfulness breaks," called the Mindful Moment Room, that is available throughout the school day. Rather than using traditional disciplinary strategies (suspensions and detentions), the Mindful Moment Room is used as an alternative calming place for students and teachers to down-regulate. In these rooms, yoga instructors lead students through mindfulness and yoga practices for about 20 minutes. Then, students return to their classroom in a more relaxed and calm state conducive to learning. Although MMP has not been formally evaluated, as a whole-school approach to mindful yoga, there is potential to positively change a school's culture by fostering greater compassion and mindfulness among students and teachers. The MMP may also affect how teachers and students approach classroom behavioral issues, with an understanding that withdrawing to a quiet place and focusing on breath work, meditation, and physical poses may be a helpful strategy for self-regulating.

Mission2Move

Mission2Move (M2M) is a Cincinnati-based non-profit organization started in 2016 by Sarah Habib (https://www.mission2move.org/). Disappointed by the lack of physical education in public schools, Habib was inspired to start a program in public schools. Cincinnati's public school students receive only 15 minutes per week of moderately vigorous to very vigorous movement, despite federal guidelines recommending 60 minutes per day of such movement (U.S. Department of Health and Human Services, 2018). In other words, Cincinnati students receive only 5% of the recommended 300 minutes of movement each week. M2M posits that a contributing factor to the chronic stress epidemic may be a lack of physical movement and emotional regulation in schools.

Chronic stress is a public health problem of epidemic proportions with roots in early childhood via exposure to ACEs (Felitti et al., 1998). In Cincinnati, preschool, elementary, and secondary school students are disproportionately impacted by ACEs relative to other cities in Ohio and across the nation. For example, nearly half (46.6%) of all children under age five living in Cincinnati are impoverished (U.S. Census Bureau, 2017). In comparison, only about one in five children (19.4%) in the Tri-State Area (Ohio, Indiana, and Kentucky) live below federal poverty levels. The purpose of M2M is to intervene early in life to alter negative trajectories by teaching emotional regulation and cognitive control strategies needed to promote resilience among youth.

The M2M program is a preventative intervention that teaches stress coping strategies (i.e., breathing, mindfulness, and physical movements that teach body-brain control) to both preschool children and their teachers. M2M merges movement strategies (e.g., Z-Health; zhealtheducation.com) and mindfulness meditation (e.g., Mindful Schools; Smith et al., 2012). The literature shows that physical activity in school is associated with better academic performance, although the mechanisms explaining this relationship are still unclear (CDC, 2010; Rasberry et al., 2011; Singh et al., 2012). By taking an early preventative approach to ACEs, M2M provides youth with movement, mindfulness, and resiliency education to aid in coping with trauma early in life rather than experiencing its untreated, unmanaged cumulative effects in adulthood. Within the context of M2M, resilience education is understood as the process of learning to adapt well in the face of adversity or significant sources of stress.

Mission2Move provides a comprehensive program that is designed to be incorporated into physical education classes and infused during academic classes so that it can be integrated more seamlessly into the regular school day and does not remove students from academic instruction to participate. The M2M program offers students three types of programming experiences during the school day: mindful movement class, academic class drop-in, and teacher-led Amazon Alexa skills. During mindful movement class, students participate in a 15-to-30-minute class once a week that consists of movements that are designed to "retrain" the brain-body connection regarding how body parts are supposed to move. This class consists of exercises including warm-ups, aerobic activity, and a "feelings circle" with hand breathing, all of which are guided by M2M's trained instructors in the gym. The movement and mindfulness exercises work in conjunction with each other to teach students how physical health is tied to social-emotional well-being and academic success. Three pilot RCTs have shown improvements in children's prosocial and problem behaviors and delayed gratification (Dariotis et al., 2020, in prep.).

During academic class drop-in, students are exposed to a five- to seven-minute lesson once a week in their homeroom class that consists of "neural drills" and hand breathing exercises led by an M2M staffer. During teacher-led Amazon Alexa skills, classroom teachers facilitate the practice of three (randomized) movement and hand-breathing exercises on a daily basis using an Amazon Alexa. Many of these exercises are replicas of the ones implemented in the mindful movement class. The variety of movements taught on the Amazon Alexa are increased as students become more familiar with them through experiences in the mindful movement class and academic class drop-in. The Amazon Alexa component on M2M minimizes classroom disruptions, eases transitions, and reduces teacher burden in implementing the techniques into the classroom. It also creates an engaging, feasible, and sustainable way for students to participate in the "neural drills," allowing for daily repetition of the exercises and facilitating integration of program elements into didactic and pedagogical routines throughout the day. The high cost associated with sending M2M instructors into the classroom to model behavior for both the teacher and the student are eventually replaced with the Amazon Alexa skills. Since COVID-19, schools using M2M have not yet widely deployed Amazon Alexas into their classrooms. As this technology became more pervasive, M2M was thought to be more likely to scale faster within a school; however, schools have largely opted for in-person implementation. Currently, the program is implemented district-wide in 45 public schools, reaching 134 classrooms and over 2,000 students every week. With the Alexa and web-based videos, teachers across the country and internationally may eventually learn how to implement the M2M program without needing an implementer in the classroom.

For teachers who are unable to participate in this three-component program, M2M has created an online training with voice-over professional development, in-classroom posters, and weekly video content that focuses on brief movement and mindfulness exercises that can be implemented by teachers in the classroom. New content is added weekly and provides teachers with 30-second lessons focusing on both movement and mindfulness to incorporate into the classroom. By making the program accessible online and generating new content on a regular basis, M2M reduces the burden of implementing mindful yoga and other movement strategies in the classroom and promotes sustainable programming for students. Further details regarding the M2M program can be obtained by visiting the program's current website: https://www.mission2move.org/.

WHERE TO START AND HOW TO RESOURCE MINDFULNESS PROGRAMMING?

Ensuring High-Quality Implementation

Implementing school-based mindful programs requires consideration of several potential issues, including barriers and facilitators of working with schools, as well as program-specific needs. Common to all programs is the need to gain entry into schools through administrative staff and to establish buy-in with students and teachers, which are no small feats. Building relationships with schools and establishing a partnership takes time and is vulnerable to administration and teacher turnover. Several studies have published lessons learned about facilitators and barriers related to mindful yoga programming in schools (Dariotis et al., 2017; Gould et al., 2014; Mendelson et al., 2013; Miller et al., 2014). Typical barriers are the gatekeepers, including teachers who refuse to release students from class to attend the program, lack of support from administrators (e.g., failure to provide space or arrange time and scheduling), ineffective communication between program implementers and school staff (e.g., teachers and principals), and the program conflicting with other school activities students prefer (e.g., lunch and resource time). Typical facilitators include positive instructor qualities (e.g., respectful, fair, nice), giving students a choice to voluntarily participate, demonstrating to teachers that the program will positively impact the classroom, and training teachers in mindful yoga practices.

Several recommendations for working with schools to implement programs, including mindful yoga, have been offered in the literature (Dariotis et al., 2017; Forman et al., 2009; Mendelson et al., 2013) and follow the guiding principles of community-based participatory research (CBPR; Israel et al., 1998). This discussion focuses on five major recommendations (for more detailed recommendations, see Dariotis et al., 2017 and Mendelson et al., 2013). First, plan for sufficient time to develop relationships and partnerships with schools and stakeholders. Relationships take substantial time, connections, and communication to foster. Such efforts should be built into the development and planning stages of the mindful yoga program. Both trust and expectations need to be established. Schools need to recognize the value-added of these programs for students and teachers to reinforce their investment. The benefits of the program should be well articulated and agreed upon.

Second, engage key stakeholders during the development stage of a program. It is important to engage school leadership (e.g., principals, assistant principals, superintendents, curriculum directors), teachers who will be impacted by the mindful yoga program, parents of children who will participate, a subset of students from the target population, and researchers or evaluators responsible for documenting program progress and outcomes. Having these key stakeholders involved from the outset will promote buy-in and, equally vital, will inform how best to implement a program. These stakeholders can serve as advocates for program implementation support and will know (a) what modifications, if any, are needed to make the program context culturally and developmentally informed, (b) pitfalls to avoid in program implementation, (c) feasibility of program elements, (d) how to secure needed resources, and (e) what data will need to be collected to demonstrate program efficacy or effectiveness. Planning a mindful yoga program and its implementation without engaging stakeholders during the development phase may result in resentment and perceptions that this is "just another program" being forced on the school, teachers, and students. Such negative perceptions can hinder the ability of programming to demonstrate positive effects.

Third, it is essential to have open and consistent communication to set clear expectations and to avoid or clarify misunderstandings. Given how long it sometimes takes to develop a mindful yoga program and implementation plan, stakeholder turnover is likely and constraints within schools may change (e.g., how many weeks a program may be implemented may be decreased). Keeping communication open and having previous stakeholders included in transition plans is ideal so that new leadership and teachers do not perceive they have inherited a program they do not know much about or that is not a high priority. Assuming everyone involved is busy and has competing demands, reminders and check-ins help to keep all parties informed and connected, especially when changes need to be made in real-time. Part of communication includes updates on program progress and dissemination of findings, as school stakeholders want to know how the program is unfolding and what, if any, outcomes emerge.

Fourth, flexibility and adaptability are essential, given that implementation plans may need to change at any moment to accommodate challenges that occur in schools (e.g., school closings, leadership and teacher turnover, changes in testing schedules). If a mindful yoga program has the flexibility to be delivered over a short time or with less frequency while still implementing core components, the likelihood of program success is greater. Programs that allow for problem-solving, adaptation, and adjustments are therefore likely to have more success in schools compared to rigid programming. Furthermore, incorporating the techniques and principles of mindful yoga into the academic curriculum ensures that participation does not take substantial time away from academic programming—and prevents against the mindful yoga programming having the feel of an "add-on" program.

Finally, it is important to ensure schools have the necessary resources for successful implementation. Schools need to provide space for mindful yoga programs—physical space as well as time or schedule space for implementation. Having a clean, dedicated physical space during the time programming is scheduled to occur is critical for successful program implementation. Other resources, however, should be provided by program implementers rather than schools. Many schools, especially public schools in impoverished areas, are operating on shoestring budgets that struggle to cover even necessary academic costs. Thus, there are likely minimal additional resources for programming needs (e.g., coordinator, yoga mats, computers, or paper for data collection administration). It is therefore important to provide those supplies and support program staff needed to implement the mindful yoga program, thereby reducing the amount of time teachers spend on program logistics (unless teachers are implementing the program). The goal is to reduce any disruption to the regular school day that could otherwise occur with new program implementation.

Resource Considerations

There are several mindful yoga programs to select from when considering school-based programming. It is critical to review the literature for programs that have been researched and evaluated in school settings to increase confidence in the effectiveness of the chosen program. It can also be helpful to reach out to program developers to inquire about their program, manuals, trainings, implementation supports, and trouble-shooting recommendations. Several reviews mentioned in this chapter contain a great deal of program information (e.g., Felver et al., 2016; Khalsa & Butzer, 2016; Zenner et al., 2014). Some of these programs are proprietary and may have costs associated with materials, yet there are some free online resources as well (e.g., Pure Edge; http://pureedgeinc.org). It is important to note that even though mindful yoga programs have been evaluated and researched, adaptations and modifications may be needed based on the current setting, contextual factors, characteristics, and needs of the population. Additionally, local mindful yoga practitioners and yoga studios may provide valuable resources, especially coupled with the use of existing curricula. Even with a curriculum, however, it may be necessary to secure funding to implement and evaluate a program. Possible sources of funding may include community or national foundations (e.g., W.T. Grant Foundation, Annie E. Casey Foundation, Doris Duke Charitable Foundation), state departments of education or health departments and funding entities, and federal funding agencies (e.g., National Institutes of Health, Substance Abuse and Mental Health Services Administration, U.S. Department of Education).

FUTURE DIRECTIONS FOR MINDFUL YOGA IN SCHOOLS

Research and Evaluation Efforts

Determining which components of mindful yoga programs—breathing, physical activity, meditation—are effective, in what combination, with what level of exposure (e.g., program duration), and with what other programming (e.g., mental health programs) has been understudied. For this reason, future studies need to identify and isolate the effect of mindful yoga components using precision-based research designs (Fishbein & Dariotis, 2019). Using the multiphase optimization strategy (MOST; Collins et al., 2009; Collins et al., 2016) or the sequential multiple assignment randomized trial (SMART; Almirall et al., 2014; Collins et al., 2007), a sequence of studies can identify components and dosage of mindful yoga that most effectively impact mechanisms underlying emotion regulation to produce a cost-efficient, optimized intervention for ready scaling. MOST enables researchers and evaluators to determine what components of an intervention produce the greatest effects (optimization), in which participants (moderation), and how it exerts those effects (mediation). MOST requires a factorial design, which means multiple schools or classrooms within schools could be randomized to different combinations of intervention (e.g., breathing only; physical poses only; meditation only; breathing and poses; breathing, poses, and meditation) or control conditions.

Barriers to MOST and SMART studies include funding and, in some settings, the inability to randomize students, classrooms, or schools to conditions. In general, MOST and SMART studies are expensive, as multiple conditions often require additional funding. Schools are often reluctant to allow randomization, especially if they know there is a possibility of receiving no intervention (e.g., waitlist or receiving "usual care" or "standard care"). This is understandable yet impedes our ability to know what program components are working, for whom, at what dosage, and in what context. Beyond this more detailed level of analysis, there is also a general need to fund program evaluation. Although mindful yoga programs are cost-effective, funding is still needed to rigorously evaluate these programs to document their efficacy and effectiveness and to move toward establishing them as evidence-based interventions.

There is also a need to focus future mindful yoga research more intentionally on youth populations. Mindful yoga is increasingly being integrated into the treatment of adult psychiatric disorders (e.g., anxiety, depression, pain, and insomnia; e.g., Brown & Gerbarg, 2005; Farb et al., 2012) and medical diseases (e.g., heart disease, high blood pressure, and diabetes; e.g., Bijlani et al., 2005). Yet the research base is lacking in regard to high-need children, from preschool through transition-aged youth who suffer from regulatory dysfunction (cf. Singh et al., 2013). Studies exploring the effects of mindful yoga programming among preschool youth, elementary school youth, adolescents, and those living in poverty are largely absent from the literature. Most of the research base focuses on adults and, thus, more programming and research is needed with younger populations.

Finally, given that mindful yoga programs in schools tend to focus on the benefits for students and youth, the potential benefits for teachers, administrators, and parents/caregivers are unknown. Students have reported sharing mindful yoga strategies learned in school-based programs with their parents, family members, and peers (Dariotis et al., 2016b). Yet this expansion of mindful yoga practices to affect other populations that are connected to schools and their stakeholders needs to be further explored. For example, it is still unknown to what extent implementing mindful yoga might influence a school's climate, such that it is characterized by greater compassion and positive stress coping and reactivity. Similarly, it is unknown how programming in one or more schools might impact a district. More research and evaluation studies are needed to explore and document efforts to expand the reach of school-based mindful yoga programs beyond students to their caregivers and the wider community.

Implementation Approaches

Systemic approaches that integrally involve school personnel are needed to better integrate mindful yoga into classrooms and schools. Training teachers on mindful yoga components during pre-service preparation programs and in-service professional development opportunities may be the most effective way to reach schools, classrooms, and students. Schools of education are quite effective at training future teachers to impart content knowledge (e.g., math, science, and language arts) to students, but they usually do not equip future teachers with techniques to effectively manage their own stress, regulate their emotions and thoughts, and have compassion for self or others—or with the competencies to impart such knowledge and skills to students. Given burnout is quite high among teachers, and teachers may model suboptimal and even detrimental stress management to students, having required (rather than elective) courses on mindfulness-based strategies for personal and classroom implementation, such as mindful yoga, has the potential to spark change in educational systems. Training future teachers to practice mindfulness themselves and to use it to translate positive stress coping strategies and self-care to students is of utmost importance.

Roeser and colleagues (e.g., Roeser et al., 2012) have conducted some of the first studies on the use of mindfulness training with teachers in urban and suburban settings. Although yoga practices were not a focus of this research, the findings are relevant and instructive. Development, feasibility, and efficacy studies have demonstrated that mindfulness training is feasible for teachers and that it improves teachers' attention, mindful awareness, and emotion regulation—with training-induced changes in mindful awareness mediating the effects of the program on teachers' well-being (Benn et al., 2012; Roeser et al., 2013; Taylor et al., 2016). Although mindfulness training has been implemented as part of teachers' professional development (Roeser et al., 2012), it has not been studied as part of pre-service and in-service teacher preparation programs. Incorporating mindful yoga training into the educational training of teachers may have long-standing effects for the educational systems, as it may remove the burden on districts or schools to incorporate such training as part of teachers' professional development.

By systemically changing how educational settings as well as related higher-education training programs (e.g., social work, school counseling, school psychology, and educational leadership) train and prepare the next generation of primary and secondary teachers, counselors, and principals to address their own mental and physical health needs via mindfulness and mindful yoga practices, benefits will transfer to students. In turn, these structural changes promise to promote more positive classroom environments (e.g., less need for classroom behavioral management by teachers), school climates (e.g., a shift toward greater compassion), and adaptive functioning of teachers and students (Harris et al., 2016; Jennings et al., 2013). Such changes in teacher preparation may ultimately result in more sustainable training and farther-reaching exposure and impacts compared to typical "one-and-done" program approaches, because teachers may be able to continuously implement these practices, reaching new cohorts of students each year. This is especially important as states begin to integrate daily or weekly time devoted to relaxation for stress reduction and fostering social-emotional learning and positive mental health. For example, Illinois State Bill 2872 proposes 20 minutes weekly for relaxation in schools and has passed both the state House and Senate.

In addition to changes in training, studying how technology can assist with mindful yoga program implementation is another future direction for the field. As described earlier in the chapter, the M2M program is using the Amazon Alexa and web-based videos to assist preschool teachers with program implementation. By asking Alexa to play a M2M 30-second lesson or by viewing M2M videos, teachers are equipped to implement lessons in their classroom on a daily basis without incurring the cost of an interventionist in the classroom. Furthermore, the HLF uses audio recordings to sustain mindful moments in schools. Smart phones can also be used to remind the user to practice breath work or other strategies learned in mindful yoga sessions, which may increase implementation integrity or exposure, thereby boosting the effectiveness of programming. Although these technology-based strategies are typically utilized after in-person training and demonstration with implementers, the use of technology has implications for scalability and sustainability of mindful yoga, not only for school-based programming but also for translation to other settings. For example, audio or video materials may promote home practice of skills taught in school or encourage the sharing of such skills with other family members and friends. Studies that rigorously research and evaluate the efficacy and effectiveness of technology-assisted implementation will thus expand the research base regarding mindful yoga implementation approaches in schools.

CONCLUSION

In conclusion, there is a growing body of evidence to suggest that school-based mindful yoga programs improve students' emotional and behavioral regulation, executive cognitive functioning, and stress reactivity. Such positive findings suggest that increasing availability of mindful yoga programs may be a highly worthwhile objective for schools. School-based mindful yoga programs have been successfully implemented in schools both as individual add-on programs and whole-school initiatives. Several programs exist as models for practitioners who would like to incorporate mindful yoga into their educational settings. Recommendations for starting the process include developing relationships with stakeholders in educational settings, engaging stakeholders from the onset of program planning and development, maintaining open and consistent communication, building flexibility into programs to accommodate adaptations, and ensuring that schools have the necessary resources for program implementation. And for future directions, there is a need for additional research to further establish mindful yoga programs as evidence-based interventions for youth, ongoing evaluation to integrate mindfulness training into teacher preparation and related higher-education programs, exploring the degree of impact for specific mindful yoga program components and dosage, expanding the reach of program effects beyond schools, and investigating technology-assisted program implementation. Although there is much more work to be done, this is an exciting time for mindful yoga research and evaluation.

REFERENCES

Almirall, D., Nahum-Shani, I., Sherwood, N. E., & Murphy, S. A. (2014). Introduction to SMART designs for the development of adaptive interventions: With application to weight loss research. *Translational Behavioral Medicine*, *4*(3), 260–274. doi:10.1007/s13142-014-0265-0

Benn, R., Akiva, T., Arel, S., & Roeser, R. W. (2012). Mindfulness training effects for parents and educators of children with special needs. *Developmental Psychology*, *48*, 1476–1487. doi:10.1037/a0027537

Bierman, K. L., Nix, R. L., Greenberg, M. T., Blair, C., & Domitrovich, C. E. (2008). Executive functions and school readiness intervention: Impact, moderation, and mediation in the Head Start REDI program. *Development and Psychopathology*, *20*(3), 821–843. doi:10.1017/S0954579408000394

Bijlani, R. L., Vempati, R. P., Yadav, R. K., Ray, R. B., Gupta, V., Sharma, R., Mehta, N., & Mahapatra, S. C. (2005). A brief but comprehensive lifestyle education program based on yoga reduces risk factors for cardiovascular disease and diabetes mellitus. *Journal of Alternative & Complementary Medicine*, *11*(2), 267–274.

Blair, C., Raver, C. C., & Berry, D. J. (2014). Two approaches to estimating the effect of parenting on the development of executive function in early childhood. *Developmental Psychology*, *50*(2), 554. doi:10.1037/a0033647

Briere, J., Hodges, M., & Godbout, N. (2010). Traumatic stress, affect dysregulation, and dysfunctional avoidance: A structural equation model. *Journal of Traumatic Stress*, *23*(6), 767–774. doi:10.1002/jts.20578

Brown, R. P., & Gerbarg, P. L. (2005) Sudarshan Kriya yogic breathing in the treatment of stress, anxiety and depression: Part II—clinical applications and guidelines. *The Journal of Alternative and Complementary Medicine*, *11*, 711–717. doi:10.1089/acm.2005.11.711

Brown, R. P., & Gerbarg, P. L. (2009). Yoga breathing, meditation, and longevity. *Annals of the New York Academy of Sciences*, *1172*(1), 54. doi:10.1111/j.1749-6632.2009.04394.x

Carlson, L. E. (2012). Mindfulness-based interventions for physical conditions: A narrative review evaluating levels of evidence. *ISRN Psychiatry*, *2012*. doi:10.5402/2012/651583

Carsley, D., Khoury, B., & Heath, N. L. (2018). Effectiveness of mindfulness interventions for mental health in schools: A comprehensive meta-analysis. *Mindfulness*, *9*, 693–707. doi:10.1007/s12671-017-0839-2

Centers for Disease Control and Prevention. (2010). *The association between school based physical activity, including physical education, and academic performance.* US Department of Health and Human Services.

Collins, L. M., Dziak, J. J., & Li, R. (2009). Design of experiments with multiple independent variables: A resource management perspective on complete and reduced factorial designs. *Psychological Methods*, *14*(3), 202–224.

Collins, L. M., Kugler, K. C., & Gwadz, M. V. (2016). Optimization of multicomponent behavioral and biobehavioral interventions for the prevention and treatment of HIV/AIDS. *AIDS and Behavior*, *20*(1), 197–214.

Collins, L. M., Murphy, S. A., & Strecher, V. (2007). The multiphase optimization strategy (MOST) and the sequential multiple assignment randomized trial (SMART): New methods for more potent eHealth interventions. *American Journal of Preventive Medicine*, *32*(5), S112–S118.

Dariotis, J. K., Cluxton-Keller, F., Mirabal-Beltran, R., Gould, L. F., Greenberg, M. T., & Mendelson, T. (2016a). "The program affects me 'cause it gives away stress": Urban students' qualitative perspectives on stress and a school-based mindful yoga intervention. *Explore: The Journal of Science and Healing*, *12*(6), 443–450.

Dariotis, J. K., Habib, S. F., Toraman, S., & Mabisi, K. (2020). *A preschool-based mindful movement intervention: An experimental study of the Mission2Move program.* Paper presentation at the Society for Prevention Research, May 26–May 29, 2020, Washington, DC. COVID-19 interference.

Dariotis, J. K., Mabisi, K., Jackson-Gordon, R., Rose, E. J., Fishbein, D. H., & Mendelson, T. (2023a). Perceived benefits of mindfulness and health education programs for minoritized adolescents: A qualitative analysis. *Mindfulness*, *14*(6), 1346–1361.

Dariotis, J. K., Mabisi, K., Jackson-Gordon, R., Yang, N., Rose, E. J., Mendelson, T., & Fishbein, D. H. (2023b). Implementing adolescent wellbeing and health programs in schools: Insights from a mixed methods and multiple informant study. *Prevention Science*, *24*(4), 663–675.

Dariotis, J. K., Mabisi, K., Yang, N., Jackson-Gordon, R., & Habib, S. F. (in preparation). A Preschool-Based Mindful Movement Intervention: Two Experimental Studies of the Mission2Move Program.

Dariotis, J. K., Mirabal-Beltran, R., Cluxton-Keller, F., Gould, L. F., Greenberg, M. T., & Mendelson, T. (2016b). A qualitative evaluation of student learning and skills use in a school-based mindfulness and yoga program. *Mindfulness*, *7*, 76–89.

Dariotis, J. K., Mirabal-Beltran, R., Cluxton-Keller, F., Gould, L. F., Greenberg, M. T., & Mendelson, T. (2017). A qualitative exploration of implementation factors in a school-based mindfulness and yoga program: Lessons learned from students and teachers. *Psychology in the Schools*, *54*, 53–69.

Davidson, R. J., Kabat-Zinn, J., Schumacher, J., Rosenkranz, M., Muller, D., Santorelli, S. F., Urbanowski, F., Harrington, A., Bonus, K., & Sheridan, J. F. (2003). Alterations in brain and immune function produced by mindfulness meditation. *Psychosomatic Medicine*, *65*(4), 564–570.

Davis, J. M., Fleming, M. F., Bonus, K. A., & Baker, T. B. (2007). A pilot study on mindfulness based stress reduction for smokers. *BMC Complementary and Alternative Medicine*, *7*(1), 2.

Duggan, K., & Julliard, K. (2018). Implementation of a mindfulness moment initiative for healthcare professionals: Perceptions of facilitators. *Explore, 14*(1), 44–58.

Dunning, D. L., Griffiths, K., Kuyken, W., Crane, C., Foulkes, L., Parker, J., & Dalgleish, T. (2019). Research review: The effects of mindfulness-based interventions on cognition and mental health in children and adolescents—A meta-analysis of randomized controlled trials. *Journal of Child Psychology and Psychiatry, 60*(3), 244–258. doi:10.1111/jcpp.12980

Eisenberg, N., Spinrad, T. L., & Eggum, N. D. (2010). Emotion-related self-regulation and its relation to children's maladjustment. *Annual Review of Clinical Psychology, 6*, 495. doi:10.1146/annurev.clinpsy.121208.131208

Ernst, M., Pine, D. S., & Hardin, M. (2006). Triadic model of the neurobiology of motivated behavior in adolescence. *Psychological Medicine, 36*, 299–312. doi:10.1017/S0033291705005891

Farb, N. A., Anderson, A. K., & Segal, Z. V. (2012). The mindful brain and emotion regulation in mood disorders. *Canadian Journal of Psychiatry, 57*(2), 70. doi:10.1177/070674371205700203

Feldman, G., Hayes, A., Kumar, S., Greeson, J., & Laurenceau, J. P. (2007). Mindfulness and emotion regulation: The development and initial validation of the Cognitive and Affective Mindfulness Scale-Revised (CAMS-R). *Journal of Psychopathology and Behavioral Assessment, 29*(3), 177–190. doi:10.1007/s10862-006-9035-8

Felitti, V. J., Anda, R. F., Nordenberg, D., Williamson, D. F., Spitz, A. M., Edwards, V., & Marks, J. S. (1998). Relationship of childhood abuse and household dysfunction to many of the leading causes of death in adults: The adverse childhood experiences (ACE) study. *American Journal of Preventive Medicine, 14*(4), 245–258. doi:10.1016/j.amepre.2019.04.001

Felver, J. C., Celis-de Hoyos, C. E., Tezanos, K., & Singh, N. N. (2016). A systematic review of mindfulness-based interventions for youth in school settings. *Mindfulness, 7*(1), 34–45. doi:10.1007/s12671-015-0389-4

Fishbein, D. (2000). The importance of neurobiological research to the prevention of psychopathology. *Prevention Science, 1*(2), 89–106.

Fishbein, D. H., & Dariotis, J. K. (2019). Personalizing and optimizing preventive intervention models via a translational neuroscience framework. *Prevention Science, 20*, 10–20. doi:10.1007/s11121-017-0851-8

Fishbein, D. H., Stahl, M., Eldreth, D., Hyde, C., Paschall, M. J., Ialongo, N., Hubal, R., & Hubbard, S. (2006). Mediators of the stress-drug use relationship in high-risk urban adolescents. *Prevention Science, 7*, 113–126. doi:10.1007/s11121-006-0027-4

Fjorback, L. O., Arendt, M., Ørnbøl, E., Walach, H., Rehfeld, E., Schröder, A., & Fink, P. (2013). Mindfulness therapy for somatization disorder and functional somatic syndromes—Randomized trial with one-year follow-up. Journal of Psychosomatic Research, 74(1), 31–40. https://doi.org/10.1016/j.jpsychores.2012.09.006

Flook, L., Goldberg, S. B., Pinger, L., & Davidson, R. J. (2015). Promoting prosocial behavior and self-regulatory skills in preschool children through a mindfulness-based kindness curriculum. *Developmental Psychology, 51*, 44–51. doi:10.1037/a0038256.supp

Forman, S. G., Olin, S. S., Hoagwood, K. E., Crowe, M., & Saka, N. (2009). Evidence-based interventions in schools: Developers' views of implementation barriers and facilitators. *School Mental Health, 1*(1), 26–36. doi:10.1007/s12310-008-9002-5

Fox, N. A., & Calkins, S. D. (2003). The development of self-control of emotion: Intrinsic and extrinsic influences. *Motivation and Emotion, 27*(1), 7–26.

Froeliger, B. E., Garland, E. L., Modlin, L. A., & McClernon, F. J. (2012). Neurocognitive correlates of the effects of yoga meditation practice on emotion and cognition: A pilot study. *Frontiers in Integrative Neuroscience, 6*. doi:10.3389/fnint.2012.00048

Gard, T., Noggle, J. J., Park, C. L., Vago, D. R., & Wilson, A. (2014). Potential self-regulatory mechanisms of yoga for psychological health. *Frontiers in Human Neuroscience, 8*, 770. doi:10.3389/fnhum.2014.00770

Garland, E. L., Froeliger, B., & Howard, M. O. (2013). Mindfulness training targets neurocognitive mechanisms of addiction at the attention-appraisal-emotion interface. *Frontiers in Psychiatry*, 4. doi:10.3389/fpsyt.2013.00173

Garland, E. L., Hudak, J., Hanley, A. W., & Nakamura, Y. (2020). Mindfulness-oriented recovery enhancement reduces opioid dose in primary care by strengthening autonomic regulation during meditation. *American Psychologist, 75*(6), 840–852. https://doi.org/10.1037/amp0000638

Goldin, P. R., & Gross, J. J. (2010). Effects of mindfulness-based stress reduction (MBSR) on emotion regulation in social anxiety disorder. *Emotion, 10*(1), 83–91. doi:10.1037/a0018441

Gould, L. F., Dariotis, J. K., Mendelson, T., & Greenberg, M. T. (2012). A school-based mindfulness intervention for urban youth: Exploring moderators of intervention effects. *Journal of Community Psychology, 40*(8), 968–982. doi:10.1002/jcop.21505

Gould, L. F., Mendelson, T., Dariotis, J. K., Ancona, M., Smith, A. S., Gonzalez, A. A., Smith, A. A., & Greenberg, M. T. (2014). Assessing fidelity of core components in a mindfulness and yoga intervention for urban youth: Applying the CORE process. *New Directions for Youth Development, 2014*(142), 59–81. doi:10.1002/yd.20097

Greenberg, M. T., & Harris, A. R. (2012). Nurturing mindfulness in children and youth: Current state of research. *Child Development Perspectives, 6*(2), 161–166. doi:10.1111/j.1750-8606.2011.00215.x

Harris, A. R., Jennings, P. A., Katz, D. A., Abenavoli, R. M., & Greenberg, M. T. (2016). Promoting stress management and wellbeing in educators: Feasibility and efficacy of a school-based yoga and mindfulness intervention. *Mindfulness, 7*(1), 143–154. doi:10.1007/s12671-015-0451-2

Hofmann, W., Schmeichel, B. J., & Baddeley, A. D. (2012). Executive functions and self-regulation. *Trends in Cognitive Sciences, 16*(3), 174–180. doi:10.1016/j.tics.2012.01.006

Hölzel, B. K., Carmody, J., Vangel, M., Congleton, C., Yerramsetti, S. M., Gard, T., & Lazar, S. W. (2011a). Mindfulness practice leads to increases in regional brain gray matter density. *Psychiatry Research: Neuroimaging, 191*(1), 36–43. doi:10.1016/j.pscychresns.2010.08.006

Hölzel, B. K., Lazar, S. W., Gard, T., Schuman-Olivier, Z., Vago, D. R., & Ott, U. (2011b). How does mindfulness meditation work? Proposing mechanisms of action from a conceptual and neural perspective. *Perspectives on Psychological Science, 6*, 537–559. doi:10.1177/1745691611419671

Hsu, N. S., Novick, J. M., & Jaeggi, S. M. (2014). The development and malleability of executive control abilities. *Frontiers in Behavioral Neuroscience, 8*, 221. doi:10.3389/fnbeh.2014.00221

Israel, B. A., Schulz, A. J., Parker, E. A., & Becker, A. B. (1998). Review of community-based research: Assessing partnership approaches to improve public health. *Annual Review of Public Health, 19*(1), 173–202. doi:10.1146/annurev.publhealth.19.1.173

Iyengar, B. K. S. (1966). *Light on yoga*. Allen & Unwin.

Jennings, P. A., Frank, J. L., Snowberg, K. E., Coccia, M. A., & Greenberg, M. T. (2013). Improving classroom learning environments by Cultivating Awareness and Resilience in Education (CARE): Results of a randomized controlled trial. *School Psychology Quarterly, 28*(4), 374–390. doi:10.1037/spq0000035

Jerath, R., Crawford, M. W., Barnes, V. A., & Harden, K. (2015). Self-regulation of breathing as a primary treatment for anxiety. *Applied Psychophysiology and Biofeedback, 40*(2), 107–115. doi:10.1007/s10484-015-9279-8

Kabat-Zinn, J. (2003). Mindfulness-based interventions in context: Past, present, and future. *Clinical Psychology: Science and Practice, 10*(2), 144–156. doi:10.1093/clipsy.bpg016

Kabat-Zinn, J., Massion, A. O., Kristeller, J., & Peterson, L. G. (1992). Effectiveness of a meditation-based stress reduction program in the treatment of anxiety disorders. *The American Journal of Psychiatry, 149(7)*, 936–943.

Khalsa, S. B. S., & Butzer, B. (2016). Yoga in school settings: A research review. *Annals of the New York Academy of Sciences, 1373*(1), 45–55. doi: 10.1111/nyas.13025

Khalsa, S. B., Hickey-Schultz, L., Cohen, D., Steiner, N., & Cope, S. (2012). Evaluation of the mental health benefits of yoga in a secondary school: A preliminary randomized controlled trial. *Journal of Behavioral Health Services & Research, 39*(1), 80–90. doi:10.1007/s11414-011-9249-8

Khoury, B., Lecomte, T., Fortin, G., Masse, M., Therien, P., Bouchard, V., Chapleau, M., Paquin, K., & Hofmann, S. G. (2013). Mindfulness-based therapy: A comprehensive meta-analysis. *Clinical Psychology Review, 33*(6), 763–771. doi:10.1016/j.cpr.2013.05.005

Klingbeil, D. A., Renshaw, T. L., Willenbrink, J. B., Copek, R. A., Chan, K. T., Haddock, A., . . . Clifton, J. (2017). Mindfulness-based interventions with youth: A comprehensive meta-analysis of group design studies. *Journal of School Psychology, 63*, 77–103. doi:10.1016/j.jsp.2017.03.006

Kristeller, J. L., Baer, R. A., & Quillian-Wolever, R. (2006). Mindfulness-based approaches to eating disorders. In R. A. Baer (Ed.), *Mindfulness-based treatment approaches: Clinician's guide to evidence base and applications* (pp. 75–91). Academic Press.

McEwen, B. S., & Morrison, J. H. (2013). The brain on stress: Vulnerability and plasticity of the prefrontal cortex over the life course. *Neuron, 79*, 16–29. doi:10.1016/j.neuron.2013.06.028

Mendelson, T., Dariotis, J. K., Gould, L. F., Smith, A. S. R. A., Smith, A. A., Gonzalez, A. A., & Greenberg, M. T. (2013). Implementing mindfulness and yoga in urban schools: A community-academic partnership. *Journal of Children's Services, 8*(4), 276–291. doi:10.1108/JCS-07-2013-0024

Mendelson, T., Greenberg, M. T., Dariotis, J., Gould, L. F., Rhoades, B., & Leaf, P. J. (2010). Feasibility and preliminary outcomes of a school-based mindfulness intervention for urban youth. *Journal of Abnormal Child Psychology, 38*, 985–994. doi:10.1007/s10802-010-9418-x

Miller, S., Herman-Stahl, M., Fishbein, D., Lavery, B., Johnson, M., & Markovits, L. (2014). Use of formative research to develop a yoga curriculum for high-risk youth:

Implementation considerations. *Advances in School Mental Health Promotion*, *7*(3), 171–183. doi:10.1080/1754730X.2014.916496

Pagnoni, G., Cekic, M., & Guo, Y. (2008). "Thinking about not-thinking": Neural correlates of conceptual processing during Zen meditation. *PLoS One*, *3*(9), e3083. doi:10.1371/journal.pone.0003083

Paulson, S., Davidson, R., Jha, A., & Kabat-Zinn, J. (2013). Becoming conscious: The science of mindfulness. *Annals of the New York Academy of Sciences*, *1303*(1), 87–104. doi:10.1111/nyas.12203

Pilkington, K., Kirkwood, G., Rampes, H., & Richardson, J. (2005). Yoga for depression: The research evidence. *Journal of Affective Disorders*, *89*, 13–24. doi:10.1016/j.jad.2005.08.013

Prenoveau, J. M., Papadakis, A. A., Schmitz, J., Hirsch, E. L., Dariotis, J. K., & Mendelson, T. (2018). Psychometric properties of the Child and Adolescent Mindfulness Measure (CAMM) in racial minority adolescents from low-income environments. *Psychological Assessment*, *30*(10), 1395–1400. doi:10.1037/pas0000630

Rasberry, C. N., Lee, S. M., Robin, L., Laris, B. A., Russell, L. A., Coyle, K. K., & Nihiser, A. J. (2011). The association between school-based physical activity, including physical education, and academic performance: A systematic review of the literature. *Preventive Medicine*, *52*, S10–S20. doi:10.1016/j.ypmed.2011.01.027

Reynolds, A. J., Temple, J. A., Robertson, D. L., & Mann, E. A. (2001). Long-term effects of an early childhood intervention on educational achievement and juvenile arrest: A 15-year follow-up of low-income children in public schools. *Journal of the American Medical Association*, *285*, 2339–2346. doi:10.1001/jama.285.18.2339

Ricard, M., Lutz, A., & Davidson, R. J. (2014). Mind of the meditator. *Scientific American*, *311*(5), 38–45.

Rocha, K. K. F., Ribeiro, A. M., Rocha, K. C. F., Sousa, M. B. C., Albuquerque, F. S., Ribeiro, S., & Silva, R. H. (2012). Improvement in physiological and psychological parameters after 6 months of yoga practice. *Consciousness and Cognition*, *21*(2), 843–850. doi:10.1016/j.concog.2012.01.014

Roeser, R. W., Schonert-Reichl, K. A., Jha, A., Cullen, M., Wallace, L., Wilensky, R., Oberle, E., Thomson, K., Taylor, C., & Harrison, J. (2013). Mindfulness training and reductions in teacher stress and burnout: Results from two randomized, waitlist-control field trials. *Journal of Educational Psychology*, 105, 787–804. doi:10.1037/a0032093

Roeser, R. W., Skinner, E., Beers, J., & Jennings, P. A. (2012). Mindfulness training and teachers' professional development: An emerging area of research and practice. *Child Development Perspectives*, *6*(2), 167–173. doi:10.1111/j.1750-8606.2012.00238.x

Rose, E. J., Dariotis, J. K. [first co-authors], Lewis, G., Eldreth, D. A., Mendelson, T., and Fishbein, D. H. (in press). Distinct latent profiles predict associations between stress physiology and risk for conduct problems in 'at-risk' youth. *Journal of Research on Adolescence*. Special issue: Advancing studies of adolescent development from bench science to preventive interventions and policy through interdisciplinary research.

Schmalzl, L., Powers, C., & Blom, E. H. (2015). Neurophysiological and neurocognitive mechanisms underlying the effects of yoga-based practices: Towards a comprehensive theoretical framework. *Frontiers in Human Neuroscience*, *9*, 235. doi:10.3389/fnhum.2015.00235

Schonert-Reichl, K. A., Oberle, E., Lawlor, M. S., Abbott, D., Thomson, K., Oberlander, T. F., & Diamond, A. (2015). Enhancing cognitive and social-emotional development through a simple-to-administer mindfulness-based school program for elementary school children: A randomized controlled trial. *Developmental Psychology*, *51*, 52–66. doi:10.1037/a0038454

Schore, A. N. (2005). Attachment, affect regulation, and the developing right brain: Linking developmental neuroscience to pediatrics. *Pediatrics in Review*, *26*(6), 204–217. doi:10.1542/pir.26-6-204

Semple, R. J., Droutman, V., & Reid, B. A. (2017). Mindfulness goes to school: Things learned (so far) from research and real-world experiences. *Psychology in the Schools*, *54*(1), 29–52. doi:10.1002/pits.21981

Singh, A., Uijtdewilligen, L., Twisk, J. W., Van Mechelen, W., & Chinapaw, M. J. (2012). Physical activity and performance at school: A systematic review of the literature including a methodological quality assessment. *Archives of Pediatrics & Adolescent Medicine*, *166*(1), 49–55. doi:10.1001/archpediatrics.2011.716

Singh, N. N., Lancioni, G. E., Winton, A. S., Karazsia, B. T., & Singh, J. (2013). Mindfulness training for teachers changes the behavior of their preschool students. *Research in Human Development*, *10*(3), 211–233. doi:10.1080/15427609.2013.818484

Smith, A., Guzman-Alvarez, A., Westover, T., Keller, S., & Fuller, S. (2012). *Mindful Schools program evaluation*. Unpublished manuscript. Center for Education and Evaluation Services, University of California at Davis.

Steinberg, L. (2005). Cognitive and affective development in adolescence. *Trends in Cognitive Sciences*, *9*(2), 69–74. doi:10.1016/j.tics.2004.12.005

Stuss, D. T. (2011). The future of cognitive neurorehabilitation. *Neuropsychological Rehabilitation*, *21*(5), 755–768. doi:10.1080/09602011.2011.605590

Tang, Y. Y., Ma, Y., Wang, J., Fan, Y., Feng, S., Lu, Q., & Posner, M. I. (2007). Short-term meditation training improves attention and self-regulation. *Proceedings of the National Academy of Sciences*, *104*(43), 17152–17156. doi:10.1073/pnas.0707678104

Taylor, C., Harrison, J., Haimovitz, K., Oberle, E., Thomson, K., Schonert-Reichl, K., & Roeser, R. W. (2016). Examining ways that a mindfulness-based intervention reduces stress in public school teachers: A mixed-methods study. *Mindfulness*, *7*(1), 115–129. doi:10.1007/s12671-015-0425-4

Teper, R., Segal, Z. V., & Inzlicht, M. (2013). Inside the mindful mind: How mindfulness enhances emotion regulation through improvements in executive control. *Current Directions in Psychological Science*, *22*(6), 449–454. doi:10.1177/0963721413495869

Tomasino, B., Chiesa, A., & Fabbro, F. (2014). Disentangling the neural mechanisms involved in Hinduism- and Buddhism-related meditations. *Brain and Cognition*, *90*, 32–40. doi:10.1016/j.bandc.2014.03.013

Tracy, J. I., & Osipowicz, K. Z. (2011). A conceptual framework for interpreting neuroimaging studies of brain neuroplasticity and cognitive recovery. *NeuroRehabilitation*, *29*(4), 331–338. doi:10.3233/NRE-2011-0709

Tull, M. T., Bardeen, J. R., DiLillo, D., Messman-Moore, T., & Gratz, K. L. (2015). A prospective investigation of emotion dysregulation as a moderator of the relation between posttraumatic stress symptoms and substance use severity. *Journal of Anxiety Disorders*, *29*, 52–60. doi:10.1016/j.janxdis.2014.11.003

U.S. Census Bureau. (2017). *Cincinnati City, Ohio population estimates: July 2017*. Retrieved from https://www.census.gov/quickfacts/cincinnaticityohio

U.S. Department of Health and Human Services. (2018). *Physical activity guidelines for Americans* (2nd ed.). Author.

Venkatakrishnan, A., & Sandrini, M. (2012). Combining transcranial direct current stimulation and neuroimaging: Novel insights in understanding neuroplasticity. *Journal of Neurophysiology*, *107*(1), 1–4. doi:10.1152/jn.00557.2011

Vøllestad, J., Nielsen, M. B., & Nielsen, G. H. (2012). Mindfulness- and acceptance-based interventions for anxiety disorders: A systematic review and meta-analysis. *British Journal of Clinical Psychology*, *51*(3), 239–260. doi:10.1111/j.2044-8260.2011.02024.x

Weare, K. (2013). Developing mindfulness with children and young people: A review of the evidence and policy context. *Journal of Children's Services*, *8*(2), 141–153.

Zenner, C., Herrnleben-Kurz, S., & Walach, H. (2014). Mindfulness-based interventions in schools—A systematic review and meta-analysis. *Frontiers in Psychology*, *5*, 603. doi:10.3389/fpsyg.2014.00603

Zoogman, S., Goldberg, S. B., Hoyt, W. T., & Miller, L. (2014). Mindfulness interventions with youth: A meta-analysis. *Mindfulness*, *6*(2), 290–302. doi:10.1007/s12671-013-0260-4

9

Dialectical Behavior Therapy Skills in Schools

JAMES J. MAZZA AND ELIZABETH DEXTER-MAZZA ■

The concept of teaching mindfulness in schools has gained considerable traction over the past 10 years (Carsley et al., 2018; Zenner et al., 2014). This trend has not come without controversy, yet the data collected from recent studies appears to show support for the effectiveness of mindfulness-based interventions at elementary, middle, and high school levels (Carsley et al., 2018).

Although the concept of mindfulness being taught in schools is fairly recent (Felver et al., 2016; Tan, 2016), the implementation of mindfulness strategies in schools with adolescents has been ongoing for over a decade with dialectical behavior therapy (DBT; Miller et al., 2007) and has been used in eastern meditational and spiritual practices for hundreds of years (Kabat-Zinn, 1994). Kabat-Zinn (1994), who developed the treatment called mindfulness-based stress reduction (MBSR; Kabat-Zinn et al., 1992), defines mindfulness as: "paying attention in a particular way, on purpose, in the present moment, and nonjudgmentally" (p. 4).

In DBT, mindfulness is not taught as a particular meditation, religion, or spirituality, but rather as a set of skillful behaviors that allows individuals to focus on living in the present moment and learning how to control their attention to the here and now (Mazza et al., 2016). The DBT mindfulness skills developed by Linehan (1993, 2015a) are grounded in the practice of mindfulness from the Zen tradition (as compared to other Buddhist mindfulness traditions, such as Tibetan or Vipassana, or Christian Contemplative Prayer). Although the concept of mindfulness as trained in DBT is fairly easy to grasp, the implementation of effective mindfulness skills takes practice and dedicated time to learn and integrate into one's life.

James J. Mazza and Elizabeth Dexter-Mazza, *Dialectical Behavior Therapy Skills in Schools*. In: *Using Mindfulness to Promote Mental Health in Schools*. Edited by: Tyler L. Renshaw and Shane R. Jimerson, Oxford University Press.
 DOI: 10.1093/9780190880507.003.0009

This chapter focuses on mindfulness as it relates to school-based settings and uses the framework of DBT to describe the different components of mindfulness-based practices. Additionally, this chapter highlights related skills and strategies that are taught within a universal (school-wide) curriculum designed for middle and high school students: *DBT Skills in Schools: Skills Training for Emotional Problem Solving for Adolescents* (DBT STEPS-A; Mazza et al., 2016). This chapter also integrates current research in the area of mindfulness through a school-based DBT lens, showing how mindfulness skills are essential in providing the foundation for the acquisition of other DBT skills. Finally, this chapter discusses current gaps in the field regarding school-based mindfulness research as well as limitations and barriers related to using mindfulness from a DBT perspective.

WHAT IS DBT?

Because the lens of DBT is used throughout this chapter, it is important to understand what it is. In short, DBT is a comprehensive, empirically based treatment for individuals who have pervasive problems of emotional dysregulation (Linehan, 1993, 2015a). More specifically, DBT is a behavioral change-based treatment that dialectically weaves in acceptance strategies. It is based on a dialectical philosophy that two opposing things can be true and present at the same time. For example, we may say that a student is doing the best they can *and* that the student has to do more. In DBT, the primary dialectic present throughout the treatment is the continual balance of acceptance and change. The four modules of DBT skills also follow this dialectic: the Core Mindfulness and Distress Tolerance skills of DBT are considered acceptance-based skills, whereas the Emotion Regulation and Interpersonal Effectiveness skills are change-based skills.

Although initially focused on individuals diagnosed with borderline personality disorder, DBT has been shown to be effective for improving numerous mental health difficulties, such as post-traumatic stress disorder (PTSD), depression, anxiety, substance abuse, and self-harming/suicidal behavior (McCauley et al., 2018; Mehlum et al., 2014, 2016; Neacsiu et al., 2014; Pistorello et al., 2012). This broad application of DBT is important to highlight, as it parallels the breadth of mental health difficulties that are experienced by adolescents and young adults in schools (Carsley et al., 2018; Mazza, 2019). Research has shown that most mental health difficulties are first experienced during adolescence and emerging adulthood (American Psychiatric Association, 2013), thus, providing a strong rationale for delivering evidence-based mental health programs in schools—particularly for middle and high school students (Gouda et al., 2016; Lau & Hue, 2011; Metz et al., 2013).

Comprehensive outpatient DBT has been adapted by Miller and colleagues (Miller et al., 1997; Rathus & Miller, 2002) for adolescents and modified for use in school-based mental health programs with high-risk students. This adaptation is now referred to as "comprehensive school-based DBT" (CSB-DBT). In CSB-DBT, students identified by school-based clinicians as in need of DBT would receive the comprehensive treatment model in their school, including individual DBT therapy, a DBT-skills group, and as-needed skills coaching. The DBT clinicians would also attend weekly DBT consultation team meetings. Within the DBT skills group and individual therapy settings, students learn DBT skills from the four core skills modules: Core Mindfulness, Emotion Regulation, Distress Tolerance, and Interpersonal Effectiveness skills, plus the adolescent DBT skills module of Walking the Middle Path. The mindfulness skills taught in the CSB-DBT skills group are discussed in more detail below. In more recent years, Mazza and colleagues (2016) have further adapted DBT skills into a social-emotional learning (SEL) curriculum designed to be implemented with all middle and high school students at the universal (school-wide) level. The implementation of *DBT Skills in Schools: Skills Training for Emotional Problem Solving for Adolescents* (DBT STEPS-A) provides an increased opportunity for a greater number of students to learn effective decision-making and coping skills, including mindfulness skills.

DBT STEPS-A is a universal social-emotional learning (SEL) curriculum designed to teach middle and high school students decision-making skills and coping strategies for effectively navigating emotional distress. The primary behavioral targets of DBT STEPS-A are skills related to reducing the likelihood of experiencing emotional dysregulation while enhancing decision-making and coping strategies. The curriculum comprises 30 50-minute lessons that teach skills across the four core modules of DBT: Core Mindfulness, Distress Tolerance, Emotion Regulation, and Interpersonal Effectiveness. DBT STEPS-A is designed to be taught by school-based professionals in middle and high school settings, including general education teachers, school psychologists, school social workers, school counselors, and school nurses. The curriculum structure is designed for one lesson per week for the academic year or two lessons per week for an academic semester. Adaptations for elementary schools and students with cognitive challenges are being developed.

Currently, there are two randomized clinical trials that have evaluated the effectiveness of comprehensive DBT for adolescents (McCauley et al., 2018; Mehlum et al., 2014, 2016). Both trials reported a significant decrease in suicidal and nonsuicidal self-injurious behaviors (i.e., cutting, burning, head banging). Further, the Mehlum study (2014) also reported a decrease in self-reported measures of depression in adolescents. Additionally, over the years DBT for adolescents has been adopted for use in a variety of treatment settings and tested in open trials, including juvenile detention centers (Trupin et al., 2002), residential treatment centers (Sunseri, 2004), inpatient psychiatric units (Hashim et al., 2013), and schools (Mazza et al., 2016; Sally et al., 2002). As DBT has grown in popularity as an evidence-based treatment, multiple open trials evaluating DBT for specific problem areas also have been conducted. These open trials show favorable outcomes for DBT in treating adolescents with eating disorders (Fischer & Peterson, 2015; Safer et al., 2007), school refusal (Chu et al., 2015), and bipolar disorder (Goldstein et al., 2015).

Unfortunately, sometimes comprehensive DBT is not an option for treatment providers, and in some places, DBT skills groups are the only available treatment. However, DBT skills groups alone have been also evaluated and shown to be effective for some disorders. Several studies have shown that a DBT skills group–only intervention provided significant reductions in problems related to eating disorders, substance abuse, childhood abuse, attention deficit hyperactivity disorder (ADHD), depression, and anxiety-related behavior (Bradley et al., 2003; Hirvikoski et al., 2011; Neacsiu et al., 2014; Safer et al., 2001). Further, a component analysis comparing comprehensive DBT (individual DBT plus DBT skills group) with individual-DBT-only and DBT-skills-group-only demonstrated improvements in problems related to suicide and non-suicidal self-injury, depression, anxiety, anger, emotion regulation, and relationship difficulties across all conditions (Linehan, 2015a), highlighting the effectiveness of the DBT-skills-group-only training component.

There are two primary limitations to the field of research as it pertains to DBT skills. The first is that most research is done only on clinical populations and is therefore difficult to generalize to adolescents with lower levels of disorder and non-clinical populations. The second is that research on DBT skills has typically been conducted examining the accumulation effect as part of a four- to six-month DBT skills group. Recent studies by Flynn et al. (2018), Martinez et al. (2022), and Hastings et al. (2022) have helped fill in this gap, as all three studies support the use of DBT STEPS-A in school-based settings. Limited research has been conducted on specific skills or smaller combinations of skills to determine which skills may be essential to providing effective outcomes for both clinical and non-clinical populations of adolescents.

MINDFULNESS IN DBT

Mindfulness in DBT is described by Linehan as "the act of consciously focusing the mind in the present moment without judgement and without attachment to the moment" (Linehan, 2015a, p. 151). From a DBT perspective, the ultimate goal of mindfulness is to live mindfully: to live in the world with full awareness of the present while accepting reality as it is right now. In order to live mindfully, one needs to practice mindfulness daily or regularly. In mindfulness practice, skills are repeatedly practiced through a variety of exercises that focus on the strengthening of the different DBT mindfulness skills. This approach to living mindfully means walking around the world with one's "eyes wide open" to accept reality. To quote Linehan: "If we want to accept what's happening to us, we have to know what's happening to us" (p. 152).

Core Mindfulness Skills is one of four modules of skills that are taught as part of the original comprehensive DBT for adults (Linehan, 1993, 2015b; Miller et al., 2007; Rathus & Miller, 2015; note: there are five modules in the adolescent version of comprehensive DBT). The ability to be aware of the present moment, both internally (e.g., bodily sensations, thought, and emotions) and externally (e.g., environment) assists the individual in determining what coping strategy and/or decision-making skill may be warranted for the next moment. Because these skills are essential to accurate processing of information, the skills taught in this module are called Core Mindfulness Skills (Linehan, 2015a, p. 153) and become the foundation for the use of all other DBT skills. The core mindfulness skills that are taught to adults in comprehensive DBT are the same skills that are taught to adolescents in middle and high school, and even to children in elementary schools.

There are three primary goals of mindfulness, according to Linehan (2015a): (a) to increase control of one's mind, (b) to experience reality as it is and to increase overall awareness of the current moment, and (c) to reduce suffering and increase happiness. Each of these goals is described below.

a) *To increase control of one's mind.* The goal of increasing control of one's mind is to increase your ability to focus your attention where you want it to be, rather than allowing your mind to wander, such as daydreaming in class and missing 10 minutes of a lecture. It is equally important for one to be able to put one's attention on one task as it is to be able to notice when the mind becomes distracted and shift attention back to the task (Mazza et al., 2016). It is the difference between walking home and wondering how you got there versus noticing the path home and paying attention to the experience of walking. The former would be considered mindlessness, while the latter is mindfulness (Mazza et al., 2016).
b) *To experience reality as it is and increase overall awareness of the current moment.* In contrast to focusing your mind, increasing awareness is the ability to expand your attention to the current moment. For example, one may be aware of his or her own emotions and contributing factors as they are increasing in intensity in the current moment, rather than not noticing the emotion until it has reached extremely high intensity. Furthermore, this goal focuses on increasing one's ability to be present to experience life as it truly is versus thinking about how life is supposed to be or should be. It focuses on connecting with life in the present moment and is the opposite of avoiding or escaping problems (Mazza et al., 2016).
c) *To reduce suffering and increase happiness.* This goal is based on research findings from clinical and non-clinical settings that show that practicing mindfulness is correlated with a reduction in anxiety, depression, and anger, while increasing one's perception of self (Kabat-Zinn et al., 1992; Kaviani et al., 2011; Vøllestad et al., 2012). It is important to note that practicing mindfulness does not necessarily take away one's pain; rather, it can help reduce the suffering associated with pain while increasing one's freedom and the capacity for joy on a daily basis (Mazza et al., 2016).

DBT CORE MINDFULNESS SKILLS

In order to accomplish the three goals stated above, DBT teaches seven specific skills to enhance one's ability to live mindfully in the moment. The seven skills are: (a) Wise Mind, (b) the three "What" skills: Observe, Describe, and Participate, and (c) the three "How" skills: One-mindfully, Non-judgmentally, and Effectively. Each skill is described below.

Wise Mind

In comprehensive DBT and DBT STEPS-A, the first mindfulness skill that is taught to students is Wise Mind (Mazza et al., 2016; Rathus & Miller, 2015). In teaching this particular skill, students are oriented to three states of mind: Reasonable Mind, Emotion Mind, and Wise Mind (Mazza et al., 2016). Reasonable Mind is where decisions and behaviors are being guided or directed by logic and reason in the complete absence of emotion. There are times and professions where being in Reasonable Mind is appropriate, such as when one is engaged in the activities of dentists, computer science engineers, or surgeons. In these situations, the inclusion of emotions may create less effective behavior. In contrast, Emotion Mind is where thoughts, decisions, and behaviors are being directed by intense emotions and completely disregard reason or logic. Being in Emotion Mind can be highly problematic. For example, when one's emotions are so intense that one says something hurtful to someone they care about; or when one is so distraught about losing the state championship game that they engage in self-medicating or harmful behaviors. In Emotion Mind, it's as if the amygdala, the emotion control center of the brain, has completely hijacked the prefrontal cortex, the area of the brain responsible for executive functioning, problem-solving, and decision making.

The synthesis of Reasonable Mind and Emotion Mind is what is called Wise Mind in DBT. Wise Mind is where decisions, thoughts, and behaviors are directed and guided by both Reasonable and Emotion Minds. This is not simply a compromise between Reasonable and Emotion Minds; rather, it is a place where wise-minded decisions acknowledge and honor both the logical thoughts and the emotions one is experiencing. Thus, being in Wise Mind can mean that both reason and emotion are in complete balance or that one's mind might be weighted more to one side (reason) or the other (emotion). For example, if a student just won a state championship game and is extremely excited and celebrating, we still want some level of Reasonable Mind to be present so that the student does not engage in emotion-driven behaviors that can result in danger (e.g., the student is so excited that they begin driving recklessly and honking their horn repeatedly in the school parking lot). Another example is with a student who receives a failing grade on a test. In Emotion Mind, this student may be experiencing intense shame and anxiety. This may lead to thoughts of failing the class, fears of parents' anger and punishment, which leads to extreme thoughts of how to avoid or escape the situation. Without Reasonable Mind (the prefrontal cortex) engaged and Emotion Mind in control, the student may end up skipping school, using substances, or engaging in high-risk or life-threatening behaviors such as making a suicide attempt, as they are unable to see any other possible solutions to the failing grade.

Ultimately, Wise Mind is the state of mind where an individual sees reality for what it is and experiences the emotions of that reality without being overwhelmed by the intensity of the emotions (Mazza et al., 2016). In practice, one can invoke Wise Mind by asking oneself questions such as, "What does my Wise Mind say in this situation?" and "If I am in Emotion Mind right now, how do I get myself into Wise Mind?" In Wise Mind, the student with the failing grade may be able to recognize the fear of punishment from their parents and logically know that their parents also love them and that, together, they can find an effective solution. In addition, by teaching this language to students, the adults in the school and the student now share a common language. Educators can shift language to be less judgmental and ask questions to their students, such as, "Do you think this is an Emotion Mind or Wise Mind choice?" and "What does your Wise Mind tell you to do?"

The "What" Skills

The "What" skills are three skills that are practiced sequentially, meaning that you can only engage in one of these skills at a time. In comprehensive DBT and DBT STEPS-A, students are taught to use "What" and "How" skills as a means for accessing Wise Mind. There are three "What" skills: Observe, Describe, and Participate. Each of these skills is described below.

Observe

The Observe skill in mindfulness is to simply notice or observe sensations, situations, and events that are happening either inside or outside ourselves, without putting words to the observations. This is referred to as "wordless watching." The five senses are used to gather information about the outside world, while thoughts and emotions provide information through internal sensations. The Observe skill refers to one's ability to practice noticing where your attention is at any given moment and, if distracted, to notice that and bring one's attention back to the task at hand. When developing this skill, it is important to note that one cannot directly observe the internal information of others, meaning that one cannot observe thoughts, emotions, or intentions in other people. Rather, outside information through our senses allows us to observe others' behaviors and facial expressions (Mazza et al., 2016), which leads to interpretations of others' internal information that sometimes may be inaccurate. We often remind students that it is just as important, if not more important, to notice when your attention has wandered and you are distracted as well as holding your focus on one thing.

Describe

Describe is the second "What" skill and refers to putting words to sensations, situations, and/or events we just observed. We call this "wordful watching." This skill is sequential and second to the Observe skill, because one cannot describe what one does not observe. Thus, the Describe skill is to mindfully describe the observable facts without judgment, interpretation, or opinion (Mazza et al., 2016). For example, you might see a person who you think is angry. However, anger is an internal experience and is therefore not something you can directly observe in another person. But you can describe that you observe a person yelling loudly, waving fists in the air, and displaying a furrowed brow and a red face. The Describing skill is used to access or move toward Wise Mind while also moving one away from interpretations of events where adding judgmental thoughts and interpretations may fuel the intensity of Emotion Mind. We will often ask students, "Are you making an observation or an interpretation?" This will help students to notice and restate what they observed.

Participate

The last of the three "What" skills is Participate, which involves completely and mindfully engaging in an activity or event without judgment. This means thoroughly throwing oneself into the current moment, while letting go of what has happened in the past or what will happen in the future. The principle behind Participate is to become fully engaged in the present moment without being self-conscious or judgmental. Similar to the other "What" skills, when mindfully participating, one is not observing or describing (Mazza et al., 2016). Students can often recognize that they are fully participating when they are "in the zone" when doing an activity such as performing in a concert or in theater, playing in an athletic event, or focusing while taking an exam.

The "How" Skills

The "How" skills also comprise three key skills. Yet, in contrast to the "What" skills, all three "How" skills can be done simultaneously. The three "How" skills are: Non-judgmentally, One-mindfully, and Effectively. As the name implies, the "How" skills describe the process of doing the "What" skills, meaning the "How" skills guide the process of Observing, Describing, and Participating (Mazza et al., 2016).

Non-Judgmentally

The skill of Non-judgmentally is to Describe in a way that is without judgment, simply describing what you observed. This "How" skill is challenging, because humans are judgmental by nature (Linehan, 2015a). Thus, being aware of this tendency and refraining from being judgmental is a challenging task, especially when one is first learning mindfulness skills. Judgments are often considered to be shorthand descriptions of the consequences of a behavior that are deemed "good" or "bad." For example, being a jerk is bad, whereas being a sweetheart is good. In both descriptions of jerk and sweetheart, one misses the opportunity to describe exactly what behaviors the individual engaged in, focusing instead on the judgment of the behaviors. Thus, if one wants to change their behavior, they must Describe what specific behaviors they observed non-judgmentally. Furthermore, the intensity of emotions is often fueled by judgments, so the more judgmental one tends to be, the more intense that person experiences the emotion (Mazza et al., 2016). For example, if after the student receives a failing test grade, they begin calling themselves "stupid, lazy, and idiotic," the intensity of the student's fear and shame will continue to increase and last as long as the judgments continue. Thus, being able to Describe events and experiences Non-judgmentally can decrease the intensity of an emotion and therefore assist in moving from Emotion Mind to Wise Mind.

One-Mindfully

The skill of One-mindfully means doing only one thing at a time in the moment. The One-mindfully skill is the opposite of multitasking. The purpose of this skill is to focus one's attention on the task-at-hand in the moment, ignoring what happened in the past and not worrying or thinking about what is going to happen in the future—allowing one to participate fully in the moment. For example, if a student is attempting to complete an assignment in class while continuing to think about the failing test grade from the class before and how their parents will react, that student is not focusing completely on the current assignment and therefore may jeopardize their grade on this task as well. In this situation, the skill of One-mindfully can help the student to keep their focus on the current assignment; each time the student Observes that their attention has wandered back to the previous test grade, they can bring it back to the current assignment.

Effectively

The skill of Effectively focuses on doing what works or is needed in this moment. For instance, students might ask themselves, "Is this behavior or decision in line with my long-term goals? Is this what I want *now* or is it what I want *most*?" These questions assist students to use the skill of doing things Effectively, because it helps them understand whether their behavior is based on the short-term situation or in line with their long-term Wise Mind goals. Thus, the skill is the opposite of making a decision or taking action based on the principle of the matter, which often leads one away from their long-term goals (Mazza et al., 2016). For example, if the student's goal is to pass a class so they don't have to retake it and won't be punished by parents, the student would want to Effectively respond to the teacher who says, "You really failed this test. Did you even care to study?" If the student responds in Emotion Mind and based on the principle of the matter (e.g., high shame and anger), believing that the teacher shouldn't have called them out publicly, then they may say something rude and ineffective, such as "Screw you! Did *you* even try to shower this morning?" This response is likely to decrease the teacher's willingness to help the student improve their grade; it is also likely to result in disciplinary action, which will increase the parent's anger and consequences. An Effective and Wise-Minded response may be for the student to simply respond with, "Yes, I studied for 4 hours and I am not sure how I did so poorly."

APPLICATION OF DBT MINDFULNESS SKILLS

As stated earlier, the seven interrelated mindfulness skills in DBT are called "core" skills and are essential for students who are building greater Emotion Regulation skills. Specific to DBT, the mindfulness skills are fundamental in obtaining and practicing the other DBT skills—Emotion Regulation, Distress Tolerance, and Interpersonal Effectiveness—on a day-to-day basis (Linehan, 2015a). This is because one DBT skill is rarely used in isolation. For example, if a student needs to ask a teacher a difficult question and is highly anxious about the request, then the student might use multiple DBT skills to accomplish the task. The student may first have to make a Wise-Minded decision over Emotion Mind to approach the teacher, recognizing that it is their anxiety about talking to the teacher that is blocking them from making the request. Then they may need to be able to observe their internal indicators of anxiety (e.g., butterflies in the stomach, tense shoulders, thoughts that the teacher doesn't care and won't help or doesn't like the student). Once the student can mindfully observe and describe those indicators non-judgmentally, then they can begin to tolerate the urge to avoid the teacher by using the DBT Emotion Regulation skill of Mindfulness to Current Emotion (also called the "Wave" skill). The goal in this situation is for the student to experience the emotion without avoiding and then implement an effective DEAR MAN (an interpersonal effectiveness skill that guides what to say in the request), which is an acronym for an interpersonal effectiveness skill (Linehan, 2015a; Mazza et al., 2016), for asking the teacher for assistance. This sequence of skill use is referred to in DBT as "stacking the skills" on top of one another. Thus, mindfulness skills are the first steps of self-awareness inside the body and outside awareness in the surrounding environment. As such, these skills play a significant role in adolescents' emotion regulation and decision-making processes (Mazza et al., 2016).

As it pertains to DBT, mindfulness skills are on the acceptance side of the primary dialectic of acceptance and change (Linehan, 1993, 2015a). Mindfulness skills are designed to increase one's awareness and accept the reality of the situation and one's emotions without trying to directly refute or push away or change those emotions. Mindfulness skills are also used in Acceptance and Commitment Therapy (ACT; Hayes et al., 2012), where clients are encouraged to be aware of and accepting toward their cognitions, experiences, and emotions, as opposed to trying to control them (see Chapter 10 in this volume). The importance of understanding that mindfulness skills are part of the acceptance side of the dialectic cannot be overstated, because mindfulness skills are not designed to directly change thoughts, behaviors, or emotions. From a DBT perspective, mindfulness skills provide awareness to the current moment, which includes painful moments and emotions.

With the ultimate goal of being in Wise Mind, the other mindfulness skills facilitate a student's ability to engage in more adaptive decision-making skills. However, we caution schools to teach not only mindfulness skills to students. Given mindfulness skills focus only on the acceptance strategy of emotional awareness, they may potentially make students aware of the difficulty of their current emotional state without teaching them effective strategies for problem-solving or experiencing the emotion without engaging in impulsive or other problematic behaviors. For example, if a student is only taught to be aware of the uncomfortable physical sensations (i.e., heavy weight or tightness in chest, tension in shoulders) or thoughts associated with shame or anxiety (e.g., everybody will laugh at me; I can never go back to school; I'll never pass that test), they may resort to avoiding the anxiety-provoking event (e.g., test-taking or social interactions) as a means of decreasing their shame or anxiety in the short term. Thus, mindfulness skills can heighten one's awareness of emotion intensity (i.e., how awful one feels); yet this experience is only one side of the dialectic (acceptance skills) that focuses on increasing awareness of the problem, with the other side of the dialectic (change skills) being needed to make meaningful behavioral or emotional change that assist the student in solving the problem. By adding in additional acceptance skills (Distress Tolerance) and change-based skills (Emotion Regulation and Interpersonal Effectiveness), a student can build a balanced approach to emotional awareness and regulation.

A model taught in the Distress Tolerance skills is our AAA model. The AAA model stands for Awareness–Acceptance–Action. First, an individual needs to be aware of their situation (i.e., emotions, thoughts, problems . . .), and then one must find Acceptance of the situation based on the current reality by describing it non-judgmentally (a mindfulness How skill) and without interpretation (a mindfulness What skill) of how they "want things to be." And only once we have Acceptance can a person move into effective (a mindfulness How skill) Action.

APPLICATION OF DBT SKILLS TO THE MINDFULNESS MOLECULE

There are numerous mindfulness programs, curricula, and strategies that are implemented in schools to help students enhance their academic performance while also reducing disciplinary problems and promoting positive mental health (Carsley et al., 2018; see Chapters 2, 6, 7, 8, 10, 11, and 12 in this volume). One conceptual structure that has been suggested to help increase mental health professionals' understanding of mindfulness is the Mindfulness Molecule (Renshaw & O'Malley, 2014). An illustration of the mindfulness molecule is in Figure 9.1, with the DBT skills aligned to the different components of the molecule.

In expanding Renshaw and O'Malley's (2014) description of a mindfulness molecule to DBT mindfulness skills, we would label the entire structure as a Wise Mind Mindfulness Molecule. Renshaw and O'Malley describe the center of the molecule as the mindfulness nucleus, consisting of the substance or components that comprise mindfulness. The outer ring of the Mindfulness Molecule is (comparable to electrons) composed of additional properties that constitute mindfulness and give the molecule its identity. As illustrated in Figure 9.1, applying DBT skills to the nucleus of the Mindfulness Molecule results in the substance of mindfulness as the "What" skills. The "How" skills of DBT then comprise the outer ring around the molecule's nucleus and represent the processes of developing mindfulness. In this illustration, purposeful awareness is consistent with DBT's One-Mindfully, necessitating present-moment focus as an essential feature. Intentionality is represented by DBT's Effectively, doing what works and being intentional in using a strategy that is consistent with one's long-term goals. Finally, the "How" skill of Non-judgmentally is analogous to receptive attitude, in that internal thoughts and emotions as well as external situations and events are accepted openly, without pretense, as a part of life. Thus, the Wise Mind Mindfulness Molecule represents an integration of the six DBT mindfulness skills that comprise the seventh and overarching skill: Wise Mind.

SCHOOL BARRIERS IN IMPLEMENTING DBT MINDFULNESS SKILLS

Schools are complex systems. When introducing new curricula or content into the already complex system, there are several foreseeable barriers that may prevent or hinder such implementation. When working with schools to implement the teaching of the DBT STEPS-A curriculum, including the mindfulness module, there have been several barriers to effective implementation. First and foremost, there needs to be administrative support. Whether this is from the principal at the school or the superintendent of the district, the implementation of DBT STEPS-A needs to have leadership support from the top. In addition, with administrative support, there is a greater likelihood of integrating DBT STEPS-A with other school-based intervention frameworks that already may be in place, such as traditional SEL programs, positive behavior interventions and supports (PBIS), multitiered systems of support (MTSS), or school mental health programming. The synergies that could be created by integrating DBT mindfulness skills that align with skill-specificity and practice within a larger school-wide framework, such as PBIS and MTSS, are likely to help schools establish an academic environment that is supportive of students' social-emotional needs and well-being.

The second barrier to implementation is scheduling and determining when and where the DBT STEPS-A skills are going to be taught within the school schedule. There are several variables related to this barrier; for example, are the lessons going to be taught by a general education teacher or one of the school's mental health

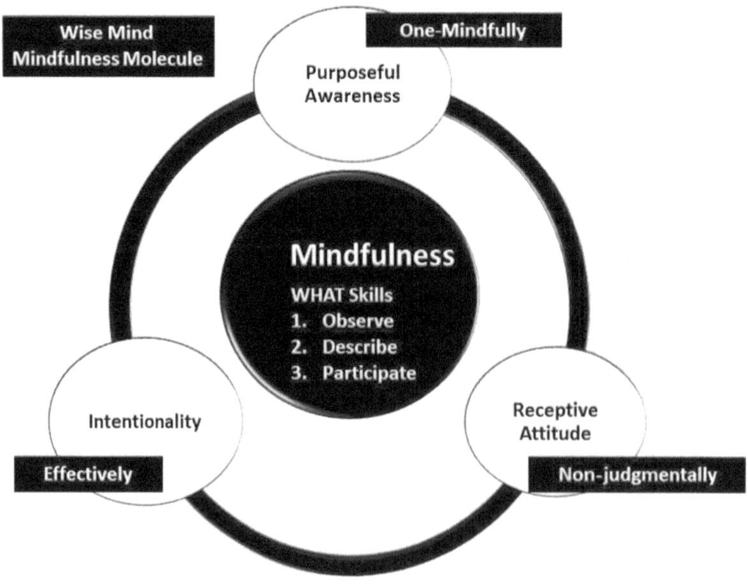

Figure 9.1 Applying DBT Skills to the Mindfulness Molecule. Adapted from Renshaw and O'Malley (2014).

professionals? If the DBT STEPS-A lessons are going to be taught by a mental health professional, will it be an independent course, or will a staff member have to push-in to another class? At times, scheduling can be difficult due to limitations of mental health staff's availability for pushing-in or classroom teachers' decisions to override the SEL content or prioritize other content. Thus, DBT STEPS-A lessons were developed so that general education staff can teach the lessons. It is not required to have a mental health background in order to teach these skills. Finally, are the DBT skills going to be taught at a universal (school-wide) level, or will students be selected or referred for more targeted intervention based on other social-emotional criteria? These scheduling and scoping issues are important to address as preemptive steps prior to implementing the DBT STEPS-A curriculum.

The third barrier to implementation is evaluation. When implementing any type of curriculum, whether academic or SEL, there needs to be an evaluation component that examines if the curriculum is being implemented in accordance with several variables, such as acceptability, appropriateness, and fidelity (Proctor et al., 2011). Too often, school personnel give up on the implementation of new SEL curricula because they are not seeing the immediate outcomes they had hoped for—or because the new curriculum lessons are perceived as being awkward to teach (Mazza & Miller, 2015). Yet, when evaluations are conducted, results show that some teachers have eliminated key components of the SEL skills or are not implementing the instructional guidelines designed to help students learn and acquire those skills, which impacts outcomes and usability (Flynn et al., 2018). Along similar lines, student outcomes need to be measured in order to evaluate if the program is having the intended impact. Outcome evaluation is an added step above and beyond teaching DBT STEPS-A skills and requires additional time. However, the evaluation of outcomes, along with implementation variables, parallels key features of the MTSS framework, where progress monitoring is used to make data-based decisions for determining program effectiveness and next steps.

A fourth barrier to implementation is the confusion that mindfulness and meditation are the same. In DBT, the definition of meditation "is the practice of mindfulness while sitting or standing quietly for a period of time" (Linehan, 2015a, p. 152). Linehan also states that some people mistakenly view meditation as the core of mindfulness, which is not accurate. Even though meditation as defined in DBT does entail mindfulness, the reverse is not true; mindfulness does not necessitate one to meditate. This is an important distinction, because everyone has the ability to practice mindfulness, while not everyone can sit or stand still to practice meditation (Linehan, 2015a).

There are many ways in which one can practice mindfulness. We often think of the different mindfulness exercises in the DBT STEPS-A curriculum as practice drills, similar to the way dribbling drills are done at a soccer or basketball practice. Practice drills are run repeatedly during practice in order to make the behaviors of dribbling and maneuvering a soccer ball during a game more automatic. We apply that same principle to our mindfulness exercises. They are practice drills for each of the different mindfulness skills we want the students to strengthen so that when they are out living their lives, they are more automatically living more mindfully through observing, describing, and participating non-judgmentally, one-mindfully and effectively. For example, one mindfulness exercise we utilize in the DBT STEPS-A curriculum is a game called "Sound Ball." In this game, students practice "throwing" random sounds with their voices and bodies, followed by another student "catching" the sound by repeating it with their voice and body and then "throwing" a new sound to someone else who will catch it. Throughout this exercise, the students are practicing participating one-mindfully and non-judgmentally. An exercise like this gives students the opportunity to practice letting go of their own judgments and throwing themselves fully into an activity. The more they can practice these skills, the more automatic they will become in their lives. An example of this is when someone is running a race; they often need to be one-mindfully aware of their pace, the conditions of the course/road, and who is in front of them while being non-judgmental about themselves or others. Thus, mindfulness skills would be very important in such a performance, though very few people would consider running a competitive race mindfulness.

Relatedly, because many religions utilize contemplative practices that require mindful meditation, the practice of mindfulness and the teaching of mindfulness skills in schools are sometimes perceived (incorrectly) as teaching religion. This faulty assumption leads some school personnel and parents to resist the idea of implementing mindfulness-based practices in schools, despite the evidence that such practices work to improve students' emotion regulation, coping strategies, and academic attainment (Carsley et al., 2018).

The last barrier to implementing DBT skills in schools is lack of patience. Any time a new curriculum is implemented, there is a learning curve. It is important that school personnel not set the bar too high for immediate results and that school administrators offer continued support during at least the first years of implementation. Equally important is that teachers of DBT STEPS-A do not give up too quickly because they are not seeing the results they wanted or students are not practicing the skills as intended. Like learning to swim, teaching and learning new skills—including DBT skills—takes time and practice. Thus, encouraging implementers to practice the mindfulness skills themselves and patience while teaching DBT STEPS-A to students is important and consistent with DBT's "How" skills of Non-judgmentally and Effectively.

CONCLUSION

The implementation of DBT STEPS-A, including mindfulness skills, in schools offers an evidenced-based approach to helping students develop coping strategies and emotion regulation skills (Flynn et al., 2018). Comprehensive DBT has been shown to be effective with adolescents in school-based settings (Miller et al., 1997; Sally et al., 2002), outpatient settings (McCauley et al., 2016; Mehlum et al., 2014), and inpatient settings (Hashim et al., 2013). Overall, the evidence suggests that schools might provide DBT skills to students to help meet their social-emotional needs and promote well-being.

As described throughout this chapter, there are seven DBT mindfulness skills: Wise Mind; the "What" skills of Observe, Describe, and Participate; and the "How" skills of One-mindfully, Non-judgmentally, and Effectively. Together, these skills can be used in schools to help students reach the three goals of mindfulness: (1) to increase control of one's mind, (2) to increase awareness and accept reality as it is, and (3) to reduce suffering and increase capacity for joy. While DBT STEPS-A mindfulness skills provide a proactive approach to teaching mental wellness in the area of social-emotional learning, mindfulness alone is not the panacea for all problems related to emotion regulation. It is important to understand that mindfulness skills are on the acceptance side of the dialectic and that other skills are needed to make behavioral and emotional changes. Finally, there are important barriers that need to be addressed to ensure successful implementation of DBT skills in school-based settings. Given the broad reach and positive effects that mindfulness can have on academic and social-emotional learning, expanding the lens of education to include DBT skills can be a proactive approach for helping students improve their social-emotional functioning while obtaining their educational goals.

REFERENCES

American Psychiatric Association. (2013). *Diagnostic and statistical manual of mental disorders* (5th ed.). https://doi.org/10.1176/appi.books.9780890425596

Bradley, R. G., & Follingstad, D. R. (2003). Group therapy for incarcerated women who experienced interpersonal violence: A pilot study. *Journal of Traumatic Stress, 16*(4), 337–340. https://doi.org/10.1023/A:1024409817437

Carsley, D., Khoury, B., & Heath, N. L. (2018). Effectiveness of mindfulness interventions for mental health in schools: A comprehensive meta-analysis. *Mindfulness, 9*(3), 693–707. https://doi.org/10.1007/s12671-017-0839-2

Chu, B. C., Rizvi, S. L., Zendegui, E. A., & Bonavitacola, L. (2015). Dialectical behavior therapy for school refusal: Treatment development and incorporation of web-based coaching. *Cognitive and Behavioral Practice, 22*(3), 317–330. https://doi.org/10.1016/j.cbpra.2014.08.002

Felver, J. C., Celis-de Hoyos, C. E., Tezanos, K., & Singh, N. N. (2016). A systematic review of mindfulness-based interventions for youth in school settings. *Mindfulness, 7*(1), 34–45. https://doi.org/10.1007/s12671-015-0389-4

Fischer, S., & Peterson, C. (2015). Dialectical behavior therapy for adolescent binge eating, purging, suicidal behavior, and non-suicidal self-injury: A pilot study. *Psychotherapy, 52*(1), 78. https://doi.org/10.1037/a0036065

Flynn, D., Joyce, M., Weihrauch, M., & Corcoran, P. (2018). Innovations in practice: Dialectical behaviour therapy–skills training for emotional problem solving for adolescents (DBT STEPS-A): Evaluation of a pilot implementation in Irish post-primary schools. *Child and Adolescent Mental Health, 23*(4), 376–380. https://doi.org/10.1111/camh.12284

Goldstein, T. R., Fersch-Podrat, R. K., Rivera, M., Axelson, D. A., Merranko, J., Yu, H., . . . Birmaher, B. (2015). Dialectical behavior therapy for adolescents with bipolar disorder: Results from a pilot randomized trial. *Journal of Child and Adolescent Psychopharmacology*, *25*(2), 140–149. https://doi.org/10.1089/cap.2013.0145

Gouda, S., Luong, M. T., Schmidt, S., & Bauer, J. (2016). Students and teachers benefit from mindfulness-based stress reduction in a school-embedded pilot study. *Frontiers in Psychology*, *7*, 590.

Hashim, B. L., Vadnais, M., & Miller, A. L. (2013). Improving adherence in adolescent chronic kidney disease: A dialectical behavior therapy (DBT) feasibility trial. *Clinical Practice in Pediatric Psychology*, *1*(4), 369. https://doi.org/10.1037/cpp0000024

Hastings, S. E., Swales, M. A., Hughes, J. C., Jones, K., & Hastings, R. P. (2022). Universal delivery of dialectical behaviour therapy skills programme (DBT STEPS-A) for adolescents in a mainstream school: Feasibility study. *Discover Psychology*, *2*(1), 21. https://doi.org/10.1007/s44202-022000021-x

Hayes, S. C., Strosahl, K. D., & Wilson, K. G. (2012). *Acceptance and commitment therapy: The process and practice of mindful change.* Guilford.

Hirvikoski, T., Waaler, E., Alfredsson, J., Pihlgren, C., Holmström, A., Johnson, A., . . . Nordström, A. L. (2011). Reduced ADHD symptoms in adults with ADHD after structured skills training group: Results from a randomized controlled trial. *Behaviour Research and Therapy*, *49*(3), 175–185. https://doi.org/10.1016/j.brat.2011.01.001

Kabat-Zinn, J. (1994). *Wherever you go there you are: Mindfulness meditation in everyday living.* Hyperion.

Kabat-Zinn, J., Massion, A. O., Kristeller, J., Peterson, L. G., Fletcher, K. E., Pbert, L., Lenderking, W. R., & Santorelli, S. F. (1992). Effectiveness of a meditation based stress reduction program in the treatment of anxiety disorders. *American Journal of Psychiatry*, *149*, 936–943. https://doi.org/10.1176/ajp.149.7.936

Kaviani, H. J., Javaheri, F., & Hatami, N. (2011). Mindfulness-based cognitive therapy (MBCT) reduces depression and anxiety induced by real stressful setting in non-clinical population. *International Journal of Psychology & Psychological Therapy*, *11*, 285–296.

Lau, N. S., & Hue, M. T. (2011). Preliminary outcomes of a mindfulness-based programme for Hong Kong adolescents in schools: Well-being, stress and depressive symptoms. *International Journal of Children's Spirituality*, *16*(4), 315–330.

Linehan, M. M. (1993). *Skills training manual for treating borderline personality disorder.* Guilford.

Linehan, M. M. (2015a). *DBT skills training manual* (2nd ed.). Guilford.

Linehan, M. M. (2015b). *DBT skills training handouts and worksheets* (2nd ed.). Guilford.

Martinez, R. R., Marraccini, M. E., Knotek, S. E., Neshkes, R. A., & Vanderburg, J. (2022). Effects of dialectical behavioral therapy skills training for emotional problem solving for adolescents (DBT STEPS-A) program of rural ninth-grade students. *School Mental Health*, *14*, 165–178. https://doi.org/10.1007/s12310-021-09463-5

Mazza, J. J. (2019, February). *Proactively addressing emotional dysregulation: DBT skills for middle and high school students.* Workshop presented at the annual conference of the National Association of School Psychologists, Atlanta, GA.

Mazza, J. J., Dexter-Mazza, E. T., Miller, A. L., Rathus, J. L., & Murphy, H. E. (2016). *DBT skills in the schools: The skills training for emotional problem solving for adolescents* (DBT STEPS-A) *curriculum.* Guilford. https://doi.org/10.1093/oxfordhb/9780198758723.013.21

Mazza, J. J. & Miller, A. L. (2015, April). *Applying DBT to school-based settings.* Workshop presented at the annual conference of the American Association of Suicidology, Atlanta, GA.

McCauley, E., Berk, M. S., Asarnow, J. R., Adrian, M., Cohen, J., Korslund, K., . . . Linehan, M. M. (2018). Efficacy of dialectical behavior therapy for adolescents at high risk for suicide: A randomized clinical trial. *JAMA Psychiatry*, *75*(8), 777–785. https://doi.org/10.1001/jamapsychiatry.2018.1109

Mehlum, L., Ramberg, M., Tørmoen, A. J., Haga, E., Diep, L. M., Stanley, B. H., . . . Grøholt, B. (2016). Dialectical behavior therapy compared with enhanced usual care for adolescents with repeated suicidal and self-harming behavior: Outcomes over a one-year follow-up. *Journal of the American Academy of Child & Adolescent Psychiatry*, *55*(4), 295–300. https://doi.org/10.1016/j.jaac.2016.01.005

Mehlum, L., Tørmoen, A. J., Ramberg, M., Haga, E., Diep, L. M., Laberg, S., . . . Grøholt, B. (2014). Dialectical behavior therapy for adolescents with repeated suicidal and self-harming behavior: A randomized trial. *Journal of the American Academy of Child & Adolescent Psychiatry*, *53*(10), 1082–1091. https://doi.org/10.1016/j.jaac.2014.07.003

Metz, S. M., Frank, J. L., Reibel, D., Cantrell, T., Sanders, R., & Broderick, P. C. (2013). The effectiveness of the learning to BREATHE program on adolescent emotion regulation. *Research in Human Development*, *10*(3), 252–272. http://dx.doi.org/10.1080/15427609.2013.818488

Miller, A. L., Rathus, J. H., Leigh, E., Landsman, M., & Linehan, M. M. (1997). Dialectical behavior therapy adapted for suicidal adolescents. *Journal of Practicing Psychiatry and Behavioral Health*, *3*, 78–86. http://dx.doi.org/10.1097/00131746-199703000-00002

Miller, A. L., Rathus, J. H., & Linehan, M. M. (2007). *Dialectical behavior therapy with suicidal adolescents*. Guilford.

Neacsiu, A. D., Eberle, J. W., Kramer, R., Wiesmann, T., & Linehan, M. M. (2014). Dialectical behavior therapy skills for transdiagnostic emotion dysregulation: A pilot randomized controlled trial. *Behaviour Research and Therapy*, *59*, 40–51. https://doi.org/10.1016/j.brat.2014.05.005

Pistorello, J., Fruzzetti, A. E., MacLane, C., Gallop, R., & Iverson, K. M. (2012). Dialectical behavior therapy (DBT) applied to college students: A randomized clinical trial. *Journal of Consulting and Clinical Psychology*, *80*(6), 982. https://doi.org/10.1037/e525102013-007

Proctor, E., Silmere, H., Raghavan, R., Hovmand, P., Aarons, G., Bunger, A., . . . Hensley, M. (2011). Outcomes for implementation research: Conceptual distinctions, measurement challenges, and research agenda. *Administration and Policy in Mental Health and Mental Health Services Research*, *38*(2), 65–76. http://dx.doi.org/10.1007/s10488-010-0319-7

Rathus, J. H., & Miller, A. L. (2002). Dialectical behavior therapy adapted for suicidal adolescents. *Suicide and Life-Threatening Behaviors*, *32*, 146–157. http://dx.doi.org/10.1521/suli.32.2.146.24399

Rathus, J. H., & Miller, A. L. (2015). *DBT skills manual for adolescents*. Guilford.

Renshaw, T. L., & O'Malley, M. D. (2014). Cultivating mindfulness in students. In M. J. Furlong, E. S. Huebner, & R. Gilman (Eds.), *Handbook of positive psychology in schools* (2nd ed., pp. 245–259). Routledge.

Safer, D. L., Couturier, J. L., & Lock, J. (2007). Dialectical behavior therapy modified for adolescent binge eating disorder: A case report. *Cognitive and Behavioral Practice*, *14*(2), 157–167. https://doi.org/10.1016/j.cbpra.2006.06.001

Safer, D. L., Telch, C. F., & Agras, W. S. (2001). Dialectical behavior therapy for bulimia nervosa. *American Journal of Psychiatry*, *158*(4), 632–634. https://doi.org/10.1176/appi.ajp.158.4.632

Sally, M., Jackson, L., Carney, J., Kevelson, J., & Miller, A. L. (2002). *Implementing DBT skills training groups in an underperforming high school.* Poster presented at the annual meeting of the International Society for the Improvement and Training of DBT, Reno, NV.

Sunseri, P. A. (2004). Preliminary outcomes on the use of dialectical behavior therapy to reduce hospitalization among adolescents in residential care. *Residential Treatment for Children & Youth*, *21*(4), 59–76. https://doi.org/10.1300/J007v21n04_06

Tan, L. B. (2016). A critical review of adolescent mindfulness-based programmes. *Clinical Child Psychology and Psychiatry*, *21*(2), 193–207. https://doi.org/10.1177/1359104515577486

Trupin, E. W., Stewart, D. G., Beach, B., & Boesky, L. (2002). Effectiveness of a dialectical behaviour therapy program for incarcerated female juvenile offenders. *Child and Adolescent Mental Health*, *7*(3), 121–127. https://doi.org/10.1111/1475-3588.00022

Vøllestad, J. N., Nielsen, M. B., & Høstmark, G. (2012). Mindfulness- and acceptance-based interventions for anxiety disorders: A systematic review and meta-analysis. *British Journal of Clinical Psychology*, *51*, 239–260. http://dx.doi.org/10.1111/j.2044-8260.2011.02024.x

Zenner, C., Herrnleben-Kurz, S., & Walach, H. (2014). Mindfulness-based interventions in schools—A systematic review and meta-analysis. *Frontiers in Psychology*, *5*, 603. https://doi.org/10.3389/fpsyg.2014.00603

10

DNA-V

The Youth Model of Acceptance and Commitment Therapy for Social-Emotional Learning in Schools

LOUISE HAYES AND JOSEPH CIARROCHI ■

We are in the midst of a mindfulness revolution. Two decades of research have shown that mindfulness is beneficial to many aspects of human functioning. Mindfulness is said to help people handle negative events, have self-control, build productive relationships, reduce chronic stress, improve mental performance, and overcome bad habits (Keng et al., 2011). And yet, the methodology in many of the early mindfulness intervention studies was preliminary. Recently, among studies with more rigorous methodology, we have seen evidence that mindfulness interventions can be ineffective in some contexts (Noone & Hogan, 2018). When it comes to young people, many mindfulness interventions have focused narrowly on structured meditation.

In this chapter, we argue that a narrow focus on mindfulness as structured meditation is problematic because it deemphasizes mindfulness-based interventions that do not have formal meditation. One might practice mindfulness while engaging in a conversation, playing a sport, walking in nature, or during the few seconds before a difficult social interaction. We present here a mindfulness intervention for young people called DNA-V, which allows one to more flexibly employ mindfulness in day-to-day life. This intervention is based on the theory underlying acceptance and commitment therapy (ACT; Hayes et al., 2012) and evidence-based social-emotional learning (SEL) programs (Durlak et al., 2011).

There has been considerable work done on best-practice SEL interventions with youth, and mindfulness approaches should build on those evidence-based principles rather than stand alone. For example, mindfulness-based programs would do well to follow the SAFE guidelines: they should involve sequenced (S) and

Louise Hayes and Joseph Ciarrochi, *DNA-V*. In: *Using Mindfulness to Promote Mental Health in Schools*. Edited by: Tyler L. Renshaw and Shane R. Jimerson, Oxford University Press. © Oxford University Press (2025).
DOI: 10.1093/9780190880507.003.0010

coordinated activities, employ active (A) experiential exercises that are focused (F) on developing mindfulness skills, and explicitly (E) target the core SEL skills of self-awareness, self-management, social awareness, relationship skills, and responsible decision-making (Durlak et al., 2011). A meta-analysis examining 213 school-based SEL programs, involving over a quarter of a million kindergarten through high school students (Durlak et al., 2011), revealed that SEL programs led by teachers were effective for improving youth outcomes in all six of the following categories: social and emotional skills, attitudes toward self and others, positive social behaviors, conduct problems, emotional distress, and academic performance. This meta-analysis indicates that SEL programs produced an average of an 11-percentile-points gain in students' academic achievement (Durlak et al., 2011). We believe mindfulness-based and SEL interventions are already implicitly integrated to some extent, in that both seek to increase awareness of self and others. We speculate that youth outcomes can be improved even further if mindfulness and SEL interventions are more deliberately and explicitly integrated.

We present in this chapter a model that is consistent with what a mindfulness-based SEL program ought to look like. It is a systemic model that brings together all behavior, thoughts, and feelings into four psychological processes, and then intervenes where these processes occur: in the contexts of the self and the social world. These psychological processes can be used by interventionists to hypothesize how developmental events might have an influence on youth well-being and prosocial behavior, to conceptualize the social-emotional skill level of a young person in the present, and to provide strategies to increase the social-emotional skills and growth of a young person.

CONTEXTUAL BEHAVIORAL SCIENCE

Our model for a mindfulness-based SEL program is derived from principles and techniques that comprise ACT. ACT is nested inside a scientific view called Contextual Behavioral Science (CBS). A brief overview of CBS will allow readers to understand how our approach in this chapter is grounded. CBS begins broadly, using the evolutionary science principles of variation, selection, and retention to understand how young people are adapting to their context. Adaptation and selection by consequences is examined at multiple levels, starting within the individual (cellular, behavioral, symbolic, and cultural) and extending outward to the level of social groups (Wilson et al., 2014). A CBS approach allows us to shape learning in young people by using Skinnerian operant principles for overt behavior and principles from relational frame theory (RFT) for covert behavior such as thoughts and feelings (Hayes et al., 2001).

ACT (Hayes et al., 2012) is an applied technology underpinned by CBS. The purpose of ACT is to help people accept what they can't change (e.g., the distress that occurs during the natural course of life) and commit to valued action even in the presence of distress. Like other forms of cognitive behavioral therapy, ACT seeks to undermine unhelpful cognitions (e.g., low self-esteem), but it does so by targeting mindfulness of cognitions rather than seeking to directly change the content of cognitions themselves (see later in this chapter for more on this point). ACT has strong evidence for promoting well-being and valued action in adults (A-Tjak et al., 2015), good emerging evidence for promoting well-being and valued action in adolescents (e.g., Hayes et al., 2011), and is an important target for social-emotional education and growth in young people (Williams et al., 2012). From these foundations, we developed DNA-V, which is a developmentally sensitive, ACT-informed, mindfulness-based approach to SEL. DNA-V is not intended to treat psychological distress only; rather, we conceptualize it as a bottom-up model that considers how humans grow (socially, emotionally, and behaviorally) from birth into adulthood and how we can facilitate this growth at multiple levels, including biological, individual, and social levels. In this chapter, we focus on how to use DNA-V in schools. In other work, we have focused on its application for traditional therapy, with families, and with community groups (Hayes & Ciarrochi, 2015).

DNA-V is a process-based approach rather than a package-based approach to intervention (Hayes et al., 2019). That is, DNA-V is built up from evidence-based processes of change, such as experiential acceptance and mindful awareness of feelings. We do not view DNA-V as a unitary thing—it is not a trademarked package that needs to be evaluated against every other mindfulness-based treatment package. The comparing of such treatment packages has no ending, given new packages can be created every day. There are perhaps already numerous mindfulness-based treatment packages. Rather than focusing on packages, one can focus on the processes targeted in the package, which are drawn from theory and empirical evidence.

Thus, DNA-V may target the same evidence-based processes but be delivered using different packages and procedures. For example, one package may focus on art, whereas another may utilize classroom discussion. The interventions may explicitly use the acronym DNA-V or not. The key element that makes the different packages "DNA-V" is the focus on core intervention processes (reviewed later in this chapter). We have conducted a thorough review of the evidence for each of the DNA-V processes. This review is beyond the scope of the present chapter, but the curious reader is encouraged to read our open access review of the evidence (Ciarrochi et al., 2016).

DNA-V: A CONTEXTUAL APPROACH TO THRIVING YOUNG PEOPLE

DNA-V is a model for how we develop and improve, socially and emotionally. It consists of four psychological processes that can be used to conceptualize much human activity. The letters D, N, and A refer to three processes that we have labeled "discoverer" (D), "notice" (N), and "advisor" (A). These processes can be understood as classes of behavior that are ideally used in the service of building the fourth process, which represents the V in the model: vitality, or valued action.

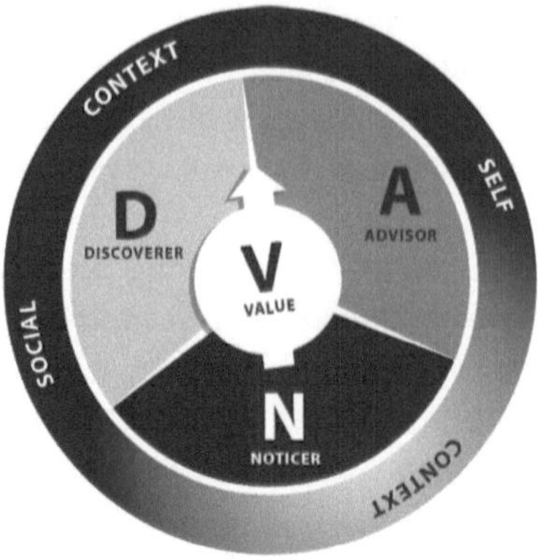

Figure 10.1 DNA-V Model

D, N, A, and V are assumed to be reciprocally influenced and changed by two perspectives, the social or nurturing context (or social view) and the context of the self (or self-view). As we will explain below, mindfulness plays an essential role in all four of these processes.

We often use biological DNA as a metaphor to describe our model because, just as we all have DNA in our cells that can be expressed in different ways, we also all have D, N, A, and V behaviors that can be shaped and expressed in different ways. Just like biological DNA, the DNA-V behaviors in our model are influenced by contextual factors such as environment and nurturing. Finally, just like biological DNA, our DNA-V behaviors can be influenced at the biological, behavioral, symbolic, and cultural levels, both within the individual and within groups.

The DNA-V model (see Figure 10.1) aims to help educators and mental health professionals draw together empirically supported techniques into a cohesive strategy for intervention. DNA-V describes a set of psychological processes that cover key behavior that helps people to adapt to an environment and thrive. Therefore, intervention techniques can be brought in from other traditions and used to target core psychological processes, provided they are adapted to meet the underlying theory. For example, we can help youth clarify their values (targeting the V in the DNA-V model) using art, song, sport, dance, or card-sorting tasks. The diversity of potential intervention techniques can help youth identify and verbally express what is important to them.

In the remainder of this chapter, we describe each of the four core psychological processes and the two perspectives that comprise DNA-V. We first describe *what* each aspect of the model is. Then we discuss *why* each aspect of the model is important, touching on the empirical evidence supporting it. Finally, we briefly describe *how* each aspect of the model can be used with young people. A more detailed account of intervention strategies derived from the DNA-V model can be found in *The Thriving Adolescent* intervention manual (Hayes & Ciarrochi, 2015) or at https://thrivingadolescent.com.

THE NOTICER

The "noticer" is the process that describes our ability to notice what is going on inside and outside our bodies—and then to choose our responses. We all start life as noticers; from birth, we begin seeing, hearing, touching, tasting, and smelling our world. Noticing starts as the behavior of simply being present with our experiences without verbal evaluation. For example, as babies, we cry when uncomfortable, we laugh when happy, and we *do not* verbally evaluate any of these experiences.

From birth, our noticer behavior also includes responding to danger that, like all mammals, is sensed through our bodies. External messages of safety or danger bring changes to our heart rate, bronchi, vocalization, middle ear, and facial expressivity (Porges, 2011). Children who grow up in harsh or socially unsupportive environments become hypersensitive to cues that relate to threat and safety (Szalavitz & Perry, 2010), whereas children who grow up in a nurturing environment learn noticer skills that allow them to be more sensitive to cues that indicate novelty and elicit curiosity and exploration (Ainsworth et al., 2015). If we are soothed by loving caregivers when upset, we will learn how to listen to the signals in our bodies, to trust our bodies, and to trust that we can connect with others and seek their help if needed (Ainsworth et al., 2015). Children who have been nurtured and supported when they felt unsafe will be set to respond well to the emotional ups and downs of adolescence. They will have developed skills that allow their emotions to come and go, understanding that they are signals about the world, not threats that need to be squashed or controlled. These children will be able to stay in the present moment some of the time, and view life with curiosity and, sometimes, awe (Williams & Ciarrochi, 2020; Williams et al., 2012). Highly skilled noticers are also able to be non-reactive to inner experience, such as impulses or self-doubt, and can practice non-attachment or non-clinging to pleasant experiences and feelings (Sahdra et al., 2016).

There are three basic, foundational noticer skills we want to strengthen in young people:

1. Understand that difficult thoughts and feelings are normal, transitory events that do not need to be avoided or clung to.
2. Bring feelings and thoughts into awareness by noticing and labeling them.
3. Learn to pause and respond—or not—to inner and outer experiences, depending on what best serves one's values.

First, we want young people to understand the valuable function of noticing and to become aware that humans are keenly sensitive to detecting change in our world. We liken noticing to the way that a cell phone is constantly scanning for a signal and can alert us to a message at any time. Our body, just like a cell phone, is a receiver of signals from around us. For example, we notice instantly if someone stands too close to us, if another's facial expression signals danger, or if the touch of a friend is loving. Our body is the instrument to detect and notice. Our task with young people is to help them understand that they are exquisitely tuned to the world and that messages come and go constantly. Just as we would not smash our cell phone for receiving unwanted calls, our bodies are not something to fear, to cut, to burn, or to hate because we receive unwanted messages through them. Just as we accept that a cell phone might ring outside our control, we help young people understand that feelings of sadness, happiness, anger, and frustration might also come uninvited or unexpectedly. Feelings are messages, and with time, we can learn how to receive and accept them rather than trying to control them or shut them up.

In the second step, we teach the basic skill of learning to become aware of signals inside us, to name them, and to add a feeling label, if appropriate. This skill might seem overly simple, but many adolescents are unable to do this effectively. Being able to identify and label our incoming signals is enormously important to humans; it helps us make sense of ourselves and the world. Those who struggle to identify their feelings tend to develop emotional problems and poor social networks (Ciarrochi et al., 2016), substance use (Lindsay & Ciarrochi, 2009), and have poor health outcomes (Kauhanen et al., 1996). It is for these reasons that awareness and acceptance of sensory input are the foundation of developmental emotional awareness programs for youth and trauma therapies (Van der Kolk, 2006).

To build this second aspect of the noticer skill, we use the acronym A-N-D to help youth remember to pause and become aware (A) of their bodies or breath, to name (N) any sensations that are currently present, and then to describe (D) these sensations with a feeling label. This acronym and exercise can also be used in reverse order—if an adolescent begins by saying they feel very angry, we can ask them to name the sensations in their bodies that are linked to this feeling label, and then to become aware of that sensation. We teach this aspect of the noticer skill through experiential learning rather than just telling. For example, we might say:

> *We are going to take a moment to learn the A-N-D skill. We start with A, or awareness of the breath. Take a few moments to notice your breath.* [Pause.] *Now we move to N: notice the sensations in your body. See if you can name that sensation, like a scrunched-up face or heavy chest. Next, we move to D: describe what you are feeling.*

After we have walked a young person through the A-N-D steps and they understand the basic skill, we can help them practice this sequence as they move about in the world. For example, for someone taking on a challenge in school, we might say:

> *As you walk into the class, try the A-N-D practice to see what you notice about yourself. You may find that sometimes you need to respond to the signals, and sometimes you can let them pass. The important thing is that you get to choose. Practice the A-N-D skill and you will have time and space to choose to react to feelings, or just let them go.*

We hope that, over time, young people will get better at receiving their bodies' signals, labeling them, and letting go of the urge to control them, squash them, or run away from them.

The final step of the noticer skill is to learn to allow or respond to feelings with awareness instead of "pushing away" or "clinging." When young people are aware of their feelings, they are better able to choose their responses. We teach young people to allow or welcome their experiences because we know that responding in this way can make experiencing negative emotions less aversive (Brockman et al., 2017). Furthermore, allowing discomfort helps a young person be able to engage in valued activities (Coutu et al., 2010). For example, we might ask, "Are you willing to feel scared in order to ask someone on a date?" It is okay if the young person says "No" to a question like this—it simply means our task is to help them practice more noticing skills, or that we need to help them to see the value inside their scared feelings. The pairing of allowing discomfort with a valued activity helps youth learn that if they say "No" to the feeling, they are also saying "No" to the valued activity. Over time, we hope to help young people understand that emotional vulnerability is normal. If we want love, we have to allow for rejection; if we want to achieve, we have to allow for fear and failure.

Once the basic three steps of noticing (as described above) are shared with a young person, we can introduce further mindfulness skills. The intent is to help youth develop skills for noticing their inner and outer experiences, to appreciate the present moment, and to choose their actions. Formal mindfulness exercises with young people can be easier if they begin with external sensations, such as mindfulness of sounds, smells, music, or sights. Then we can introduce mindfulness of internal experiences, such as mindful breathing, eating, and body scan. Physical activities such as yoga, martial arts, and running are useful for helping youth practice being present with their bodies. Creative exercises such as painting, cooking, building, and knitting are also useful for this purpose. There are several available apps and media clips that can be used to help young people develop their mindfulness skills (see examples at https://thrivingadolescent.com).

THE ADVISOR

The "advisor" is a metaphorical term we use to describe our self-talk and the behaviors of predicting events, believing, judging, generating rules, evaluating, and problem-solving. Mindfulness is an essential component of strong advisor skill. Mindfulness can be used to become aware of self-talk as it unfolds and the consequences of listening to (or not listening to) that self-talk. For example, young people may learn to recognize when they are thinking "I am not smart enough to get a good grade" and be aware that when they study, despite this self-advice, they do well. Thus, they learn to ignore some self-talk while listening to other self-talk (e.g., "It is natural to feel confused when studying something new").

The advisor is based largely on what we have learned from the past and how we use these experiences to predict what to do next. Initially, when we are young children, our parents are the primary source of verbal information about the world, telling us if we are tired, hungry, or need to come inside because it is going to rain. Eventually, as we mature, we learn to develop our own inner voice that helps us learn from the past and navigate the present and future.

Additionally, the advisor comprises a large part of our symbolic language behavior. It is an application of RFT's account of human language and cognition and its operant principle of arbitrary applicable derived relational responding (Hayes et al., 2001). Aspects of the advisor relate closely to other terms used in psychological theories for describing the relationship among thinking, feeling, and behaving—like "self-talk," "self-concept," "hope," "dysfunctional beliefs," "automatic negative thoughts," and "schema." The advisor also relates to interventions used in cognitive therapy, such as psychoeducation, cognitive reappraisal, and problem-solving (Beck, 1995).

From an evolutionary perspective, it makes little sense that humans would evolve self-talk just to say positive things to themselves; self-talk is most likely a tool that evolved to aid survival and therefore must include a significant amount of negativity. Research shows many examples of the benefit of both positive and negative thinking. Concerning positive self-talk, better academic and well-being outcomes are achieved if people believe that they can accomplish their goals (authentic hope), that they have social worth (authentic self-esteem), and that problems are more of a challenge rather than an overwhelming threat (Ciarrochi et al., 2015; Marshall et al., 2014). Concerning negative self-talk, self-doubt can motivate change or contribute to avoidance (Marshall et al., 2014). Meanwhile, cognitive reappraisal may fail to work if it is done in a way that does not consider the individual and their specific needs. Indeed, some research suggests that higher use of reappraisal may be associated with increased negative affect among adolescents (Brockman et al., 2017). Thus, when we work with the advisor skill, we do not challenge all negative self-advice; rather, it all depends on how this advice is being used by a particular person, in a particular situation.

To summarize, with DNA-V we hope to show young people how to use their advisor skill in ways that promote flexible thoughts and behavior. Flexibility would be present if they listened to their advisor when it was useful (e.g., "You can do this if you put the effort in") and not follow the advice when it is not useful (e.g., "You will never be good at anything").

We begin with four basic steps to develop effective advisors:

1. Understand the normality of negative and positive self-talk and know that a primary function of our advisor is to watch out for danger.
2. Decide on the helpfulness of self-talk based on its function, considering questions like, "Does this kind of thinking help you build value?"
3. Learn to unhook if stuck inside unhelpful self-talk by stepping outside the advisor to the noticer or discoverer skills.
4. Create helpful rules and evaluations to navigate the world flexibly.

We begin teaching the advisor skill by helping young people get acquainted with the purpose of language and cognition, which is to normalize all the different ways in which humans think. Given a few years of growing and developing in a culture, most young people will have absorbed the culture's dominant views on negative and positive thinking. They will often believe that positive thinking is good and negative thinking is bad. So, in this first step, our aim is to help youth understand that both kinds of thinking are normal and functional, and that a contextual view helps us use self-talk more flexibly. We do this by introducing the idea that self-talk is like an inner advisor. We might say something like, "All humans have the ability to talk to themselves, and we call this giving yourself advice—or your advisor."

In the second step, we help young people learn to connect their self-talk with what they care about as a way of deciding if their advisor is helpful or unhelpful. We might say something like:

> *It can be hard to know whether our advisor is useful or not, so we suggest one way to decide is to connect with what is in your heart, or what you really care about. This can be tricky because the advisor's job is to keep us safe. That means the advisor, or inner voice, tells us not to do something because we are worried we might fail or look foolish. Yet when we connect with what we value, we might decide that our value is more important than fear of failure.*

The following experiential exercise can help us connect the advisor's self-talk to values and gives practice in deciding whether the advisor is helpful or unhelpful. In this exercise, we first step into the values space and ask a young person to imagine that they are about to engage in a value that they really care about. To do this, we might have the value written on a sheet of paper and ask them to stand on the paper. We want youth to really imagine that they are doing the valued experience *now*. As they imagine themselves doing this, we ask them to become aware of what their advisor is telling them. We prompt them to say all of the negative things as well as the positive things that they would tell themselves and note these thoughts down on a second sheet of paper called the "advisor page." Next, we ask them to step from their value space (the first piece of paper) into their advisor space (the second piece of paper). Now they can pause, look at all of the things that the advisor tells them, and have a shared discussion about which thoughts are helpful in terms of connecting with the value space (over there on the first piece of paper) and which statements may be protective, avoidant, or unhelpful and not in the service of the value space. Whenever we do this exercise, we are always careful to emphasize that their advisor is not bad, nor is it split into a good advisor and a bad advisor. Rather, their task is to learn to distance their *self* from their *self-talk* by practicing perspective-taking on their advisor.

In step three, we aim to teach experiential ways to unhook from habitual critical, painful, or sticky thoughts. DNA-V provides an easy way to unhook by practicing stepping out of the advisor space and into the noticer or discoverer space. In the noticer space, we can pause, take a breath, look at our self-talk, and notice how it makes us feel. In the discoverer space (discussed in more detail later in this chapter), we can track what has happened when we followed our self-advice with actions. We might also ask young people to draw what their advisor might look like, to create a name or caricature of their self-talk (remembering to keep the good and the bad). Then when critical thoughts arise, we ask them to playfully recall the character they have created of themselves and decide if these thoughts are useful advice. Also, in step three, we might use any of the classic ACT defusion exercises to help de-couple the link between thoughts and action (see Hayes et al., 2012).

Finally, we can help youth train their adviser in flexibility. We do this by embracing the advisor skill as a powerful way to navigate the world, to problem-solve, to take the past and use it to predict the future. One might even consider the advisor the ultimate human skill. Learning to use our advisor well requires self-rules that need to be tested and modified. We can help youth create new DNA-V rules, such as "Everybody gets stuck in their discoverer, noticer, or advisor space, and with practice we can learn to be DNA-V shifters." We also test out new rules with young people, such as, "Growth is always possible" or "Everyone can build their DNA-V skills." And last, if the young person cannot do it for themselves, there are times when adults can scaffold their own hopeful rules. For example, we can tell youth: "I have hope for you." The aim in learning to use one's advisor well is to help young people try out their problem-solving, advice, evaluations, and beliefs, learn to hold their self-rules lightly, and expand with new rules, as needed, that help them live more flexibly and more in tune with their values.

THE DISCOVERER

"Discoverer" is the term for the behavior of using trial-and-error learning in order to expand one's skills and resources. Mindfulness is essential for effective discoverer behavior. For example, mindfulness helps young people to become aware of the antecedents and consequences of their behavior (e.g., they discover what works and doesn't work). Mindfulness also helps them become aware of and accept the distress (an antecedent) of going out of their comfort zone and doing something new or different in their life. It also helps them to notice the consequences of this different behavior—how acting differently may (or may not) make their life better.

Discoverer behaviors begin very early in life. Consider a baby in a high chair, pushing their toast off the side of the tray, seeing it fall to the floor, watching their parent pick it up, and then repeating this sequence. In this way, children discover their agency—as well as its antecedents and consequences—through play and exploration. Compared to childhood discovery, adolescent discovery has a different function: it is trying out adult-like roles and behaviors. Adolescence is commonly characterized by love of novelty, sensation-seeking, and risk-taking. These patterns of behavior are seen in human and non-human adolescents alike (Spear, 2004). For example, adolescent mice have been shown to take more risks and seek out new sensations compared to younger and older mice. If placed in a maze environment where there is a cliff, adult and child mice avoid the cliff, while adolescent mice take risks, explore, and ultimately walk along the cliff's edge (Laviola et al., 2003). These behaviors are likely to have an evolutionary adaptive value for adolescents. In non-human adolescents, these behaviors facilitate leaving the nest and finding a mate. In human adolescents, these behaviors help youth develop independence, learn adult roles, become sexually active, and practice adult-like relationships. Our understanding of the discoverer is based on a broad range of research streams, including (a) adaptive risk-taking across species (Ellis et al., 2012), (b) broaden and build theories of positive psychology (Fredrickson, 2001), (c) contingency-shaping that begins in childhood, and (d) behavioral activation interventions for mental health problems (Cuijpers et al., 2007).

With DNA-V, we facilitate discoverer skills in order to help young people find ways to direct their actions toward valued ends rather than impulsive reward-seeking. By necessity, adolescents make many mistakes, so in the discovery space we help them track the antecedents and consequences of their actions and continually examine the workability of new and old behaviors toward valued ends. Given that we expect mistakes, we intentionally create contexts where failure is understood as learning. To put this into mindfulness terms, we teach young people to intentionally notice and accept the distress that comes from trying something new as well as to be aware of and accepting toward the antecedents and consequences of their actions.

We build discoverer skills using four steps:

1. Tracking what is working (i.e., training awareness of antecedent–behavior–consequence sequences).
2. Building strengths.
3. Creating values.
4. Exploring new and untested behavior.

Step one, tracking what is working, is more technically called a "functional assessment." This is where we help a young person understand the context in which their behavior occurs, including the antecedents, the behavior itself, and the consequences of their behavior. Ultimately, we want to ask these questions: "Did this behavior work for you? Did it help you connect to what you care about?" We ask these questions about workability in the service of values, because it is common for humans to keep repeating the same behavior over and over again while expecting a different outcome. For example, youth sometimes acquiesce to a bully, expecting each time that the bully will stop, only to be bullied more. We want to explore the discoverer space experientially to help young people have an "ah-ha" realization, because humans often learn more effectively by doing than by being told what to do. To help a young person track their behavior, we can role-play the situation, re-enact the situation, or step through the antecedents and consequences using an interview approach (e.g., "What happened just before? . . . And then what did you do? . . . And then what happened next?"). We might also playfully try out different behaviors—even those that seem outrageous or silly—just to see what we notice when our repertoire changes.

Step two involves helping a young person see the strengths they have and creating dialogue around strengths they would like to develop. When we do strengths-based work, we want to look at strength behaviors that young people engage in, not merely labels they have for themselves. For example, "I try to be honest" is a strength behavior, whereas "I am an honest person" is a strength label. We want to help connect a young person's strengths to what they value, and then help them see how they might use their strengths for building more value. We also want to discover when and how they use that strength, given that it is a repertoire that they are familiar and comfortable with. For example, a young person may identify that they have the strength of being honest, so we explore when and how they use this honest behavior. We might then explore how we can help build their strength of honesty to enhance friendships (their value). Yet we can also help them see how their strength can sometimes take them away from their value, such as being blunt in one's feedback at a time when tactfulness is a more appropriate response to a friend. We can identify youths' strengths by discussing current behaviors or by using a strengths questionnaire or card-sort task. (Interested readers can download a strengths card-sort task or questionnaire from https://thrivingadolescent.com.)

Step three aims to help young people create vitality and value from their activities and behaviors. Technically, we define "values" as a transformative rule about life meaning or purpose—in other words, using words to state what you care about. We attempt to connect youths' activities and experiences with discussion and reflection to create "values dialogue." For example, we might say, "You've mentioned going to the movies a few times; what is it that you love about the movies?" We assume our task is to help youth create values through discussing and sharing the experiences they are engaging in.

Finally, in step four of the discoverer, we shape and reinforce testing and trying out new behaviors. We set achievable goals to work toward outside of the session and revisit basic tracking skills to help young people decide if the new behaviors they are engaging in (i.e., the goals they are working toward) are worthwhile. We continually circle back to the notion that success in life is not the absence of failure, but the willingness to try, to broaden and build our repertoires for the purpose of connecting to a life of meaning.

THE VALUER

At the center of the DNA-V model is value and vitality (see Figure 10.1). We want young people to learn how to use their D, N, and A behaviors to build their Mindfulness can be useful in helping people to discriminate between what they value and find personally important (intrinsic and autonomous motivation) versus what they do out of a sense of pressure, guilt, or external coercion (controlled motivation). Research suggests that high levels of mindfulness tend to be linked with higher levels of autonomous motivation (Donald et al., 2020). Autonomous motivation, in turn, is linked to higher well-being and achievement (Ryan & Deci, 2017).

We argue that a form of value is present from birth; babies value contact and connection with the humans who provide nurturing and secure attachment (Ainsworth et al., 2015). As we grow, we learn to use language to construct values statements, such as "I love dancing." Note that the ability to speak of value is dependent on growing up in contexts where adults also model and practice speaking and acting on valued meaning. By adolescence, value becomes a kind of verbal behavior that can transform experience and help young people move beyond immediate reward-seeking. For example, a teen can use value statements to transform a "boring dance rehearsal" into something that "helps her become a better dancer." We group value into six broad areas derived from research on well-being, vitality, and life satisfaction. These domains are: connecting with others, giving, being active, connecting with the present moment, challenging oneself and learning, and caring for oneself (Hayes & Ciarrochi, 2015). We shape young people to speak of values and connect to them by asking questions like, "What do you care about?" or "What are you doing this for?" We do not assume that all youth can initially connect their behavior to values, but we hope that we can eventually shape behavior in this direction. There is evidence that creating value statements can lead to improved health, education, relationships, and grades, as well as reduced psychological distress and increased willingness to experience pain in the service of value (Cohen & Sherman, 2014).

We help young people use their discoverer, noticer, and advisor skills to build values every time we work with them. This might be as simple as a class discussion on what young people hope for in a general sense. Over time, as youth become more flexible with their thoughts and feelings, we engage in experiential exercises that connect them to profound experiences they have had, and we use this connection to help them learn about themselves, what they love, what is in their heart, and what actions they might take to further connect with their values. For example, we may have them review the big and small events they reported on social media during the past year, noticing which of these events reflect their values as a person.

CONTEXTUAL PERSPECTIVES OF DNA-V

"Context" forms the outer circle of our DNA-V model (see Figure 10.1) and refers to all the evolutionary history, one's life history, and immediate events that exert an organizing influence on a young person's D, N, and A behavior. It is important to note that, from a functional contextualist perspective, there is no *a priori* way to specify what is context and what is behavior. Context can be history, memories, time, feelings, and stimuli that is either a setting event or an antecedent. For example, a distressing thought about one's childhood (e.g., "No one ever loved me") can become an antecedent in a moment of relationship stress with a partner. In short, behavior refers to what is of interest to the interventionist at a particular point in time, and context refers to all the factors that may affect behavior. Within the DNA-V model, two contextual factors are important to target in young people's development: social context and self-context.

Social Context for DNA-V

Humans have evolved to need each other as much as we need food and air. Many interventions for young people focus on what is happening *within* the young person, such as the occurrence of automatic negative thoughts. These interventions often neglect the social context or pay it only cursory attention, despite its importance. We know, for example, that adolescents continue to need secure attachment with parents and report that parents are the primary source of information when making important decisions (Helsen, Vollebergh, & Meeus, 2000). We also know that harsh versus nurturing social environments can differentially shape how young people seek to get their needs met (Ellis et al., 2012). In the social world, adolescents need friendships to thrive—yet 79% report being lonely sometimes or often (Heinrich & Gullone, 2006). Social isolation is a risk factor for obesity, impaired thinking, mental health problems, and, ultimately, early death (Hawkley & Cacioppo, 2010).

With DNA-V, we can consider how discoverer, noticer, and advisor skills are influenced by contextual factors, such as parents, schools, and friends. For example, a young person who grows up with yelling, criticism, and harshness—in the home or at school—is likely to develop an inner advisor that is self-critical or destructive. We also know that young people are able to influence the social context around them, so we use DNA-V for interventions to build stronger classrooms, stronger communities, and stronger friendship groups. We do this by incorporating Ostrom's (1990) principles of prosocial behavior into all DNA-V group interventions, from families to community groups. These principles include (a) having a clear group identity linked to values, (b) participatory decision-making in developing and implementing rules, (c) effective monitoring of the rules, (d) appropriate sanctions when rules are broken, and (e) quick and fair conflict resolution.

One social intervention might involve having young people role-play different social situations, using DNA-V to structure the process. For example, young people might explore how to deal with a bully by first identifying what they want or value in the situation. Then they might become aware of their self-talk (advisor), feelings (noticer), and past behaviors (discover) in response to the bully. Finally, they may role-play new behaviors (discover) and notice what shows up in their body (noticer) and their self-talk (advisor) as a result. Finally, they may seek to implement the new behavior in real life and see if it works to obtain the valued outcome (discover). There is insufficient space to describe more interventions related to the social context in this chapter, but the interested reader can find information on using DNA-V in social groups in *The Thriving Adolescent* intervention manual (Hayes & Ciarrochi, 2015).

Self-Context for DNA-V

Finally, we come to the self-context, which is an important developmental space for adolescents. One's *self* can be thought of as a perspective that emerges from DNA-V behavior. For example, we might think: "I am not good enough" (advisor), "I am feeling irritable now" (noticer), "I am not enjoying this activity at all" (discoverer), and "I care about being a good friend" (values). The self can also be thought of as a context for influencing how D, N, and A are expressed. For example, a young person who believes he must act masculine at all times may use D, N, and A to pursue and be successful at stereotypically masculine activities (e.g., boxing), but may ignore activities that he believes are stereotypically feminine (e.g., expressing emotions).

We argue that the self is not a fixed *thing*; rather, the self is a class of behaviors that we engage in (Hayes et al., 2001). It often involves relating a verbal "I" to an evaluation. For example, when a small child struggles at school with catching a ball, they might say to themselves, "I am clumsy." If this behavior occurs often enough, the label may become something they attach to. Sometime in the future, for instance, they may recall "I am clumsy"—and even though they want to become a chef, they can be afraid they are too clumsy for it. In DNA-V, we could test this selfing behavior with new discoverer tasks that use physical coordination. Or we could bring the embarrassing event into the present and have the young person be a noticer: becoming aware of how it feels to do something clumsy and allowing it to just be. Or we could ask the young person to consider how their advisor acquired the "clumsy" label, perhaps as a way of protecting them from looking clumsy in front of others when they were a child. The purpose of all of these strategies is to help the young person unhook from the label ("clumsy") that is now unhelpful.

With DNA-V, we help young people relate to their past history with self-compassion and to see themselves as capable of change or as having a growth mindset (Marshall et al., 2015). DNA-V fosters self-compassion by helping youth to notice negative self-evaluations (advisor), know that these thoughts are part of them but do not define them, and recognize that self-evaluations are normal and often useful sources of information. We help young people engage in new advisor rules that build a growth mindset, engage in self-kindness actions toward themselves (discoverer), and practice allowing feelings to come and go without needing to control them (noticer). Research supports the value of self-compassion, showing its linkage to improved well-being and ability to manage setbacks (Marshall et al., 2015). Ultimately, we want young people to recognize that they are more than their thoughts and feelings, more even than their D, N, and A behavior. For example, they learn that they do not have to be defined by their past mistakes (discover); by previous, self-destructive avoidance strategies (noticer); or by self-doubt (advisor). Instead, they can transcend their past behavior and build a better life.

SUMMARY AND CONCLUSION

DNA-V can be conceptualized as a mindfulness-based approach to SEL programming in schools. Mindfulness processes such as awareness, acceptance, and non-reactivity pervade every aspect of DNA-V. Discover skills involve becoming mindful and accepting of distress when one leaves the comfort zone and tries new things. It also involves mindfulness of consequences when trying out different strategies—whether these work or don't work. Noticer skills involve awareness and acceptance of sensations and emotions and also of external stimuli. Advisor skills involve being mindful and non-reactive to thoughts and accepting that thoughts are often and naturally threat-oriented and negative.

The DNA-V model does not assume that adolescents are broken and need to be fixed. Rather, it views youths' behavior as adaptations to context. Grounded in CBS, DNA-V uses operant principles to examine how a young person's behavior is selected by consequences, and it employs RFT to understand how their symbolic or cognitive world grows. We look at the match between youths' environment and individual needs and consider how to help them grow strengths and increase psychological flexibility using principles of variation, selection, and retention across the different streams of understanding—from biology to learning to cultural transmission. The context in which a young person grows is central to the DNA-V model; we look at their social context and self-context to inform and guide interventions.

In terms of application, DNA-V uses principles and techniques from ACT to understand why young people become distressed and stuck in unhelpful behavioral patterns as well as how we can intervene to help them let go of unhelpful behavior and develop new, more helpful repertoires. DNA-V also makes use of positive psychology techniques to consider how to broaden youths' repertoires and build their strengths. We conceptualize this approach to intervention through three psychological processes that we call "discoverer," "noticer," and "advisor." The ultimate goal of the DNA-V model is to help young people use these D, N, and A skills to connect with greater vitality and valued living.

REFERENCES

A-Tjak, J. G. L., Davis, M. L., Morina, N., Powers, M. B., Smits, J. A. J., & Emmelkamp, P. M. G. (2015). A meta-analysis of the efficacy of acceptance and commitment therapy for clinically relevant mental and physical health problems. *Psychotherapy and Psychosomatics*, *84*(1), 30–36.

Ainsworth, M. D., Blehar, M. C., Waters, E., & Wall, S. N. (2015). *Patterns of attachment: A psychological study of the strange situation*. Psychology Press.

Beck, J. S. (1995). *Cognitive Therapy*. The Guilford Press.

Brockman, R., Ciarrochi, J., Parker, P., & Kashdan, T. (2017). Emotion regulation strategies in daily life: Mindfulness, cognitive reappraisal and emotion suppression. *Cognitive Behaviour Therapy*, *46*(2), 91–113.

Ciarrochi, J., Atkins, P. W. B., Hayes, L. L., Sahdra, B. K., & Parker, P. (2016). Contextual positive psychology: Policy recommendations for implementing positive psychology into schools. *Frontiers in Psychology*, *7*, 1561.

Ciarrochi, J., Parker, P., Kashdan, T. B., Heaven, P. C., & Barkus, E. (2015). Hope and emotional well-being: A six-year study to distinguish antecedents, correlates, and consequences. *The Journal of Positive Psychology*, *10*, 520–532.

Cohen, G. L., & Sherman, D. K. (2014). The psychology of change: Self-affirmation and social psychological intervention. *Annual Review of Psychology*, *65*, 333–371.

Coutu, M. F., Baril, R., Durand, M. J., Côté, D., Rouleau, A., & Cadieux, G. (2010). Transforming the meaning of pain: An important step for the return to work. *Work*, *35*(2), 209–219.

Cuijpers, P., van Straten, N., & Warmerdam, L. (2007). Behavioral activation treatments for depression: A meta-analysis. *Clinical Psychology Review, 27*, 318–326.

Donald, J. N., Bradshaw, E. L., Ryan, R. M., Basarkod, G., Ciarrochi, J., Duineveld, J. J., Guo, J., & Sahdra, B. K. (2020). Mindfulness and its association with varied types of motivation: A systematic review and meta-analysis using self-determination theory. *Personality and Social Psychology Bulletin, 46*(7), 1121–1138. https://doi.org/10.1177/0146167219896136

Durlak, J., Weissberg, R., Dynmicki, A., Taylor, R., & Schellinger, K. (2011). The impact of enhancing students' social and emotional learning: A meta-analysis of school-based universal interventions. *Child Development, 82*, 405–432.

Ellis, B. J., Del Giudice, M., Dishion, T. J., Figueredo, A. J., Gray, P., Griskevicius, V., . . . Volk, A. A. (2012). The evolutionary basis of risky adolescent behavior: Implications for science, policy, and practice. *Developmental Psychology, 48(*3), 598.

Fredrickson, B. L. (2001). The role of positive emotions in positive psychology: The broaden-and-build theory of positive emotions. *American Psychologist, 56*(3), 218–226.

Hayes, L., Boyd, C. P., & Sewell, J. (2011). Acceptance and commitment therapy for the treatment of adolescent depression: A pilot study in a psychiatric outpatient setting. *Mindfulness, 2*(2), 86–94.

Hayes, L., & Ciarrochi, J. (2015). *The thriving adolescent: Using acceptance and commitment therapy and positive psychology to help young people manage emotions, achieve goals, and build positive relationships*. Context Press.

Hayes, S. C., Barnes-Holmes, D., & Roche, B. (Eds.). (2001). *Relational frame theory: A post-Skinnerian account of human language and cognition*. Kluwer Academic.

Hayes, S. C., Hofmann, S. G., Stanton, C. E., Carpenter, J. K., Sanford, B. T., Curtiss, J. E., & Ciarrochi, J. (2019). The role of the individual in the coming era of process-based therapy. *Behaviour Research and Therapy, 11*, 40–53.

Hayes, S. C., Strosahl, K. D., & Wilson, K. G. (2012). *Acceptance and commitment therapy: The process and practice of mindful change* (2nd ed.). Guilford Publications.

Hawkley, L. C., & Cacioppo, J. T. (2010). Loneliness matters: A theoretical and empirical review of consequences and mechanisms. *Annals of Behavioral Medicine, 40*(2), 218–227.

Heinrich, L. M., & Gullone, E. (2006). The clinical significance of loneliness: A literature review. *Clinical Psychology Review, 26*(6), 695–718. https://doi.org/10.1016/j.cpr.2006.04.002

Helsen, M., Vollebergh, W., & Meeus, W. (2000). Social support from parents and friends and emotional problems in adolescence. *Journal of Youth and Adolescence, 29*(3), 319–335. https://doi.org/10.1023/A:1005147708827

Kauhanen, J., Kaplan, G. A., Cohen, R. D., Julkunen, J., & Salonen, J. T. (1996). Alexithymia and risk of death in middle-aged men. *Journal of Psychosomatic Research, 41*, 541–549.

Keng, S. L., Smoski, M. J., & Robins, C. J. (2011). Effects of mindfulness on psychological health: A review of empirical studies. *Clinical Psychology Review, 31*(4), 1041–1056.

Laviola, G., Macrì, S., Morley-Fletcher, S., & Adriani, W. (2003). Risk-taking behavior in adolescent mice: Psychobiological determinants and early epigenetic influence. *Neuroscience & Biobehavioral Reviews, 27*(1), 19–31.

Lindsay, J., & Ciarrochi, J. (2009). Substance abusers report being more alexithymic than others but do not show emotional processing deficits on a performance measure of alexithymia. *Addiction Research & Theory*, 17(3), 315–321.

Marshall, S., Parker, P., Ciarrochi, J., & Heaven, P. C. (2014). Is self-esteem a cause of consequence of social support: A five-year longitudinal study. *Child Development, 85,* 1275–1291.

Marshall, S., Parker, P., Ciarrochi, J., Sahdra, B., Jackson, C., & Heaven, P. (2015). Self-compassion protects against the negative effects of low self-esteem: A longitudinal study in a large adolescent sample. *Personality and Individual Differences, 74,* 116–121.

Noone, C., & Hogan, M. J. (2018). A randomised active-controlled trial to examine the effects of an online mindfulness intervention on executive control, critical thinking and key thinking dispositions in a university student sample. *BMC Psychology, 6,* no. 13. https://doi.org/10.1186/s40359-018-0226-3

Ostrom, E. (1990). *Governing the commons: The evolution of institutions for collective action.* Cambridge University Press.

Porges, S. W. (2011). *The polyvagal theory: Neurophysiological foundations of emotions, attachment, communication, and self-regulation.* WW Norton & Company.

Ryan, R. M., & Deci, E. L. (2017). *Self-determination theory: Basic psychological needs in motivation, development, and wellness.* Guilford Publications.

Sahdra, B., Ciarrochi, J., & Parker, P. (2016). Nonattachment and mindfulness: Related but distinct constructs. *Psychological Assessment, 28*(7), 819–829.

Spear, L. P. (2004). Adolescent brain development and animal models. *Annals of the New York Academy of Sciences, 1021,* 23–26.

Szalavitz, M., & Perry, B. D. (2010). *Born for love.* William Morrow.

Van der Kolk, B. A. (2006). Clinical implications of neuroscience research in PTSD. *Annals of the New York Academy of Sciences, 1071*(1), 277–293.

Williams, K. E., & Ciarrochi, J. (2020). Perceived parenting styles and values development: A longitudinal study of adolescents and emerging adults. *Journal of Research on Adolescence, 30*(2), 541–558. https://doi.org/10.1111/jora.12542

Williams, K., Ciarrochi, J., & Heaven, P. (2012). Inflexible parents, inflexible kids: A six-year longitudinal study of parenting style and the development of psychological flexibility in adolescents. *Journal of Youth and Adolescence, 41,* 1053–1066.

Wilson, D., Hayes, S., Biglan, A., & Embry, D. (2014). Evolving the future: Toward a science of intentional change. *Behavioral and Brain Sciences, 37,* 395–460.

11

Brief Mindfulness Interventions

Soles of the Feet for Students and Guided Mindfulness Practices

JOSHUA C. FELVER

Mindfulness-based interventions (MBIs) have become an increasingly popular topic of scientific inquiry over the past 30 years (Baer, 2003; Brown et al., 2007; Khoury et al., 2015). Emerging research indicates that MBI can reduce stress and improve well-being in adults (Khoury et al., 2015). In parallel with research conducted with adult populations, clinicians and researchers are also interested in exploring the utility of MBIs with youth (Greenberg & Harris, 2012; Zoogman et al., 2015) and in school settings (Felver & Schutt, 2021; Felver et al., 2016; Felver & Jennings, 2016; Mind and Life Education Research Network (MLERN) et al., 2012; Zenner et al., 2014). As examples of this surge in focused research activity, there have been several peer-reviewed journal special issues devoted to the topic of MBIs in school settings, including *Mindfulness* (Felver & Jennings, 2016; Roeser et al., 2023), *Psychology in the Schools* (Renshaw & Cook, 2017), *Contemporary School Psychology* (Renshaw et al., 2017), and *ECNU Review of Education* (Felver & Wang, 2025) as well as entire books devoted to the topic, including the *Handbook of Mindfulness in Education* (Schonert-Reichl & Roeser, 2016) and the present edited volume.

To illustrate the nascent state and the pace of research exploring the utility of MBIs with student populations, using the PsycINFO electronic database and keywords "mindfulness" and "school," as of summer 2024 there were 140 studies involving youth (i.e., subjects under the age of 18) that have been published in academic peer-reviewed journals. Restricting this search to only articles published since 2019, one finds that 46% ($n = 65$) of the existing literature has been published in the last five years alone. Clearly, people are interested in MBIs, and

Joshua C. Felver, *Brief Mindfulness Interventions*. In: *Using Mindfulness to Promote Mental Health in Schools*. Edited by: Tyler L. Renshaw and Shane R. Jimerson, Oxford University Press. © Oxford University Press (2025).
DOI: 10.1093/9780190880507.003.0011

the empirical evidence supporting the utility of these practices is mounting; however, research exploring MBIs with youth in school settings is a relatively new area of scientific inquiry.

To gain perspective on the current state of any field of scientific inquiry, it is useful to periodically conduct literature reviews to synthesize findings and to identify areas in need of further study. Zenner and colleagues (2014) conducted a meta-analysis of the existing literature published through 2012. This review found great variability in the existing MBI. For example, programming ranged in school-based sessions from 4 to 24 weeks of training, yielding total student mindfulness practice time ranging from 160 to 3700 minutes. Felver and colleagues (2016) conducted a systematic review of the literature published through 2014 and found similar results, with high heterogeneity in MBI that included program length lasting anywhere from 2 to 24 weeks and including between 75 and 2160 minutes of direct service delivery to students. Both of the aforementioned reviews, as well as more recent meta-analytic reviews (Carsley et al., 2018; Dunning et al., 2019; Klingbeil et al., 2017), have noted that although MBI is a promising approach to supporting students, the existing heterogeneity in programming makes it difficult to draw conclusions about the effectiveness of MBI as a whole; thus, replication studies are recommended. Felver and colleagues also recommended that the field would benefit from identifying key intervention components that are shared across MBIs (e.g., basic mindful breathing practice), as a more thorough understanding of these common elements would inform future MBI development.

In parallel with growing academic interest in MBIs, school systems are increasingly interested in MBI technology; however, the challenges faced by contemporary public education systems pose unique barriers to implementing additional programming. A common sentiment among school administrators and staff is that school systems are consistently being asked to do more with fewer resources. Given these increasing demands placed on school systems, the prospect of adding time-intensive programing to an already full school schedule is a daunting proposition. It is therefore understandable that many, if not most, school districts would be reluctant to implement an MBI that could require the upper-range of in-class time (i.e., 24 weeks of programming totaling more than 2,000 minutes of student time; Felver et al., 2016) or require expensive external interventionists or training programs to support implementation. Conversely, briefer MBIs that require minimal interventionist training may be more desirable, given they place relatively reduced demands on school systems' already tight budgets and schedules.

The focus of this chapter is to detail two brief MBIs for use in school settings: an evidence-based (Felver et al., 2022) five-session curriculum for student disruptive behavior called *Soles of the Feet* (SoF; Felver & Singh, 2020) and basic guided mindfulness practices. These brief MBIs may offer several advantages over other more intensive forms of mindfulness programming. Specifically, brief formats make it easier to conduct replication studies by virtue of their simplicity. SoF has been empirically replicated in several studies using single-case experimental research designs, providing compelling evidence for its effectiveness relative to MBI that have demonstrated results in fewer clinical trials. Less complicated curricular formats are also easier to subject to intervention component analyses, as there are fewer programming elements to scrutinize. Basic daily guided mindfulness practices are ubiquitous across MBIs, offering a simpler method to employ a potentially effective intervention component with lower resource allocation. There is also empirical evidence that indicates both SoF and daily guided mindfulness practices improve student functioning. In the absence of data backing claims that more time-intensive MBIs yield superior results to less time-intensive programming, it seems desirable to implement less intensive programming whenever possible in schools in order to efficiently deploy finite resources.

SOLES OF THE FEET FOR STUDENTS

Soles of the Feet (SoF) was originally developed as a brief MBI to reduce aggressive behavior among adults with disabilities (Singh et al., 2003). Since its inception, it has been adapted for different populations, including students with and without disabilities. This section provides an overview of SoF, a brief literature review of the empirical evaluation of SoF, and an introduction to how SoF is currently being implemented in school settings in its modified form: *Soles of the Feet for Students* (Felver & Singh, 2020).

Overview of Soles of the Feet

Soles of the Feet is a brief MBI that teaches a simple routine for responding to situations that elicit unpleasant emotional arousal states (e.g., anger) and eventually disruptive behavior (e.g., physical aggression). The goal of SoF is to support individuals in learning and establishing behavioral fluency with a three-part self-control strategy. The first aspect of this self-control strategy is to develop mindful awareness of the precursors to unpleasant emotional arousal and disruptive behavior. Individuals are given instruction on how to simply notice (i.e., self-regulate attention toward) the conditions that immediately precede unpleasant emotional arousal (e.g., anger) and disruptive behavior. This noticing is done without judgment of the condition as "good" or "bad," and with an attitudinal quality of acceptance, or allowing the condition to simply be as it is. These two elements of non-judgment and acceptance are defining features of any MBI, including SoF. Individuals are also taught that these preceding conditions (also referred to as "triggers" or "antecedents") can be either external (occurring in the environment outside the person) or internal (occurring within oneself in the form of thoughts, feelings, or physiological arousal states). In sum, the first aspect of SoF involves basic didactic instruction and opportunities to practice identifying, accepting, and non-judgmentally observing these conditions without trying to change them in any way.

The second aspect of SoF involves teaching individuals a procedure of moving attention away from the aforementioned external or internal conditions and toward an emotionally neutral part of one's body: the feet. Individuals repeatedly practice a sequence of noticing the somatic experience of their feet (e.g., wiggling toes to feel their socks, noticing pressure on their heel) until they gain mastery of and automaticity with self-regulating attention to their feet. The feet are specifically selected as the part of the body to focus attention on because feet are not typically associated with unpleasant feelings such as anger (as opposed to, for example, the hands, which may become clenched into fists), are rich with somatic information to notice (as oppose to, for example, the back, which has relatively little somatic sensation), and are easily accessible for attention whether sitting, walking, or standing. By moving attention away from the external or internal conditions that lead to unpleasant emotional arousal and disruptive behavior and toward a neutral sensation in the body, the pattern of escalating emotional or behavioral reaction is naturally disrupted and, thus, de-escalated.

After individuals can mindfully notice the conditions that precede maladaptive emotional and behavioral reactions and can use the attentional regulation procedure to de-escalate and return to a calmer emotional state, the third aspect of SoF involves instructing individuals to choose how to respond to the condition. Because individuals are no longer *reacting* to the immediate conditions during a state of heightened emotional arousal, they can *respond* in an intentional manner that is in their best interests (e.g., not engaging in disruptive behavior such as verbal or physical aggression). The actual responses that individuals choose to use during this third part of SoF are not explicitly instructed, as these are unique to the individual and their particular circumstances. Rather, the *quality* of choosing how to respond in an adaptive manner is emphasized, not the response itself. Students typically know what they "should do" during unpleasant situations (and if they do not, this can easily be identified with the support of an adult); the challenge is that students cannot use these adaptive responses because intense unpleasant emotions interfere with their decision making or because they have an entrenched pattern of non-adaptive problem behavior.

As a case example, an elementary school student was referred to learn SoF because of disruptive off-task behavior that occurred during silent independent seatwork (e.g., pushing materials off of their desk and talking to classmates). Their disruptive behavior resulted in the student being sent out of the classroom to the guidance office, which allowed the student to escape (functionally) from their assignment. After learning SoF, the student was able to identify that independent seatwork was "not fair and boring!" and was triggering for their feelings of intense anger (first aspect—mindfully identifying reaction to unpleasant experience). The student also learned to use the SoF procedure to calm themselves down (second aspect—de-escalating during unpleasant experience) and, finally, to adaptively respond to their identified trigger by raising their hand and asking for help (third aspect—choosing alternative adaptive responses). This student was well aware that the adaptive response in this particular situation was to raise their hand if they needed teacher support (indeed, virtually every student knows this from an early age); they were simply unable to use this adaptive response because of an established pattern of reactive disruptive behavior that interfered with their ability to use this response during moments of strong unpleasant feelings. Thus, SoF was effective for this student because it equipped them with an effective coping strategy to de-escalate themselves during an intense period of unpleasant internal and external experience, which afforded a calmer state of mind to choose a response that was in their best interests.

The SoF curriculum includes five sessions, each lasting approximately 30 minutes (see Table 11.1). These sessions are sequenced iteratively such that by the end of the fifth session students develop fluency with identifying the proximal antecedent conditions that elicit disruptive behavior, directing themselves through the SoF procedure (i.e., self-regulating attention to somatic experience of feet) to nullify or mitigate the escalated unpleasant feelings, and then returning to their school activity while making a decision that is in their best interests. Students' fluency with SoF procedures is also scaffolded through these five sessions, beginning with mastery of the component steps (Session1), to being able to use the entire procedure with verbal direction from the instructor and visual support in the form of provided worksheets (Sessions 2 and 3), and then, finally, to being able to use the entire routine without any external supports (Sessions 4 and 5).

Throughout the SoF curriculum, students are given multiple practice opportunities to develop the skill of moving attention to the somatic experience of their feet. During Session 1, students practice a SoF script that instructs the step-by-step process of paying attention to different anatomical locations on their feet. Session 2 involves students verbally recounting a recent situation that elicited a pleasant emotional experience (e.g., "happy"), which the clinician then verbally repeats back to the student in order to elicit the pleasant emotional and physiological response *in vivo*. After the student evidences observable behaviors indicating that they are experiencing the emotional state (e.g., a smile on their face), the clinician instructs the student to use the SoF script and to place all of their attention on the somatic experiences of their feet. Post-practice discussion centers on the student describing how their positive affective state was nullified or mitigated by moving their attention away from the pleasant memory of the recounted event. Sessions 3 and 4 involve students recounting experiences that elicited unpleasant emotional/physiological experiences (e.g., anger) and resulting disruptive behavior (e.g., aggression), which are then similarly recounted by the clinician and used as opportunities for *in vivo* practice with the SoF script. In these sessions, post-practice discussion revolves around students understanding that if they notice these unpleasant emotional or physiological states and then use the SoF script, they can avoid engaging in disruptive behavior that is often associated with negative life consequences. Session 5 of the curriculum reviews the content of the previous four sessions and then creates concrete plans for when and how students will generalize the SoF routine throughout their day-to-day lives.

Empirical Support for Soles of the Feet

SoF has empirically demonstrated beneficial clinical outcomes in several published studies using single-case research design methodology. The first study of SoF demonstrated that an adult with dual diagnoses of intellectual disability and psychotic disorder not otherwise specified was able to significantly reduce high rates of aggressive behavior following completion of the manualized intervention (Singh et al., 2003). These preliminary results prompted two follow-up studies utilizing multiple-baseline research designs, which demonstrated similarly significant reductions in aggressive behavior for adults with severe psychiatric diagnoses (Singh, Lancioni, Winton, Adkins, Wahler, et al., 2007) and moderate intellectual disabilities (Singh, Lancioni, Winton, Adkins, Singh, et al., 2007).

Since these initial studies, SoF has been replicated several times and consistently demonstrated significant reductions in aggressive behavior in adult populations in various settings, including individuals with intellectual disabilities in a forensic mental health facility (Singh et al., 2008) and individuals with intellectual disabilities and mental illness in community-based assisted living homes (Adkins et al., 2010). Following the success of the aforementioned studies that demonstrated reductions in aggressive behavior among adults with intellectual and/or psychiatric disabilities, a two-group randomized controlled trial (RCT) was conducted in which participants with intellectual disabilities (mean age = 23 years old; $n = 34$) were randomized to SoF and waiting list control conditions (Singh et al., 2013). Results from this RCT showed that participants receiving SoF demonstrated statistically significant reductions in physical and verbal aggressive behavior.

SoF has also been used with non-adult populations to reduce aggressive behavior. The first trial of SoF with youth involved a multiple-baseline design research study of three typically developing adolescents with conduct disorder (Singh, Lancioni, Joy, Wintom, Sabaawi, et al., 2007). Following SoF training, these adolescents evidenced significant reductions in their aggressive and antisocial behavior (e.g., fire-setting, cruelty to animals). Two other single-case research design studies explored the utility of SoF with adolescents with autism spectrum disorder; both demonstrated significant reductions in instances of aggressive behavior (Singh, Lancioni, Manikam, et al., 2011; Singh, Lancioni, Singh, et al., 2011).

Given the effectiveness of SoF for reducing disruptive behavior among individuals with intellectual, developmental, and psychiatric disabilities, researchers have also explored the use of SoF in school settings with students with disruptive behavior. More specifically, researchers adapted the SoF protocol with minor modifications to fit within a school-based setting (Felver & Singh, 2020). Examples of these modifications include creating fill-in-the-blank worksheets to teach vocabulary about parts of the foot and handouts that describe the SoF procedure to use during home practice. The first study to use SoF in schools recruited typically developing third-grade students with high rates of off-task behavior in the classroom (Felver et al., 2014). Using a multiple-baseline research design, students demonstrated significant reductions in their off-task behavior and increases in their academically engaged behavior following completion of the SoF intervention. Post-intervention data collected from students and teachers also indicated that SoF was a socially acceptable and feasible intervention. Building on the results of Felver et al.'s (2014) study, use of the SoF in schools was replicated with four students (Grades 4–7) receiving special education services under the disability categories of Other Health Impairment and Emotional and Behavioral Disability (Felver et al., 2017). Results from this single-case design study demonstrated a similar pattern of results as the earlier study (Felver et al., 2014), with all students showing significant reductions in disruptive classroom behavior and significant increases in academically engaged behavior following SoF intervention.

To summarize the extant literature, a meta-analysis was conducted to explore SoF intervention effects for reducing disruptive behavior (Felver et al., 2022). Following a literature review, 15 publications were identified that met established criteria for high-quality single-case research design (SCRD) studies (Horner et al., 2005; Kratochwill et al., 2013). These studies included 49 participants ranging in age from 9 to 72 years ($M = 23.1$, $SD = 15.9$) with diverse diagnostic/disability classifications, and about half of the participants (53%) were younger than 18 years of age. Employing a non-parametric statistical approach for estimating effect sizes in SCRD studies (Tau-U; Parker et al., 2011), SoF demonstrated a large aggregated effect size for reducing disruptive behavior (Tau-U = −0.87; $SE = 0.03$, 95% CI [−0.93 to −0.81]). Moderator analyses indicated that SOF's effectiveness was robust across participant age, whether or not participants had an intellectual disability, adaptations (session frequency and duration) to delivery format, and SoF interventionist experience level. These results indicate that SOF is an effective evidence-based practice for disruptive behavior (Horner et al., 2005).

School-Based Adaptation of Soles of the Feet

During the process of implementing the aforementioned school-based applications of SoF (Felver et al., 2014, 2017), the curriculum was modified to meet the unique needs of youth in school settings (Felver & Singh, 2020). As one example of these modifications, many younger students had difficulty with the instruction "noticing the *ball* of your feet." It was determined that students lacked the anatomical knowledge to follow this instruction, and thus additional materials and curricular content were required. To develop their vocabulary, fill-in-the-blank worksheets (a common instructional format in school settings) were created that included a basic drawing of the foot, a word bank, and arrows pointing to different parts of the foot that students could fill in with words selected from the word bank. Experiential activities were also developed to give students an opportunity to practice using these words. For example, to teach about the ball of the foot, students were asked to stand up and lean forward as far as they could, without taking a step and without going up on their toes, and then asked what part of the foot they were using. These modifications were pilot-tested in school-based contexts with both children and adolescents, in both individual and group settings, and the insights gleaned from these pilot tests were used to iteratively refine the SoF manual. The final revised SoF manual, entitled *Mindfulness in the Classroom: An Evidence-Based Intervention to Reduce Disruptive Behavior and Increase Academic Engagement* (Felver & Singh, 2020), was formatted and written so that it could be accessible for the intended audience of school-based service providers (e.g., teachers, school psychologists, school-based mental health professionals). The session outline for this adapted-for-school version of SoF is presented in Table 11.1.

Table 11.1. Soles of the Feet for Students: Session Outline and Criterion for Mastery

Session	Criterion for advancing to next session
Session 1 Introducing Soles of the Feet	Fluency with diaphragmatic mindful breathing Memorization of vocabulary describing anatomy of the foot
Session 2 Practicing with a Strong Positive Feeling	Able to use SoF routine by following verbal instructions Able to identify the feeling of happiness Experience of nullifying or mitigating the feeling of happiness
Session 3 Practicing with a Strong Negative Feeling	Able to use SoF routine with visual aid Able to identify the feeling of anger Experience of nullifying or mitigating the feeling of anger
Session 4 Practicing with the Triggers to Negative Feelings	Able to use SoF routine without (or with minimal) external supports during session Able to identify trigger(s) to feeling of anger Experience of applying SoF routine to trigger(s) of anger, thus nullifying or mitigating the feeling of anger
Session 5 Planning to use Soles of the Feet in Daily Life	Fluency with using SoF routine outside of session with minimal or no external supports Fluency with using SoF during proximal antecedents of anger, and while feeling angry Able to identify settings/events/times when they can use SoF

The first adaptation to ready SoF for use in schools was to explicitly outline the criterion necessary for students to progress through each of the five sessions of the curriculum (see Table 11.1). This modification was included to ensure that students gained fluency with prerequisite skills before moving on to further curricular content that built upon skills developed during earlier sessions. As an example, the final objective of the intervention is that students become fluent with the full SoF procedure: identifying that they are becoming unpleasantly emotionally or physiologically aroused, moving their attention to their feet, and then returning and responding adaptively within the setting. However, to meet this final objective, students must first be able to identify the different somatic experiences in their feet and then be fluent with a memorized script for self-guiding how they allocate attention. Paying attention to feet is taught to students in a scaffolded and sequential process, beginning with developing vocabulary of the anatomy of feet (e.g., toes, balls of the feet, arches), followed by practice using the SoF script to guide attention to the feet (e.g., "Now shifting attention to the feet . . . all of your attention is on the soles of your feet . . . wiggling your toes . . ."). Students initially use the SoF script with printed visual support, then by reciting the memorized script aloud, and finally by internally using the SoF script when needed. By explicitly detailing these steps, the adapted SoF curriculum provides students and school-based service providers with a structured process that ensures each earlier element is mastered before proceeding to the next step.

The second modification to ready SoF for use in schools was to include materials and adjunctive activities that students and school-based clinicians would be accustomed to using to support the learning process. Examples of these materials include worksheets that students can use to learn how to identify anatomical areas of feet, handouts that detail the practice assignment (i.e., homework) for students to use between sessions to develop fluency with target skills, and practice stickers that students affix to their desktops as a visual prompt to use the SoF script during class when they notice triggers to disruptive behavior. These materials make the SoF procedure more familiar to students and school staff, which may contribute to the acceptability of the curriculum. Activities and materials were intentionally developed to make the content approachable for younger individuals. As an example, rather than verbally discussing the anatomy of the foot and accompanying physical sensations, students are guided through a brief movement activity to help identify the parts of their feet (e.g., standing up and leaning forward as far as they can, without falling, to identify the balls of the feet). By incorporating more experiential activities into the curriculum than the original version of SoF, the adapted-for-school curriculum is more accessible to younger students who may disengage with lengthy discussions and didactic activities.

The third modification to ready SoF for use in schools was to create supplementary material to facilitate school-based clinicians' use of the manual. Minor supplementary materials include an implementation fidelity checklist to code for structural and process elements of the intervention (Century et al., 2010) and worksheets for gathering detailed, multi-sensory reports of emotionally evocative life events that students describe during *in vivo* exposure activities. For example, a clinician would first use a worksheet to gather detailed information from a student about an event that happened during the previous week, and then recite back to the student the details, such as, "remembering that time last Tuesday during math class when you were told by your teacher to stop talking or you would get a detention . . . recalling the sounds of students snickering . . . and you started thinking to yourself 'that wasn't fair!'" Major supplementary materials include a full description of a booster session to be used after the sequence of regular sessions in the manual is completed as well as details regarding how to use the SoF procedure with groups or classrooms of students. Although these major supplementary materials have not been empirically evaluated, they have been used by several school-based interventionists who reported their effectiveness with various student populations.

DAILY GUIDED MINDFULNESS PRACTICES

Perhaps the most common shared programmatic element across all MBIs is the utilization of basic guided mindfulness practices. Guided practices entail verbally delivered instructions that specify a given mindfulness-based meditation exercise. This format of instruction has been used to train novice meditation practitioners in non-secular contexts (e.g., Buddhism) for centuries; however, the instructions themselves are usually secular in nature. As an example, a common introductory activity for individuals learning mindfulness for the first time is seated awareness-of-breath meditation (Lippelt et al., 2014). Individuals learning this practice are instructed to find a comfortable seated position on a padded floor mat (e.g., *zabuton*), by sitting on a cushion (e.g., *zafu*) cross-legged with one's knees touching the ground. The instructor directs individuals to sit upright with their chin slightly tucked, and then to pay close attention to the somatic sensations of breathing (e.g., movement of the abdomen during diaphragmatic contractions or sensations of air moving into and out of the nose). For the next 20 to 40 minutes, the instructor directs individuals to notice when their attention has gone elsewhere (e.g., remembering a past event or planning for the future), and then to return their attention to the sensation of breathing with an attitude of curiosity, self-kindness, and non-judgment. Following this practice period, the instructor de-briefs the individuals' experiences during the guided practice, answering questions that typically center on the fact that individuals found their attention moving off of the breath repeatedly during the activity (which is to be expected for novice practitioners). Guided mindfulness practices could also include other meditation practices, such as open monitoring or loving kindness meditation (Lippelt et al., 2014). But most formal meditation training traditions (e.g., Vipassana Buddhism) typically begin with versions of the aforementioned focused attention practices as a way of building attentional stability before moving on to other practices.

Western mindfulness-based therapeutic practices, such as mindfulness-based stress reduction (Kabat-Zinn, 1990) and mindfulness-based cognitive therapy (Segal et al., 2012), also rely heavily on guided mindfulness practices. In addition to guided practices being delivered in person by an instructor, most current MBIs make use of pre-recorded guided meditation exercises, which are used outside of sessions to support individuals as they establish their own personal practice. As an example, the MBSR curriculum (Kabat-Zinn, 1990) includes daily meditation practices that individuals are instructed to engage in between weekly group sessions. These practices include the aforementioned focused attention awareness of breathing practice and also other practices, such as open monitoring meditation, in which individuals are instructed to simply notice any external (e.g., sound or somatic sensation) or internal (e.g., feeling or thought) experiences without attempting to change the experiences in any way.

Despite the ubiquity of practices such as focused attention and open monitoring meditations in well-established MBIs and some promising evidence for their efficacy, little research has investigated these component practices in controlled laboratory settings independent of larger curricula. For example, laboratory-based research has found that as few as four days of 20-minute mindfulness practices have significant beneficial effects on behavioral measures of attention and executive processing relative to an active control condition (Zeidan et al., 2010). As another example, three days of 25-minute mindfulness meditation practice was found to alter self-reported stress-reactivity relative to an active control condition following an acute stress induction in a laboratory setting (Creswell et al., 2014). The current state of this limited literature suggests that brief component practices may offer benefits that are similar to the larger interventions from which they are typically employed (e.g., MBSR). Thus, there have been calls for additional research into standardized basic mindfulness practices conducted in laboratory settings to more fully understand the benefits of MBI's core components (Morton et al., 2019).

Guided Mindfulness Practices as a Component of MBI

Given their ubiquity in adult MBIs, daily guided mindfulness practices have also been incorporated into programming targeting youth and in school settings. As one example of such programming, the Learning to BREATHE (Broderick, 2013) protocol for adolescents combines thematic and curricular elements of MBSR with more standard social-emotional learning competencies (Payton et al., 2000). Among the programmatic elements, L2B involves adolescents listening to 10-minute guided mindfulness practices on a daily basis outside of school. These practices include the aforementioned awareness-of-breath focused attention practices as well as open monitoring, loving kindness, and body scan meditations (Broderick, 2013). Several studies have found that the full L2B curriculum is beneficial for addressing adolescent stress and psychosocial well-being (Broderick & Metz, 2009; Felver et al., 2019; Metz et al., 2013); however, these studies have not investigated the unique contributions of the daily home practice element that emphasizes students' use of guided mindfulness practices.

To address the aforementioned limitation, researchers have begun to explore effects of daily mindfulness practice. For example, the Mind Body Laboratory at Syracuse University recently conducted a randomized controlled trial of classrooms receiving L2B ($n = 33$) compared to typical classroom programming ($n = 31$). The trial found no significant differences over time between these groups on a total scale score of a commonly used measure of behavioral and emotional functioning (BASC-3 Behavioral and Emotional Screening System [BESS]; Reynolds & Kamphaus, 2015), $F(1,62) = 0.45$, $p = 0.833$, $\eta_p{}^2, = .001$. However, when analyzing home practice logs for students assigned to the L2B condition, students' total days of guided mindfulness practice was significantly predictive of change scores on the total scale score of the BESS, $r(31) = -0.39$, $p = 0.03$, even though these students' BESS scores didn't change as a group between pre- and post-intervention time points, $t(30) = 0.46$, $p = 0.65$, Cohen's $d = 0.05$ (Felver, 2016). These data suggest that there may be unique benefits of daily guided meditation practice that are not observable by simply receiving a manualized MBI in a classroom context.

Guided Mindfulness Practices as a Stand-Alone Intervention

Guided meditation practices delivered independently of multi-component MBIs have also received empirical support among school-aged populations. As one example, researchers have investigated the utility of awareness-of-breath meditation on systolic blood pressure among African-American adolescents at risk for developing cardiovascular disease (Barnes et al., 2008; Gregoski et al., 2011). Adolescents were led through guided mindfulness breathing practices by their teachers for 10 minutes per day during school days, and they were asked to practice 10 minutes at home outside of school. Results indicated that following three months of daily mindful breathing practice, the teenagers in the intervention condition had significantly reduced systolic blood pressure relative to control conditions (Barnes et al., 2008; Gregoski et al., 2011). It is notable that in these studies the teachers were required to undergo minimal training (e.g., a single part-day workshop) to guide students through these 10-minute practices.

The effects of basic guided mindfulness practices have also been explored with elementary school students. In one study, researchers explored the utility of a series of 10-minute guided mindfulness practices among third-grade general education students (Bakosh et al., 2016). The guided practices included 35 unique audio recordings that led students through common practices of MBSR (Kabat-Zinn, 1990) that had been adapted to their developmental level. Teachers played these audio tracks daily in their classroom during normal academic instructional periods. Results indicated that students in these classrooms evidenced improved quarterly grades relative to a no-intervention control condition. In addition to being one of the first studies to have demonstrated achievement benefits for youth who receive MBI, this study is also notable in that it required virtually no training on the part of teachers, as the MBI was implemented by simply playing an audio recording during class.

CONCLUSIONS AND FUTURE DIRECTIONS

The empirical evidence supporting the utility of MBIs in school settings is still emerging. In this nascent field of scientific inquiry, there are already many MBI protocols that have demonstrated benefits for students; however, these MBIs are highly heterogeneous in terms of their content and intensity (Felver et al., 2016; Zenner et al., 2014). This chapter reviewed interventions that are relatively brief and that require relatively fewer resources to implement compared with more complex school-based MBIs: SoF for students and daily guided mindfulness practices. Given the time and resource constraints of many school systems, these more basic interventions may offer benefits for schools with limited resources that are seeking to implement MBI with students. However, there are also many empirical questions regarding these more basic mindfulness practices that have yet to be addressed.

One currently unanswered question regards the amount of training required for an interventionist to implement brief MBIs—such as SoF or other guided meditation—with fidelity. Most MBI curricula and facilitator manuals recommend that potential interventionists have a well-developed personal mindfulness practice prior to seeking to teach mindfulness to others; however, research that directly explores this question has not yet been completed. Future studies should consider directly exploring this topic by, for example, systematically manipulating the amount of prerequisite mindfulness experience of interventionists and then evaluating their fidelity of implementation. As discussed earlier, a potential benefit of the brief MBIs reviewed in this chapter is that they likely require far less interventionist training. In particular, using pre-recorded audio tracks to guide mindfulness practices offers an avenue for school-based personnel to implement MBIs without any background training.

Furthermore, although there is convincing support for MBIs as an approach for improving student social and emotional functioning (Felver et al., 2016; Zenner et al., 2014), a pressing question for intervention scientists interested in MBI is how this technology may benefit student academic achievement. Future research should consider evaluating the effects of MBIs on students' grades and standardized test scores. As an example of how this could be accomplished, the Syracuse University Mind Body Laboratory is currently investigating the utility of SoF for adolescents in schools with test-taking anxiety. Preliminary evidence from pilot studies suggests that students who utilize the SoF procedure for their feelings of anxiety outperformed active control conditions during high-stakes testing situations (Felver, 2018).

Ultimately, brief MBIs may offer a more appealing format of intervention service delivery in schools compared with more time- and resource-intensive mindfulness programming. Brief MBIs also have the advantage of being more easily replicated and subjected to intervention component analyses. As discussed earlier, researchers have called for further investigation into the "active ingredients" of mindfulness-based curricula and treatment packages, and thus brief MBIs should be strongly considered as candidates for component analysis studies. Taken together, the evidence exploring the utility of brief MBIs is promising, and future work exploring the extent of these benefits, particularly compared with more intensive MBI programming, will be exciting to monitor in the years to come.

REFERENCES

Adkins, A. D., Singh, A. N., Winton, A. S., McKeegan, G. F., & Singh, J. (2010). Using a mindfulness-based procedure in the community: Translating research to practice. *Journal of Child and Family Studies*, *19*(2), 175–183.

Baer, R. A. (2003). Mindfulness training as a clinical intervention: A conceptual and empirical review. *Clinical Psychology: Science and Practice*, *10*(2), 125–143. https://doi.org/10.1093/clipsy.bpg015

Bakosh, L. S., Snow, R. M., Tobias, J. M., Houlihan, J. L., & Barbosa-Leiker, C. (2016). Maximizing mindful learning: Mindful awareness intervention improves elementary school students' quarterly grades. *Mindfulness*, *7*(1), 59–67. https://doi.org/10.1007/s12671-015-0387-6

Barnes, V. A., Pendergrast, R. A., Harshfield, G. A., & Treiber, F. A. (2008). Impact of breathing awareness meditation on ambulatory blood pressure and sodium handling in prehypertensive African American adolescents. *Ethnicity & Disease*, *18*(1), 1–5.

Broderick, P. C. (2013). *Learning to breathe: A mindfulness curriculum for adolescents to cultivate emotion regulation, attention, and performance* (1st ed.). New Harbinger Publications.

Broderick, P. C., & Metz, S. (2009). Learning to BREATHE: A pilot trial of a mindfulness curriculum for adolescents. *Advances in School Mental Health Promotion*, *2*(1), 35–46. https://doi.org/10.1080/1754730X.2009.9715696

Brown, K. W., Ryan, R. M., & Creswell, J. D. (2007). Mindfulness: Theoretical foundations and evidence for its salutary effects. *Psychological Inquiry*, *18*(4), 211–237. https://doi.org/10.1080/10478400701598298

Carsley, D., Khoury, B., & Heath, N. L. (2018). Effectiveness of mindfulness interventions for mental health in schools: A comprehensive meta-analysis. *Mindfulness*, *9*(3), 693–707.

Century, J., Rudnick, M., & Freeman, C. (2010). A framework for measuring fidelity of implementation: A foundation for shared language and accumulation of knowledge. *American Journal of Evaluation*, *31*(2), 199–218. https://doi.org/10.1177/1098214010366173

Creswell, J. D., Pacilio, L. E., Lindsay, E. K., & Brown, K. W. (2014). Brief mindfulness meditation training alters psychological and neuroendocrine responses to social evaluative stress. *Psychoneuroendocrinology*, *44*, 1–12. https://doi.org/10.1016/j.psyneuen.2014.02.007

Dunning, D. L., Griffiths, K., Kuyken, W., Crane, C., Foulkes, L., Parker, J., & Dalgleish, T. (2019). Research review: The effects of mindfulness-based interventions on cognition and mental health in children and adolescents—A meta-analysis of randomized controlled trials. *Journal of Child Psychology and Psychiatry, and Allied Disciplines*, *60*(3), 244–258. https://doi.org/10.1111/jcpp.12980

Felver, J. C. (2016). *Evaluation of school-based mindfulness curriculum "Learning to BREATHE."* Unpublished raw data.

Felver, J. C. (2018). *Brief effective strategies for test-stress (BEST)*. Unpublished raw data.

Felver, J. C., Clawson, A. J., Ash, T. L., Martens, B., Wang, Q., & Singh, N. (2022). Meta-analysis of mindfulness-based program Soles of the Feet for disruptive behaviors. *Behavior Modification*, *46*, 1488–1516. https://doi:10.1177/01454455211073738

Felver, J. C., Clawson, A. J., Morton, M. L., Brier-Kennedy, E., Janack, P., & DiFlorio, R. (2019). School-based mindfulness intervention supports adolescent resiliency: A randomized control pilot study. *International Journal of School and Educational Psychology*, *7*(sup1), 111–122. https://doi.org/10.1080/21683603.2018.1461722

Felver, J. C., Felver, S. L., Margolis, K. L., Ravitch, N. K., Romer, N., & Horner, R. H. (2017). Effectiveness and social validity of the Soles of the Feet mindfulness-based intervention with special education students. *Contemporary School Psychology*, *21*(4), 358–368. https://doi.org/10.1007/s40688-017-0133-2

Felver, J. C., Frank, J. L., & McEachern, A. D. (2014). Effectiveness, acceptability, and feasibility of the Soles of the Feet mindfulness-based intervention with elementary school students. *Mindfulness*, *5*(5), 589–597. https://doi.org/10.1007/s12671-013-0238-2

Felver, J. C., Hoyos, C. E. C., Tezanos, K., & Singh, N. N. (2016). A systematic review of mindfulness-based interventions for youth in school settings. *Mindfulness*, *7*(1), 34–45. https://doi.org/10.1007/s12671-015-0389-4

Felver, J. C., & Jennings, P. A. (2016). Applications of mindfulness-based interventions in school settings: An introduction. *Mindfulness*, *7*(1), 1–4. https://doi.org/10.1007/s12671-015-0478-4

Felver, J. C., & Schutt, M. K. A., (2021). Mindfulness in education. In N. N. Singh & S. D. S. Joy (Eds.), *Mindfulness-based interventions with children and adolescents: Research and practice* (pp. 57–73). Springer.

Felver, J. C., & Singh, N. N. (2020). *Mindfulness in the classroom: An evidence-based intervention to reduce disruptive behavior and increase academic engagement.* New Harbinger Publications.

Felver, J. C. & Wang, Q. (2025). Mindfulness-based programming for students and teachers in public school settings: Present findings and future directions. *ECNU Review of Education*, *8*(1), 203–208. https://doi.org/10.1177/20965311241306764

Greenberg, M. T., & Harris, A. R. (2012). Nurturing mindfulness in children and youth: Current state of research. *Child Development Perspectives*, *6*(2), 161–166. https://doi.org/10.1111/j.1750-8606.2011.00215.x

Gregoski, M. J., Barnes, V. A., Tingen, M. S., Harshfield, G. A., & Treiber, F. A. (2011). Breathing awareness meditation and LifeSkills Training programs influence upon ambulatory blood pressure and sodium excretion among African American adolescents. *The Journal of Adolescent Health: Official Publication of the Society for Adolescent Medicine*, *48*(1), 59–64. https://doi.org/10.1016/j.jadohealth.2010.05.019

Horner, R. H., Carr, E. G., Halle, J., McGee, G., Odom, S., & Wolery, M. (2005). The use of single subject research to identify evidence-based practice in special education. *Exceptional Children*, *71(2)*, 165–179. https://doi.org/10.1177/001440290507100203

Kabat-Zinn, J. (1990). *Full catastrophe living: Using the wisdom of your body and mind to face stress, pain, and illness.* Dell.

Khoury, B., Sharma, M., Rush, S. E., & Fournier, C. (2015). Mindfulness-based stress reduction for healthy individuals: A meta-analysis. *Journal of Psychosomatic Research*, *78*(6), 519–528. https://doi.org/10.1016/j.jpsychores.2015.03.009

Klingbeil, D. A., Renshaw, T. L., Willenbrink, J. B., Copek, R. A., Chan, K. T., Haddock, A., . . . Clifton, J. (2017). Mindfulness-based interventions with youth: A comprehensive meta-analysis of group-design studies. *Journal of School Psychology*, *63*, 77–103. https://doi.org/10.1016/j.jsp.2017.03.006

Kratochwill, T. R., Hitchcock, J. H., Horner, R. H., Levin, J. R., Odom, S. L., Rindskopf, D. M., & Shadish, W. R. (2013). Single-case intervention research design standards. *Remedial and Special Education*, *34(1)*, 26–38. https://doi.org/10.1177/0741932512452794

Lippelt, D. P., Hommel, B., & Colzato, L. S. (2014). Focused attention, open monitoring and loving kindness meditation: Effects on attention, conflict monitoring, and creativity—A review. *Frontiers in Psychology*, *5*. https://doi.org/10.3389/fpsyg.2014.01083

Metz, S. M., Frank, J. L., Reibel, D., Cantrell, T., Sanders, R., & Broderick, P. C. (2013). The effectiveness of the Learning to BREATHE program on adolescent emotion regulation. *Research in Human Development*, *10*(3), 252–272. https://doi.org/10.1080/15427609.2013.818488

Mind and Life Education Research Network (MLERN). Davidson, R. J., Dunne, J., Eccles, J. S., Engle, A., Greenberg, M., . . . Vago, D. (2012). Contemplative practices and mental training: Prospects for American education. *Child Development Perspectives, 6*(2), 146–153. https://doi.org/10.1111/j.1750-8606.2012.00240.x

Morton, M. L., Helminen, E. C., & Felver, J. C. (2019). A systematic review of mindfulness interventions on psychophysiological responses to acute stress. Manuscript submitted for publication.

Parker, R. I., Vannest, K. J., Davis, J. L., & Sauber, S. B. (2011). Combining nonoverlap and trend for single-case research: Tau-U. *Behavior Therapy, 42*(2), 284–299. https://doi.org/10.1016/j.beth.2010.08.006

Payton, J. W., Wardlaw, D. M., Graczyk, P. A., Bloodworth, M. R., Tompsett, C. J., & Weissberg, R. P. (2000). Social and emotional learning: A framework for promoting mental health and reducing risk behavior in children and youth. *Journal of School Health, 70*(5), 179–185.

Renshaw, T. L., & Cook, C. R. (2017). Introduction to the special issue: Mindfulness in the schools—Historical roots, current status, and future directions. *Psychology in the Schools, 54*(1), 5–12. https://doi.org/10.1002/pits.21978

Renshaw, T. L., Fischer, A. J., & Klingbeil, D. A. (2017). Mindfulness-based intervention in school psychology. *Contemporary School Psychology, 21*(4), 299–303. https://doi.org/10.1007/s40688-017-0166-6

Reynolds, R. W., & Kamphaus, C. R. (2015). *BASC-3 behavioral and emotional screening system: BASC-3 BESS*. Pearson.

Roeser, R. W., Schussler, D., Baelen, R. N., & Galla, B. M. (2023). Mindfulness for students in pre-K to secondary school settings: Current findings, future directions. *Mindfulness, 14*(2), 233–238. https://doi.org/10.1007/s12671-022-02036-w

Schonert-Reichl, K. A., & Roeser, R. W. (Eds.). (2016). *Handbook of mindfulness in education: Integrating theory and research into practice*. Retrieved from //www.springer.com/us/book/9781493935048

Segal, Z. V., Williams, J. M. G., Teasdale, J. D., & Kabat-Zinn, J. (2012). *Mindfulness-based cognitive therapy for depression*. (2nd edition). The Guilford Press.

Singh, N. N., Lancioni, G. E., Joy, S. D. S., Winton, A. S. W., Sabaawi, M., Wahler, R. G., & Singh, J. (2007). Adolescents with conduct disorder can be mindful of their aggressive behavior. *Journal of Emotional and Behavioral Disorders, 15*(1), 56–63. https://doi.org/10.1177/10634266070150010601

Singh, N. N., Lancioni, G. E., Karazsia, B. T., Winton, A. S., Myers, R. E., Singh, A. N., . . . Singh, J. (2013). Mindfulness-based treatment of aggression in individuals with mild intellectual disabilities: A waiting list control study. *Mindfulness, 4*(2), 158–167.

Singh, N. N., Lancioni, G. E., Manikam, R., Winton, A. S., Singh, A. N., Singh, J., & Singh, A. D. (2011). A mindfulness-based strategy for self-management of aggressive behavior in adolescents with autism. *Research in Autism Spectrum Disorders, 5*(3), 1153–1158.

Singh, N. N., Lancioni, G. E., Singh, A. D., Winton, A. S., Singh, A. N., & Singh, J. (2011). Adolescents with Asperger syndrome can use a mindfulness-based strategy to control their aggressive behavior. *Research in Autism Spectrum Disorders, 5*(3), 1103–1109.

Singh, N. N., Lancioni, G. E., Winton, A. S., Adkins, A. D., Singh, J., & Singh, A. N. (2007). Mindfulness training assists individuals with moderate mental retardation to maintain their community placements. *Behavior Modification, 31*(6), 800–814.

Singh, N. N., Lancioni, G. E., Winton, A. S., Adkins, A. D., Wahler, R. G., Sabaawi, M., & Singh, J. (2007). Individuals with mental illness can control their aggressive behavior through mindfulness training. *Behavior Modification*, *31*(3), 313–328.

Singh, N. N., Lancioni, G. E., Winton, A. S., Singh, A. N., Adkins, A. D., & Singh, J. (2008). Clinical and benefit—Cost outcomes of teaching a mindfulness-based procedure to adult offenders with intellectual disabilities. *Behavior Modification*, *32*(5), 622–637.

Singh, N. N., Wahler, R. G., Adkins, A. D., & Myers, R. E. (2003). Soles of the Feet: A mindfulness-based self-control intervention for aggression by an individual with mild mental retardation and mental illness. *Research in Developmental Disabilities*, *24*(3), 158–169. https://doi.org/10.1016/S0891-4222(03)00026-X

Zeidan, F., Johnson, S. K., Diamond, B. J., David, Z., & Goolkasian, P. (2010). Mindfulness meditation improves cognition: Evidence of brief mental training. *Consciousness and Cognition*, *19*(2), 597–605.

Zenner, C., Herrnleben-Kurz, S., & Walach, H. (2014). Mindfulness-based interventions in schools—A systematic review and meta-analysis. *Frontiers in Psychology*, *5*. https://doi.org/10.3389/fpsyg.2014.00603

Zoogman, S., Goldberg, S. B., Hoyt, W. T., & Miller, L. (2015). Mindfulness interventions with youth: A meta-analysis. *Mindfulness*, *6*(2), 290–302. https://doi.org/10.1007/s12671-013-0260-4

12

Mindfulness for Teachers

Evidence-Based Models to Promote Well-Being

PATRICIA A. JENNINGS

Teachers play a critical role in creating caring and supportive classroom environments that promote students' social, emotional, and academic learning (Jennings & Alamos, 2024; Jennings & Greenberg, 2009). This involves successfully building a supportive relationship with each student (Hamre & Pianta, 2001). Such relationships can make all the difference in a child's success in school and in life, especially for students exposed to risk factors such as poverty and trauma (Birch & Ladd, 1998; Jennings, 2019). However, increasing levels of teacher stress and psychological distress can impair teachers' ability to perform this critical role (Greenberg et al., 2016). This chapter describes cutting-edge research showing that when teachers learn and engage with mindful awareness and compassion practices on a regular basis and develop emotion regulation skills, their ability to manage classroom stress and consciously respond to students' needs and challenging behaviors improves. These improvements make it less likely that teachers will unconsciously react in ways that may impair their relationships with students or negatively impact students' learning and well-being.

TEACHING IS STRESSFUL

There is growing evidence that teaching is an especially demanding profession, both cognitively and emotionally (Greenberg et al., 2016). For example, most of the day teachers must constantly shift their attention from individual students to the whole class, while maintaining awareness of the curricular content and directing engaging learning activities. This requires high levels of attentional

Patricia A. Jennings, *Mindfulness for Teachers*. In: *Using Mindfulness to Promote Mental Health in Schools*. Edited by: Tyler L. Renshaw and Shane R. Jimerson, Oxford University Press. © Oxford University Press (2025).
DOI: 10.1093/9780190880507.003.0012

acuity and flexibility as well as strong working memory. Emotional demands include managing sometimes strong emotions in response to challenging student behavior while teaching, without privacy or an opportunity to take a break to self-regulate. An effective professional response requires composure that may be difficult to maintain, especially after repeated incidents. Teachers, especially those teaching younger students, rarely get a break and must maintain this high level of cognitive engagement and emotional labor for hours at a time. To top it off, teachers and students are confined to the classroom for long periods of time, virtually captives. No one has the freedom to leave at will, even to take care of basic physical needs. Feeling physically confined adds to the level of stress that both teachers and students experience, especially for those with a trauma history (Jennings, 2019, 2021).

These demands may lead to a "burnout cascade," where increasing levels of teacher exhaustion result in ineffective responses to students' challenging behaviors and, thus, an increase in these behaviors, which in turn results in increasing levels of emotional exhaustion for teachers (Jennings & Greenberg, 2009). Teachers' emotional reactivity in response to student behaviors associated with exposure to trauma and chronic stress can be particularly harmful to such students, because it reinforces students' perceptions of being threatened by a more powerful adult (Jennings, 2019).

Added to these stressors are the demands of high-stakes accountability evaluations, time-consuming record-keeping, and challenging parents and colleagues. Teachers report disproportionately high rates of mental health problems, compared with rates found among other occupational groups (Schonfeld et al., 2017). Teacher stress has a negative impact on teaching quality and student engagement and progress in learning (Wong et al., 2017). Teacher mental health difficulties negatively impact the quality of classroom interactions and student behavior and learning (Jennings, 2015a; McLean & Connor, 2015; Milkie & Warner, 2011; Oberle & Schonert-Reichl, 2016). Thus, finding ways to support teachers' social and emotional competencies and dispositions that support coping with these demands is critical (Greenberg et al., 2016).

Added to their responsibilities as educators, teachers and other school staff are often required to deliver both universal and targeted mental health services to their students. Indeed, school professionals are among the most frequent providers of mental health services to children and youths (Green et al., 2013; Rones & Hoagwood, 2000). Universal interventions include social-emotional learning (SEL) programs (Collaborative for Academic, Social, and Emotional Learning [CASEL], n.d.). Teaching SEL involves modeling social and emotional skills and coaching students through a variety of socially and emotionally challenging situations that occur day-to-day in a typical classroom (Jennings & Frank, 2015).

To successfully perform this role of SEL interventionist, teachers themselves require strong social and emotional competencies (SEC) that can be cultivated with mindful awareness and compassion practices (Roeser et al., 2012). The prosocial classroom model explains how these competencies relate to classroom and student outcomes (Jennings & Greenberg, 2009; see Figure 12.1). The model employs the social and emotional competencies articulated by the Collaborative

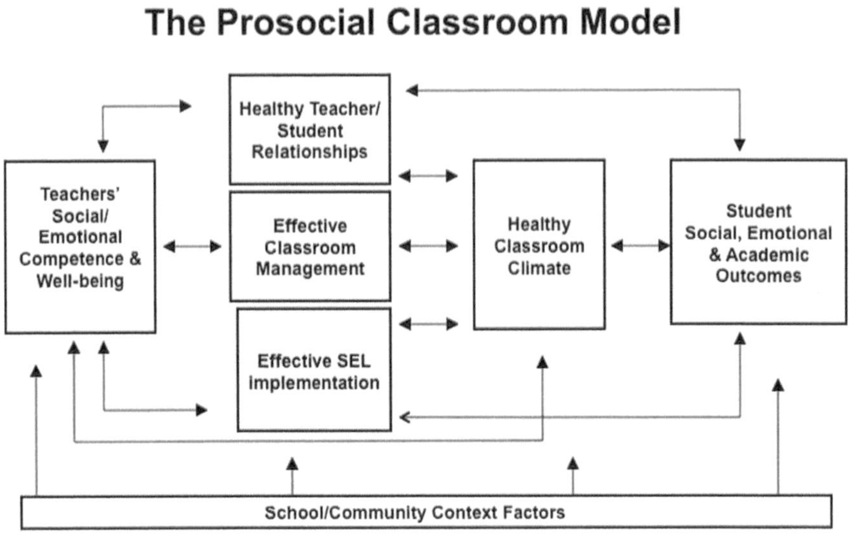

Figure 12.1 A Model of Teacher Well-Being and Social and Emotional Competence, Support, and Classroom and Student Outcomes
From: Jennings, P. A., & Greenberg, M. T. (2009). The prosocial classroom: Teacher social and emotional competence in relation to student and classroom outcomes. *Review of Educational Research, 79*, 491–525. Reprinted with permission from SAGE Publications, Inc.

for Academic, Social and Emotional Learning (CASEL, n.d.): self-awareness, self-management, social awareness, relationship skills, and responsible decision-making. While many adults have cultivated these skills to some degree, Jennings and Greenberg (2009) argue that these skills are context dependent and that teachers may require specialized training to cultivate the specific skills required to successfully build supportive relationships with students, manage classrooms with firmness and warmth, and teach SEL. For example, although teaching can be emotionally demanding, a teacher's self-awareness can help her notice when feelings of stress begin to arise. She recognizes the tension in her shoulders and jaw that signal frustration. She is aware of her emotional habit patterns and the types of situations and student behaviors that are most likely to trigger her strong emotions. This heightened self-awareness promotes greater self-management; the teacher can proactively respond to situations with thoughtfulness, rather than react automatically and take the situation personally. Social awareness helps her understand and consciously orchestrate the social dynamics of the classroom. With this understanding, she is more able to cultivate a supportive learning environment and healthy peer relationships (Gest et al., 2014). A teacher with strong relationship skills also understands the feelings and needs of individual students and how to support them socially, emotionally, and academically. Finally, she can apply these competencies to make professional decisions that account for the complex and sometimes conflicting demands of each teaching situation.

THE HISTORY OF MINDFULNESS-BASED INTERVENTIONS FOR TEACHERS

There is growing evidence that mindfulness-based interventions (MBIs) may support the development of teachers' social and emotional competencies, resulting in improved classroom learning environments and student learning (Klingbeil & Renshaw, 2018; Zarate et al., 2019). Several professional learning programs have been developed based on a model that grew from a dialog held in 2000 between the Dalai Lama and scientists sponsored by the Mind and Life Institute. Entitled "Destructive Emotions," the meeting was documented in a book by Daniel Goleman (2003) with the same title. During this meeting, emotion researcher Paul Ekman and contemplative teacher Alan Wallace joined forces to develop a new program called Cultivating Emotional Balance (CEB). At the time, CEB was unique in that it combined mindful awareness and compassion practices with emotion skills instruction—with the aim of reducing emotions that are destructive to oneself and others. At the University of California San Francisco (UCSF), Ekman and, subsequently, Margaret Kemeny, examined the efficacy of CEB in a randomized control trial (RCT) involving 82 female preK–12 teachers. Teachers were chosen as the target population for these studies because researchers recognized that teachers experience high levels of emotional stress in their work and that their behavior has a substantial impact on students' well-being. The eight-week CEB program integrates didactic presentations, discussion, and practice related to both mindful reflection and emotional experience. CEB involves various forms of mindfulness practice, including directive practices designed to promote compassion toward others. The CEB model also includes training in the features of emotions, their elicitors and consequences, methods for recognizing emotions, understanding relations between emotion and cognition, and techniques for recognizing one's own emotional patterns. Further details regarding the content of the CEB can be obtained at the program's website: http://cultivating-emotional-balance.org.

Results from the RCT indicated that, at both post-test and five-month follow-up, teachers who participated in CEB had significantly reduced self-reported depression, anxiety, negative affect, and rumination, as well as increased emotional self-awareness, positive affect, and mindfulness compared with controls. In experimental tasks, CEB teachers also demonstrated greater compassion in response to suffering and greater congruence between explicit and implicit measures of affect, indicating greater emotional self-awareness compared with control teachers (Kemeny et al., 2012).

Following this RCT, a team of researchers examined whether CEB had a significant positive impact on the quality of observed classroom interactions in another RCT involving 31 preschool teachers. Despite the positive effects on teachers' subjective well-being, CEB did not improve the observed teacher-student interactions (e.g., emotional and instructional support or classroom organization, as measured by the Classroom Assessment Scoring System [Pianta et al., 2008]) critical to student success (Jennings et al., 2011). These results suggested that the skills cultivated in CEB needed to be tailored to the specific stressors and challenges teachers face, so that teachers could apply these skills while teaching.

Following these early studies, three professional learning programs have been developed and tested that build on the CEB research: Cultivating Awareness and Resilience in Education (CARE), Mindfulness-Based Emotional Balance (MBEB; also called SMART in Education), and Community Approach to Learning Mindfully (CALM for Educators). While these programs share many elements in common, they provide examples of three different modes of delivery. Like CEB, MBEB is typically delivered in weekly sessions over eight weeks, with a single one-day retreat. CARE was typically delivered in a more intensive format across five full days of training that are spread out over the course of several months; however, more recently, the model has been condensed into three days. The CALM program was designed to be presented within the school building for 20 minutes each day (typically before school), four days per week, for a semester.

All of these programs (CARE, MBEB, and CALM) are designed to apply mindful awareness to the specific challenges of teaching—to cultivate the social and emotional competencies teachers need to successfully create and maintain supportive learning environments. All of these programs include a variety of mindful awareness and compassion practices, mindful movement, and emotion skills instruction to build teachers' social and emotional competencies (as described earlier). All three programs have shown positive impacts on teachers' well-being and social and emotional competence (Benn et al., 2012; Braun et al., 2018; Harris et al., 2015; Jennings et al., 2013; Jennings et al., 2017; Jennings et al., 2019; Roeser et al., 2013). Because CARE has also demonstrated significant positive impacts on both classroom interactions and student outcomes, the remainder of this chapter focuses on this program and related research.

CULTIVATING AWARENESS AND RESILIENCE IN EDUCATION

CARE was developed by a team of former teachers and teacher-educators with support from the Garrison Institute. Similar to CEB, CARE combines mindful awareness and compassion practices with emotion skills instruction. In contrast, in CARE these skills are specifically applied to the classroom challenges teachers identify and bring to the training. CARE is offered by CREATE (https://createforeducation.org) as both a field-based in-service professional learning program, often presented at schools, and as a weeklong intensive summer retreat at the Garrison Institute in Garrison, New York. The field-based CARE program model that has been evaluated for efficacy entails four daylong sessions spread across four to five weeks of the school year (usually in the fall), with an additional daylong booster session presented several months thereafter (totaling 30 hours of in-person training). Between workshop sessions, CARE facilitators provide coaching to teachers by phone and email to help them develop a self-care routine, which includes regular mindfulness practice, and to apply the new skills and practices they have learned in their teaching. The CARE summer retreats are delivered as five-day intensive trainings, with no follow-up coaching. A program workbook and a take-home audio CD/MP3 of mindfulness practices are provided to all participants in both programs (Jennings et al., 2018a). Trainers implement the CARE program using a comprehensive facilitator manual (Jennings et al., 2018b) and associated measures of program quality and fidelity. These implementation materials have been refined over the course of several studies, with some evidence showing links between CARE implementation quality and program uptake (Doyle et al., 2018). Furthermore, CREATE for Education has developed a facilitator training and certification process to build capacity to deliver CARE more broadly.

Program Components

Designed to apply best practices for adult learning, CARE introduces material by sequentially blending didactic instruction with experiential and interactive learning activities. Following is a brief overview of core CARE components; more detail regarding these components can be found in other publications (e.g., Jennings, 2011, 2015a, 2016).

Self-Care

CARE begins with the premise that to care for others requires self-care. Participants review and assess their current self-care routines to see how well they are balancing their physical, emotional, intellectual, and psychological/spiritual developmental needs. Teachers identify and reflect on the gaps in their self-care routines in relation to these domains of personal growth. At the end of the program, participants develop a feasible self-care plan that integrates mindful awareness practices (MAPs) and other practices learned throughout the program, so teachers can sustain what they have learned.

Intention Setting

At the beginning of the program, participants learn the practice of setting intention and repeatedly revisit this practice throughout the program to monitor whether their behavior is aligning with their intention. The program builds on teachers' own ethical frameworks and values by inviting participants to recall their reasons for becoming a teacher and the values they hold that motivate them to continue teaching. After reflecting on this, participants are invited to imagine themselves at their best and set an intention based on this vision. Setting intention involves focusing attention on the intention using words spoken silently to oneself or imagining oneself acting as intended. For example, one common intention teachers share is to slow down and let go of feeling rushed all the time. When teachers set this intention, they may tell themselves, "My intention is to slow down and take it easy today," or they may imagine themselves relaxed and taking it easy at work. Participants learn how intention setting can help to orient their thoughts and behavior to align with their values and vision, without the pressure and fear of failure that often comes with goal-setting. To support intention setting, participants are invited to share their intention with an "intention buddy" and are encouraged to periodically check in and remind one another of their intention. Periodically during the program, participants are given the opportunity to reflect on their intention to see how they are doing and to modify it, if needed.

Emotion Skills Instruction

To support teachers' ability to manage the emotional demands of teaching, CARE provides psychoeducation regarding the latest neuroscientific findings on the role of emotions within the brain and how they affect teaching and learning. Participants learn that emotions are normal, biological, and psychological processes that have a purpose and are neither "bad" nor "good." A model of emotional mastery called "The Four Rs" (respect, recognition, regulation, responsiveness) is introduced early in the program. These elements, or "Rs," reflect a process of emotional mastery that can be viewed as linear and cyclical, but elements can also occur simultaneously. The Four Rs help teachers synchronize the dimensions of their experience (physical, emotional, and mental) so their emotions don't take them by surprise, which may lead to actions they later regret.

The first "R" stands for respect, which involves appreciating the adaptive functions of emotions and the power they have to affect us and others. Teachers learn that emotions evolved to support survival; how anger (or the "fight" response) unleashes powerful energy in the form of hormones and neurotransmitters that give us the strength to fight for our lives. They learn that fear (the "flight" or "freeze" response) musters similar energy that enables us to run for our lives or freeze to become unnoticed by a predator. Teachers also learn how the stress response can impair our health when it is elevated for too long and that our stress response is often triggered by psychological and social situations. However, the stress response is often not adaptive for solving such situations and can actually interfere with responses that may be most adaptive. For example, if a parent of a student is angry because her daughter received a poor grade, the stress response immediately goes into high gear, because the parent feels threatened. However, this is a psychosocial threat, not a real physical threat, so all the neurotransmitters and hormones being pumped through the parent's body are not helpful. Expressions of anger or fear in this situation may be completely inappropriate, but managing this automatic response is challenging. To begin building emotional mastery, teachers must first understand and respect their emotional experience.

The second "R" is for recognition. To master their emotions, it helps for teachers to recognize the physical sensations, thoughts, and behaviors that are typically associated with them. For example, a teacher may notice tension in her neck and shoulders and a change in the tone of her voice and facial expressions when she's beginning to feel frustrated. She may also notice a tendency to excessively judge another and the situation as the anger arises, interfering with her ability to empathize and show understanding and compassion. Teachers learn skills for recognizing pleasant emotional states in the classroom, like joy and enthusiasm, and how to point them out and savor them with the students. This ability to recognize emotional experiences and how they affect one's perceptions, thoughts, and physical sensations is critical to emotional mastery.

The next "R" is for regulation, which is the ability to monitor and modify the intensity level of emotional experience and expression. Depending on the situation, regulation can involve reducing or increasing the intensity of emotional experience in response to situational needs. Self-regulation helps teachers use emotions more consciously to affect the emotional climate in their classroom. Participants learn about the parts of the brain involved in the fight, flight, or freeze response and the role of the prefrontal cortex in helping engage higher-order cognitive processes to appropriately manage behavioral tendencies during a strong emotion. The aim of this "R" is not to suppress emotions but to take a moment—a pause—to allow oneself to calm down and consider the broader implications of the situation. For example, a teacher might ask herself, "Is the student *really* trying to ruin my day? Or is she just having a bad day herself?" This pause gives teachers an opportunity to re-appraise the situation so they can take the next step and respond appropriately.

The culmination of the process of respecting, recognizing, and regulating is the fourth "R": responding. When teachers master their emotions, they can respond to situations more thoughtfully, rather than reacting unconsciously. Once teachers are calm, they can observe the situation with greater mindfulness and compassion. They can take the perspectives of others in the situation and consider these in their responses. When teachers are composed, they can apply their higher-order mental functions and knowledge to tailoring a response that matches the needs of the situation. To help participants further explore their own habitual emotional patterns (called "scripts") and learn how to re-appraise emotionally provocative situations, experiential activities such as reflections and role-plays are used.

Mindful Awareness Practices

CARE introduces a series of core MAPs, beginning with breath awareness practice. This basic, secular mindfulness practice involves focusing attention on the sensations of the breath, feeling the air going in and out of the body. When attention wanders into thinking or another distraction, the practice is to notice that attention is no longer focused on the sensations of the breath and the nature of the distraction, then to return attention to the breath. Participants are instructed to do this practice with kindness and curiosity, rather than criticism and judgment. Given that mind-wandering is a normal state of mind, the intention of this practice is not to stop thinking, but to allow thoughts to settle—to let them go, rather than to hold on to thinking. Over time, participants begin to notice their habitual thought patterns and their tendency to rush through things, promoting a greater sense of calm presence while teaching. Teachers learn not to become identified with thoughts, emotions, desires, and other mental and physical experience that may capture their attention. The practice helps them recognize that they are not their thoughts; thus, they are less disturbed by distressing thoughts. This reduced reactivity to thought content, described as "de-centering," is thought to be the mechanism through which MBIs affect improvements in mental health (Bernstein et al., 2015).

Applying mindful awareness to emotional states while teaching can improve the quality of teacher-student interactions. When experiencing high levels of stress, teachers may take student behavior personally, imagining that it is intentionally directed toward upsetting them. This tendency can lead to coercive responses to students and power struggles, resulting in more student disruption and teacher stress (Jennings, 2015b). CARE helps teachers recognize this tendency by applying mindful awareness to noticing physical sensations and thoughts associated with emotion and how this process can distort their perception of what's occurring (Schussler et al., 2018).

Applying mindfulness to cultivate body awareness is also part of the CARE program. Teachers learn that developing body awareness helps them recognize stress and emotions before they become overwhelming and difficult to manage. It also helps them become more aware of their physical and emotional needs. One MAP that serves this purpose is the "body scan." This guided practice involves focusing attention on each part of the body sequentially, simply noticing tension or other sensations. Another MAP, called "centering," involves standing and focusing attention on the feeling of the body's weight pressing against the floor as well as the center of gravity of the body located in the middle of the abdomen. This practice is a preparation for the MAP called "mindful walking," which involves focusing attention on the soles of the feet as the weight of the body shifts from one foot to the other with each step. Like the breath awareness practice, mindful walking involves noticing distractions and then returning attention to the soles of the feet and the sensation of the transfer of weight with each step. The CARE program involves supporting teachers' application of these MAPs into their lives. For example, the sequence of mindful walking practices begin with slow, formal mindful walking that transitions, after some practice, toward walking faster, similar to a normal pace, so that teachers can eventually practice mindfulness during ordinary walking.

Caring and Listening Practices

An important element of CARE is cultivating empathy and compassion for oneself and others. Caring practice, which is a secularized version of Buddhist *metta* (loving-kindness) practice, is a core part of this element. During this practice, participants silently generate feelings of loving-kindness and care to themselves and others. Evidence shows that regularly engaging in this caring practice promotes well-being (Fredrickson et al., 2008). A series of mindful listening activities also promotes care and compassion. These activities begin with simple partner practices and build into role-plays in which participants reflect on their thoughts, emotions, and scripts (mental schema) linked to emotional experience. A key aspect of these practices is "holding space" for a speaker by mindfully listening, without responding, interrupting, fixing, or judging, while noticing any impulses to do so. During these activities, teachers are instructed to generate feelings of care and compassion to the speaker as they listen. The speaker, in turn, applies mindfulness to speech by noticing any emotions, thoughts, or sensations that arise as they are speaking.

Research on CARE

A series of studies have confirmed that CARE improves teachers' social and emotional competencies and well-being, their classroom interactions, and student learning. After a pair of pilot studies indicated that the program was valuable and feasible, a randomized controlled study was conducted involving 50 pre-K–12 teachers in a northeast metropolitan area (Jennings et al., 2013). These teachers were randomly assigned to receive CARE or be in a waitlist control group. At post-assessment, teachers assigned to CARE reported significantly higher levels of mindfulness, teaching efficacy, personal accomplishment, emotion regulation by reappraisal, and reductions in daily physical symptoms and stress caused by hurry compared with control teachers. Effect sizes ranged from small to large. These results demonstrated CARE's promise for promoting teachers' emotional skills and reducing their stress and burnout.

To better understand how CARE affected these outcomes, several qualitative studies were conducted with this sample. One study involved a series of focus groups with a total of 44 study participants (Schussler et al., 2016). Teachers described how the combination of mindfulness and psychoeducation about emotions helped them become more aware of the physical sensations of stress. Participants also described how CARE helped them develop an enhanced awareness of both their physical and emotional responses to stress, along with strategies to regulate their emotions more effectively. For example, one teacher commented: "I take a minute and calm myself down before I try to take care of the situation" (Schussler et al., 2016, p. 137). Another noted: "I think [CARE] helps you make that connection between your physical feelings and your mental state of being. . . . When you feel tired, to realize that that's affecting how you are going to think about things and how you are going to react to things in turn. I think it heightens the awareness of that" (Schussler et al., 2016, p. 137). Furthermore, teachers described how they became better at catching themselves when they were reacting too quickly to situations, especially in response to their students' behavior. For example, one teacher noted:

> I'm quicker to catch things coming out of my mouth or quicker to not react as fast which helps in the classroom. . . . I think it has helped me work through some of my ADHD tendencies of wanting to jump all the time, to think and be mindful of what and how I'm feeling and reacting.
>
> (Schussler et al., 2016, p. 137)

The most recent trial of CARE involved the largest and most rigorous study of an MBI for teachers to date. This cluster RCT examined the efficacy of CARE for improving teachers' well-being, the quality of their classroom interactions, and student learning and behavioral outcomes (Brown et al., 2023; Jennings et al., 2017a). Researchers randomized 224 teachers to receive CARE or be in a waitlist control group. Analyses of student outcomes accounted for the nesting of the data (i.e., multiple students nested within classrooms taught by the same teacher) by utilizing hierarchical linear modeling. Post-test results showed that CARE had significant direct positive impacts on mindfulness, adaptive emotion regulation, psychological distress, and time urgency on teachers who were randomly assigned to CARE compared to those assigned to the waitlist control group. Effect sizes were generally modest. Researchers also collected follow-up data from teachers nine and a half months after program completion. CARE teachers showed continued significant decreases in psychological distress and physical symptoms, and continued significant improvements in emotion regulation. Again, these effects were modest; however, given that the sample was normative (e.g., most teachers' scores were not in the clinical ranges of these measures), modest effects were anticipated. These results indicate that even without additional intervention during the following school year, CARE teachers continued to report benefits (Jennings et al., 2019).

As part of this cluster RCT, researchers blind to teachers' group assignment observed all classrooms at pre- and post-intervention and coded classroom interactions using the Classroom Assessment Scoring System (CLASS; Pianta et al., 2008). CARE had significant positive impacts with modest effect sizes on the CLASS domain of emotional support and two subdimensions of emotional support: positive climate (reflecting the teacher's warmth and supportive relationships with students) and teacher sensitivity (reflecting the teacher's awareness of and responsiveness to students' needs). CARE had a marginally significant positive impact with modest effect sizes on the CLASS domain of classroom organization and the subdimension of productivity (the efficiency of the classroom operations). Although no significant impacts were found on the instructional support domain of the CLASS, researchers did not expect such changes would occur, because CARE does not focus on content related to academic instruction.

To address other outcomes of interest in this cluster RCT, teachers completed surveys reporting on their perceptions of students' behavior ($N = 5{,}200$). CARE had a direct significant positive impact on teacher-reported student engagement, motivation, and reading competence (Brown et al., 2023). The sizes of the intervention effects were modest, but comparable to those commonly found in universal prevention research (Greenberg & Abenavoli, 2017). Taken together, these different strands of evidence indicate the positive impacts CARE can have on both the quality of the learning environment and student outcomes.

In addition to promoting positive classroom and student outcomes, teachers consistently report satisfaction with CARE. In response to evaluation surveys, 80% of participants across all trials reported that the program improved their self-awareness and well-being. More than 75% reported that CARE helped them be more able to establish and maintain supportive relationships with students and better able to manage classroom behaviors effectively and compassionately. Furthermore, more than 87% of participants "strongly agreed" or "agreed" that CARE or a similar program should be integrated into preparation and in-service training for all teachers. Teachers' responses to open-ended questions provided further evidence of their program satisfaction and learning. For example, one teacher described CARE as "the most valuable, personally rewarding and important class that [she has] ever taken" (Jennings, 2016, p. 139). Another teacher noted, "Now I have the tools to stay calm, reflective, appreciative, joyful and grateful every day, which will help me interact positively with my students and colleagues" (p. 140).

CONCLUSION

There is now well-established evidence that MBIs designed for teachers can have significant positive impacts on teachers' well-being. The recent CARE research demonstrates that MBIs targeted to teaching can also have a significant positive impact on teachers' classroom interactions and student engagement (Brown et al., 2023; Jennings et al., 2017). Nevertheless, more research is needed to determine whether such programs impact students' self-reports and objective measures of well-being, academic learning, and behavioral outcomes. In addition, more research is required to understand the causal mechanisms and moderating factors that influence these findings. For example, the following questions still await empirical answers: How does teachers' improved emotion regulation affect classroom interactions and student engagement? For which teachers and students are programs like CARE most helpful? What are the long-term impacts of teacher-focused MBIs on student outcomes? Can programs like CARE boost the effectiveness of mindfulness-based programs for students?

An important caveat for future research and practice in this area is that teachers' lack of social and emotional skills is only one cause of teacher stress. There are structural and employment issues that are beyond the scope of teachers' capacity to control (Greenberg et al., 2016; Jennings et al., 2019). However, given the stress teachers face today, MBIs are an important means for helping teachers reduce stress so they are more able to build supportive relationships with students and cultivate quality learning environments that promote student engagement and learning. Ultimately, MBIs targeted to teaching may be one cost-effective approach among many for supporting teachers' occupational health and well-being.

REFERENCES

Benn, R., Akiva, T., Arel, S., & Roeser, R. W. (2012). Mindfulness training effects for parents and educators of children with special needs. *Developmental Psychology, 48*(5), 1476–1487. http://doi.org/10.1037/a0027537

Bernstein, A., Hadash, Y., Lichtash, Y., Tanay, G., Shepherd, K., & Fresco, D. M. (2015). Decentering and related constructs. *Perspectives on Psychological Science, 10*(5), 599–617. http://doi.org/10.1177/1745691615594577

Birch, S. H., & Ladd, G. W. (1998). Children's interpersonal behaviors and the teacher-child relationship. *Developmental Psychology, 3*, 934–946. http://dx.doi.org/10.1037/0012-1649.34.5.934

Braun, S. S., Roeser, R. W., Mashburn, A. J., & Skinner, E. (2018). Middle school teachers' mindfulness, occupational health and well-being, and the quality of teacher-student interactions. *Mindfulness, 37*(2), 57–11. http://doi.org/10.1007/s12671-018-0968-2

Brown, J. L., Jennings, P. A., Rasheed, D., Doyle, S., Cham, H., Frank, J. L., Davis, R., & Greenberg, M. (2023). Direct and moderating impacts of the CARE mindfulness-based professional learning program for teachers on children's academic and social-emotional outcomes. *Applied Developmental Science, 29*(1), 14–33. https://doi.org/10.1080/10888691.2023.2268327

Collaborative for Academic, Social, and Emotional Learning. (n.d.). Core SEL Competencies. Retrieved from https://casel.org/core-competencies/.

Doyle, S., Jennings, P. A., Brown, J. L., DeWeese, A., Rasheed, D., Frank, J. L., Turksma, C., & Greenberg, M. T. (2018). Exploring the relationship between implementation quality and uptake of the Cultivating Awareness and Resilience in Education (CARE) for Teachers Program. *Mindfulness, 10*, 122–130. https://doi.org/10.1007/s12671-018-0958-4

Fredrickson, B. L., Coffey, K. A., Pek, J., Cohn, M. A., & Finkel, S. M. (2008). Open hearts build lives: Positive emotions, induced through loving-kindness meditation, build consequential personal resources. *Journal of Personality and Social Psychology, 95*, 1045–1062. http://doi.org/10.1037/a0013262

Gest, S. D., Madill, R. A., Zadzora, K. M., Miller, A. M., & Rodkin, P. C. (2014). Teacher management of elementary classroom social dynamics. *Journal of Emotional and Behavioral Disorders, 22*(2), 107–118. http://doi.org/10.1177/1063426613512677

Goleman, D. (2003). *Destructive emotions: A scientific dialogue with the Dalai Lama*. Bantam.

Green, J. G., McLaughlin, K. A., Alegría, M., Costello, E. J., Gruber, M. J., Hoagwood, K., . . . Kessler, R. C., (2013). School mental health resources and adolescent mental health service use. *Journal of the American Academy of Child & Adolescent Psychiatry, 52*, 501–510. https://doi.org/10.1016/j.jaac.2013.03.002

Greenberg, M. T., & Abenavoli, R. (2017). Universal interventions: Fully exploring their impacts and potential to produce population-level impacts. *Journal of Research on Educational Effectiveness, 10*(1), 40–67, https://doi.org/10.1080/19345747.2016.1246632

Greenberg, M. T., Brown, J. L., & Abenavoli, R. M. (2016). *Teacher stress and health* (pp. 1–14). Robert Wood Johnson Foundation.

Hamre, B. K., & Pianta, R. C. (2001). Early teacher-child relationships and the trajectory of children's school outcomes through eighth grade. *Child Development, 72*, 625–638. http://dx.doi.org/10.1111/1467-8624.00301

Harris, A. R., Jennings, P. A., Katz, D. A., Abenavoli, R. M., & Greenberg, M. T. (2015). Promoting stress management and wellbeing in educators: Feasibility and efficacy of a school-based yoga and mindfulness intervention. *Mindfulness, 7*, 143–154. http://doi.org/10.1007/s12671-015-0451-2

Jennings, P. A. (2011). Promoting teachers' social and emotional competencies to support performance and reduce burnout. In A. Cohan & A. Honigsfeld (Eds.), *Breaking the mold of pre-service and in-service teacher education: Innovative and successful practices for the 21st century* (pp. 133–143). Rowman and Littlefield.

Jennings, P. A. (2015a). Early childhood teachers' well-being, mindfulness, and self-compassion in relation to classroom quality and attitudes towards challenging students. *Mindfulness, 6*(4), 732–743. http://doi.org/10.1007/s12671-014-0312-4

Jennings, P. A. (2015b). *Mindfulness for teachers: Simple skills for peace and productivity in the classroom*. WW Norton.

Jennings, P. A. (2016). CARE for teachers: A mindfulness-based approach to promoting teachers' social and emotional competence and well-being. In K. A. Schonert-Reichl, & R. W. Roeser (Eds.), *Handbook of mindfulness in education* (pp. 133–148). Springer New York. http://doi.org/10.1007/978-1-4939-3506-2_9

Jennings, P. A. (2019). *The trauma-sensitive classroom: Building resilience with compassionate teaching*. WW Norton.

Jennings, P. A. (2021). *Teacher burnout turnaround: Strategies for empowered educators*. W. W. Norton.

Jennings, P. A., & Alamos, P. (2024). What is educator social and emotional learning (SEL)? Why is it important? How can it be promoted? In J. A. Durlak, C. E. Domitrovich, & J. L. Mahoney (Eds.), *Handbook of social and emotional learning* (2nd ed.; pp. 129–141). Guilford.

Jennings, P. A., Brown, J. L., Frank, J. L., Doyle, S., Oh, Y., Davis, R., . . . Greenberg, M. T. (2017). Impacts of the CARE for Teachers program on teachers' social and emotional competence and classroom interactions. *Journal of Educational Psychology, 109*(7), 1010–1028. http://doi.org/10.1037/edu0000187

Jennings, P. A., Doyle, S., Yoonkyung, O., Doyle, S., Rasheed, D., Frank, J. L., & Brown, J. L. (2019). Follow-up impacts of the CARE for Teachers professional development program on teachers' social and emotional competence. *Journal of School Psychology, 76*, 186–202. https://doi.org/10.1016/j.jsp.2019.07.009

Jennings, P. A., Foltz, C., Snowberg, K. E., Sim, H., Kemeny, M. E. (2011). *The influence of mindfulness and emotion skills training on teachers' classrooms: The effects of the Cultivating Emotional Balance training*. Pennsylvania State University. Retrieved from ERIC database (ED518584).

Jennings, P. A., & Frank, J. L. (2015). Inservice preparation for educators. In J. A. Durlak, C. E. Domitrovich, R. P. Weissberg, & T. P. Gullotta (Eds.), *Handbook of social and emotional learning: Research and practice* (pp. 422–437). Guilford Press.

Jennings, P. A., Frank, J. L., Snowberg, K. E., Coccia, M. A., & Greenberg, M. T. (2013). Improving classroom learning environments by Cultivating Awareness and Resilience in Education (CARE): Results of a randomized controlled trial. *School Psychology Quarterly, 28*(4), 374–390. http://doi.org/10.1037/spq0000035

Jennings, P. A., & Greenberg, M. T. (2009). The prosocial classroom: Teacher social and emotional competence in relation to student and classroom outcomes. *Review of Educational Research, 79*(1), 491–525. http://doi.org/10.3102/0034654308325693

Jennings, P. A., Minnici, A., & Yoder, N. (2019). Creating the working conditions to enhance teacher social and emotional well-being. In D. Osher, M. Mayer, R. Jagers, K. Kendziora, & L. Wood (Eds.), *Keeping students safe and helping them thrive: A collaborative handbook for education, safety, and justice professionals, families, and communities*, Vol. 1, Chapter 9. Praeger.

Jennings, P. A., Turksma, C., & Brown, R. (2018a). *Cultivating Awareness and Resilience in Education (CARE) participant workbook*. Garrison Institute.

Jennings, P. A., Turksma, C., & Brown, R. (2018b). *Cultivating Awareness and Resilience in Education (CARE) facilitator manual*. Garrison Institute.

Kemeny, M. E., Foltz, C., Cavanagh, J. F., Cullen, M., Giese-Davis, J., Jennings, P., Ekman, P. (2012). Contemplative/emotion training reduces negative emotional behavior and promotes prosocial responses. *Emotion, 12*(2), 338–350. http://doi.org/10.1037/a0026118

Klingbeil, D. A., & Renshaw, T. L. (2018). Mindfulness-based interventions for teachers: A meta-analysis of the emerging evidence base. *School Psychology Quarterly, 33*(4), 501–511. https://doiorg.proxy1.library.virginia.edu/10.1037/spq0000291

McLean, L., & Connor, C. M. (2015). Depressive symptoms in third-grade teachers: Relations to classroom quality and student achievement. *Child Development, 86*(3), 945–954. http://doi.org/10.1111/cdev.12344

Milkie, M. A., & Warner, C. H. (2011). Classroom learning environments and the mental health of first grade children. *Journal of Health and Social Behavior, 52*(1), 4–22. http://doi.org/10.1177/0022146510394952

Oberle, E., & Schonert-Reichl, K. A. (2016). Stress contagion in the classroom? The link between classroom teacher burnout and morning cortisol in elementary school students. *Social Science & Medicine, 159*(c), 30–37. http://doi.org/10.1016/j.socscimed.2016.04.031

Pianta, R. C., La Paro, K. M., & Hamre, B. K. (2008). *Classroom assessment scoring system manual*. Brookes Publishing.

Roeser, R. W., Schonert-Reichl, K. A., Jha, A., Cullen, M., Wallace, L., Wilensky, R., . . . Harrison, J. (2013). Mindfulness training and reductions in teacher stress and burnout: Results from two randomized, waitlist-control field trials. *Journal of Educational Psychology*, *105*(3), 787–804. http://doi.org/10.1037/a0032093

Roeser, R. W., Skinner, E., Beers, J., & Jennings, P. A. (2012). Mindfulness training and teachers' professional development: An emerging area of research and practice. *Child Development Perspectives*, *6*(2), 167–173. http://doi.org/10.1111/j.1750-8606.2012.00238.x

Rones, M., & Hoagwood, K. (2000). School-based mental health services: A research review. *Clinical Child and Family Psychology Review*, *3*, 223–241. https://doi.org/10.1023/A:1026425104386

Schonfeld, I. S., Bianchi, R., & Luehring-Jones, P. (2017). Consequences of job stress for the mental health of teachers. In T. M. McIntyre, S. E. McIntyre, & D. J. Francis (Eds.), *Educator stress: An occupational health perspective* (pp. 55–75). Springer International.

Schussler, D. L., DeWeese, A., Rasheed, D., DeMauro, A. A., Brown, J. L., Greenberg, M. T., & Jennings, P. A. (2018). Stress and release: Case studies of teacher resilience following a mindfulness-based intervention. *American Journal of Education*, *125*, 1–28. https://doi.org/10.1086/699808

Schussler, D. L., Jennings, P. A., Sharp, J. E., & Frank, J. L. (2016). Improving teacher awareness and well-being through CARE: A qualitative analysis of the underlying mechanisms. *Mindfulness*, *7*, 130–142. http://doi.org/10.1007/s12671-015-0422-7

Wong, V. W., Ruble, L. A., Yu, Y., & McGrew, J. H. (2017). Too stressed to teach? Teaching quality, student engagement, and IEP outcomes. *Exceptional Children*, *83*(4), 412–427. http://doi.org/10.1177/0014402917690729

Zarate, K., Maggin, D. M., Passmore, A. (2019). Meta-analysis of mindfulness training on teacher well-being. *Psychology in the Schools*, 1–16. https://doi.org/10.1002/pits.22308

13

Mindfulness-Based Parent Training

STACY L. BENDER

Positive parent-childinteractions are important , given that they contribute to a secure attachment (consistent warmth and responsiveness), which lays the foundation for favorable social-emotional, behavioral, and academic outcomes for children (e.g., World Health Organization, 2016). Parenting children across all levels of development can be rewarding as well as challenging. For young children, the unique period of early childhood development is unlike any other period because of children's rapid growth during this time. During the preschool years, self-regulation skills are emerging, language and communication skills are developing (e.g., Shonkoff & Phillips, 2000), and adults are often needed to facilitate everyday tasks and problem solving (Kerns et al., 2006). During middle childhood, as children grow and develop, parents must adjust their expectations and rework their level of guidance provided to the child to promote independence and autonomy (Bradley et al., 2017). When children move through adolescence, parents' perceived conflict and emotional lability with their adolescent increases and reported closeness decreases (e.g., Marceau et al., 2014). For children and adolescents who experience social-emotional, behavioral, and academic difficulties, it is reported that parents experience additional challenges and higher levels of stress (e.g., Woodman et al., 2015).

Given the stress parents may experience, some research has emphasized mindfulness as an essential stress-management skill (Bluth & Wahler, 2011). Over time, parents and children can develop an automaticity, or habitual patterns of behavior, in their interactions with one another (Dumas, 2005). This automaticity is "performed with little or no conscious awareness" and is often resistant to change (Dumas, 2005, p. 781). This is particularly true during discipline. Therefore,

Stacy L. Bender, *Mindfulness-Based Parent Training*. In: *Using Mindfulness to Promote Mental Health in Schools*. Edited by: Tyler L. Renshaw and Shane R. Jimerson, Oxford University Press. © Oxford University Press (2025). DOI: 10.1093/9780190880507.003.0013 enhancing awareness of one's thoughts, emotional state, and interactions in the moment that they are occurring is one way to improve parents' responses to their child (Dumas, 2005; Kabat-Zinn & Kabat-Zinn, 1997; Steinberg, 2004). Recent research suggests that when parents are mindful during parent-child interactions, positive outcomes emerge for parents and their children (e.g., Bögels & Restifo, 2014). Therefore, mindfulness-based interventions are becoming more widely implemented for parents and families. More specifically, mindfulness-based parent training (MBPT) is becoming more commonly implemented and evaluated in school settings (e.g., Benn et al., 2012). Compared to parent training offered in other community or clinical settings, implementation of MBPT in schools may be beneficial given that families may be more likely to have access to and familiarity with their child's school, may feel less stigma receiving services at schools, and may have more opportunities to receive free or affordable services at schools. This is especially true for families who might not otherwise have access to services.

The purpose of this chapter is to describe the framework of mindful parenting and MBPT. An overview of the empirical support for this approach is provided, along with a brief description of MBPT programs that have been evaluated. The chapter closes with two case examples of MBPT implemented in school settings. The first example describes a six-week, one-hour, parent group for preschool families, and the second describes a three-week, one-and-a-half-hour parent mindfulness workshop for families in a school district. Parent recruitment, rationale for implementation, and topics covered in these programs are discussed for each case.

Given that adults raising, supporting, and caring for children are not always their parents, the author acknowledges that "caregivers" would be a more inclusive and accurate term. However, the terms "parents" and "parenting" are used throughout the chapter, to stay consistent with the literature and language used to described "parent training" and MBPT.

FOUNDATIONS AND CORE CONCEPTS OF MINDFUL PARENTING

Jon Kabat-Zinn (2003) describes mindfulness as "the awareness that emerges through paying attention, on purpose, in the present moment, and nonjudgmentally to the unfolding experience, moment by moment" (p. 145). Given that mindfulness has been suggested as an essential skill for parenting (Kabat-Zinn & Kabat-Zinn, 1997; Steinberg, 2004), a framework for mindful parenting has been proposed (Duncan et al., 2009a). Mindful parenting is described as "intentionally bringing moment to moment awareness to the parent-child relationship" (Duncan et al., 2009a, p. 255). The authors of this framework apply Kabat-Zinn's original definition of mindfulness to the parenting context and parent-child relationship. Additionally, the mindful parenting framework makes use of "concepts and practices of psychological mindfulness, mindfulness-based interventions, and contemporary theoretical and empirical writing about parenting" (Duncan et al., 2009a, p. 255). The focus of this framework is on engaging mindfulness during parenting/caregiving interactions, for the purpose of allowing mental, emotional, and physiological balance. When parents/caregivers are aware of themselves, they are more likely to be aware of their child and their interactions with their child. Research suggests that parent dispositional mindfulness, as well as mindful parenting, is linked to positive parent-child relationship quality across young childhood, middle childhood, and adolescence (Parent et al., 2016).

Duncan and colleagues (2009a) discuss five dimensions of mindful parenting:

1. *Listening with full attention*, where the parent is sensitive to the child's facial expressions, body language, content of conversations, and tone of the child's voice. Listening in this way helps parents better understand what it is the child is saying (or not saying) and provides context to the message the child is sending during the interaction.
2. *Non-judgmental acceptance of self and child*, where the parent allows clear awareness and attention to the present moment to fully understand what is occurring and accepts what is happening during the interaction. Duncan and colleagues (2009a) are careful to highlight that non-judgmental acceptance does not mean the parent must accept behavior that does not meet expectations. But rather it suggests parents take a step back and accept that there are struggles in the parent-child relationship, that parenting can be challenging, and that what is occurring in the moment is what it is. Negative thoughts (e.g., "I'm a bad parent," "my child will never learn") or feelings (e.g., blame, guilt, shame) that often arise during difficult interactions with children can be distressing to parents, and non-judgmental acceptance is what allows them to be kinder to themselves. Additionally, this aspect of mindful parenting emphasizes the importance of general acceptance of the child for who they are and providing guidance on appropriate expectations for the child.
3. *Emotional awareness of self and child*, where the parent is aware of their own and their child's emotions/feelings. Emotions can quickly lead to thoughts and behaviors that may or may not be effective in the current context. For example, a parent may tell their child in a sharp or sarcastic tone to "clean your room!" This may be the first time the parent is asking the child to clean their room that day, so the child is confused or reacts in a defensive or non-compliant manner. Prior to saying "clean your room!" in a sharp or sarcastic tone, the parent might be thinking, "Why do I have to remind them to clean their room every day?" The emotion/feeling underlying this thought and subsequent command is anger, annoyance, and frustration. Understanding that emotions, thoughts, and behaviors are often linked—and being in tune with one's own emotional state and aware of the child's emotional state—can help parents/caregivers acknowledge these feelings and be more aware of the thoughts and behaviors that may follow.
4. *Self-regulation in the parenting relationship*, where parents pause before reacting to a child's behavior. While parents may have an automatic reaction to their child, particularly during a challenging interaction, taking a breath and pausing before reacting allows parents to select the

parenting practice that is most consistent with their values, rather than impulsively reacting in a way that is inconsistent with their values or that they may later regret. To effectively self-regulate in the parenting relationships, it could be helpful to ask oneself, "What is happening during this current interaction with my child?," "Am I saying or doing things that are disproportionate to what is occurring in this moment?," and "What am I bringing to this interaction?"

5. *Compassion for self and the child*, where the parent actively "projects empathic concern for one's child and for oneself as a parent" (Duncan et al., 2009a, p. 260). Compassion, or the desire to alleviate suffering, helps parents comfort their child and meet their child's needs. Furthermore, this aspect of mindful parenting highlights the importance of compassion toward oneself as the parent. Having compassion for oneself gives parents permission to be less harsh toward themselves and more forgiving of their parenting efforts.

MINDFULNESS-BASED PARENT TRAINING PROGRAMS

Parent training is not a new concept in schools. Behavioral parent training programs have been found to be effective for improving parents' skills and reducing child behavior problems by teaching parenting practices (e.g., giving effective commands, delivery of positive reinforcement) that help improve their management of their child's behavior (e.g., Incredible Years; Webster-Stratton, 2001). What differentiates behavioral parent training from MBPT is that the latter emphasizes the teaching and use of mindfulness skills, such as awareness, attention, and compassion (Townshend et al., 2016).

In a literature review conducted by Townshend and colleagues (2016), the key change processes identified for MBPT programs were skills targeting listening, emotional awareness, emotional regulation, attentional regulation, attunement, attention to variability, intentionality, reperceiving, compassion, and non-judgmental acceptance. In 2005, Dumas constructed the first MBPT model, which aimed to reduce the automaticity and mindlessness that often occurs for parents, particularly during difficult interactions with children. This model described three strategies that could be implemented to facilitate mindful parenting. Dumas (2005) describes these three strategies as follows:

- *Facilitative listening* is "a form of communication fostering understanding and nonjudgment acceptance of thoughts, feelings, and actions—our own and those of others." (p. 783)
- *Distancing* is "a form of communication with ourselves designed to put some psychological separation between our thoughts and feelings about a particular situation and the ways in which we act in that situation." (p. 784)
- *Motivated action plans* (MAP) involve "training parents to anticipate and be ready to give a careful, immediate, and nonjudgmental attention to

> childrearing challenges as they arise" (p. 785). MAP also involve parents creating a plan for what they will say and do during especially difficult interactions with their child.

The frameworks and strategies outlined by Duncan and colleagues (2009a; i.e., listening with full attention, non-judgmental acceptance of self and child, emotional awareness of self and child, self-regulation in the parenting relationship, and compassion for self and the child), Dumas (2005; i.e., facilitative listening, distancing, and motivated action plans [MAP]), and Townshend and colleagues (2016; i.e., listening, emotional awareness, emotional regulation, attentional regulation, attunement, attention to variability, intentionality, reperceiving, compassion, and non-judgmental acceptance) can be found within many of the current MBPT programs implemented within schools. Furthermore, mindfulness programs for parents have also been created by adapting Kabat-Zinn's (1990) seminal mindfulness-based stress reduction (MBSR) program to implement with parents in various contexts. Commonly found MBPT programs in the literature include mindful awareness for parenting stress (Neece, 2014) and mindful families stress reduction (Felver et al., 2014), which are based on or adapted from MBSR, and the mindful parenting program (Bögels & Restifo, 2014). These three programs are the most pure examples of MBPT, as they specifically focus on mindfulness skill development and its application to parenting.

Another way mindfulness training has been offered to parents is as an adjunct to a preexisting evidence-based parenting program. One example of this is the mindfulness-enhanced strengthening families (MSFP) intervention, which integrated mindfulness training with the original strengthening families program for parents and youth 10–14 years (SFP 10–14; Coatsworth et al., 2015). The original SFP 10–14 program is used to prevent alcohol and substance abuse among adolescents. Overall, results suggested that MSFP was as effective as SFP 10–14 in improving mindfulness in parenting, parent-child relationship quality, behavior management, and parent well-being. Interestingly, while the mindfulness training did not have the value-added effect for mothers, it did for fathers. Stronger effects of MSFP were found for fathers immediately after the intervention as well as at follow-up (Coatsworth et al., 2015). Additional research to understand why mindfulness training did not have value-added effects for mothers would be important, as mothers are often the participants in intervention research. Along the same lines, MBPT outcomes for fathers is especially needed, to both understand why these differences emerged between mothers and fathers and to add to the outcome literature for fathers, who are often underrepresented in intervention research.

EMPIRICAL SUPPORT FOR MINDFULNESS-BASED PARENT TRAINING

The research examining MBPT programs has continued to expand during recent years following pioneering pilot studies demonstrating positive outcomes and discussion of future research needed in this area. The field has moved from single-case design analyses (see Klingbeil et al., 2017, for a meta-analysis), small samples, and pilot studies (e.g., Duncan et al., 2009b) to larger samples in randomized and well-controlled studies. Implementation of MBPTs in school settings has also been more recently examined (e.g., Burke et al., 2017), compared to their implementation in other clinical settings (e.g., outpatient, hospital, community mental health). Recent studies have examined feasibility and acceptability of mindfulness training for a range of parent populations, such as parents of children with developmental delays (e.g., Roberts & Neece, 2015), parents of preschool students (e.g., Bender et al., in press), and parents of students with disabilities in schools (e.g., Benn et al., 2012). Furthermore, as described earlier, both parent outcomes (e.g., Bögels & Restifo, 2014) and child outcomes (e.g., Felver et al., 2014) associated with MBPT have been evaluated.

Studies have revealed acceptable feasibility and satisfaction among parents who participate in MBPTs. For instance, Benn and colleagues (2012) found that parents of students with disabilities who participated in a mindfulness program had high levels of satisfaction with the program in regard to content, structure, and instruction quality. Bender and colleagues (in press) examined retention, satisfaction, and beneficial aspects of programming in a sample of parents of preschoolers (with and without disabilities) who completed either a six-week MBPT or a six-week traditional behavioral parent training. Bender et al. reported that retention for both groups was 100% and that mean scores on the Client Satisfaction Questionnaire-8 for the MBPT group and traditional behavioral parent training group were 30 and 30.5, respectively, out of a possible score of 32. On balance, these results suggest high levels of satisfaction with MBPT program content and skills learned.

A recent systematic review conducted by Townshend and colleagues (2016) examined the effectiveness of MBPT programs and outcomes for parents and children. Overall, the review concluded that MBPTs led to improved parental emotional awareness of themselves and their children, improved compassion and acceptance of oneself and their children, and enhanced mindfulness during parent-child interactions (Coatsworth et al., 2010, 2015). Furthermore, decreases in parenting stress, emotionally dismissive behaviors, and emotionally dismissive beliefs were found in the studies they reviewed (Havighurst et al., 2010; Neece, 2014; Wilson et al., 2012). Further support for MBPTs producing positive outcomes was highlighted for parents of students with disabilities in a study conducted by Benn and colleagues (2012), where researchers found improvements in mindfulness skills, self-compassion, empathic concern, forgiveness, and personal growth, alongside decreases in stress and anxiety. Additionally, Bögels and colleagues (2014) found improved self-awareness and mindfulness skills for parents who participated in MBPTs.

Examining children's outcomes after parents participate in MBPTs is an important area of research, yet these secondary or indirect effects have been examined to a lesser extent compared to the primary or direct effects of MBPTs on parents themselves. When child outcomes are included, externalizing behavior is often the outcome evaluated. In the previously mentioned systematic review by Townshend and colleagues (2016), the authors reviewed child outcomes in relation to MBPTs. Of the seven studies that met the researchers' systematic review criteria, five included child outcomes. Three studies examined externalizing child behavior, one study examined externalizing and internalizing child behavior, and one study examined children's attention regulation. Studies testing the indirect effect of MBPTs on youth suggested increased attentional processes (Felver et al., 2014), reduced attention-deficit/hyperactivity disorder–related problems (Neece, 2014), and reduced aggression, non-compliance, and self-injury (Singh et al., 2006).

CASE EXAMPLES OF MINDFULNESS-BASED PARENT TRAINING IN SCHOOLS

An important consideration for the MBPT programs described in this chapter (and commonly found in the literature) is the settings in which these programs are implemented. Historically, mindfulness-based interventions have been implemented in clinical settings (e.g., outpatient, inpatient, hospitals, community mental health institutions) and, more recently, have been adapted for school settings. Given this history, practitioners are often left with taking existing MBPT programs and adapting them to be more feasible, acceptable, and resource-efficient for use in schools. Limited research has suggested how to effectively adapt existing MBPTs. To illustrate two examples of adapting MBPTs for use in schools, the following case examples include descriptions of a six-week mindfulness group for parents of preschool students in an integrated preschool and a three-week mindfulness workshop for K–12 parents. Considering that practitioners have to carefully consider the culture, resources, and needs of their school(s), these case examples are shared to describe a few ways practitioners could consider using MBPTs in a school setting, not to prescribe a uniform template for school-based MBPT implementation.

Mindful Parenting Program for Parents of Preschoolers

School mental health professionals, teachers, and administrators may express interest in implementing MBPTs for families in their schools/district; however, the common concern expressed is feasibility of implementation. Often, the feasibility concern is related to how many weeks and hours per week the training will last, as well as who will lead implementation. Given this concern, the following case example describes the implementation of a MBPT program for parents of preschool students that was adapted from *Mindful Parenting* (Bögels & Restifo, 2014), which is a mental health practitioner guide.

For some background about the implementation, the author and administrator of a preschool discussed potential ways that the author could provide support to families in the school. The principal reported that in conversations with parents, many reported being highly stressed and were looking for support from other parents. Thus, the administrator believed that a MBPT program would be beneficial to address parents' concerns. To inform parents of the program, flyers were distributed, announcements were made at family orientation night and open houses, and the principal mentioned the program in informal conversations with families that regularly sought support.

For two years, MBPT groups were offered to parents at the preschool in the fall and spring of each year. MBPT groups lasted for one hour each week for six weeks total. In consultation with the administrator, it was determined that sessions would take place during the school day in an empty classroom. Composition of groups included no more than eight parents of preschoolers, to allow time for parents to engage in discussion and fully participate in each session. Approximately half of the parents in all of the groups had a preschool-age child with a developmental disability. Groups were led by a doctoral student in school psychology who has a master's degree in counseling psychology, is a certified yoga instructor, and is working toward their mindfulness-based stress reduction (MBSR) certification. A second doctoral student, who has a master's degree in school psychology, was also present in groups to observe implementation fidelity. Facilitators and implementation logistics were closely supervised by the author, who is a licensed psychologist with extensive experience implementing mindfulness groups for parents. Parents had the option of completing questionnaires before and after the MBPT groups. The data suggested that participation improved parents' overall mindfulness skills, mindfulness skills used during parent-child interactions, and reduced parenting stress. Parents also reported high levels of satisfaction with the MBPT groups and that they specifically enjoyed learning various mindfulness meditations and other ways to cope with stress.

The following overview describes the purpose and nature of the six weekly MBPT sessions. Almost every session begins and ends with a mindfulness practice, parents are encouraged to practice mindfulness outside of sessions, and handouts are provided at the end of each session that contain a brief overview of the topic discussed and resources (e.g., books, websites, videos, phone apps) parents could explore for further information about the topic.

Session 1: Introduction and Understanding Automatic Parenting

During the first session, the facilitator introduces themselves, parents introduce themselves, and group guidelines are established. The purpose of the MBPT session is described, followed by discussion of how mindfulness will be learned and how it may benefit parents and their children. The focus of this first session is to become aware of parenting on autopilot during interactions with their children and while stressed. It is acknowledged that all parents experience stress and have various reactions to stress (e.g., fight, flight, freeze). Parents learn that although reactions to stress can become habitual, by pausing and responding intentionally they may reduce their stress and improve their interactions with others. This is an important concept, as it provides the foundation for the remaining sessions. To help parents practice mindfulness by using their senses, recognize that their senses provide them with a window of awareness, and practice experiencing something in a new way, an exercise using a small piece of chocolate or a raisin is conducted. During this activity, parents each receive a bit of chocolate/raisin. They are asked to look at it for one minute, smell it for one minute, unwrap it for one minute, touch it for one minute, then place it in their mouth (without eating it) for one minute. The group facilitator prompts parents during each of the tasks and then facilitates discussion afterward. The facilitator may ask "What did you notice?," "What was this like for you?," "Did your mind wander while looking, smelling, touching, or tasting?," "What did you do to gently bring yourself back to the moment?" Parents may bring up, for example, that it was challenging to maintain attention, that they engaged in negative self-talk to bring their awareness back to the task, that they liked/didn't like the food, that it reminded them of something else, or that they were thinking of their to-do list. The point of this exercise is to discuss that thoughts and feelings can distract their attention away from the present moment, and that they can be mindful of these experiences by learning how to be non-judgmental when it occurs, recognize when it happens, and gently bring oneself back to the task at hand. The session closes with a brief mindful breathing meditation.

Session 2: Beginner's Mind

Starting with session 2, a brief mindful breathing meditation opens each session. The focus of the session, beginner's mind, is described and discussion is facilitated about what this means for parents. When stressed, or during difficult interactions, people usually operate on autopilot, which may result in ignoring what is really occurring during that moment and therefore reacting in a way that is not consistent with the situation at hand. To illustrate, various examples are provided in session, such as this one:

> Imagine you ask your child to clean up their toys. In the past you have had to ask numerous times, each time growing in frustration when your child responds by crying or telling you "No." In this moment, you ask your child to clean up their toys and they respond by whining quietly and slowly beginning to clean up. Your reaction is to elevate your voice and say, "I'm tired of having to tell you over and over again to clean up your toys! Hurry up!"

This is an example that parents often smile, nod, and quietly laugh about, because it describes an experience they can relate to. The facilitator discusses how parents' previous history of interactions with their children—particularly, difficult or annoying interactions—can play a role in their current interactions with their children. In the earlier example, the child quietly whined and began cleaning up slowly. While that might still not meet parental expectations, the parent's reaction in this interaction (i.e., raising their voice and expressing frustration with the child) may be more automatic than responsive—failing to match the current moment. The session ends with a brief mindful breathing meditation.

Session 3: Reconnecting With Our Body

A brief visualization meditation opens the session, which encourages parents to imagine and focus on a particular image (e.g., leaves floating down a stream, balloons released into the air). Discussion surrounding what the experience was like for parents during this type of meditation is conducted. After reflecting on this meditation, the facilitator highlights that sometimes it is easier for parents to identify what is stressful about their lives than it is for them to identify how their body actually responds to stress. Much of the session focuses on the facilitator describing the mind-body connection. Examples of not paying attention to one's physical being (e.g., ignoring a headache, hunger, or muscle pain) and how it may affect one's thoughts or feelings (e.g., becoming irritable or overwhelmed) and interactions with others (e.g., inconsistent discipline of children because one is feeling drained and has low energy) are discussed. Several questions are posed and discussed to help parents become more aware of their body: "Am I hungry—what have I eaten so far today?" "Am I thirsty—how much have I had to drink today?" "Am I tired—how much sleep have I had this week?" "Am I achy, tight, or tingly anywhere? If so, describe it." "Am I clenching my teeth, tightening my shoulders, biting my nails, or exhibiting other signs of stress? If so, acknowledge it." To help parents connect with their body in session beyond *thinking* of answers to these questions, a guided mindful body scan meditation is conducted to help them *feel* their body. A brief discussion afterward helps parents process what this experience was like for them. This body scan exercise and accompanying discussion close the session.

Session 4: Responding vs. Reacting

A mindful body scan meditation is conducted to open the session. The aim of this session is to discuss the difference between responding and reacting in interactions with their children, reactions people have to stress (e.g., fight, flight, freeze), and how pausing during interactions may allow parents to re-orient themselves to the present moment. To further highlight the different ways parents may react to a problem or stress, parents are encouraged to consider a particularly challenging interaction or situation they find themselves in with their child. While imagining this situation, parents are asked to reflect on the thoughts, feelings, and behaviors they experience during this interaction. The facilitator describes how common reactions to children may fall into the fight, flight, or freeze categories, and parents are asked to consider alternatives to these reactions that can help facilitate supportive and consistent parent-child connection, even during challenging times. The steps to devising a plan with intention are outlined as follows: (1) create a goal (what do you want to achieve?); (2) create a strategy (how can you help your child complete the task?); (3) join with your child (how can you demonstrate empathy and shared effort with your child?); (4) identify life skills to teach (identify, model, and reinforce the skills you want your child to learn); and (5) lead with lightness (approach the plan as a way to shift the mood). An example vignette is read by the facilitator, and parents discuss how the five steps could be applied in the situation. The point is not that all parents will arrive at the same plan or that particular plans are right or wrong. Rather, it is to help parents think through various goals, skills, and strategies to improve the mood of their child and themselves during interactions. To close the session, parents engage in guided deep belly-breathing exercises. The power of breath and the sensations parents experience during deep belly-breathing are discussed. Orienting to one's breath is described as a tool to help parents stop and pause—to become present and respond (as opposed to react) to the present moment.

Session 5: Loving Kindness

A visualization meditation, similar to one used in session 3, is used to open the session. After reflecting on the experience of the visualization exercise, the facilitator discusses the concept of kindness toward oneself, including one's thoughts (often labeled as "positive" or "negative") and feelings (often labeled as "good" or "bad"). For an activity to illustrate the relationship among thoughts, feelings, behavior, and kindness, the facilitator asks parents in the group to close their eyes and imagine they are observing a parent and child walking into school. The parent has their hands full with the child's backpack, lunchbox, and several papers. It appears that the parent is teary-eyed and is in a rush, saying, "Hurry up, you're already late and I'm going to be late!" The child is yelling, "I don't want to go to school today!" and falling to the ground. Afterward, parents discuss their thoughts (e.g., "I've been there before!"), feelings (e.g., empathy, embarrassment), and behavior (e.g., asks parent if they need help, asks if parent wants to go for a cup of coffee) as these relate to the imagined scenario. Later in the session, the same vignette is read again, but this time, the facilitator asks parents to imagine that they were in this situation, instead of observing another parent. Afterward, parents again discuss their thoughts (e.g., "This happens every morning!" "I'm going to be late to work." "Am I the only parent that can't get this right?"), feelings (e.g., embarrassment, anger, frustration), and behavior (e.g., yelling, carrying child into school) as these relate to the imagined scenario. An important concept drawn out during this discussion is that when parents were imagining others in this situation, they were more likely to have kinder thoughts, feelings, and behaviors toward them; however, when they imagined themselves in the same situation, they described more negative and harsh evaluations of themselves and their child. The take-home message is that taking a third-person observer's stance during especially difficult interactions with their children allows parents to take a step back and be kinder toward themselves and others. A mindful breathing exercise closes the session.

Session 6: Mindful Path Through Parenting and Wrap-Up

The last session opens with a mindful body scan meditation. During the last session together, the facilitator highlights the topics discussed and the mindfulness exercised practiced throughout the duration of the program. Parents are encouraged to reflect on what the experience of participating in the group has been like for them and whether their experience in the group has affected their lives outside of session. The facilitator leads a discussion on how parents can continue mindful parenting practices after the group ends. Parents create a list of mindfulness-based practices that were particularly meaningful or effective for them as well as action plans for how they may use these practices in the future. The session ends with a final mindful breathing meditation.

Mindful You Workshop for Parents of K–12 Students

Another way to expose parents to mindfulness and offer training in mindfulness skills in a school setting is through a MBPT workshop. The author and a colleague worked with a school district that was offering a variety of workshops to the community as a way to improve family engagement with schools (Bender & Daniels, 2018). The district indicated that mindfulness was a topic of interest for families, therefore a MBPT workshop series was developed. The workshop was offered over the course of three weeks (one and a half hours each week) in the evening at one of the district's elementary schools. Parents could select if they wanted to attend one, two, or three workshops; however, the topics for each workshop did build off one another and were created to be sequential in nature. The workshop series was created and facilitated by the author based on prior mindfulness programs and MBPT content (described earlier in this chapter). Given that any parent in the district could participate, the goal was to develop an approach that would be appropriate for a short, educational workshop series for parents of all K–12 students. A total of 10 parents participated in the mindfulness workshop.

The following overview briefly describes the purpose and sequence of the three-part MBPT workshop series. When workshops were held, parents were also encouraged to practice the mindfulness activities outside of the workshop. Video and audio clips were utilized to help facilitate guided mindfulness meditations and activities. Handouts were provided at the end of each workshop session that contain a brief overview of the topic discussed and resources (e.g., books, websites, videos, phone apps) parents could explore for further information about the topic. These handouts included developmentally appropriate resources for youth, given that parents expressed interest in introducing mindfulness to their children. At the end of each workshop, parents could complete a brief, three-question satisfaction survey; results from this survey were used by facilitators to gauge what went well and what could be improved or adjusted in future workshops. Evaluation of the MBPT workshop series revealed that parents enjoyed the material and activities, with average scores in the "above average" range for post-workshop satisfaction questions.

Mindfulness Workshop 1

During the first workshop, introductions are made and the workshop is described. It was shared with parents that the overall goals of the workshop series were to describe mindfulness, engage in a variety of mindfulness practices, and understand how mindfulness may benefit parents and their children. The first workshop discussed the history and benefits of mindfulness. Additionally, three mindfulness activities were conducted, including the mindful eating activity, deep belly-breathing, and a mindfulness visualization exercise (see the descriptions of these activities provided earlier in this chapter).

Mindfulness Workshop 2

The workshop opens with an agenda followed by a brief review of mindfulness (referencing material from Workshop 1). A discussion of thoughts, feelings, behaviors, and loving kindness is described by the facilitators, accompanied by vignettes used to illustrate the relationship among these concepts. A mindfulness visualization exercise and short mindful body scan meditation are then conducted. The purpose of these activities and parents' reactions to their experiences is discussed. The workshop ends with facilitators describing how mindfulness benefits youth and how the activities practiced in the workshop can be helpful for both improving their own parenting as well as their children's well-being.

Mindfulness Workshop 3

The workshop opens with an agenda followed by asking how parents practiced mindfulness since the last workshop. After discussing the various types of mindfulness practices parents engaged in, deep belly-breathing and mindfulness visualization exercises are practiced. The discussion about how mindfulness affects parenting is continued by defining mindful parenting and considering how mindfulness practices learned in the workshop(s) could be beneficial to the parenting relationship. Finally, a recap of the three-part workshop is provided, and additional resources for information about mindfulness are shared.

CONCLUSION

Mindful parenting is described as "intentionally bringing moment to moment awareness to the parent-child relationship" (Duncan et al., 2009a, p. 255) and is considered an essential skill for parenting (Kabat-Zinn & Kabat-Zinn, 1997; Steinberg, 2004). MBPT teaches mindfulness skills such as listening with full attention, non-judgmental acceptance, emotional awareness, self-regulation within the context of the parenting relationship, and compassion for self and others. These skills enhance a parents' ability to be present and responsive with their child, deepen their relationship with their child, and reduce parenting stress. Use of MBPT is expanding across settings, with schools becoming a viable place where mindfulness can be implemented and accepted. Given that the literature on MBPT has been linked to positive outcomes for parents, children, and adolescents, it appears to be a promising intervention for meeting the needs of families, students, and schools. Although there are several benefits to implementing MBPT in schools, feasibility concerns (e.g., number of weeks the training will last, number of hours per training session, who will lead implementation) may still preclude some school mental health practitioners from engaging in mindfulness-based interventions. The overview of MBPT and case examples provided in this chapter illustrate a few ways that school mental health practitioners can adapt and implement MBPT in schools.

REFERENCES

Bender, S. L., & Daniels, B. (2018). *Understanding mindfulness for parents and children*. A 3-part series of family engagement workshops at Billerica Public Schools in Billerica, MA.

Bender, S. L., Lawson, T., Janze, J., Cathcart, S., & Li, K. (in press). Evaluating acceptability of the mindful parenting program for preschool parents. *Massachusetts School Psychologists Association Newsletter*.

Benn, R., Akiva, T., Arel, S., & Roeser, R. W. (2012). Mindfulness training effects for parents and educators of children with special needs. *Developmental Psychology, 48*, 1476–1487. doi: 10.1037/a0027537

Bluth, K., & Wahler, R. G. (2011). Parenting preschoolers: Can mindfulness help? *Mindfulness, 2*, 282–285. doi: 10.1007/s12671-011-0071-4

Bögels, S. M., & Restifo, K. (2014). *Mindful parenting: A guide for mental health practitioners*. Springer.

Bradley, R. H., Iida, M., Pennar, A., Owen, M. T., & Vandell, D. L. (2017). The dialectics of parenting: Changes in the interplay of maternal behaviors during early and middle childhood. *Journal of Child and Family Studies, 26*, 3214–3225. doi: 10.1007/s10826-017-0805-6

Burke, M. M., Chan, N., & Neece, C. L. (2017). Parent perspectives of applying mindfulness-based stress strategies to special education. *Intellectual and Developmental Disabilities, 55*, 167–180. doi: 10.1352/1934-9556-55.3.167

Coatsworth, J. D., Duncan, L. G., Greenberg, M., & Nix, R. (2010). Changing parents' mindfulness, child management skills and relationship quality with their youth: Results from a randomized pilot intervention trial. *Journal of Child and Family Studies, 19*, 203–217. doi: 10.1007/s10826-009-9304-8

Coatsworth, J. D., Duncan, L. G., Nix, R. L., Greenberg, M. T., Gayles, J. G., Bamberger, K. T., . . . Demi, M. A. (2015). Integrating mindfulness with parent training: Effects of the mindfulness-enhanced strengthening families program. *Developmental Psychology, 51*, 26–35. doi: 10.1037/a0038212

Dumas, J. E. (2005). Mindfulness-based parent training: Strategies to lessen the grip of automaticity to families with disruptive children. *Journal of Clinical Child & Adolescent Psychology, 34*, 779–791. doi: 10.1207/s15374424jccp3404_20

Duncan, L. G., Coatsworth, J. D., & Greenberg, M. T. (2009a). A model of mindful parenting: Implications for parent-child relationships and prevention research. *Clinical Child and Family Psychology Review, 12*, 255–270. doi: 10.1007/s10567-009-0046-3

Duncan, L. G., Coatsworth, J. D., & Greenberg, M. T. (2009b). Pilot study to gauge acceptability of a mindfulness-based, family-focused preventive intervention. *The Journal of Primary Prevention, 30*, 605–618. doi: 10.1007/s10935-009-0185-9

Felver, J. C., Tipsord, J. M., Morris, M. J., Racer, K. H., & Dishion, T. J. (2014). The effects of mindfulness-based intervention on children's attention regulation. *Journal of Attention Disorders, 21*, 872–881. doi: 10.1177/1087054714548032

Havighurst, S., Wilson, K., Harley, A., Prior, M., & Kehoe, C. (2010). Tuning in to kids: Improving emotion socialization practices in parents of preschool children—Findings from a community trial. *Journal of Child Psychology and Psychiatry, 51*, 1342–1350. doi: 10.1111/j.1469-7610.2010.02303.x

Kabat-Zinn, J. (1990). *Full catastrophe living: Using the wisdom of your body and mind to face stress, pain, and illness*. Dell Publishing.

Kabat-Zinn, J. (2003). Mindfulness-based interventions in context: Past, present, and future. *Clinical Psychology: Science and Practice*, *10*, 144–156. doi: 10.1093/clipsy/bpg016

Kabat-Zinn, M., & Kabat-Zinn, J. (1997). *Everyday blessings: The inner work of mindful parenting*. Hyperion.

Kerns, K. A., Tomich, P. L., & Kim, P. (2006). Normative trends in children's perceptions of availability and utilization of attachment figures in middle childhood. *Social Development*, *15*, 2–21. doi: 10.1111/j.1467-9507.2006.00327.x

Klingbeil, D. A., Fischer, A. J., Renshaw, T. L., Bloomfield, B. S., Polakoff, B., Willenbrink, J. B., . . . Chan, K. T. (2017). Effects of mindfulness-based interventions on disruptive behavior: A meta-analysis of single-case research. *Psychology in the Schools*, *54*, 70–87. doi: 10.1002/pits.21982

Marceau, K., Ram, N., & Susman, E. J. (2014). Development and lability in the parent-child relationship during adolescence: Associations with pubertal timing and tempo. *Journal of Research on Adolescence*, *25*, 474–489. doi: 10.1111/jora.12139

Neece, C. L. (2014). Mindfulness-based stress reduction for parents of young children with developmental delays: Implications for parental mental health and child behavior problems. *Journal of Applied Research in Intellectual Disabilities*, *27*, 174–186. doi: 10.1111/jar.12064

Parent, J., McKee, L. G., Anton, M., Gonzalez, M., Jones, D. J., & Forehand, R. (2016). Mindfulness in parenting and coparenting. *Mindfulness*, *7*, 504–513. doi: 10.1007/s12671-015-0485-5

Roberts, L. R., & Neece, C. L. (2015). Feasibility of mindfulness-based stress reduction intervention for parents of children with developmental delays. *Issues in Mental Health Nursing*, *36*, 592–602. doi: 10.3109/01612840.2015.1017063

Shonkoff, J. P., & Phillips, D. A. (2000). *From neurons to neighborhoods: The science of early childhood development*. National Academy Press.

Singh, N. N., Lancioni, G. E., Winton, A. S. W., Fisher, B. C., Wahler, R. G., McAleavey, K., . . . Sabaawi, M. (2006). Mindful parenting decreases aggression, noncompliance, and self-injury in children with autism. *Journal of Emotional and Behavioral Disorders*, *14*, 169–177. doi: 10.1177/10634266060140030401

Steinberg, L. (2004). *The 10 basic principles of good parenting*. Simon & Schuster.

Townshend, K., Jordan, Z., Stephenson, M., & Tsey, K. (2016). The effectiveness of mindful parenting programs in promoting parents' and children's wellbeing: A systematic review. *JBI Database of Systematic Reviews and Implementation Reports*, *14*, 138–180. doi: 10.11124/JBISRIR-2016

Webster-Stratton, C. (2001). *The parents and children series: A comprehensive course*. The Incredible Years, Inc.

Wilson, K. R., Havighurst, S. S., & Harley, A. E. (2012). Tuning in to kids: An effectiveness trial of a parenting program targeting emotion socialization of preschoolers. *Journal of Family Psychology*, *26*, 56–65. doi: 10.1037/a0026480

Woodman, A. C., Mawdsley, H. P., & Hauser-Cram, P. (2015). Parenting stress and child behavior problems within families of children with developmental disabilities: Transactional relations across 15 years. *Research in Developmental Disabilities*, *36*, 264–276. doi: 10.1016/j.ridd.2014.10.011

World Health Organization. (2016). Advancing early childhood development: From science to scale. *The Lancet*. Retrieved from: http://www.thelancet.com/series/ECD2016

14

Mindfulness-Based Programs for Classrooms and Schools

TYLER L. RENSHAW, JOHN D. BARR, CALEB D. FARLEY, THOMAS K. FRANZMANN, MARY L. PHAN, STEPHANIE A. VINAL, SEAN N. WEEKS, AND SHANE R. JIMERSON ■

Many schools are implementing programs that use mindfulness training to promote the social, emotional, behavioral, and mental health of the students (Felver et al., 2016; Palacios et al., 2023; Phan et al., 2022; Renshaw, 2020; Renshaw & Cook, 2017; Roeser et al., 2023). The aim of most school-based mindfulness programs is to increase students' awareness of how thoughts and emotions influence speech and behavior, thereby promoting more skillful and appropriate choices within the school context (Semple et al., 2017). "Mindfulness" is defined as a nonjudgmental, present-moment awareness that acknowledges and accepts feelings, thoughts, and sensations as they arise (Bishop et al., 2004). According to Hölzel et al. (2011), the benefits of mindfulness stem from two interrelated components: regulating attention to focus on immediate experiences, and approaching experiences with curiosity, openness, and acceptance. Mindfulness-based interventions (MBIs) can therefore be understood as any intentional efforts to train mindfulness skills for the purpose of improving youth's outcomes (Renshaw, 2020). Many schools are adopting MBIs because they are easy to learn and they help students become more responsive, calm, and focused, while reducing stress and distractions (Garrison Institute, 2005).

It is important to recognize that not all MBIs are the same. Some MBIs rely on training mindfulness skills as the core intervention component (e.g., Learning to BREATHE; Broderick, 2013), whereas others infuse the training of mindfulness skills alongside other core non-mindfulness interventions, such as social skills and emotional regulation training (e.g., Strong Kids; Carrizales-Englemann

Tyler L. Renshaw et al., *Mindfulness-Based Programs for Classrooms and Schools*. In: *Using Mindfulness to Promote Mental Health in Schools*. Edited by: Tyler L. Renshaw and Shane R. Jimerson, Oxford University Press.
 DOI: 10.1093/9780190880507.003.0014

et al., 2016). There is also a difference between mindfulness-based *treatments* like acceptance and commitment therapy (ACT; Day et al., 2022) and dialectical behavior therapy (DBT; Fang & Ding, 2020), which are provided to intervene with clients with significant mental health concerns in outpatient or inpatient settings, and mindfulness-based *programs* like MindUP (https://mindup.org) and Mindfulness in Schools Project (https://mindfulnessinschools.org), which are prevention-focused and provided to youth in school settings. This variability among MBIs has allowed them to be used successfully to support youth across various settings—including schools, homes, community agencies, hospitals, and private practices—for the purposes of improving a variety of desirable outcomes.

This chapter focuses on school-based mindfulness programs (SBMPs). These are MBIs that rely on mindfulness as either the primary or a supplementary intervention component and that are prevention-focused, provided to youth at the small-group or classroom levels in schools. SBMPs focus on developing mindfulness skills through specific practices such as mindful breathing, body scans, and meditation. They are usually structured as curricula that can be implemented by educators, mental health professionals, or even paraprofessionals working in the school setting. For instance, Learning to BREATHE is an SBMP for use with adolescents, with structured lesson plans for teaching mindfulness techniques to improve emotional regulation, reduce stress, and enhance overall well-being (Broderick, 2013). As another example, Strong Kids is a social-emotional learning (SEL) program that integrates mindfulness activities within its broader curriculum aimed at promoting emotional resilience, social competence, and coping skills among children and adolescents (Carrizales-Englemann et al., 2016). While the proportion of activities spent on training mindfulness skills differs drastically between Learning to BREATHE and Strong Kids, these are both considered SMBPs because they both rely on training mindfulness as a core intervention component and because they are intended to be implemented with students in schools at the small-group and classroom levels.

SBMPs are typically designed with flexibility and context in mind. These programs often provide a general framework for mindfulness practices that is operationalized into lesson plans that can be tailored to different age groups or grade levels, school contexts, and local needs. SBMPs also account for classroom dynamics, time constraints, and variability among implementers regarding their level of familiarity with mindfulness, ensuring that mindfulness practices are both practical and effective within the school context (Schonert-Reichl et al., 2015). These usability considerations have likely contributed to the spread of SBMPs in schools throughout the last decade as well as increased research in this area. Roeser et al. (2023) report that both publication and citation trends for studies on SBMPs have drastically and positively increased since 2015. Relatedly, a recent systematic review of the quality and effects of SBMPs conducted by Phan et al. (2022) covered 77 studies with 12,359 students across five continents. Syntheses of the literature on SBMPs, to date, conclude that they are safe and effective for promoting an array of desirable student outcomes, including broad improvements in their psychosocial and educational functioning (Renshaw et al., 2022).

The purpose of this chapter is to highlight the core components of SBMPs and describe how they can be used to successfully promote the psychosocial and educational outcomes of youth in schools. The chapter begins with an overview of key features of SMBPs more generally, discussing findings from recent scholarship on this topic. This information should be useful for guiding professionals in understanding the commonalities and differences among SBMPs. Following, the chapter includes a selective review of two exemplar SBMPs, providing background on each program's development, insight into each program's structure and implementation, and an appraisal of each program's empirical support and limitations. This information should likewise be valuable for professionals considering the implementation of SBMPs as it raises awareness regarding the distinctions and limitations that can manifest when choosing and implementing a program in schools. Finally, the chapter closes with a discussion of future directions for advancing research and practice on SBMPs.

KEY FEATURES OF SCHOOL-BASED MINDFULNESS PROGRAMS

This section highlights key features of SBMPs, providing further insight into the foundations of the curricula and strategies employed by many of the programs mentioned earlier in this chapter—and provides a broader perspective on the state of practice related to SBMPs. Over the last decade, several overview articles have described *how* SBMPs can be implemented for prevention-oriented purposes in schools, focusing mostly on ways that mindfulness training can be flexibly adapted within a multitiered system of supports in schools to fit the aims of universal (Tier 1), targeted (Tier 2), and intensive (Tier 3) interventions (e.g., Felver et al., 2016; Renshaw et al., 2017; Renshaw, 2020). Yet few studies have narrowed in on *what* the key features of these SBMPs are, regardless of the tier or level of support they may be implemented at in schools. Following is a review of findings from recent landmark studies that synthesize key features of SBMPs, describing their general program characteristics, common categories of techniques, and core program components. These findings are largely focused on SBMPs that have been designed and implemented at the universal (Tier 1) level of service delivery in schools, which are intended to promote well-being and buffer the onset or exacerbation of problems among a population of youth. But these findings are likewise applicable to SBMPs used at the targeted (Tier 2) and intensive (Tier 3) levels in schools, for supporting students presenting with elevated levels of psychosocial risk.

General Program Characteristics

The first scoping review of the characteristics of SBMPs was conducted by Roeser et al. (2022), who analyzed features of 36 different programs. This review found that about 30% of SBMPs were adaptations of mindfulness programs originally designed for adults (e.g., MBSR), around 50% were novel and designed originally and specifically for use in schools (e.g., for prevention-oriented or SEL purposes), and the remaining 20% were composed of brief mindfulness practices that were not necessarily formalized into a programmatic structure. Furthermore, greater than half of SBMPs were implemented by external facilitators, around one-third were implemented by educators, and the remainder were implemented by a mixture of both (Roeser et al., 2022). This review also noted substantial variability in the amount of implementation effort (or dosage) for SBMPs, with about one-quarter of the programs requiring 6 hours or less, around half requiring 6–15 hours, and the remainder requiring 15+ hours for implementation in classrooms. The most common targeted outcomes of SBMPs were self-regulation competencies, followed by internalizing and externalizing problems, and then subjective well-being (Roeser et al., 2022). Taken together, the findings of this review provided a snapshot of the common implementation characteristics of mindfulness programming in schools.

Common Categories of Techniques

A follow-up study, conducted by Palacios et al. (2023), built on the work of Roeser et al. (2022) by providing a systematic review of articles on SMBPs that were published in nine school psychology journals between 2006 and 2020: *School Psychology Review*, *School Psychology Forum*, *Journal of School Psychology*, *Journal of Applied School Psychology*, *School Psychology (Quarterly)*, *International Journal of School and Educational Psychology*, *Contemporary School Psychology*, *Psychology in the Schools*, and *School Psychology International*. The researchers identified 46 total articles about SBMPs, 23 (50%) of which focused on implementation in schools. A content analysis of the intervention techniques described in these articles, based on descriptions provided by authors of the articles, yielded eight categories of commonly used mindfulness practices (Palacious et al., 2023):

1. *Breathing*: techniques focused on the breath, involving any practice wherein attending to the breath or the process of breathing is central.
2. *Body scan or body sweep*: systematically focusing on different parts of the body, usually starting at the toes and moving to the head.
3. *Awareness*: practices enhancing awareness of the body, sensations, emotions, and thoughts, including mindful movement and mindfulness of sounds.
4. *Heartfulness*: techniques fostering compassion, kindness, gratitude, and reducing self-judgment, emphasizing the "warmer" aspects of mindfulness.
5. *Yoga*: a set of practices integrating mind and body techniques for stress relief, relaxation, and transcending material concerns.
6. *Mandala coloring*: engaging in coloring intricate mandala patterns to foster a focused and mindful state.
7. *Meditation*: exercises including various forms of meditation, such as sitting and centering meditation, aimed at training the mind toward peaceful thoughts.

Table 14.1. Common Mindfulness Techniques and Associated Citations for School-Based Studies

Technique Category	Citations for School-Based Studies Using the Technique Category
Awareness	Bannirchelvam et al. (2017), Britton et al. (2014), Dariotis et al. (2017), Devcich et al. (2017), Felver et al. (2017), Felver et al. (2019), Kang et al. (2018), Kielty et al. (2017), Long et al. (2018), Luiselli et al. (2017), Rush et al. (2017).
Breathing	Bannirchelvam et al. (2017), Britton et al. (2014), Dariotis et al. (2017), Devcich et al. (2017), Frank et al. (2014), Idler et al. (2017), Kang et al. (2018), Kielty et al. (2017), Luiselli et al. (2017), Rush et al. (2017), Terjestam et al. (2016), Wood et al. (2018)
Meditation	Dariotis et al. (2017), Felver et al. (2019), Flook et al. (2010), Frank et al. (2014), Idler et al. (2017), Kurth et al. (2020), Luiselli et al. (2017), Milligan et al. (2017)
Yoga	Bray et al. (2012), Felver, et al. (2015), Frank et al. (2014), Idler et al. (2017), Milligan et al. (2017), Wood et al. (2018)
Body Scan	Bannirchelvam et al. (2017), Britton et al. (2014), ElGarhy & Liu (2016), Flook et al. (2010), Kang et al. (2018), Kielty et al. (2017), Luiselli et al. (2017), Terjestam et al. (2016)
Heartfulness	Devcich et al. (2017), Felver et al. (2019), Terjestam et al. (2016), Wood et al. (2018)
Mandala	Carsley et al. (2015), Carsley et al. (2018)
Visualization	Bannirchelvam et al. (2017), Terjestam et al. (2016)

Note: Technique categories and associated citations are drawn from the systematic review conducted by Palacios et al. (2023).

8. *Visualization*: techniques for controlling mental imagery, managing perceptual information originating from imagination rather than physical stimuli.

Figure 14.1 uses a mandala to illustrate these eight common categories of techniques for training mindfulness in schools. Moreover, Table 14.1 lists these eight categories of techniques and provides citations, drawn from Palacios et al.'s (2023) review, for relevant studies featured in school psychology journals.

Core Program Components

The latest article to make a substantial contribution toward this end was published by Felver et al. (2023), who conducted a Delphi study with experts in the field—including researchers and program instructors—to identify consensus

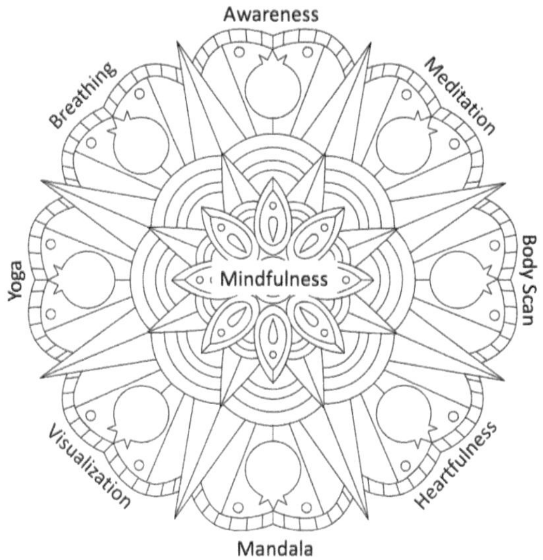

Figure 14.1 Mandala Representation of Common Categories of Mindfulness Techniques Used in Schools

regarding the core components of mindfulness programming with youth. Importantly, this study included SBMPs but was not limited to school-based programs only, also accounting for MBIs provided with youth in other service settings. The researchers defined "core program components" as "the essential aspects of a program, including the practices, processes, and principles that are hypothesized to be causally linked to outcomes" (Felver et al., 2023, p. 280). In Round 1 of the Delphi study, qualitative responses from 19 mindfulness researchers were analyzed to yield 22 potentially different core program components. In Round 2 of the study, 21 mindfulness instructors joined the group of researchers in rating and providing feedback on each of the potential core components resulting from Round 1. In Round 3, all experts again rated the importance of each potential program component in an effort to identify consensus opinions (i.e., $\geq$ 75% endorsement across experts). Ultimately, results indicated that 9 of the original 22 components achieved consensus endorsement across the researchers and instructors. Following are the names and descriptions of these components, as provided by Felver et al. (2023, p.285):

1. *Acceptance*: "embracing and being open to internal/external experiences without need to change."
2. *Compassion*: "concern for, and interest in, alleviation of suffering for self and others."
3. *De-centering*: "developing an experiential understanding that thoughts and feelings are transient events."
4. *Focused attention*: "deliberate and sustained attention allocated to a targeted internal/external experience for a sustained period of time."

5. *Non-judging*: "interpretation of internal/external experience without good/positive or bad/negative interpretation."
6. *Non-reacting*: "ability to observe pleasant/unpleasant/neutral internal/external experiences without taking immediate action to alter the experience."
7. *Orienting to present moment*: "moment-to-moment awareness of transient internal/external experiences."
8. *Self-awareness*: "experiential understanding of thoughts, actions, and emotional states, and the interrelation between these internal/external experiences."
9. *Somatic awareness*: "awareness of bodily sensations and/or movement."

Summary of Key Program Features

Taken together, the studies reviewed above provide a helpful understanding of the contemporary landscape of SBMPs by spotlighting their key program features. Roeser et al. (2022) describe commonalities and differences among implementation characteristics of SBMPs, which are likely to be useful for professionals considering programming logistics. Palacios et al. (2023) and Felver et al. (2023) build on these findings by outlining the core intervention elements of SBMPs. Readers may be especially interested in exploring the citations provided in Table 14.1, as these are the primary sources offering more detail regarding the nature of the mindfulness intervention strategies commonly used in schools. When considered together with the eight categories of techniques identified by Palacios et al. (2023; see Table 14.1 and Figure 14.1), the nine core program components identified by Felver et al. (2023) can be understood as highlighting the mechanisms of change that help to inform how and why the categories of techniques used in SBMPs work to produce desirable student outcomes. The next section in this chapter reviews two exemplar SBMPs that each employ several of these categories of techniques to activate many of these core components.

EXEMPLAR SCHOOL-BASED MINDFULNESS PROGRAMS

MindUP

The MindUP program (https://mindup.org) is the hallmark initiative of the Goldie Hawn Foundation, which is a not-for-profit organization that was developed to proactively address issues around youth suicide, depression, anxiety, and aggression. MindUP was designed in 2003 by Goldie Hawn (founder) in conjunction with a scientific advisory board comprising four members: Drs. Molly Lawlor, Kimberly A. Schonert-Reichl, Robert W. Roeser, and Joshua L. Brown. MindUP is a CASEL SELect program that includes programming for students in grades Pre-K–8 and demonstrates evidence of effectiveness at grades 4–7 (https://pg.casel.org/mindup/). According to its materials, the purpose of the MindUP program is to provide education and skills to children so that they can be prepared to better handle stress and regulate their emotions for the purposes of living a healthier and more balanced life. This program also intends to cultivate positivity, resiliency, kindness, and gratitude so that youth are better prepared to face the contemporary challenges of modern society. Thus far, MindUP has been taught to over six million children worldwide (https://mindup.org).

Structure and Implementation

The MindUP program originally consisted of 15 sequential lessons separated into four complementary units: (1) Getting Focused, (2) Sharpening Your Senses, (3) It's All About Attitude, and (4) Taking Action Mindfully. These original units have been revised and reorganized as follows: (1) My Mindful Brain, (2) Mindful Senses, (3) Building Well-Being With a Mindful Mindset, and (4) Mindful of Ourselves and the World. Curricula are developmentally differentiated by early years (ages 3–4), grades K–2 (ages 5–7), grades 3–5 (ages 8–10), and grades 6–8 (ages 11–14). The titles of lessons differ slightly depending on the developmental level of the curriculum, and the number of lessons now ranges from 14 to 17, but the content is largely consistent across levels. As an example, following are the sequential lesson titles for the current grades 3–5 curriculum (https://mindup.org): (1) Creating the MindUP Learning Community, (2) Understanding the Brain, (3) Learning to Be Mindful, (4) Focusing Our Awareness, (5) Mindful Listening, (6) Mindful Seeing, (7) Mindful Smelling, (8) Mindful Tasting, (9) Mindful Touch, (10) Mindful Movement, (11) So Many Feelings!, (12) Building Perspective-Taking and Empathy, (13) Practicing Optimism, (14) Savoring Happy Experiences, (15) Practicing Gratitude, (16) Acts of Kindness, and (17) Mindful Actions in Our Community.

Each MindUP lesson takes about 40–50 minutes to implement and is taught once per week over the course of a traditional school semester (Schonert-Reichl et al., 2015). The lessons are administered to students by a teacher employed within the school who has undergone an online training provided by a certified MindUP consultant. MindUP offers district-wide training, school-wide training, and individual training (e.g., for school administrators or classroom teachers) to support implementation (https://mindup.org). Compared with individual trainings, group trainings come with customized elements and access to a library of digital resources for the whole school. Although prior print versions of the MindUP curriculum (e.g., The Hawn Foundation, 2011) could be purchased independently by teachers or parents, the current version of curricula are available only when purchasing training plans (https://mindup.org).

Empirical Support and Limitations

MindUP states that the program is supported by 15+ years of independent research, including nine peer-reviewed studies and four randomized controlled trials (https://mindup.org). For example, Thierry et al. (2016) conducted a study with pre-kindergarten and kindergarten students, comparing the MindUP program to a control group that received education-as-usual over a two-year period. Results indicated that after the first year, pre-K students who received the MindUP programming demonstrated improvements in working memory, planning, and organizing abilities, compared with students in the control group. After the second year of programming, kindergartners who received MindUP showed higher scores in vocabulary and reading than did kindergartners in the control group (Thierry et al., 2016). As another example, Schonert-Reichl et al. (2015) investigated the MindUP curriculum with fourth- and fifth-graders. Results from this study demonstrated that, compared with peers who did not receive the intervention, students who received MindUP showed significant improvements in a number of outcomes: attention, stress physiology, empathy, perspective-taking, optimism, emotional control, mindfulness, depression, kindness, and math scores (Schonert-Reichl et al., 2015).

Research also shows that MindUP improves self-regulation strategies (deCarvalho et al., 2017), that it reduces aggression and stress (Matsuba et al., 2021), and that it increases optimism and happiness (Schonert-Reichl et al., 2010). A study by Maloney et al. (2014) also indicated that students reported positive perceptions regarding the program's acceptability. Specifically, of the 189 students in grades 4–7 who were surveyed, 43% reported they "liked it a lot," 35% reported they "liked it," and 10% described the program as "OK." Teachers' perceptions of the MindUP program have generally indicated positivity toward its implementation and utility, although some complaints regarding the program have been expressed about its intensive training and resource requirements for teachers and schools (Maloney et al., 2016). Taken together, findings from studies exploring the effectiveness and acceptability of MindUP are promising. However, it is noteworthy that its curricula and implementation approaches have evolved over time and vary depending on developmental level—suggesting that the effects of these various iterations have yet to be fully tested and compared with each other.

Inner Explorer

The Inner Explorer program (https://innerexplorer.org) is offered by a non-profit foundation with the same name, which intends to help students learn mindfulness skills for the purposes of handling difficult emotions such as anger, anxiety, and stress; developing compassion and connection with others; developing self-awareness and control; and fostering resilience. Inner Explorer was originally developed by Drs. Laura S. Bakosh and Janice Houlihan, both of whom are trained in MBSR. It claims to be the only audio-based SEL program for schools that is explicitly grounded in the principles of MBSR. Inner Explorer is a CASEL SELect program that includes programming for students in grades pre-K–12 and demonstrates evidence of effectiveness at grade 3 (https://pg.casel.org/inner-explorer/). The intention of Inner Explorer is to use mindfulness strategies to support youth mental health and well-being and, ultimately, transform communities through upstream prevention. The program narrows in on training mindfulness skills related to attention, self-awareness, and emotional regulation—and is interested in evaluating the effects of mindfulness skills on both psychosocial and educational outcomes. To date, Inner Explorer has been implemented with over two million students, in 100+ school districts, and in all 50 states within the United States (https://innerexplorer.org).

Structure and Implementation

Inner Explorer is structured as a daily, on-demand, audio-guided program containing 90 different lessons ranging from 5 to 10 minutes and featuring a variety of narrators from various ethnic backgrounds. Lessons are available in both English and Spanish and are adapted and differentiated by four developmental levels: pre-K–grade 1, elementary (grades 2–4), middle school (grades 5–7), and high school (grades 8–12). The program requires minimal preparation and planning following the first lesson, and no formal training in mindfulness is required to facilitate implementation. Before starting the program, teachers are advised to begin by defining and discussing mindfulness with their class, explaining the benefits of regular practice and applying specific examples of such benefits in relation to their own classroom. Once mindfulness has been introduced and classroom expectations have been set, all that is needed for implementation is a daily 10–15-minute window when teachers "press play" on the guided audio recording and engage with the class in the mindfulness practice. Starting with lesson 6, an additional one–two-minute journal reflection activity is included at the end of each practice.

The Inner Explore implementation dashboard is accessible to teachers online and comprises four sections: Toolkit, Practice, Tune In, and My Stats. The "Toolkit" page provides resources and advice for getting started. This includes guides and videos related to the science behind mindfulness, tips for supporting successful implementation, sample scripts for starting the program, sample letter drafts for families, and a Frequently Asked Questions (FAQ) section. Within the "Practice" section is a menu of all 90 mindfulness lessons and a history showing the use of these lessons across classes. The "Tune In" section provides the opportunity to share the audio lessons with the students' families and manage communications with them. The "My Stats" page provides the user with graphs of their current practice data and includes a calendar that can be used to schedule activities and events related to program implementation. Inner Explorer is offered to schools using different plans that are scaled by the scope of implementation, including school, community, and school district levels (https://innerexplorer.org).

Empirical Support and Limitations

Inner Explorer indicates that the program's effectiveness is supported by 14 independent research studies. The first published study by Bakosh et al. (2016) was a quasi-experimental trial with 191 students across four classrooms within two elementary schools. Findings revealed that, compared to the control group, students receiving the Inner Explorer intervention had better reading and science grades as well as fewer behavioral infractions in the classroom. Another substantial study was a randomized controlled trial conducted by Bakosh et al. (2018) with 337 students across 16 classrooms in two different elementary schools. Results showed that, compared to a waitlist control condition, the Inner Explorer condition was associated with small improvements in math grades, social studies grades, and overall grade-point average. Qualitative and quantitative findings from these studies also support the social validity of the program, showing that teachers had positive perceptions of the feasibility of procedures and that they found implementation of the program to have very little impact on their other instructional activities (Bakosh et al., 2016; Bakosh et al., 2018).

Notably, the Inner Explorer audio exercises have recently been adapted into a stand-alone self-guided app that is intended for use by school-aged youth outside of the regular school day. Although this app is not yet included within the primary program, findings from a recent randomized controlled trial conducted by Treves et al. (2023) with 270 children indicated that the app version of the program had small effects on reducing self-reported stress and parent-reported negative affect. The program claims that several other studies on Inner Explorer have been conducted and produced positive outcomes (https://innerexplorer.org), yet it appears most of these have yet to be published or remain in dissertation form (e.g., Dunlap, 2023; Parsons, 2023; Stager, 2022). Taken together, the few findings from published studies are encouraging, yet they are focused solely on the English version of the program with elementary-aged students. Given versions of Inner Explorer are also available for preschool and secondary students, as well as in Spanish, further research is needed to establish the generalizability of the program's effects on psychosocial and educational outcomes across cultures and grade levels.

Other Promising Programs

The MindUP and Inner Explorer programs were selected as two exemplar SBMPs in this chapter because they are both well-established (i.e., have been developed and implemented for 10+ years), publicly accessible (i.e., have public-facing websites where educators and mental health professionals can evaluate the nature and costs of these programs), developmentally comprehensive (i.e., have curriculum versions geared toward both primary and secondary school students), and empirically supported (i.e., have at least some published evidence supporting the program's claims regarding effectiveness). That said, there are several other available SBMPs that share most of these key characteristics. Professionals who are considering selecting a SBMP for use in their local practice situation are encouraged to carefully consider these other promising options, including (but not limited to) the DNA-V curriculum (https://dnav.international/dna-v-for-youth/), the DBT STEPS-A program (https://www.dbtinschools.com), the Headspace for Educators app (https://www.headspace.com/educators), the several curricula offered via the Mindful Schools Project (e.g., dots, Paws b, The Present; https://mindfulnessinschools.org), and the Soles of the Feet program (Felver & Singh, 2020; only accessible in book format).

FUTURE DIRECTIONS AND CONCLUSIONS

Over the past 10–15 years, the availability and reach of SBMPs have expanded substantially (Roeser et al., 2023). The evidence supporting SBMPs is now promising, suggesting that a variety of programs are safe and effective for promoting positive psychosocial and educational outcomes among diverse students (Phan et al., 2022; Renshaw et al., 2022; Roeser et al., 2022). This chapter highlighted the nature of SBMPs and described how they can be used to successfully promote the psychosocial and educational outcomes of youth in schools. The chapter began with an overview of key features of SMBPs more generally, discussing findings from recent scholarship on this topic (i.e., Felver et al., 2023; Palacios et al., 2023; Roeser et al., 2022). Following, the chapter transitioned to a selective review of two exemplar SBMPs—MindUP and Inner Explorer—providing background on each program's development, insight into each program's structure and implementation, and an appraisal of each program's empirical support and limitations. The information provided in this chapter should be useful for guiding professionals in understanding the commonalities and differences among SBMPs as well as for raising awareness regarding the distinctions and limitations related to choosing and implementing a program in schools.

Although the research reviewed herein is useful for understanding the landscape of SBMPs, there remain limitations in professional knowledge that should be addressed by future applied scholarship in order to truly establish an evidence-based approach to selecting and implementing SBMPs (Renshaw, 2020; Renshaw et al., 2022). One significant unknown is whether some SBMPs are more effective than others. Research has primarily focused on investigating the direct effects of various SBMPs compared to waitlist controls or education-as-usual, without evaluating their comparative effects against active controls of other SBMPs (Phan et al., 2022), leaving unclear which specific programs may be more or less beneficial for improving youths' psychosocial and educational outcomes. This lack of comparative research extends to the effectiveness of SBMPs versus other non-MBI yet prevention-oriented approaches in schools, such as SEL programs and other mental health prevention programming (Klingbeil et al., 2017). Clarifying the value-added effects of particular SBMPs compared against other SBMPs as well as other approaches to prevention is therefore a critical future direction for guiding best practice prevention programming in schools.

Furthermore, another limitation in professional knowledge is that it remains unclear whether existing SBMPs can be optimized or refined for greater efficiency and effectiveness. Most SBMPs include a variety of psychoeducational and experiential components, drawing on several of the common categories of techniques identified by Palacios et al. (2023; see Table 14.1). Most SBMPs also likely tap into several of the core program components or mechanisms of change identified by Felver et al. (2023). That said, it is unknown which specific intervention elements—or combination of intervention techniques and components—are most important and impactful for SBMPs. It may be the case that including more techniques and tapping more core components contributes to more effective SBMPs. However, it may also be the case that many techniques or core components are redundant with one another or, alternatively, that some techniques are more or less effective for tapping core components that are weaker or stronger mechanisms of change. This uncertainty is exacerbated in SBMPs that incorporate non-mindfulness elements, such as SEL programs that infuse mindfulness training as just one of many different skills-based strategies. Component analysis research is therefore needed to identify the active ingredients within SBMPs and related programs, allowing for the potential elimination of ineffective practices or the addition of effective ones.

A final but critical limitation related to contemporary research and practice is how to effectively employ culturally sensitive adaptations of SBMPs to reach and benefit diverse youth and their communities. Preliminary guidelines have recently been published regarding how to adapt evidence-based interventions used in schools with students who are racially and ethnically marginalized (e.g., Brown et al., 2018; Phan & Renshaw, 2023), as well as regarding how to specifically adapt SBMPs with this population (e.g., Loucks et al., 2022; Phan & Renshaw, 2024). Relatedly, preliminary guidelines have recently been published regarding how to adapt SBMPs for effective use in under-resourced schools (Phan et al., 2024). These recent guidelines are drawn from broader literature bases regarding how educators and mental health professionals can build awareness, knowledge, and skills for effectively serving diverse youth in schools. But, to date, there has yet to be an empirical research agenda associated with this movement toward culturally sensitive SBMPs. One important initial step in the line of work is to establish reporting guidelines for the core features and adaptations made when evaluating SBMPs with diverse youth (Baelen et al., 2023; Renshaw & Phan, 2023). Beyond that, broad lines of inquiry are warranted to apply and evaluate existing guidelines for culturally adapting SBMPs to understand how such adaptations may (a) impact the implementation process, (b) affect programming outcomes, and (c) influence the social validity of SBMPs with diverse populations.

In conclusion, the future directions described above highlight that, despite the increasing research on and reach of SBMPs, an evidence-based approach to selecting and implementing these programs in schools is still emerging and incomplete. Although research shows SBMPs are clearly safe and effective at a general level, much work remains to better understand how to tailor and adapt SBMPs to ensure their effectiveness at the local level. To advance the field, researchers should compare the effects of existing SBMPs, conduct component analyses of the intervention elements within SBMPs, and apply and evaluate emerging guidelines for adapting culturally sensitive SBMPs with diverse youth. In the meantime, educators and mental health professionals who are using SBMPs in their local practice situations are encouraged to be scrupulous consumers of the available evidence and to be wary of overzealous or uncritical support for mindfulness programs (Greenberg & Harris, 2012). Professionals who are selecting and implementing SBMPs may use the information provided in this chapter to help them understand and accurately represent the current state of practice on this topic for their school communities. Ultimately, implementers of SBMPs should (a) provide clear rationales for selecting a particular program, (b) seek to adapt key features of the program to fit their local practice situation, (c) evaluate the program's effectiveness via routine outcome monitoring, and (d) use local program evaluation data to inform further adaptations that enhance the program's effectiveness. This approach allows professionals to make data-driven decisions regarding SBMPs, relying on both research evidence and local practice evidence.

REFERENCES

Baelen, R. N., Gould, L. F., Felver, J. C., Schussler, D. L., & Greenberg, M. T. (2023). Implementation reporting recommendations for school-based mindfulness programs. *Mindfulness*, *14*(2), 255–278. https://doi.org/10.1007/s12671-022-01997-2

Bakosh, L. S., Snow, R. M., Tobias, J. M., Houlihan, J. L., & Barbosa-Leiker, C. (2016). Maximizing mindful learning: Mindful awareness intervention improves elementary school students' quarterly grades. *Mindfulness*, *7*, 59–67. https://doi.org/10.1007/s12671-015-0387-6

Bakosh, L. S., Mortlock, J. M. T., Querstret, D., & Morison, L. (2018). Audio-guided mindfulness training in schools and its effect on academic attainment: Contributing to theory and practice. *Learning and Instruction*, *58*, 34–41. https://doi.org/10.1016/j.learninstruc.2018.04.012

Bannirchelvam, B., Bell, K. L., & Costello, S. (2017). A qualitative exploration of primary school students' experience and utilisation of mindfulness. *Contemporary School Psychology*, *21*(4), 304–316. https://doi.org/10.1007/s40688-017-0141-2

Bishop, S. R., Lau, M., Shapiro, S., Carlson, L., Anderson, N. D., Carmody, J., Segal, Z. V., Abbey, S., Speca, M., Velting, D., & Devins, G. (2004). Mindfulness: A proposed operational definition. *Clinical Psychology: Science and Practice*, *11*(3), 230–241. https://doi.org/10.1093/clipsy.bph077

Bray, M. A., Sassu, K. A., Kapoor, V., Margiano, S., Peck, H. L., Kehle, T. J., & Bertuglia, R. (2012). Yoga as an intervention for asthma. *School Psychology Forum*, *6*(2), 39–49. https://www.nasponline.org/publications/periodicals/spf/volume-6/volume-6-issue-2-(summer-2012)/yoga-as-an-intervention-for-asthma

Britton, W. B., Lepp, N. E., Niles, H. F., Rocha, T., Fisher, N. E., & Gold, J. S. (2014). A randomized controlled pilot trial of classroom-based mindfulness meditation compared to an active control condition in sixth-grade children. *Journal of School Psychology*, *52*(3), 263–278. https://doi.org/10.1016/j.jsp.2014.03.002

Broderick, P. (2013). *Learning to BREATHE: A mindfulness curriculum for adolescents to cultivate emotion regulation, attention, and performance*. New Harbinger.

Brown, C., Maggin, D. M., & Buren, M. (2018). Systematic review of cultural adaptations of school-based social, emotional, and behavioral interventions for students of color. *Education and Treatment of Children*, *41*(4), 431–456. https://www.jstor.org/stable/26535286

Carrizales-Englemann, D., Feuerborn, L. L., Gueldner, B. A., & Tran, O. K. (2016). *Merrell's strong kids: Grades 6–8*. Brookes.

Carsley, D., & Heath, N. L. (2018). Effectiveness of mindfulness-based colouring for test anxiety in adolescents. *School Psychology International*, *39*(3), 251–272. https://doi.org/10.1177/0143034318773523

Carsley, D., Heath, N. L., & Fajnerova, S. (2015). Effectiveness of a classroom mindfulness coloring activity for test anxiety in children. *Journal of Applied School Psychology*, *31*(3), 239–255. https://doi.org/10.1177/0143034318773523

Dariotis, J. K., Mirabal-Beltran, R., Cluxton-Keller, F., Feagans Gould, L., Greenberg, M. T., & Mendelson, T. (2017). A qualitative exploration of implementation factors in a school-based mindfulness and yoga program: Lessons learned from students and teachers. *Psychology in the Schools*, *54*(1), 53–69. https://doi.org/10.1002/pits.21979

Day, C. M., Smith, A., Short, F. J., & Bater, L. (2022). Dialectical behavior therapy skills groups for youth in schools: A systematic review. *Adolescent Research Review*, *7*(2), 267–284. https://doi.org/10.1007/s40894-021-00155-4

de Carvalho, J. S., Pinto, A. M., & Marôco, J. (2017). Results of a mindfulness-based social-emotional learning program on Portuguese elementary students and teachers: A quasi-experimental study. *Mindfulness*, *8*(2), 337–350. https://doi.org/10.1007/s12671-016-0603-z

Devcich, D. A., Rix, G., Bernay, R., & Graham, E. (2017). Effectiveness of a mindfulness-based program on school children's self-reported well-being: A pilot study comparing effects with an emotional literacy program. *Journal of Applied School Psychology*, *33*(4), 309–330. https://doi.org/10.1080/15377903.2017.1316333

Dunlap, R. D. (2023). *An analysis of the impact of the Inner Explorer Mindfulness Program on the academic growth of elementary students* [Doctoral dissertation, The University of North Carolina at Charlotte]. ProQuest Dissertation No. 30486950.

ElGarhy, S., & Liu, T. (2016). Effects of psychomotor intervention program on students with autism spectrum disorder. *School Psychology Quarterly*, *31*(4), 491–506. https://doi.org/10.1037/spq0000164

Fang, S., & Ding, D. (2020). A meta-analysis of the efficacy of acceptance and commitment therapy for children. *Journal of Contextual Behavioral Science*, *15*, 225–234. https://doi.org/10.1016/j.jcbs.2020.01.007

Felver, J. C., Butzer, B., Olson, K. J., Smith, I. M., & Khalsa, S. B. S. (2015). Yoga in public school improves adolescent mood and affect. *Contemporary School Psychology*, *19*(3), 184–192. https://doi.org/10.1007/s40688-014-0031-9

Felver, J. C., Cary, E. L., Helminen, E. C., Schutt, M. K. A., Gould, L. F., Greenberg, M. T. . . . Schussler, D. L. (2023). Identifying core program components of mindfulness-based programming for youth: Delphi approach consensus outcomes. *Mindfulness*, *14*(2), 279–292. https://doi.org/10.1007/s12671-022-02015-1

Felver, J. C., Celis-de Hoyos, C. E., Tezanos, K., & Singh, N. N. (2016). A systematic review of mindfulness-based interventions for youth in school settings. *Mindfulness*, *7*(1), 34–45. https://doi.org/10.1007/s12671-015-0389-4

Felver, J. C., Clawson, A. J., Morton, M. L., Brier-Kennedy, E., Janack, P., & DiFlorio, R. A. (2019). School-based mindfulness intervention supports adolescent resiliency: A randomized controlled pilot study. *International Journal of School & Educational Psychology*, *7*(supl.), 111–122. https://doi.org/10.1080/21683603.2018.1461722

Felver, J. C., Felver, S. L., Margolis, K. L., Ravitch, N. K., Romer, N., & Horner, R. H. (2017). Effectiveness and social validity of the Soles of the Feet mindfulness-based intervention with special education students. *Contemporary School Psychology*, *21*(4), 358–368. https://doi.org/10.1007/s40688-017-0133-2

Felver, J. C., & Singh, N. N. (2020). *Mindfulness in the classroom: An evidence-based program to reduce disruptive behavior and increase academic engagement*. New Harbinger.

Frank, J. L., Bose, B., & Schrobenhauser-Clonan, A. (2014). Effectiveness of a school-based yoga program on adolescent mental health, stress coping strategies, and attitudes toward violence: Findings from a high-risk sample. *Journal of Applied School Psychology*, *30*(1), 29–49. https://doi.org/10.1080/15377903.2013.863259

Flook, L., Smalley, S. L., Kitil, M. J., Galla, B. M., Kaiser-Greenland, S., Locke, J., & Kasari, C. (2010). Effects of mindful awareness practices on executive functions in elementary school children. Journal of Applied School Psychology, 26(1), 70–95. https://doi.org/10.1080/15377900903379125

Garrison Institute. (2005). *Contemplation and education—A survey of programs using contemplative techniques in K-12 educational settings: A mapping report*. Available online https://www.garrisoninstitute.org/wp-content/uploads/2018/11/Contemplation-and-Education_2005.pdf

Greenberg, M. T., & Harris, A. R. (2012). Nurturing mindfulness in children and youth: Current state of the research. *Child Development Perspectives*, *6*, 161–166. https://doi.org/10.1111/j.1750-8606.2011.00215.x

Hölzel, B. K., Carmody, J., Vangel, M., Congleton, C., Yerramsetti, S. M., Gard, T., & Lazar, S. W. (2011). Mindfulness practice leads to increases in regional brain gray matter density. *Psychiatry Research*, *191*(1), 36–43. https://doi.org/10.1016/j.pscychresns.2010.08.006

Idler, A. M., Mercer, S. H., Starosta, L., & Bartfai, J. M. (2017). Effects of a mindful breathing exercise during reading fluency intervention for students with attentional difficulties. *Contemporary School Psychology*, *21*(4), 323–334. https://doi.org/10.1007/s40688-017-0132-3

Kang, Y., Rahrig, H., Eichel, K., Niles, H. F., Rocha, T., Lepp, N. E., Gold, J., & Britton, W. B. (2018). Gender differences in response to a school-based mindfulness training intervention for early adolescents. *Journal of School Psychology*, *68*, 163–176. https://doi.org/10.1016/j.jsp.2018.03.004

Kielty, M., Gilligan, T., Staton, R., & Curtis, N. (2017). Cultivating mindfulness with third grade students via classroom-based interventions. Contemporary *School Psychology*, *21*(4), 317–322. https://doi.org/10.1007/s40688-017-0149-7

Klingbeil, D. A., Renshaw, T. L., Willenbrink, J. B., Copek, R. A., Chan, K. T., Haddock, A., Yassine, J., & Clifton, J. (2017). Mindfulness-based interventions with youth: A comprehensive meta-analysis of group-design studies. *Journal of School Psychology*, *63*, 77–103. https://doi.org/10.1016/j.jsp.2017.03.006

Kurth, L., Engelniederhammer, A., Sasse, H., & Papastefanou, G. (2020). Effects of a short mindful-breathing intervention on the psychophysiological stress reactions of German elementary school children. *School Psychology International*, *41*(3), 218–238. https://doi.org/10.1177/0143034320903480

Long, A. C., Renshaw, T. L., & Camarota, D. (2018). Classroom management in an urban, alternative school: A comparison of mindfulness and behavioral approaches. *Contemporary School Psychology*, *22*(3), 233–248. https://doi.org/10.1007/s40688-018-0177-y

Loucks, E. B., Crane, R. S., Sanghvi, M. A., Montero-Marin, J., Proulx, J., Brewer, J. A., & Kuyken, W. (2022). Mindfulness-based programs: Why, when, and how to adapt? *Global Advances in Health and Medicine*, *11*, No. 21649561211068805. https://doi.org/10.1177/21649561211068805

Luiselli, J. K., Worthen, D., Carbonell, L., & Queen, A. H. (2017). Social validity assessment of mindfulness education and practices among high school students. *Journal of Applied School Psychology*, *33*(2), 124–135. https://doi.org/10.1007/s12671-016-0664-z

Maloney, J. E., Lawlor, M. S., Schonert-Reichl, K. A., & Whitehead, J. (2016). A mindfulness-based social and emotional learning curriculum for school-aged children: The MindUP program. In K. A. Schonert-Reichl & R. W. Roeser (Eds.), *Handbook of mindfulness in education, mindfulness in behavioral health* (pp. 313–334). https://doi.org/10.1007/978-1-4939-3506-2_20

Maloney, J. E., Whitehead, J. K., Lawlor, M. S., & Schonert-Reichl, K. A. (2014, October). *Children's perceptions of the MindUP program.* Poster presented at the International Symposium for Contemplative Studies, Boston, MA.

Matsuba, M. K., Schonert-Reichl, K. A., McElroy, T., & Katahoire, A. (2021). Effectiveness of a SEL/mindfulness program on Northern Ugandan children. *International*

Journal of School & Educational Psychology, 9(supl.), S113–S131. https://doi.org/10.1080/21683603.2020.1760977

Milligan, K., Cosme, R., Miscio, M. W., Mintz, L., Hamilton, L., Cox, M., Woon, S., Gage, M., & Phillips, M. (2017). Integrating mindfulness into mixed martial arts training to enhance academic, social, and emotional outcomes for at-risk high school students: A qualitative exploration. *Contemporary School Psychology, 21*(4), 335–346. https://doi.org/10.1007/s40688-017-0142-1

Palacios, A. M., Bender, S. L., & Berry, D. J. (2023). Characteristics of mindfulness-based interventions in schools: A systematic review in school psychology journals. *Contemporary School Psychology, 27*(1), 182–197. https://doi.org/10.1007/s40688-022-00432-6

Parsons, E. (2023). *Exploring the effects of a daily audio-guided mindfulness intervention for teachers* [Doctoral dissertation, The University of North Carolina at Charlotte]. ProQuest Dissertation No. 30249481.

Phan, M. L., & Renshaw, T. L. (2023). Guidelines for implementing and adapting evidence-based interventions with marginalized youth in schools. *American Journal of Orthopsychiatry, 93*(3), 256–268. https://doi.org/10.1037/ort0000676

Phan, M. L., & Renshaw, T. L. (2024). Guidelines for adapting mindfulness-based school interventions with youth who are racially and ethnically marginalized. *Journal of Educational and Psychological Consultation.* Advance online. https://doi.org/10.1080/10474412.2024.2373462

Phan, M. L., Renshaw, T. L., Caramanico, J., Greeson, J. M., MacKenzie, E., Atkinson-Diaz, Z., Doppelt, N., Tai, H., Mandell, D. S., & Nuske, H. (2022). Systematic review of the quality of mindfulness-based school interventions. *Mindfulness, 13*, 1591–1613. https://doi.org/10.1007/s12671-022-01885-9

Phan, M. L., Renshaw, T. L., & Farley, C. D. (2024). Guidelines for increasing access to mindfulness-based interventions in under-resourced schools. *Contemporary School Psychology*. Advance online. https://doi.org/10.1007/s40688-024-00508-5

Renshaw, T. L. (2020). Mindfulness-based intervention in schools. In C. Maykel & M. A. Bray (Eds.), *Promoting mind–body health in schools: Interventions for mental health professionals* (pp. 145–160). American Psychological Association. https://doi.org/10.1037/0000157-010

Renshaw, T. L., & Cook, C. R. (2017). Mindfulness in the schools—Historical roots, current trends, and future directions. *Psychology in the Schools, 54*(1), 5–12. https://doi.org/10.1002/pits.21978

Renshaw, T. L., Fischer, A. J., & Klingbeil, D. A. (2017). Mindfulness-based intervention in school psychology. *Contemporary School Psychology, 21*, 299–303. https://doi.org/10.1007/s40688-017-0166-6

Renshaw, T. L., & Phan, M. L. (2023). Using implementation reporting to advance culturally sensitive and equity focused mindfulness programs in schools. *Mindfulness, 14*, 307–313. https://doi.org/10.1007/s12671-023-02068-w

Renshaw, T. L., Weeks, S. N., Roberson, A. J., Upton, S. R., Barr, J. D., Phan, M. L., & Farley, C. D. (2022). Cultivating mindfulness in schools to promote well-being. In K. Allen, M. J. Furlong, D. Vella-Brodrick, & S. Suldo (Eds.), *Handbook of positive psychology in schools: Supporting process and practice* (3rd ed; pp. 135–148). Routledge. https://doi.org/10.4324/9781003013778-11

Roeser, R. W., Galla, B. M., & Baelen, R. N. (2022). *Mindfulness in the schools: Evidence on the impacts of school-based mindfulness programs on student outcomes in P–12 educational settings*. Policy Brief for Robert Wood Johnson Foundation. Edna Bennett Pierce Prevention Research Center, The Pennsylvania State University. Downloaded November 2022 from: https://www.prevention.psu.edu/uploads/files/PSU-Mindfullness-Brief-2022.pdf

Roeser, R. W., Greenberg, M. T., Frazier, T., Galla, B. M., Semenov, A. D., & Warren, M. T. (2023). Beyond all splits: Envisioning the next generation of science on mindfulness and compassion in schools for students. *Mindfulness*, *14*(2), 239–254. https://doi.org/10.1007/s12671-022-02017-z

Rush, K. S., Golden, M. E., Mortenson, B. P., Albohn, D., & Horger, M. (2017). The effects of a mindfulness and biofeedback program on the on- and off-task behaviors of students with emotional behavioral disorders. *Contemporary School Psychology*, *21*(4), 347–357. https://doi.org/10.1007/s40688-017-0140-3

Schonert-Reichl, K. A., & Lawlor, M. S. (2010). The effects of a mindfulness-based education program on pre- and early adolescents' well-being and social and emotional competence. *Mindfulness*, *1*, 137–151. https://doi.org/10.1007/s12671-010-0011-8

Schonert-Reichl, K. A., Oberle, E., Lawlor, M. S., Abbott, D., Thomson, K., Oberlander, T. F., & Diamond, A. (2015). Enhancing cognitive and social–emotional development through a simple-to-administer mindfulness-based school program for elementary school children: A randomized controlled trial. *Developmental Psychology*, *51*(1), 52–66. https://doi.org/10.1037/a0038454

Semple, R. J., Droutman, V., & Reid, B. A. (2017). Mindfulness goes to school: Things learned (so far) from research and real-world experiences. *Psychology in the Schools*, *54*(1), 29–52. https://doi.org/10.1002/pits.21981

Stager, A. (2022). *Determining the degree to which active use of mindfulness with elementary students affects their annual state test scores in math and reduces office referrals* [Doctoral dissertation, University of La Verne]. ProQuest Dissertation No. 29061165.

Terjestam, Y., Bengtsson, H., & Jansson, A. (2016). Cultivating awareness at school: Effects on effortful control, peer relations and well-being at school in grades 5, 7, and 8. *School Psychology International*, *37*(5), 456–469. https://doi.org/10.1177/0143034316658321

The Hawn Foundation. (2011). *The MindUp curriculum: Grades 6–8*. Author.

Thierry, K. L., Bryant, H. L., Nobles, S. S., & Norris, K. S. (2016). Two-year impact of a mindfulness-based program on preschoolers' self-regulation and academic performance. *Early Education and Development*, *27*(6), 805–821. https://doi.org/10.1080/10409289.2016.1141616

Treves, I. N., Olson, H. A., Ozernov-Palchik, O., Li, C. E., Wang, K. L., Arechiga, X. M., . . . Gabrieli, J. D. E. (2023). At-home use of app-based mindfulness for children: A randomized active-controlled trial. *Mindfulness*, *14*, 2728–2744. https://doi.org/10.1007/s12671-023-02231-3

Wood, L., Roach, A. T., Kearney, M. A., & Zabek, F. (2018). Enhancing executive function skills in preschoolers through a mindfulness-based intervention: A randomized, controlled pilot study. *Psychology in the Schools*, *55*(6), 644–660. https://doi.org/10.1002/pits.2213

INDEX

For the benefit of digital users, indexed terms that span two pages (e.g., 52–53) may, on occasion, appear on only one of those pages.

Tables and figures are indicated by an italic *t* and *f* following the paragraph number.

www.ingramcontent.com/pod-product-compliance
Ingram Content Group UK Ltd.
Pitfield, Milton Keynes, MK11 3LW, UK
UKHW012141150926
475595UK00012B/239

9 780190 880477